the complete book of SOFT FURNISHINGS

the complete book of SOFT FURNISHINGS

**UPHOLSTERY ◆ CURTAINS & BLINDS
CUSHIONS & COVERS**

DOROTHY GATES
EILEEN KITTIER
SUE LOCKE

WARD LOCK

First published 1989 by Ward Lock,
Villiers House, 41/47 Strand,
WC2N 5JE, England
125 East 23rd Street, Suite 300,
New York 10010, USA

Reprinted 1990, 1991 (twice), 1992

A Cassell imprint

Originally published as
Upholstery by Dorothy Gates 0 7063 6363 9
Curtains and Blinds by Eileen Kittier 0 7063 6364 7
Cushions and Covers by Sue Locke 0 7063 6655 7

Text filmset/set in Bauer Bodoni
by Facet

Printed and bound in Hong Kong by
Colorcraft Ltd

ISBN 0-7063-6697-2

CONTENTS

CONTENTS

CONTENTS

INTRODUCTION: DECORATING YOUR HOME

THE IMPORTANCE OF PLANNING

Having the responsibility of furnishing a home or flat can be a very rewarding experience. However, it is not until you start shopping that you begin to realize the vast choice of materials that are available. And although you may have been quite clear in your mind about the sort of look you wanted to achieve, it probably won't take too long before you've been tempted by a variety of other design ideas. To avoid becoming totally confused and frustrated by the enormous selection of goods currently available, you need to work to a plan. Spending time with pencil and paper jotting down favourite ideas and planning out your colour schemes can help to restore a sense of fun to any home furnishing projects.

The first step to furnishing your home successfully is to make a scaled drawing of all the rooms that you intend to furnish. Take a note of the dimensions and include windows, alcoves and any interesting features such as fireplaces. You will also need to pencil in the doors, making a special note of those doors that connect one room to another.

If you have already painted or papered the walls and covered the floors, then staple some left over tufts from the carpet and add a small dab of paint to your plan. These accurate colour references will be enormously helpful when you need to start selecting fabrics.

Your sketch should also include any items of furniture that you want to include in a room. Large items of furniture such as a suite or bed should also be measured, so that you can decide on paper where you want to position them in your room. If you have curtains or covers that you want to keep, make a rough copy of the pattern or texture and the colours. If you haven't a remnant available then colour in a small area on your plan keeping the colour reference as accurate as possible. All these small details when put together can start to build up a picture of the room you are planning.

Having spent time studying your room you will also need to decide whether you want to exaggerate or disguise any particular features, and make a note of this on your plan. Your budget may prevent you from buying some new units but a length of inexpensive cloth can hide a multitude of faults.

With all your furniture in place on your scaled plan you can then start to make a list of the items that you need to buy. It is advisable to make two lists, one marked essentials and the other marked extras. It is easy when out shopping to get side-tracked into buying hoards of colourful knick-knacks, then finding you haven't sufficient funds to buy those much-needed curtains for the living room. Always work your way down your list of essentials before looking for those little extras.

Budgeting is also very important. If you know you have a set amount to spend then you can start to allocate a specific amount to each of the essentials. With a price guide to work to you can then limit the range of fabrics you can choose from. However, when budgeting for curtains or re-upholstering a chair, do include all the small accessories that you will need. This may include lining, curtain poles and fringing or calico, webbing, piping and springs. Accessories can be expensive so don't simply guess – make a note when you are out shopping. The more accurate your financial planning the more likely you are to be able to afford most of the items you need. If you work with a price guide (providing it is not totally unrealistic), you won't be tempted to spend a fortune on cloth for curtains and then find you can't possibly afford to re-upholster those dining-room chairs.

Always take your plans with you whenever you go shopping, just in case something takes your eye. You can then see at a glance whether it will harmonize with your carpets and walls. Always avoid buying on impulse. Make a note of the price, colours and design of the materials then go away and think about them before you are cajoled into buying by the store's employees. If you are planning to make curtains or cover a suite, you are going to have to live with your decision for quite some time, so it is worthwhile making the right one.

If time is at a premium for you, either because of work or seeing to the needs of a young family, then you may benefit from firms that offer a mail order service. By looking at brochures and catalogues at home you can enjoy making your purchase in a more leisurely way, rather than tearing round the shops on a Saturday. Do request fabric swatches if they are offered to you, as the colours in a brochure are not always totally accurate.

THE FURNISHING SCRAPBOOK

Keeping a file or box specifically for furnishing ideas can be a handy way of renewing your enthusiasm. By simply looking at room sets and ideas that other people have used can help to show how others have co-ordinated their fabrics. And the knowledge that clever ideas and a professional look has been achieved by amateurs can be most encouraging.

Before discarding old magazines and supplements cut out any ideas that you particularly liked. This can be especially useful where people have had to work to a budget and relied on some good ideas to complete their project. This might be a simple sofa made from slats of wood and made comfortable with home-made cushions or a window seat that has been converted from an old wooden box and again topped with an attractive cushion. If you're in the slightest way practical, other people's ideas can encourage you to improvise around the home rather than buying everything ready-made.

By dividing your folder or box into sections you can allocate your tear sheets into various room ideas. When you come to decorate the bathroom or a child's bedroom you can then simply refer to that particular section of the folder. Once your folder is starting to look too full, take time every six months or so to work your way through it and discard those ideas that seem rather dated.

In addition to keeping a scrapbook of ideas you could also keep one for remnants. If you have been offered carpet samples or fabric swatches that you can keep but may not need immediately you may find they can be useful at a later date. Staple the swatches of fabric together in a book form and write on the back the name of the manufacturer and a price. Divide the fabrics so that you have one book for furnishing fabrics and one for dress fabrics, as dress fabrics can be used for decorative cushions, throw-over covers ('throws') and bedspreads. Carpet samples should be cut quite small and glued to stiff pieces of card, again with details of the supplier and cost per square metre.

If you have been tempted to buy fabric remnants in a sale keep them neatly folded in a box or cupboard. Don't be tempted to plan your entire room round one inexpensive length of cloth, unless you are quite sure it will look quite stunning as a centre-piece on a chair or covering a table. You are far safer planning your room in a more orderly fashion and then seeing if the remnant can be incorporated into one of the rooms in the house without upsetting the colour balance. If you are fortunate enough to have at least five or six rooms to furnish, it is quite likely that a remnant can be fitted into one of the colour schemes.

Attractive lengths of cloth that have been damaged and are beyond repair can be cut about and used for cushion covers or a contrasting edging on bedcovers or curtains. When you're collecting samples of fabric together check to see that you haven't any remnants stored at home before budgeting to buy everything you need.

TEXTURE

Initially it is the colour and design of a cloth that catches our eye but the texture of a cloth is also very important. Feeling a cloth to see what it is like to the touch can be just as important as the colour or design of it, particularly when we are looking at materials for chairs or sofas. Cloths such as velvet and dralon have a soft luxurious feel about them, whereas linens and cottons can be rather coarse. Touching cloth and deciding how you react towards it will help to determine the type of materials you want around you. The texture of cloth is also very evident when light hits it. You can decide whether you want a cloth with a glazed finish that will reflect the light or a dark velvety material that absorbs it. Texture of cloth can also be taken into consideration when looking at the different rooms to be furnished. Soft, silky fabrics for a bedroom, PVC cloths and washable fabrics for the bathroom, kitchen and a child's room. Looking at how a room is to be used will determine to some extent the texture of the cloth to be used in it. You may like to consider whether you wish to echo or contrast with surfaces already in your room such as a rough brick fireplace, a highly polished table or a coarse rag rug.

CONNECTING ROOMS

When you are furnishing a home it is very easy to fall into the trap of decorating a room and seeing it as entirely separate from the rest of the house or flat. Although you may decide to emphasize a particular theme or period in one area, don't ignore the fact that hallways and landings connect rooms together. A more pleasing effect can be achieved by seeing rooms in relation to each other. For example, a child's bedroom in predominantly red tones opening into a landing in shades of orange may prove to be very over-powering. When planning a room try to ensure that any neighbouring areas will either blend or contrast effectively with the room you are currently working on. By constantly working with swatches you can avoid making too many expensive mistakes.

ASSESSING YOUR NEEDS

The life you lead will determine to a great extent the type of furnishings that you require. If you have a young family, be prepared for a tremendous amount of hard wear and tear on your home in a fairly short space of time. You will need to be thinking of kitchen surfaces that can be wiped clean, chair covers that can be sponged over and flooring that is comfortable to crawl on but tough enough to withstand some indoor gymnastics! With youngsters about, furnishings need to be easy to wash and quick to dry.

Teenagers make different demands on your home. Be warned that they are likely to have very strong opinions about the decor in their room, and it is likely that you will need to compromise over colour schemes. Scarlet gloss on the woodwork and bright green walls may be the epitome of good taste to a sixteen-year-old, but strong colours such as these are difficult to disguise if your teenager decides to leave home. If your offspring likes bold colours, you could suggest looking through the advertisements in your local paper for pieces of second-hand furniture and using these as the basis for colour themes. During the teenage years, youngsters like to be able to bring friends home, provided they can have some privacy. A large bedroom can be equipped with a couple of second-hand sofas re-covered in a bright jazzy print. Alternatively, a shed or garage can be converted and, provided it has heating, lighting and somewhere to plug in a stereo, it can make a useful and cheap extension to your home.

If you and your partner are working full-time, then home needs to provide comfort at the end of a tiring day, but comfort that doesn't require too much effort. Without children to consider you can opt for pastel-coloured carpets and coverings. Covers that can be dry-cleaned can be an advantage – although expensive they will save you the bother of washing and ironing. If you regularly bring work home then you can work more efficiently with an area designated for this. Depending on the amount of space you have available, you could choose to convert a spare bedroom or screen off a corner of a large sitting room. If space really is at a premium, don't overlook large cupboards, walk-in wardrobes or a pantry. All of these can be easily adapted by using floor-to-ceiling shelving with a simple counter and stool tucked underneath for your typewriter, computer or word processor. Another area worth investigating is under the stairs. And if you don't need an office, how about a sewing area or library?

Having labelled your floor plan and decided how each area of the house is to be used, then designate each room either practical or decorative. For example, if your bedroom is simply for sleeping, you might label it decorative and feel free to use delicate and silky fabrics. However, your kitchen and dining room should be practical with walls, flooring and furnishings that are easy to clean. If you have a young family it may be wise to label each room practical apart from, perhaps, the master bedroom. You can perhaps afford to be slightly less practical with curtains in the dining and sitting rooms, but white carpets and highly polished tables with lace runners wouldn't be a very sensible choice. However, a length of PVC in a pretty print can be thrown over that polished table and will preserve the surface until the time when your children are able to appreciate the need to take care of things. Planning a practical home with youngsters about will help you to feel more relaxed. Knowing that loose covers are washable or that kitchen worktops won't easily scratch can enhance the years that you spend at home together. Creating an environment where everyone's needs are catered for isn't easy but it can be achieved provided you plan ahead. To enjoy your home you need to be realistic about the demands each member of your family is going to place upon it.

HOW MUCH TO SPEND?

Having a reasonably large amount of money to spend on 'doing up' your home can be potentially lethal. For many people there can be a very strong urge to buy things simply on impulse – things they've always wanted and could never afford, perhaps a precious antique or a set of highly expensive prints. The danger is that having splashed out on your heart's desire there is no spare change for essentials such as carpets, paint or curtains. Perhaps the impulsive shopper should leave all cash, cheques and credit cards at home, taking just enough change for the car park and a cup of coffee. This may seem rather drastic advice but how often have you bought something because it looked stunning in a window display which then looked perfectly hideous in your front room? Shops display goods so enticingly these days – everything is co-ordinated and homeware charmingly laid out in room sets, complete with soft lighting and convivial music – that it can be hard to resist.

Another dangerous time for shopping is during the sales. A genuine bargain may well prove to be no bargain at all if it simply isn't what you actually need. And because it has a 50% reduction tag you may still end up wasting the amount you do spend on it. If you leave your purse at home you can then feel free to browse without any pressure, simply collecting swatches and ideas. Should you see an item of furniture that you feel would be right then you can always ask to have it put by. Collect as many fabric swatches and carpet samples as you can as well as leaflets offering choices of paints. Spend as much time as you can window-shopping so that you can start to be clear in your mind exactly how you intend to spend your money.

Unless you have a trained eye, gained through much experience in interior designing, the art of furnishing a home successfully comes with practice. The best way of learning is to study the experts. Read magazines, borrow books from the library and visit showrooms – these techniques are all valuable ways of gaining an insight into how the professionals work.

Once you feel confident to start purchasing your goods it is useful to work out a break-down of roughly how the money will be spent. To do this make another floor plan labelling the items needed for each room – carpets, paint, curtains, furniture. Also bear in mind those rooms that you would like to be a little more extravagant with and those that you intend to economize on – for example the utility room, spare bedroom and upstairs landing. Divide your capital by the number of rooms and the requirements of each.

To some extent the amount of money you spend on a room will be determined by the priority you give it. For example, do you want wall-to-wall furniture in your bedroom; is it necessary to have a fitted kitchen or could you manage just as happily with a selection of second-hand pine? Do you want a bathroom complete with jacuzzi? If you're a keen cook then you may hanker after a fitted kitchen, but if cooking is more of a chore than anything you may prefer to invest in a sumptuous bedroom. Every householder has a different set of priorities and it is important to establish your own.

Unless you have access to unlimited capital and can afford to furnish every room lavishly, you are going to need to budget carefully. If, for example, the previous owners have left a room in good decorative order, complete with carpets and curtains to your taste, this can be a useful saving. You may also decide to spend the money you have decorating two or three rooms extravagantly and working on the remainder at a later date.

ATMOSPHERE

Creating the right sort of atmosphere for your home is perhaps the most important element. But atmosphere isn't something you can buy as it has a lot more to do with you stamping your personality on your surroundings.

It simply doesn't pay to imitate either a friend's room or one you've seen in a magazine. There is no harm in borrowing a few ideas but it can be far more of a challenge to add suggestions of our own. The secret is to work positively, to be bold and unafraid of what others may think. So long as you feel happy about the end result then that is all that counts. Few of us feel totally relaxed in other people's homes, because there are always things we would change to suit ourselves. It is that very ingredient that should deter us from simply copying. If we create a home to suit ourselves then we can be assured it will be quite unique.

Colour can contribute towards the atmosphere of a home and to some extent is a reflection of our own personality. Some colour tones have a warming effect while others are cool and create a feeling of calm. Tones of red, while giving a warm glow, should be used with care and are most effective when combined with shades of green or blue. Red is perfect as an accent colour in a rug, painting, curtains or flowers. Yellow lends a bright cheerful atmosphere to a room – a good choice for rooms with few windows and little daylight. Subtle tones of yellow are easier to work with than, say, a vivid shade of buttercup. A bright yellow can also be used as an accent colour. Shades of blue create a more formal background, but beware of making a room look cold. If you have chosen blue as your main colour use touches of warmer tones – oranges, yellows and reds – to detract from that coldness. Green tones suggest a country feel and are best contrasted with another strong colour, perhaps yellow or red. Neutral colours such as grey, beige, cream and white are very popular. These quieter shades are ideal for a background colour, particularly if you have a hoard of brightly coloured accessories – rugs, lamps, pictures and china. As your choice of colour will make a major contribution to the mood and consequently the atmosphere of your room, spend time experimenting. Use sample-size pots of paint and test them on all the walls, to consider how they look both during the day and at night. Electric light can alter the tone. Colours also create an illusion of making a room seem smaller or larger. Strong dark colours create a feeling of cosiness, making the area seem smaller, while pale colours give a feeling of light and spaciousness.

The style of furnishings that you choose can also contribute towards the atmosphere. With such a choice of furniture and accessories to choose from these days it can sometimes prove less confusing if you have decided on a particular theme. You may of course simply wish to reflect the period of your house, whether it is Georgian, Victorian or modern. The following are some of the most distinctive styles available today: country, bohemian, modern and high-tech.

Of the four mentioned the country style is currently the most popular. Even couples living in city centres want to create a rustic atmosphere complete with second-hand pine furniture, open fires and scrubbed boards. There is no doubt that the 'cottage look' conjures up pictures of homeliness and warmth, and what the advertisers would have us believe, a 'real' home should be. But only adopt this style if it is one that you have always liked. There is a very great danger of simply copying everyone else and falling in with the latest craze. If you have a secret desire to do something quite different don't allow yourself to be swayed by advertising.

It is possible to create your country cottage even if you live in a modern house with little character, although it will require more expense and more effort. A genuine Victorian house may already have wooden floors, open fireplaces, beams and solid wooden doors – all items that will need to be bought for a modern property. An effective yet simple way of achieving the cottage look is to start by painting all the walls with white emulsion. For this style it is more a case of spending less on paper and paint and more on knick-knacks such as patchwork quilts, rag rugs, rush mats, old china (even if it's chipped), faded prints in wooden or gilt frames and a comfortable three-piece suite with loose covers and lots of sumptuous cushions.

The country style is epitomized by the Laura Ashley range, but beware of co-ordinating everything. Curtains that match the wallpaper, the borders, the china and the bedspreads can look very daunting. There is a real danger with the cottage look to go completely over the top – too much china, too many frills, walls smothered in pictures and printed fabric everywhere. The essence of the cottage is in its simplicity. Stripped pine doors, boards with a few rugs, a handful of attractive prints and pretty curtains at the window can be all that is needed to set the mood. While the room should never be stark, it needs to be simple, not too cluttered, with a few carefully chosen accessories, and then you should resist the desire to keep adding more. Plain walls can take a little stencilling but furnishing fabrics should include a smattering of gorgeous floral prints – rambling roses, pansies or sweet peas. The room that above all others makes the statement about the country style is the kitchen. Scrubbed pine work surfaces and exposed brickwork are two possibilities. Quarry tiles on the floor covered with rush mats and an Aga or Rayburn chugging away in the corner are more essential ingredients. But be warned about these solid fuel types of stove as they need regular stoking and create a considerable amount of dust. Welsh dressers, or at the very least rows of pine shelves, overloaded with mismatched china and hung with bunches of dried flowers have a country flavour about them. Cover the kitchen walls with copper pots and pans and use basketware in different shapes and sizes to fill awkward corners, and to suspend from the ceiling. Country kitchens have a definite 'lived in' look but that shouldn't include rows of wet washing drying above the Aga or worktops so weighed down with home-made jars of jams and chutney that you've nowhere to prepare food.

The bohemian style of furnishing really took off in the sixties during the hippy era. Today, it is a style especially popular with students, as it can be an inexpensive way of decorating. This style of furnishing centres around the use of rich dark colours: jewel shades, such as purple, scarlet, gold and dark green. Second-hand flat weave rugs scattered over painted boards set the mood, and walls hung with Indian cotton bedspreads. Conventional sofas are taboo, replaced by large floor cushions in sumptuous silky fabrics or a paisley design. Carved wooden chests, wooden figures and brassware fit in well with this type of decorative scheme. Highly ornate Chinese lanterns with plenty of tassels are the perfect lighting accessory. If you are fortunate enough to purchase a sufficient number of rugs you can also use them as curtains to cover tables and to throw over beds.

Modern furnishings are clean and simple, typified by the Habitat range. The style isn't fussy, but it is comfortable. The modern look has none of the frilly edgings and ornate accessories so popular in the country style. Abstract prints in neutral colours are popular, along with plain-coloured carpets. Furniture is simple but well made. One or two large abstract paintings or framed posters decorate the walls, with plain-coloured china and glass vases on shelves and occasional tables.

High-tech is a style of furnishing that people tend to either love or loathe. It requires a minimal amount of furniture: plain walls, no curtains and a neutral-coloured flooring. There may be just one picture, a piece of sculpture, but definitely no knick-knacks, floral fabrics or feminine frills. The emphasis is on space and light, creating a rather austere and cold atmosphere. However, if you are disciplined enough to be able to keep your home free from clutter, then this style of furnishing can be perfect for a working couple because maintenance is so simple.

LIGHTING

Knowing how to light a room can be just as demanding as choosing a colour scheme. Creating the right sort of mood with lights can be fun but check that lighting is sufficient. Bear in mind that you need enough light to work or read by and ensure that landings, hallways and other hazardous areas are well lit, especially if you have children. If it is necessary for your house to be rewired make sure you have a sufficient number of sockets – at least eight in a kitchen. Also decide where you want the sockets, to avoid flexes winding across the floor.

In the kitchen you need sufficient light to be able to iron or cook comfortably. Strip lights are very popular but not very flattering as they give a cold, harsh light. Small fluorescent lights fitted under wall cupboards to light worktops provide an ideal compromise, with the tinted variety being more attractive. If your eating area is housed in the kitchen then consider using a central light over the table with an adjustable flex, or alternatively try a recessed ceiling spot. Create an intimate eating area but with sufficient light to see what you are eating.

For your bathroom lighting the priority has to be safety. Pull-strings are far safer than wall switches. Choose a flattering light for the bathroom mirror where you may need to apply make-up in the mornings. A set of bulbs mounted around the frame of the mirror can be fun.

For hallways and landings keep the lighting simple with just overhead lighting, using a 60 or

100 watt bulb.

Bedroom lighting needs to be designed to create a cosy atmosphere with the light centred around the bed. Bedside lamps should be positioned so that reading doesn't strain the eyes, and the switch near to hand.

The lounge area is one where you can experiment – here a dimmer switch can be particularly useful to create a low light for watching television and a brighter light for studying or simply chatting. A series of table lamps around the room create an attractive informal setting, possibly including a standard lamp to avoid using the centre light. Wall lights can be most attractive but decide whether having them fitted is worth the extra expense when table lamps can create a similar effect. Position lamps where they are likely to be most useful – on desks, either side of a sofa or on a table. Also check to see that sockets are nearby. Like most other aspects of furnishing a home, lighting comes with practice – move lamps about and, if you are not operating a dimmer switch, then experiment with different bulbs in different sizes and colours to gain the effect you want.

Spotlights can be useful for drawing attention to a particular object or painting in a room. Those with shutters attached can be used to direct light at an object with great accuracy. Spotlights on a track can be adjusted to light a group of pictures or ornaments in a room but beware of the cost involved in running them. Uplighters are floor lights used to create a beam of light that grows upwards in the room, and are often positioned behind a sofa or large plant for an interesting effect. Downlighters can be recessed or actually mounted in the ceiling and are ideal for creating a background light. Depending on the mood you want to create, use a wide, soft beam for background lighting and a narrow beam for highlighting a particular surface in the room.

A word about children's bedrooms. Safety is the absolute priority regarding anything electrical with youngsters about. Personally I would avoid any lamps in a child's room until they are at least school age. For youngsters it is worthwhile investing in a dimmer switch for the central light and sealing off sockets until young enquiring hands know the rules about safety.

In addition to lighting and colour it is your own little knick-knacks that add the final touch to atmosphere. You might for example have a passion for collecting clockwork toys, miniature houses, china animals – whatever you collect you can use it to become a point of interest in the room. Cigarette cards can be mounted in frames or displayed under the glass on a coffee table. If you have decided to collect objects from a particular country or time in history, set aside a small table and the surrounding wall to house a display. Perhaps you have a selection of gorgeous fans that can be secured to the wall – they can then become a real talking point if you use a spotlight to light them. Having a home to furnish can be the perfect opportunity to adopt a hobby for collecting, and if family and friends run short of ideas for Christmas and birthdays they can look for additional objects for your collection. Family photographs can also make a room come alive, perhaps a whole mass of them, enough to create a small gallery, dotted around on a wall or in the hall. Look out for second-hand frames or make your own with stiff cardboard and fabric.

Children's paintings and crafts can look lovely in the kitchen. Pictures of mum and dad in bright, gaudy colours can bring a sterile kitchen atmosphere to life. Samples of needlework or collages of assorted spaghetti shapes decorated with spray paints deserve hanging space. And those misshapen clay pots, first lessons in pottery, are ideal for housing paper clips, nails, loose change or small rolls of sellotape. Children love to see their handiwork on display, and it seems a pity to hide it in cupboards and drawers when you could create a small gallery in the kitchen where every child's current handiwork can be exhibited.

TEXTILES

With such a wealth of textiles to choose from in this country we can be spoilt for choice. There are linens, silks, cottons, woollens, lace, brocades and velvets, to name just a few. And the 'feel' of a cloth is just as important as how it looks. Shawls and tartan rugs woven in geometric patterns in rich dark shades of red, purple, blue and green conjure images of hillside cottages and draughty castles. The warm look of these cloths must have helped the occupants in those far-flung rural places to feel warmer and more cosy.

Brocades, velvets and chintzes remind one of more formal and elegant surroundings. The vivid colours often used on silk brocades lend an exotic air to a room. Tassels, fringing and braid in complementary colours are the perfect accompaniment to this type of textile.

Cottons and linens have a country freshness about them. Practical and hardwearing, their properties make them entirely suitable for a family house. Children can be allowed to roam free if cushions, covers and curtains made from cottons and linens can be dropped into the washing machine when they start to look grubby.

Silk and lace require special care. The delicate qualities of lace and the luxury look of silk make them destined for display purposes only in a family house. They can be ideal for table coverings, decorative small cushions or used in a master bedroom.

OLD TEXTILES

Antique fabric can be used for all sorts of decorative purposes in the home. Even if it is in very poor condition you may have enough to make several cushion covers. Alternatively, snip around a pretty motif or some embroidery and then frame it. Faded materials can be given a new lease of life if carefully dyed in a light colour, a tip certainly worth keeping in mind for faded white materials that can be dyed a light shade of blue or pink. Some pieces of antique fabric may be worth repairing while others may be too threadbare. Use them instead to cover tables and disguise the flaws with an assortment of trinkets and knick-knacks.

Old lace can be particularly lovely. You can use it to trim tablecloths, as coverings for pillows in the bedroom or tie-backs for the curtains. Old tapestry cushions and those made from faded velvet can give a lovely 'lived in' look to a newly covered suite. If you can learn to live with the odd flaws and faults to be found in old cloth then you can start to work on more adventurous projects of bringing old and new textiles to work together in a room.

If you are fortunate enough to acquire a large length of antique material, provided it is in good condition, use it just as if it were new for curtains, chair coverings, a blind or a bed throw. Really beautiful fabric can be draped over sofas and chairs or used to decorate a wall.

If you acquire a pile of antique fabric never discard it on the grounds that it is either too threadbare or that there is no place for it in a new house. The very fact that the fabric is slightly faded and the colours rather muted can be the perfect qualities for making them blend into a room.

PLAIN OR PATTERNED?

Whether you choose to use a plain or patterned fabric can make a world of difference to your room. The danger can be to use too much of one or the other: too many plain surfaces make a room appear boring and dull, while too many patterned surfaces make it confusing and muddled.

One of the popular reasons for using patterns is to disguise marks and stains. Having a plain cream-coloured suite is obviously going to involve more cleaning than one with a dark, intricate pattern. And although it is no fun to be dictated to by purely practical considerations, it can be ideal to work a mixture of plain and printed surfaces together, perhaps reserving the plain ones for those areas that receive less wear.

Patterns on every surface, however well co-ordinated, can look very over-done. So too can a room that is either predominantly all light colours or all dark ones. Ideally you need a balance of plain and printed designs that includes your carpet, walls and soft furnishings.

Different patterns can create a totally different effect. For example a cloth with strong geometric lines looks modern and bold, while a floral print in subtle colours looks delicate and old-fashioned. Patterns can be loud and bold or soft and dainty; they can work together provided there are colours that relate in each.

The most popular patterns are floral ones which can range from small all-over prints to enormous great blooms. They can be modern, old-fashioned or very ethnic depending on your taste. Many people choose floral patterns because they are 'safe'. If you have a tendency to repeat your style of furnishing, when it's time to redecorate make a conscious effort to steer away from the safe options and look at something quite different. Perhaps a bold stripe or check, or the introduction of more plain areas in your room. Adjusting to different styles takes time – just like clothes that come into fashion. If you are tempted to try something new, allow yourself time to get to really like the style you have chosen. Don't be in a hurry to buy the fabric until you are quite certain you can live with it. With such a variety of printed fabrics available today it is worth taking the opportunity when you are furnishing your home to look for something more unusual and less predictably 'you'.

WHERE TO SHOP

Having made a list of materials that you need to buy you will have to decide whether to shop in one large store or several small ones. Shopping at a hypermarket can be very convenient especially with regard to parking and being able to unload your goods with ease into your car. Personally, I would opt for buying all my basic materials such as white spirit, sandpaper, paint, paste and curtain poles from a large store and buy wallpaper, borders and fabrics from chain stores or a local furnishing showroom.

Many companies offer a mail order service which can be a bonus if you simply haven't too much time to spare. You can also enjoy shopping in the comfort of your home and browsing through catalogues before making your choice. The disadvantage of mail order is that you may have to wait for your materials, but if you're in no hurry this method may suit you best.

If money isn't a problem you may like to employ the services of a local interior designer. Those who are attached to shops prefer you to select fabrics from their ranges, while others will simply suggest colours and print ideas that they think would suit you. Interior designers can be expensive but if you find it difficult to co-ordinate a colour scheme it could be money well spent.

If you have the capital to buy everything you need to decorate your home, I would recommend that you purchase it all at one time. At the very least buy the materials for an entire room at one time. This way you can be assured that the fabric and wallpaper has been cut from the same dye batch. If you have over-estimated the amount that you need, many stores will refund your money on rolls of unopened wallpaper.

Armed with a list of things to buy, do include absolutely everything from screws and hooks to paste and brushes. It is infuriating to get halfway through a project only to find that you omitted to buy interfacing or thread.

Once you have all your materials at home, store those items that you don't need immediately for safe keeping. Furnishing fabrics can be folded and kept in plastic bags or cardboard boxes. Accessories, such as hooks, screws and nails can be kept in smaller bags or tins. Mark each package so that you know where to find it at a glance. Don't be tempted to leave cloth about as it's liable to get splashed with paint or paste.

Always keep leftover paint, wallpaper and fabric as you may need to use them if you decide to make further alterations to a room.

WHERE TO BEGIN

Having purchased the necessary paint, wallpaper, borders and so on, where should you start? With an entire house to decorate the task at this stage seems almost impossible. To restore some order, it makes sense to begin on one of the smallest and least important rooms in the house, especially if this is your first attempt at decorating. If you are desperately keen to start on a particular room first, perhaps the kitchen or sitting room, then provided you have some experience it is fine to go ahead. But if you've never papered a wall before or worked with gloss paint it is worthwhile practising in a room that is seldom used.

Trying to decorate a room that is full of furniture can be a nightmare. Not only do you have to keep shifting objects from one end of the room to the other but paint is liable to drip onto things however well you cover them. Unless you have absolutely nowhere to store things, the best solution is to move them into another room, then make sure everything is well covered with two layers of dust sheets. If you set to work in an empty room you will find that you can work a lot faster and you have the advantage of being able to leave pots of paint around and brushes soaking in white spirit ready for you to pick up where you left off when you next have a moment free. And if you have a young family you can also simply lock the door and mark the room out of bounds until all the surfaces are quite dry. If it is necessary to use the room while you're decorating, you will need to pack things away to avoid pots of paint being knocked over and things being dropped into buckets of paste. Clear a small cupboard so that decorating tools and equipment can be quickly and easily stored.

With an entire house to decorate it is tempting to

begin with one room and then see how the paint looks on a wall in another before completing the first. Try to organize yourself so that you complete one room at a time, rather than attempting several at once. Start with the ceilings, move on to the walls, then work gloss paint on doors and woodwork and finish with the flooring. Furnishing projects such as curtains and covers should be the last items on your list of things to do. Once the decorating has been completed you can at least replace all the furniture before starting work on your furnishings. After a day spent decorating it can be quite relaxing to sit and sew. Hems on curtains, tablecloths and cushion covers can be worked by hand so keep these projects for the evening.

If you feel nervous about decorating certain areas of the house – perhaps you have the stair walls to paper and the drop is rather long – you may consider hiring professional decorators. Although this can be highly expensive if you employ them to decorate throughout, for just one or two rooms it may prove to be worthwhile. Ring round for quotes and see whether this includes the cost of materials, then ask to see examples of their work. There is no doubt that the professional finish is always noticeable but you need to decide whether it is affordable. You may decide to do all the bedrooms, kitchen, upstairs landing and dining room yourself and hire a decorator for the stairs and sitting room.

Furnishing projects need to be tackled in the same way as the decorating – select the easiest project first. If you have little experience in sewing make your first attempt a simple cushion cover devoid of frills and pleats before you embark on covering a three-piece suite. Having made your cushions then move on to a pair of simple curtains for perhaps a child's bedroom, the bathroom or kitchen. The third project could be a very simple loose cover for a bed or a chair in a bedroom. Once you feel confident about making more complicated designs, then you can start to work on items for the busiest rooms in the house.

It is tempting not to bother about making simple projects and just to begin with covers for the three-piece suite or a set of long and heavy curtains for the lounge. However, gaining experience and confidence in basic sewing skills will help to ensure that as you progress from the elementary to the more complicated patterns the results will be most satisfactory. It is also highly likely that the fabric you have chosen for the main rooms in the house will have been expensive. Rushing a furnishing project can end up being a costly business with covers that don't fit and curtains that have been cut too short. Always make calico covers for your suite before cutting into expensive material and pin and tack everything before setting out your sewing machine. Do remember that fabrics such as velvet and satin will leave marks if you have to do some unpicking, so it is vital to spend time on preparation to avoid this happening.

FINISHING TOUCHES

If you're in the enviable position of having purchased a home that has been decorated recently, and to your taste, how can you make your soft furnishings blend in successfully?

If you have curtains that you don't wish to replace, try swopping them around in your new home. Curtains that hung in a bedroom before may not suit the decor in your new one, but they may look equally good in the dining room or at the landing windows. If you find that your curtains are either too short or not wide enough, you could add strips of contrasting material stitched around the side and lower edges of each curtain. You could also use the contrasting material for a pelmet. Alternatively, make some ties for the curtains or make three tubes of fabric, plait them together and use them to hold the curtains in place. If curtains are too short you can adapt them into café curtains for the kitchen or bathroom. Inexpensive curtains that you may have considered discarding can be cut up and used for cushion covers.

When it comes to adding a new item of furniture or a covering to a room you will need to decide whether you want it to become a focal point or whether you want it to blend in quite unobtrusively. For items that need to blend in you could perhaps incorporate a border around the room in colours that echo those of your sofa or curtains. For extra impact take the border around a mirror, window or door-frame.

Picture rails and skirting-boards can be repainted in a colour to tone with your furnishings. You might also like to add a new dimension to your paintwork by painting door frames and panels in a contrasting shade. Alcoves and window sills are also useful areas for using a contrasting shade of paint. Or, instead of painting the window sill, use leftover fabric to make a window seat or a blind. Scraps of leftover fabric can be used to make delightfully pretty picture frames or collages for the wall. Oddments of fabric can also be used to make patchwork cushions.

If you want your furnishing project to look really striking then you should not worry about whether it co-ordinates with anything else in the room. Objects designed to be focal points can be much admired but be prepared for them to be closely scrutinized. Do feel confident that the items you have chosen deserve pride of place in your room.

An attractively covered chair or a beautifully embroidered cloth needs to be positioned in an uncluttered corner and not squeezed in amongst a pile of furniture. Keep the surrounding area as clear as possible. A chair or sofa can be made to look even more attractive with cushions. However, beware of smothering the sofa with too many of them. If you have decided to make the curtains a focal point you will need to keep the area around them as tidy as possible. Avoid having a window sill piled high with knick-knacks and don't jam chairs, sofas or tables so tightly against the wall that they prevent the curtains hanging freely.

To reinforce the colours of your focal point, use them on small accessories arranged nearby. For example, you may wish to follow through that dominant red on your curtains with two or three plain-coloured vases, or, use a set of unusual glass bottles to echo watery green and blue shades.

Fresh or dried flowers are a delightful way of reflecting colour themes and can be matched to the colours found in floral prints.

Any focal point in a room, whether it's a sofa, chair, curtains or cushions, or a stunning throwover cover, needs to be kept in prime condition. Be prepared to have them cleaned regularly, and be on the look out for any repairs that may be needed. A loose cover can lose its appeal if the chair stuffing is trailing over the floor, and pretty cloths carefully arranged on an occasional table never look quite so pretty if the legs of the table have been badly scored and are in desperate need of some attention.

If at first glance a furnishing item doesn't seem to fit into a room, don't despair. Study the colours and see whether they can be contrasted or co-ordinated effectively with those already in the room. If this really is impossible then consider having material dyed or using the item in another room.

ON THE MOVE

If the accommodation you are living in is only temporary, then you probably won't feel inclined to spend too much money or time on it. The simplest and cheapest way to brighten a home is with paint. You can use it to cover walls, ceilings, doors, cupboards, even floors. And light, bright colours can transform a dark, dingy home into somewhere clean and inviting. To furnish temporary accommodation use rugs and mats on sanded and varnished or painted floors. Emulsion paint can be used on bedroom floors while a gloss paint is more hard-wearing and suitable for the lounge and dining area. Concrete paint can be used in the kitchen and is far less expensive than lino or cork tiles.

Blinds are less expensive than curtains and can be used in every room. However, if you prefer curtains, include a deep hem so that you can hopefully alter them to fit your next home. If your windows are small then you might consider using several metres of a cheap dress fabric such as a cotton gingham. Café curtains are also useful as they use about half the amount of cloth that ordinary lined curtains need.

If you are living in rented accommodation and you want to cover a suite cheaply, consider using throws cut from large squares of fabric in different prints with the same basic colour tones. Loose covers should be made in a cheap cotton or linen material. If you add pretty cushions to your suite in more expensive materials you can at least take them with you when you leave. As a change from paint, you can also use lengths of material to cover the walls, stapled to wooden batons screwed into the walls. You can simply remove the material when you move out.

Unsightly dining room chairs can be painted and pretty cushions with ties added to the seats and backs. Large floor cushions can be used to liven up painted boards and lengths of inexpensive cotton can be thrown over tables, boxes and beds for instant effect.

Living in temporary furnished accommodation can be a good time for experimenting with colours and having a go at techniques such as stencilling and marbling. However, remember to adopt a policy of making do, and to spend time and effort on projects that can be taken away with you rather than investing capital on someone else's furniture.

SOMETHING TO TREASURE

For most of us the need to furnish our homes is mainly a practical one. We want curtains to keep out the draught, cushions to make sofas and chairs more comfortable and bed covers to disguise sheets and blankets. But we might also like to sew something that we can treasure. We tend to think in terms of small items, such as embroidery or tapestry as things we can treasure, but it can apply to curtains, cushions and covers too.

A bed cover and matching cushions could be cut from a wedding dress, trimmed with pretty silk flowers and the edges decorated with ribbons made from a bridesmaid's dress. A family heirloom such as an antique shawl can be draped across a wall or thrown over a table, sofa or bed. And buttons from childhood sweaters can be used in upholstery projects.

In the past patchwork was used to commemorate a special occasion. Friends and neighbours would donate one or two pieces of cloth and mothers and daughters would use them to sew a quilt. You might like to ask friends and relatives to donate some remnants of their favourite fabrics to enable you to make a quilt full of memories for your home.

UPHOLSTERY

PART I

UPHOLSTERY AND RE-UPHOLSTERY

1 TOOLS AND EQUIPMENT

The following list gives a guide to the tools and equipment used during modern and traditional upholstery. A complete set of tools would be acquired over a long period.

Pair of tressles with a trough top, *or* a low table at least 1 m (1 yd) square
Sewing machine, with running foot and piping foot
Machine needles 14 to 18
Hammers: magnetic, cabriole and either two-headed or claw
Ripping chisel
Mallet
Web stretcher
Pincers
Bradawl
Scissors: blunt-end pair and one pair with 18 cm (7 in) blade
Steel rule
Metre stick
Tacks 16 mm (⅝ in), improved 13 mm (½ in) and fine 10 mm (⅜ in)
Gimp pins (assorted colours)
Mattress needles: assorted lengths, round and bayonet points
Spring needle, regulator, skewers

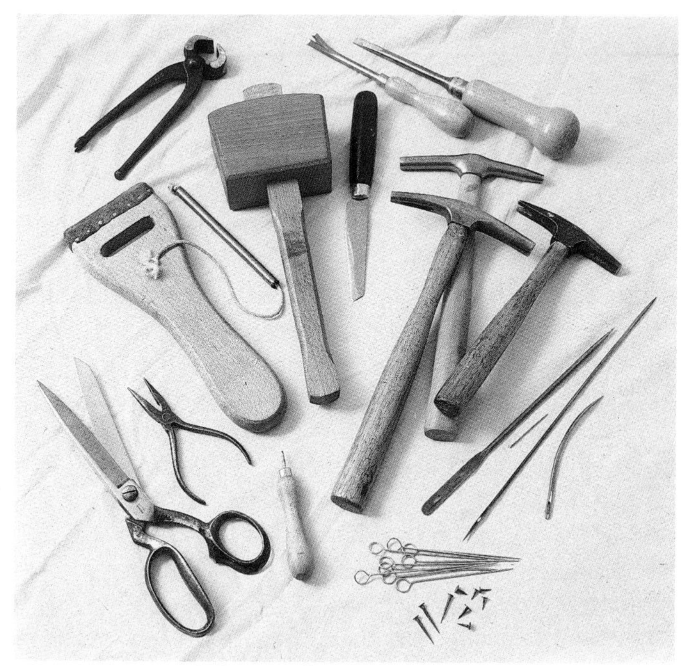

Some essential upholstery tools

Circular and cording needles
Knife
Staple gun and staples
Adhesive
Tack lifter

MATERIALS USED IN TRADITIONAL UPHOLSTERY

Algerian fibre: black in colour, is very similar to coir and has the same uses, but is more resilient.

Coir: fibre made from coconut husk, ginger in colour. It is used as a first stuffing.

Calico: a cotton fabric, made in different weights. It is used as an undercovering. A heavy calico is very strong and can be used as a top cover under loose covers.

Flock: made of cotton and waste fabrics. It can be milled and re-used as a filling but it is inclined to go 'lumpy' in use.

Hessian: a loosely-woven cloth made from jute. It is used as the main foundation in upholstery and comes in different densities. 283 g (10 oz) or 340 g (12 oz) are among the highest densities used.

Hair: usually horse hair, as this type is longer and keeps its curl (although it is not always available now). It is used as a top stuffing. It is very resilient and can be milled and re-used if in good condition. Hog's hair is sometimes used, but it is a much shorter hair and therefore lacks the qualities of horse hair.

Linette: black, fine-woven cloth used on the underside of chairs or loose seats. It is rather thin and does not stand up to a great deal of wear.

Piping cord: made from cotton strands, twisted into a cord and made in several thicknesses. It is used to make the piping (or welting) on the seams of furniture.

Scrim: a type of hessian weave made from the linen thread and therefore finer than hessian. It is used to cover the first stuffing on a seat, and when it has been stitched through, it forms a very strong stitched-up edge.

Springs: many types and sizes of spring are available. The double cone (or waisted spring) is the most commonly used; serpentine or wiggle springs are also in use. Rubber webbing can be used as a flat spring particularly on modern furniture.

Laid cord (lay cord): a thick cord used for lashing down the springs.

Linter felt: made from cotton lintas, this is a thick, soft padding used over the hair to prevent it penetrating through the outer cover. It is also used as an extra padding layer.

Threads and twine: linen thread is the strongest type. It is made in different thicknesses. Always use the best available. Twines are made from both linen and jute and can be waxed for easier handling.

Tarpaulin: a type of hessian weave that is very much heavier than ordinary hessian. It is sometimes called spring canvas and is used to cover over the springs.

Webbing: several types are available. The strongest and most expensive is the English type of webbing which is a black and white, herring-bone, linen weave. It is usually 5 cm (2 in) wide, but is also available in other widths. The other type of webbing used is made of jute, and is fawn in colour. It is very strong and available in different widths, 5 cm (2 in) being the most popular. Alternatively, polypropylene webbing is now available. It looks similar to the English webbing except that it is shiny. It is not as strong as the other types and is inclined to shred.

Wadding: sold by the metre (or yard), wadding looks like cotton wool enclosed in a thin skin. It comes in different weights and is used under the top cover to prevent wear on the fabric and to prevent hair from working its way through the top cover. Use the best one available as it is more economical to use one layer of a heavy wadding than two layers of a thin one.

MATERIALS USED IN MODERN UPHOLSTERY

Some of the materials in modern upholstery are identical to those used in traditional upholstery. In addition, however, the following materials are required.

Foam: latex foam is made from rubber which is

liquidized and poured into moulds in which air bubbles are allowed to form. It is made in different densities and types according to its function. The two types are pinhole and cavity: the pinhole is solid with air bubbles set at intervals and the cavity has a box-like construction on the inside and a moulded outer edge.

Plastic foam is made from polyether. It is made in many densities and is much lighter than rubber as well as being cheaper. It looks like a fine honeycomb and can be cut to size with a sharp knife.

Rubberized hair: made in sheets, it consists of hair covered in latex. It is usually sold approximately 5 cm (2 in) thick and can be cut to size as required.

Rubber webbing: very strong and used as a flat spring. It is sold in 5 cm (2 in) and 2.5 cm (1 in) widths.

Tension spring: a tightly wound spiral of wire covered with either a plastic or a fabric sleeve. It hooks on to either side of the frame. A row of tension springs make a spring seat or back.

Polyester or terylene wadding: similar in appearance to cotton wool. The wadding is used to wrap round cushions, to provide padding on backs and seats. Polyester wadding has a centre core and is usually thicker than terylene wadding.

Adhesives: several types are available. Each has a specific use for a particular material.

2 DROP IN SEAT

The traditional method of upholstery, or re-upholstery, requires a fair amount of skill and patience, as well as a good many years practise. It is much better to acquire the basic skills on a small item. One of the best pieces of furniture on which to practise is an overstuff seat, particularly if it is sprung. This type of chair incorporates nearly all the processes used in upholstery. A good alternative for the beginner is a drop-in dining seat which we will start on here. The first stage in re-upholstering is known as ripping out.

RIPPING OUT

Before beginning to re-upholster, the top cover and stuffings have to be removed. To do this, start at the underside of the seat and remove the bottom canvas using a ripping chisel and mallet. Insert the chisel under the head of a tack, and tap gently with the mallet until the tack starts to loosen. Exert downward pressure on the chisel, and give a hard tap on the end with the mallet;

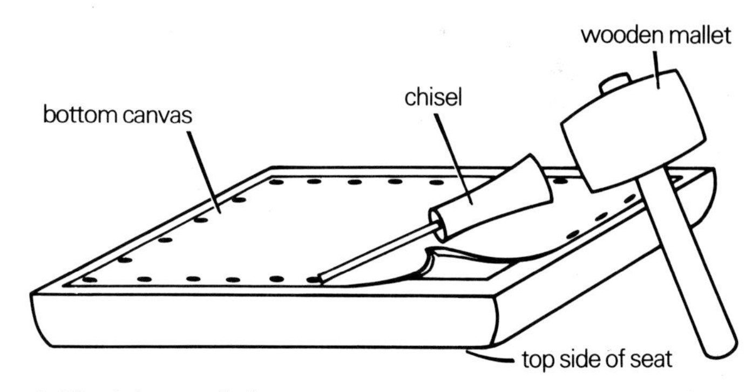

1 Ripping out a chair seat

the tack should come out clean. Always work along the grain of the wood in order not to split the frame. Before removing all the tacks, check the webbing and stuffing; sometimes a repair is all that is needed.

REMOVING BOTTOM CANVAS (HESSIAN OR LINETTE)

If the webbing and stuffing are in bad repair and need to be renewed, proceed with the removal of all the tacks. Remove the bottom canvas, the stuffing and the old webbing, making sure that no tacks are left in the frame. Check the joints for soundness and re-glue them at this stage if necessary.

WEBBING A SEAT

Using either English webbing (black and white) or a good quality jute webbing, proceed to web the seat in the following manner. Space the strips of webbing approximately 5 cm (2 in) apart, depending on the size of the seat. Do not skimp on the webbing, as this forms the main foundation for the seat. Place the first piece of webbing in position in the middle of the rail, and fold the raw end towards the centre of the seat. Place three 16 mm (5/8 in) improved tacks along the outer edge of the rail and hammer home. Place two more tacks towards the inner edge making a 'W' formation. This prevents the wood from splitting. If the rail is narrow or frail use a smaller tack 13 mm (1/2 in) fine.

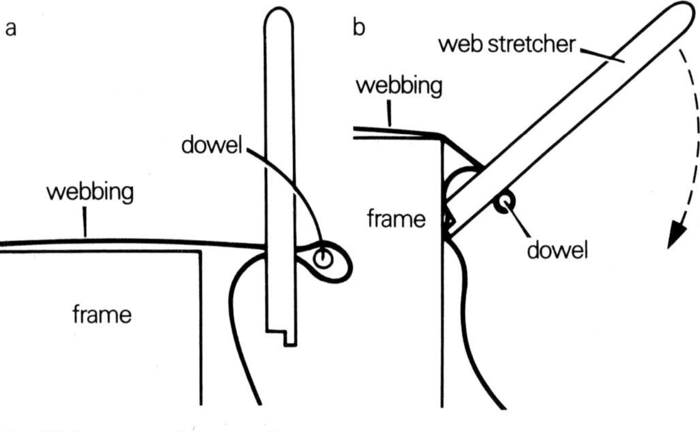

2 *Using a web stretcher*

Having fixed the webbing on one side, pull it towards the opposite side. Make a loop in the webbing, and thread it through the web stretcher. Use the web stretcher as a lever to pull the webbing until it is 'drum tight'. With three tacks fix the webbing onto this rail as before; cut the webbing, allowing enough to turn back. Turn back the end and tack down with two tacks in a 'W' formation. Continue to web the seat between the front and back rails. If the seat is wider across the front than the back, graduate the webbing to follow the frame line. When the webbing has been completed in one direction, weave the webbing, basket-fashion, from side to side and secure at each rail in the same manner as before.

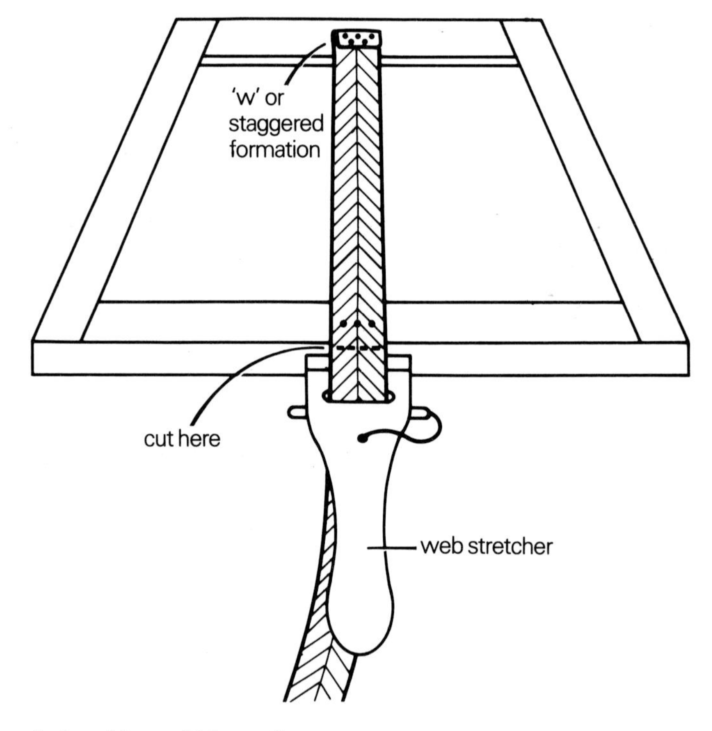

3 *Attaching webbing to frame*

4 Weaving the webbing

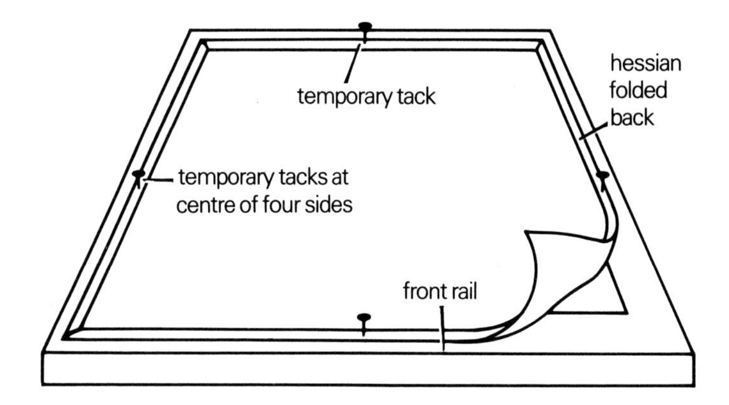

5 Applying the hessian

When the webbing has been completed, cut a length of hessian to fit the frame plus an allowance of 2.5 cm (1 in) all round to turn up. The hessian must be cut to the thread; this ensures that when it is turned over and tacked to the thread, it lies square. To apply the hessian, fold over a hem of 2.5 cm (1 in) on the front edge and place it along the front rail, so that it just covers the webbing. Place a temporary tack in the centre. (A temporary tack is one that is not tacked right home; it is a means of holding the fabric in place, and can easily be taken out and moved.)

Place a temporary tack in the centre back, centre front and centre sides. Working from the centre front, temporary tack out towards the corners, keeping the threads in the hessian straight along the front. Then repeat along the back and sides, again keeping the threads parallel to the sides. Keep the hessian taut while you tack. When you have tacked out from the four central points, work into the corners. Turn the corners over neatly and tack down. Hammer home all the tacks when satisfied that the hessian is square on the frame. The next stage is to apply bridle stitching to the hessian in order to secure the stuffing to the seat.

BRIDLE STITCHING

Bridle stitching is worked in rows across the seat using a spring needle and twine. A row of stitching every 10 cm (4 in) is about average, but the distance depends on the size of area to be covered. Use a good quality medium twine.

STUFFING

Using a good quality fibre, or hair if available, tease out the stuffing a handful at a time and push it under the

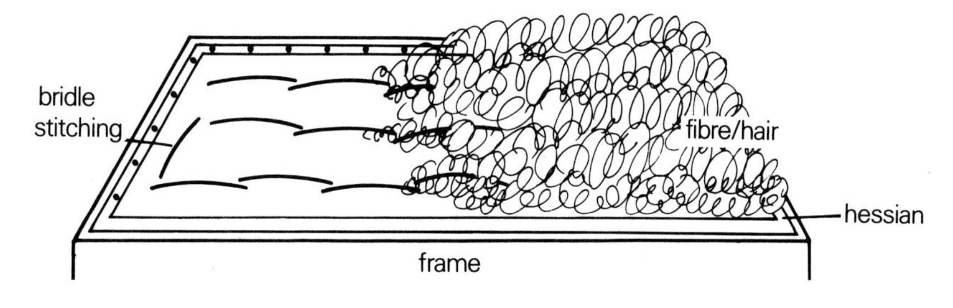

6 Section showing bridle stitching and stuffing

bridle stitching. Start at the back and work across the seat, gradually moving forwards until the whole seat is covered. Each time a handful of stuffing is added, tease it together with the stuffing around it until it all mats together. The objective is to achieve a smooth pad of evenly-distributed fibre. Add extra fibre to the centre of the seat in order to obtain a convex shape. The centre of the seat takes the most weight, and tends to flatten out or, worse still, form a hollow, if extra stuffing is not added at this stage.

COVERING WITH CALICO

After completing the stuffing, lay a piece of calico over the fibre. If the fibre or hair is very short or coarse, it may penetrate the calico. To prevent this, lay a thin layer of wadding between the fibre and the calico. The piece of calico should be long enough to cover the stuffing and the back edge of the frame.

Place a temporary tack in the centre of the back rail about 1.5 cm (5⁄8 in) from the lower edge. Do not turn the edge under, just leave it raw. (A fold would leave an impression that might show through the finished cover.)

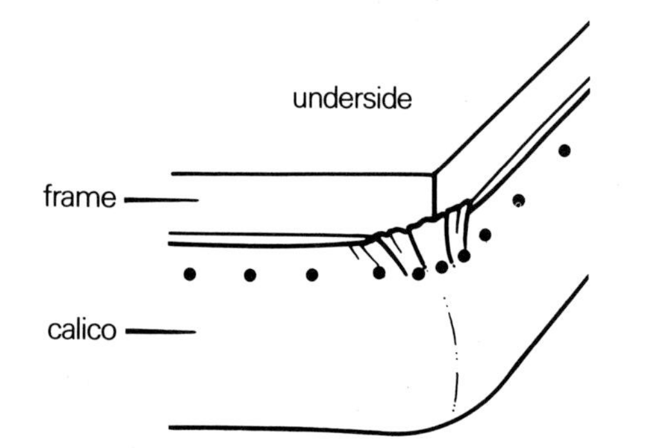

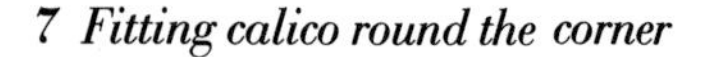
7 Fitting calico round the corner

Drop in seat with frame

Pull the calico forward and tack to the centre of the front rail, repeat this from side to side. Working out towards each corner, pull the calico with the left hand and push it with the right hand to give the maximum stretch; temporary tack in place.

When you reach the corners, pull from the centre of a corner, until the calico is stretched clean over the edge of the frame. Tack home along the underside of the frame and proceed to hammer home the remaining tacks. Cut off the excess calico just below the tack line, leaving the edge raw.

POSITIONING WADDING

Place a piece of sheet wadding on top of the calico,

making sure that it does not fall over the edge of the frame. If this happens the seat becomes too large for the chair frame, thus straining the chair joints. When positioning the wadding, do not cut it to size. It should be torn apart (between the fingers and thumb), which thins the edges making it blend with the other stuffing. The seat is now ready for the top cover.

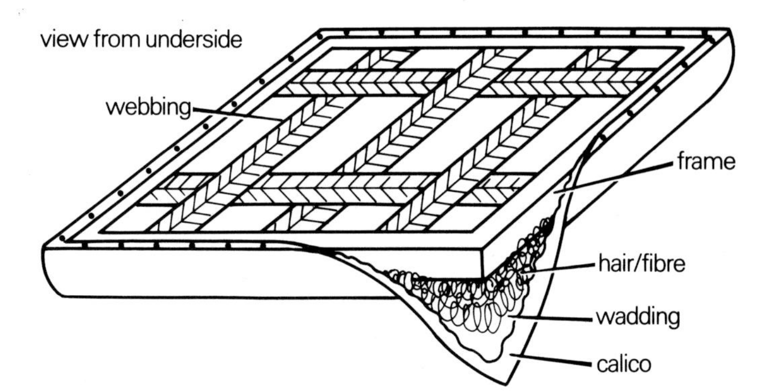

*8 **Right** View of layers from underside*

3 STOOLS AND LOOSE SEATS

Stools and loose seats are not always sprung, and in some cases they have a minimum of stuffing. The base can be either solid, or webbed on the top of the frame. To re-upholster a webbed frame, place a length of hessian over the seat, turn the edges up, and tack in position just inside the outer edge of the frame. The seat can now be padded by stitching ties into the hessian, stuffing with hair or fibre and covering with a layer of linter felt. On the solid seat, a layer of black felt or linter felt, covered by a layer of wadding, can be used. These 'webbed' and 'solid' methods are obviously more economical than the technique that follows, although the products are, of course, much harder to sit on.

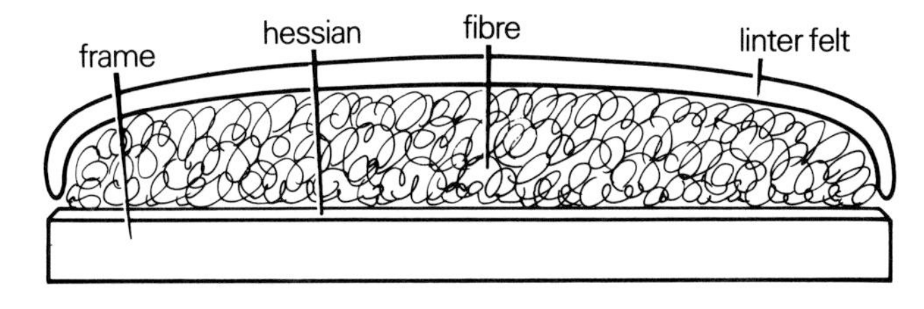

9 Section showing layers

STOOL WITH TACK ROLL

The tack roll method is used for a stool or seat that requires a built-up edge. It is a quicker alternative to making a stitched up edge (page 39). The tack roll can be used around wings, scrolls, or any edge that needs to be built up.

First web the seat (page 26) and then cut a length of hessian the same size as the seat plus 8 to 10 cm (3–4 in) extra on each side. Stretch the hessian tight across the seat, and tack in position on the edge of the frame. Starting in the middle of the back edge, take a handful of fibre and place it in a sausage shape on top of the canvas. Roll the hessian over it, packing in the stuffing as hard as possible until it makes a neat, firm roll. Then, working with about 10 cm (4 in) at a time, push the inner side of the roll against the outer edge of the frame so that it is just proud of the edge. Tack the roll in place along the inside edge of the roll.

When the corner is nearly reached, turn the extra hessian under and make a mitre on the corner. Use the regulator to ensure that the fibre is packed in evenly and

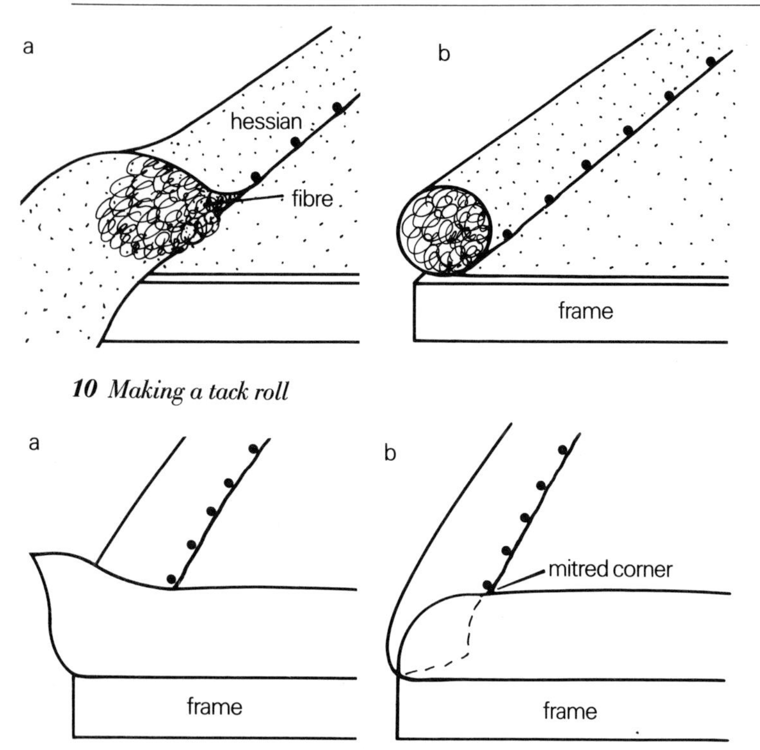

10 Making a tack roll

11 Fitting the corner of tack roll

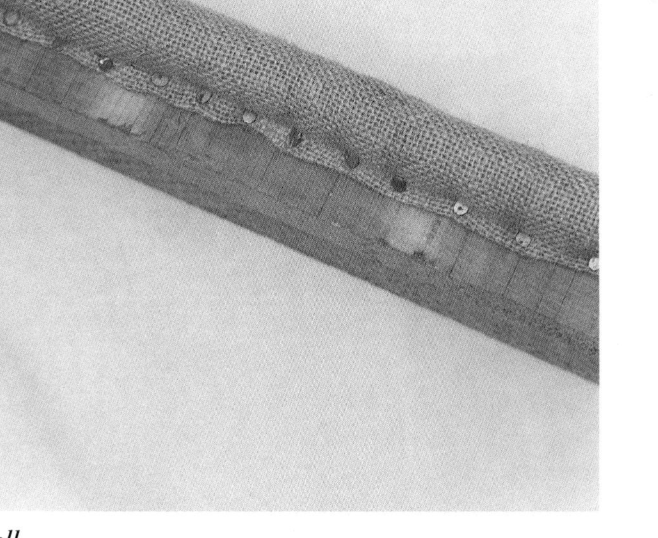

Tack roll

firmly. When the tack roll has been completed all round the edges, bridle stitch the centre section of hessian and fill with fibre until it is slightly higher than the tack roll. Cover with calico, pulling it very firmly over the edges. If the frame is show wood, finish the tack line above the rebate and cut off raw. Otherwise finish just above the lower edge. Cover the calico with a layer of wadding and the stool is ready for re-covering.

STOOL OR LOOSE SEAT USING FOAM

If the seat has rounded corners the foam must be cut 3 cm (1¼ in) wider all round and the extra 3 cm (1¼ in) should then be chamfered. But if the seat has a square edge, the foam should be cut to the exact size of the base. If the base is webbed, web and apply hessian (pages 26–7). If it is solid, the foam can be fixed directly to the base. Using 8 cm (3 in) strips of calico with adhesive or adhesive tape, stick half the strip to the foam, leaving the other half free. On rounded edges they must be stuck to the top side of the foam, whilst on the square edge stool they must be stuck on the upright edge.

Place a tack on the halfway point of each side on the underside of the seat and work out towards each corner until the foam is smooth. Trim the excess tape or calico off at the corner. Either 13 mm (½ in) fine tacks or staples may be used, finish all round and trim off the calico at the tack line. Place a thin sheet of wadding over the foam, or, for a squashy effect, use a layer of Dacron, then re-cover.

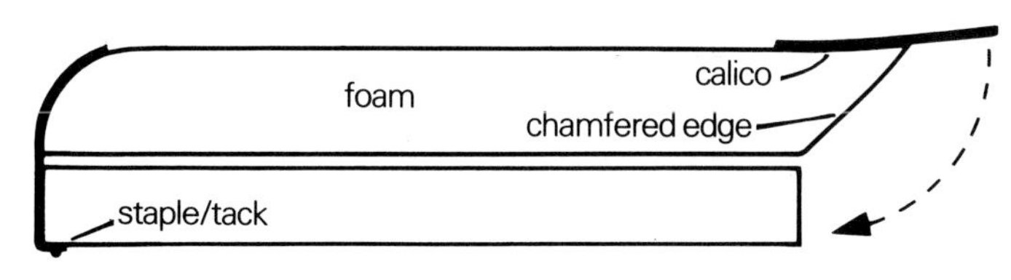

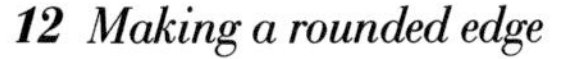
12 Making a rounded edge

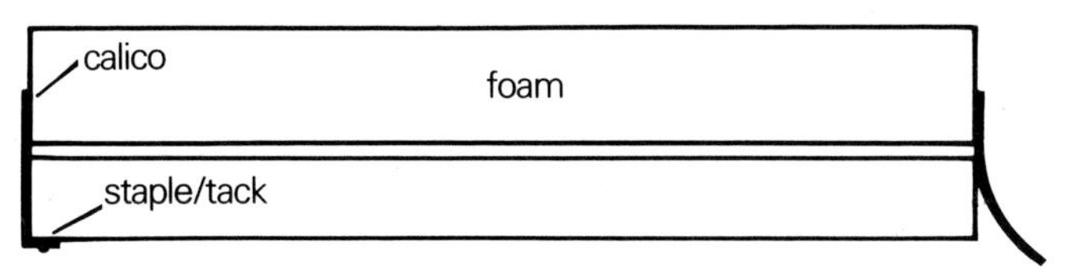

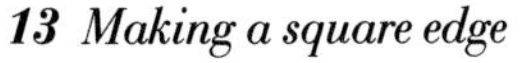
13 Making a square edge

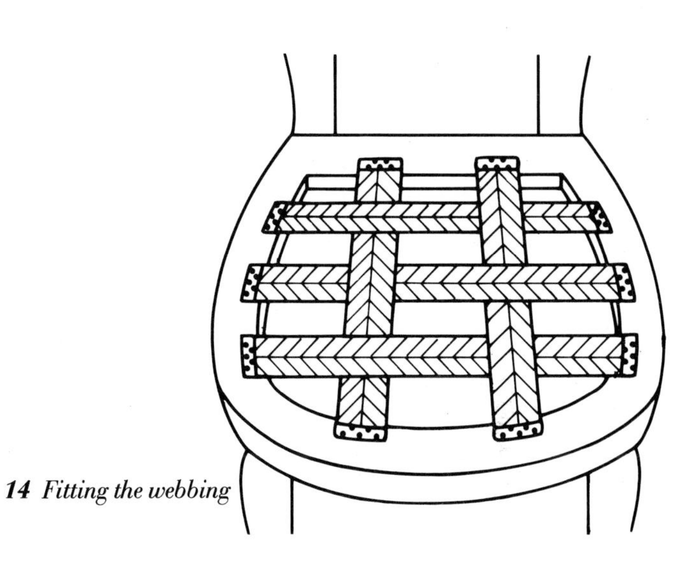
14 Fitting the webbing

PIN CUSHION SEAT

The pin cushion seat is usually found on small occasional chairs, stool tops and other types of show wood furniture. First the webbing is applied using 13 mm (½ in) fine tacks so as not to damage or split the frame. Web in the same manner as for the drop in seat (page 26), making sure that the webbing is on the top of the frame. Where the frame is rounded, the ends of the webbing may have to be folded at an angle so that they lie parallel to the edge of the frame (fig. 14). This also applies if the uprights are in the way of the webbing.

Having applied the webbing, cut a length of hessian to cover the seat area and turnings. With the raw edge upwards, tack the hessian on to the frame, keeping inside the original hessian tack line. Turn the edges upwards. Stuff the seat with a thin layer of hair and cover it with a layer of wadding. If the fabric is very fine, use calico over the top of the hair, otherwise just cover the wadding with your chosen fabric. If calico is used, fix with very few tacks, and cut just inside the outline edge, before positioning the wadding, and finally, covering.

4 OVERSTUFF DINING CHAIR WITH SPRUNG SEAT

In the previous chapters, we dealt with simple types of seats. The re-upholstery of an overstuff seat includes all the processes involved in upholstering an easy chair seat and even larger items of furniture. If possible, practise on this type of chair before attempting a larger item, as it is much easier to handle.

We will assume that the seat needs a complete re-seat. In this case, we must remove all the old cover, stuffing, springs, and so on. Rip out in the same manner as the chair seat (page 25). After ripping out, make sure the frame is firm. If joints need re-gluing, they should be attended to at this stage. We are now ready to start the

Overstuff chair

webbing. In the case of a sprung seat, the webbing is attached to the underside of the frame. Follow the directions on page 26 for webbing a seat.

SEWING IN SPRINGS

Once the seat has been webbed, the next stage is to sew in the springs working from the underside using thread and a spring needle. First place the springs in position on top of webbing. Four springs are sufficient for an average size seat. (Five are used on a larger seat.) To start the sewing, use a slip knot. As this knot is used many times over during the upholstering, it is worth practising (fig. 15).

Stitch the twine through the material, leaving a long end and a short end. Hold on to the long end, and form the slip knot using the short end. Pull on the long end until the knot slips up tight. To lock the knot in position see fig. 15d.

Position the springs on the webbing, spaced so that they follow the frame line for maximum support. Using a spring needle and working from the underside, tie a slip knot and then make a stitch through the webbing over

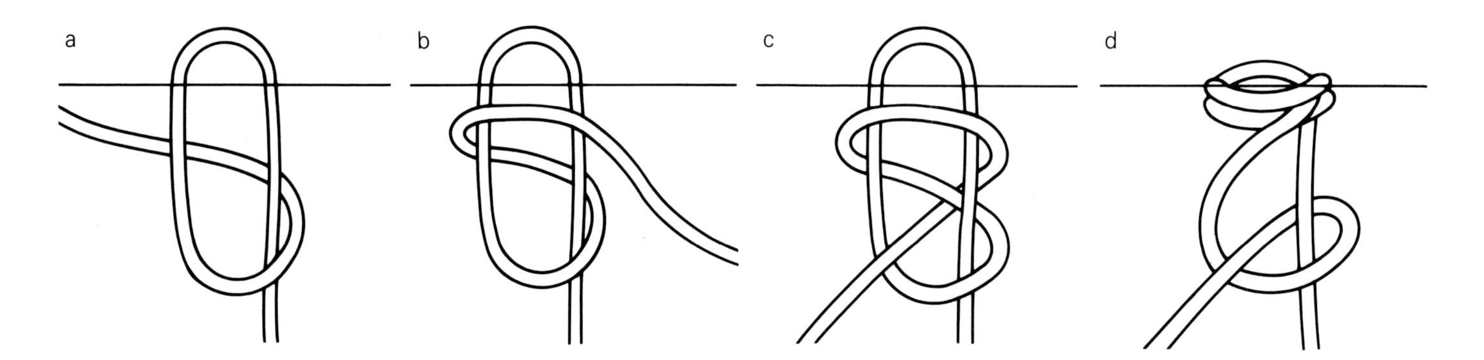

15 Above and right *Upholsterer's slip knot*

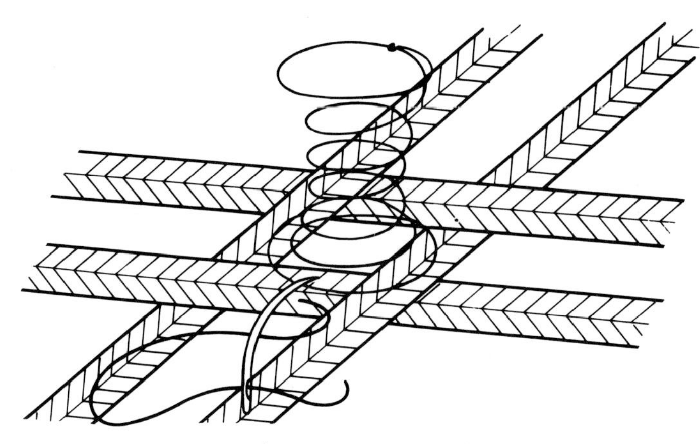

16 Sewing a spring in place

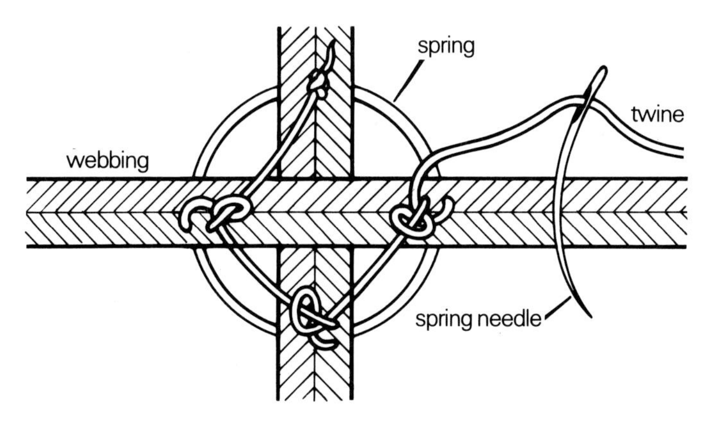

17 Stitch pattern around spring

the spring wire and back through the webbing; tie a single knot and lock it in place. Repeat on each of the four strands of web with which the spring is in contact. Proceed to stitch all the springs in place.

LASHING (LACING) THE SPRINGS

When all the springs have been stitched in place, the next stage is to lash the springs (this is sometimes called lacing). Use 16 mm (5⁄8 in) improved tacks and laid cord

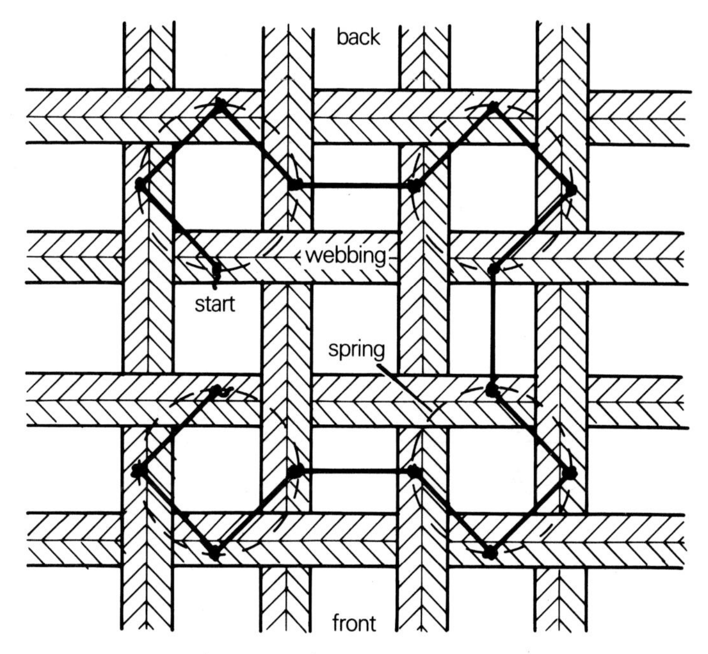

18 Stitch pattern between springs

to do this. Measure from the side edge of the frame over the top of the springs to the opposite edge, add half as much again, and cut off a piece of laid cord this length.

Place a temporary tack in one side of the frame, in line with the row of springs to be lashed. Take the length of laid cord and tie a single knot leaving enough free to stretch from the tack back to the spring. Slip the knot over the tack head, pull it tight and hammer the tack home. Leave the short end for the time being and proceed to lash down the springs with the long end in the following manner.

Compress the spring with the left hand until the initial 'give' in the spring is taken up. With the right hand, tie the first knot on the coil of the spring which is second from the top. Tie the second knot on the top coil. Stretch the cord across to the next spring, tie a knot on the top

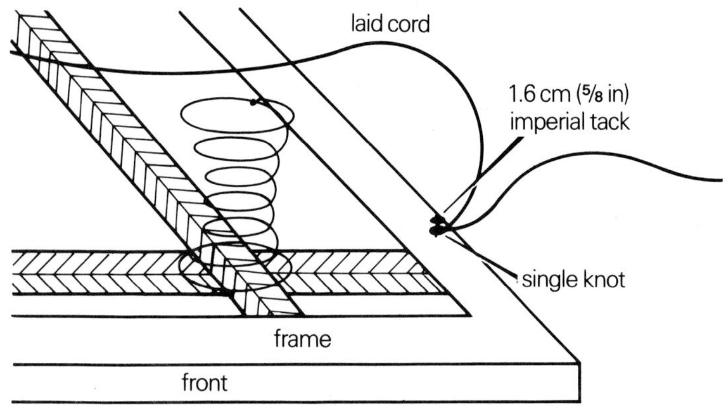

19 Attach the laid cord around a temporary tack

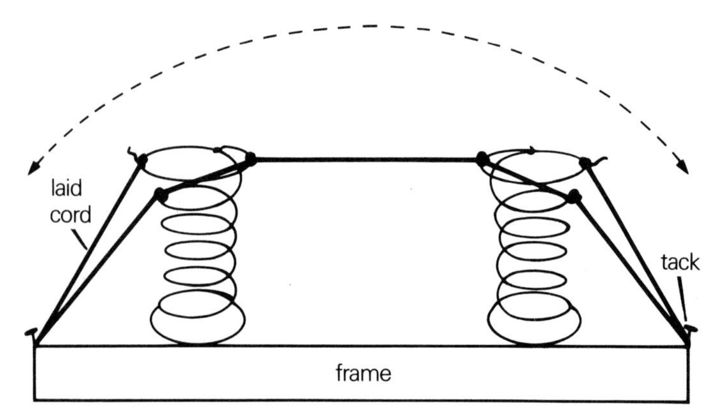

20 Laid cord lashing springs

Lashed springs on an overstuff chair

coil of the spring, and a second on the second coil on the side closest to the frame edge. (If there are more than two springs in a row, the central springs should be tied on both sides of the top coil.) Now tap a tack into the frame and secure the laid cord by knotting it round the tack and hammering it home. Tie the loose end of the laid cord securely to the top coil of the spring (on the side closest to the frame edge). Do the same with the loose end on the first side where the tying started. It is most important that the laid cord lies in a straight line and that the springs are evenly lashed down.

Knots used in lashing springs

The hitch is the first knot used after tacking down the laid cord to the frame, it is then used alternatively with the half hitch across the seat. However, always finish with a hitch even if this means tying two hitches in a row. After tying the last knot lock it with the knot immediately below, then cut off the laid cord leaving at least 3 cm (1¼ in) of cord from the knot. There are variations on the knots shown and also varying methods of tying them. Every spring can be tied with a hitch; however,

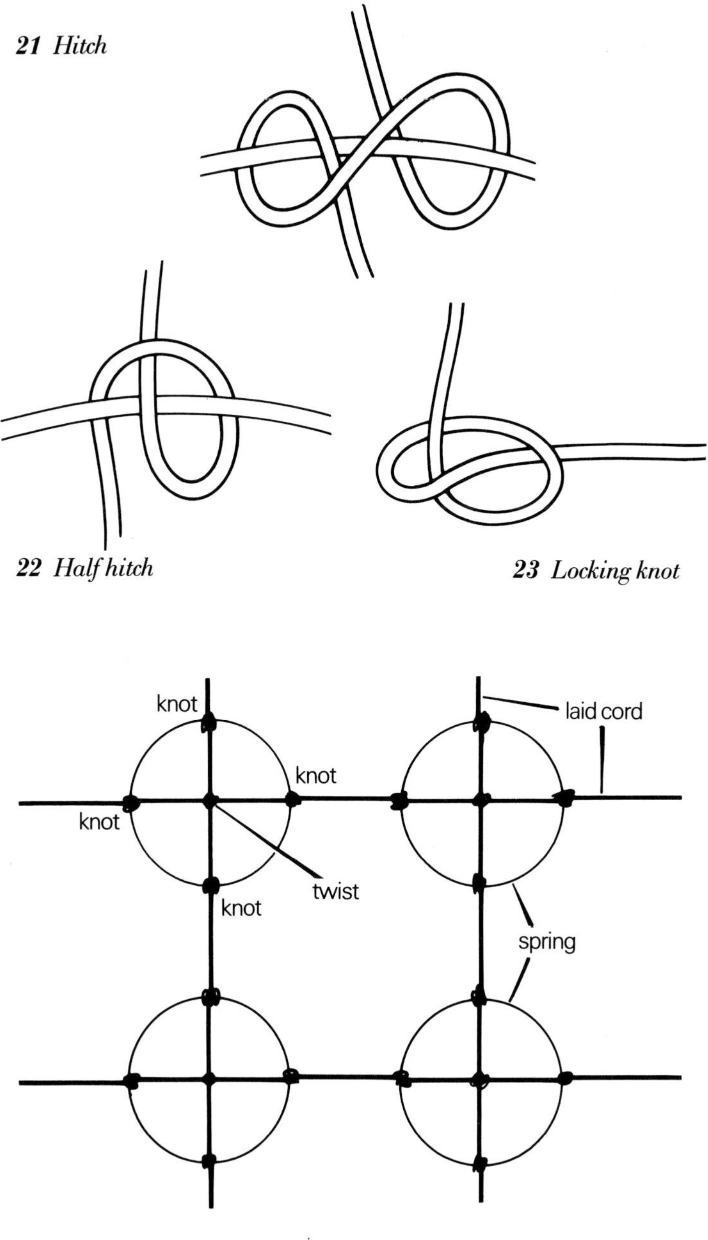

21 Hitch

22 Half hitch

23 Locking knot

24 ***Above*** *Springs lashed in both directions*
25 ***Right*** *Fitting tarpaulin around frame upright*

alternating half-hitches with hitches is suggested because, with this method, the tension can be adjusted easily while the springs are lashed in place. (Most beginners wish they had an extra pair of hands during this process.)

Having lashed all the springs from side to side, now lash them from front to back. Where the cords cross at the centres of the springs, take a twist (fig 24). If the springs are over 22 cm (8½ in) in depth, they are lashed through the middle as well as across the top, to prevent the centre bowing out. The method used is exactly the same as the lashing already described with the only difference that the knots are tied to the middle coils on each spring.

FITTING TARPAULIN (SPRING CANVAS)

When the lashing has been completed, tarpaulin must be tacked over the springs. Cut the tarpaulin approximately 5 cm (2 in) larger overall than the area to be covered. Fold the back edge over to approximately 2.5 cm (1 in) so that the raw edge faces up. Following one thread to get a straight line, fix three temporary tacks along the centre of the back edge and stretch the tarpaulin over the springs towards the front edge. Tack in position with temporary tacks all along the back edge, and then along the side edges, smoothing the excess material towards the corners. Tack home the temporary tacks; trim off the excess material around the front and sides to approxi-

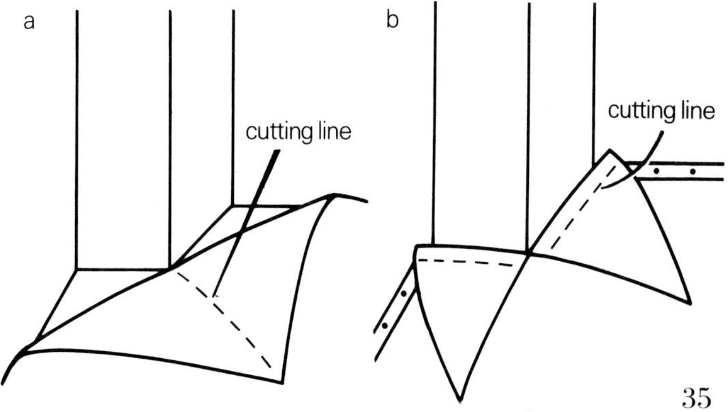

mately 2.5 cm (1 in). Where the back frame meets the seat the tarpaulin should be cut and tacked down (fig. 25).

The springs must now be stitched through the tarpaulin, using the same method as for stitching springs to the webbing. Work from spring to spring following the most logical pattern around the seat. When the stitching has been completed, finish off with a double knot. The tarpaulin is fixed on four points of the springs although if the chair has more than four springs, three fixings are sufficient, as long as they make a complete triangle. This holds the springs steady, so that they do not rub on the tarpaulin.

Now bridle stitch the tarpaulin in rows ready for stuffing. The loops should be loose enough to allow a hand to pass underneath. Follow the procedure for bridle stitching on page 27. This stitching is done over the top of the spring stitching.

FIRST STUFFING AND FITTING SCRIM

The seat is now ready for the first stuffing. Fibre is usually used for first stuffing, but hair can be used. Tease the stuffing with the fingers and then, using a handful at a time, tuck it under the loops. Start at the back, and work across and forward. Tease each handful into the next so that it masses together. Continue to cover the seat right up to the edges. Add more to the centre section to give a domed appearance. Make sure the fibre is evenly distributed over the seat, with the outer edge of the frame just covered.

Cut a length of scrim to cover the seat plus approximately 3 cm (1¼ in) extra to tuck under, between the frame and the fibre. Starting at the back, tuck the scrim under the fibre and place a tack right on the chamfered edge of the frame. (If the frame is new it must be chamfered off on the edge, using a rasp; the edge will already be chamfered if it has been upholstered before.) Temporary tack the scrim to the middle of the back, front and each side, thus holding it in position ready for the stuffing ties.

The stuffing ties are stitched right through the seat using a double-pointed needle approximately 35 cm (14 in) long, and a strong medium twine. The pattern of stitching depends on the size and shape of the seat. On a small seat, form the stitches in a square shape following the outline of the seat. On a larger seat follow the shape illustrated in fig. 27. Starting with a slip knot, push the needle right through the seat from top to bottom, pull the needle out at the bottom, and, making a stitch approximately 1.25 cm (½ in) long, push the needle back up through the seat, then proceed to take another stitch through from the top. The top stitches should be

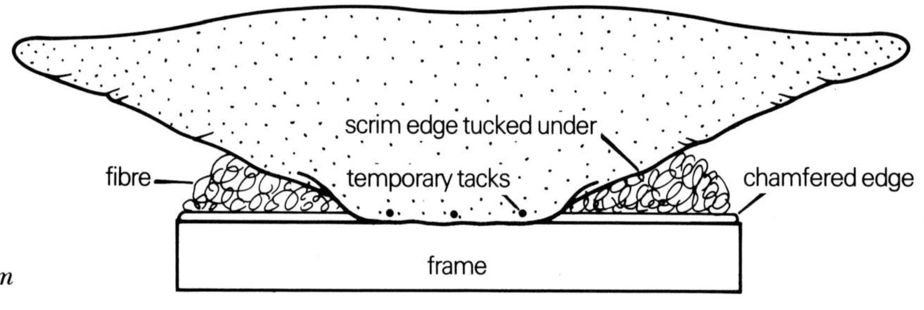

26 *Positioning scrim*

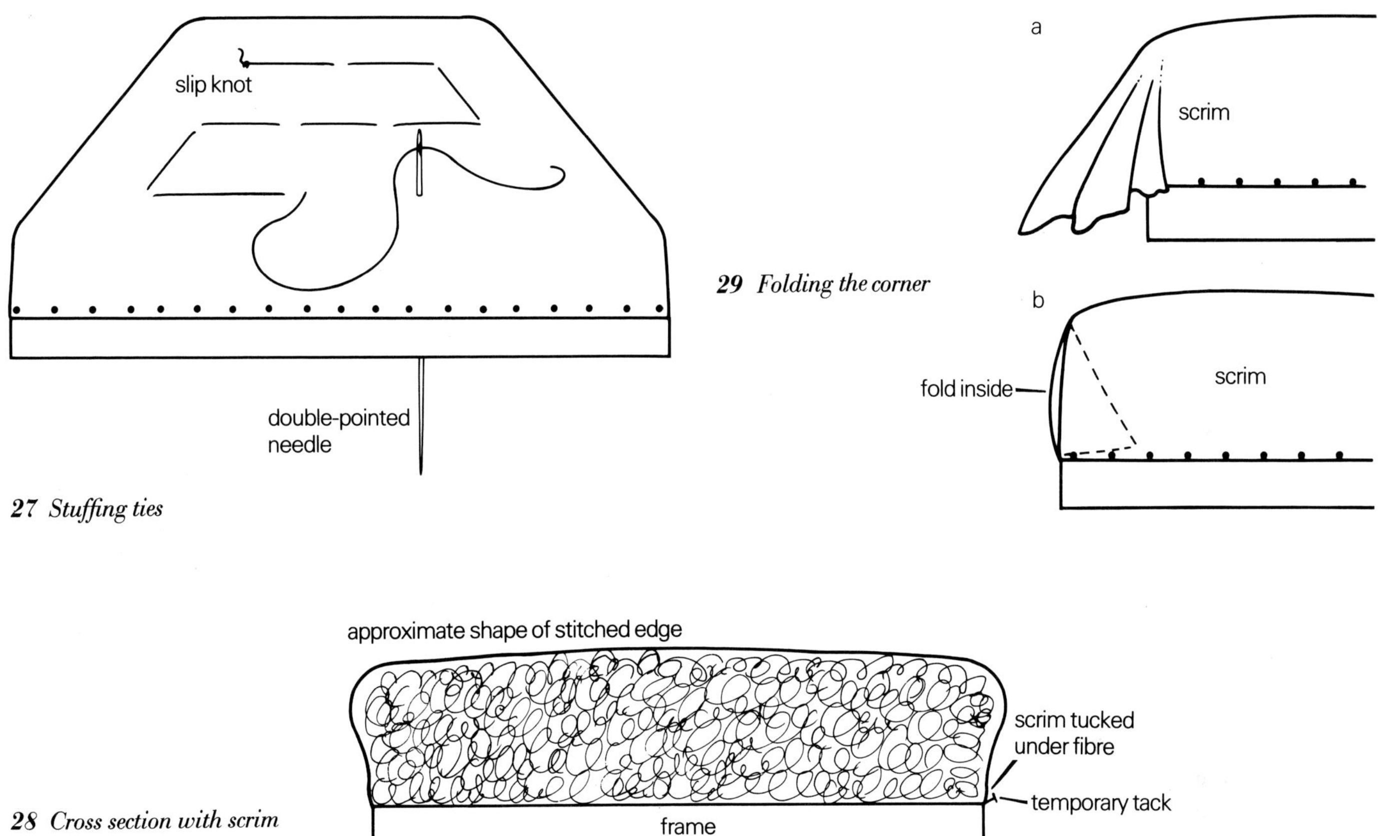

27 Stuffing ties

29 Folding the corner

28 Cross section with scrim in position

approximately 15 cm (6 in). Leave the stitching loose at this stage. When the stitching is complete, start at the back and pull on the twine, while pushing the seat down. Repeat this at each stitch, until the stuffing has been pulled down as hard as possible, leaving an indentation in the centre of the seat. When the last stitch has been reached, tie the loose end round the last stitch and knot off the twine. (Do not come out to the edge of the seat with this stitch; leave at least a 10 cm [4 in] margin.)

Ease the scrim over the fibre towards the front of the frame and tuck the excess under the fibre. To obtain the right tension takes a good deal of practise. The object is to have the scrim tight enough to enable the edge to be stitched, but not so tight that it flattens out the edge. Find the approximate position of where the stitched edge will be and pinch between thumb and forefinger to form a roll. Use this method at the front and back and both sides to gauge the tension of the scrim. Temporary tack the scrim to the frame at the back, sides and front, working from the centres towards the corners. Fold the corners under to form a good square corner exactly in line with the corner of the frame.

USING THE REGULATOR

When the stuffing ties have been completed and the scrim has been tacked down, the stuffing must be 'regulated'. This means that, using a regulator, the stuffing is distributed to exactly the area where it is needed. To use the regulator on the edge, hold the edge between the thumb and fingers, and place the point of the regulator into the stuffing a few centimetres away from the fingers. By twisting the regulator back and forth, the stuffing will be pulled towards the edge, thus making it very firm. The fingers and thumb are used to feel the stuffing and to make sure it is being regulated evenly.

BLIND STITCHING

When the stuffing is firmly in place along the top edge, the next step is to blind stitch the edges. Use the 20 cm (8 in) double-pointed needle, and thread it with a fairly long length of twine. Start at the back left of the seat and work forward, inserting the needle as low down as possible, close in to the frame, and pushing it at an angle until it comes out approximately 10 cm (4 in) from the top edge of the seat. Pull the needle *nearly* out, then push it back into the seat, so that it comes out on the bottom edge approximately 2 cm (¾ in) to the left of where it was inserted. With the two loose ends, make a slip knot and pull tight.

Form the next stitch by inserting the needle 3 cm (1¼ in) to the right and repeating the procedure. When the needle is halfway out, take the twine on the left side and wind it round the needle for three turns. Continue to pull the needle out, and then place it out of the way on the worktop (it is not necessary to unthread it). Pull the twine first to the left and then to the right, until it is as tight as possible. To prevent the twine from cutting the hands wear an old leather glove on the right hand. At the corner let the needle come out through the same point at the top until the corner has been turned. Continue to blind stitch all round the edge of the seat. The blind stitching will have moved the stuffing towards the edges, so use the regulator again.

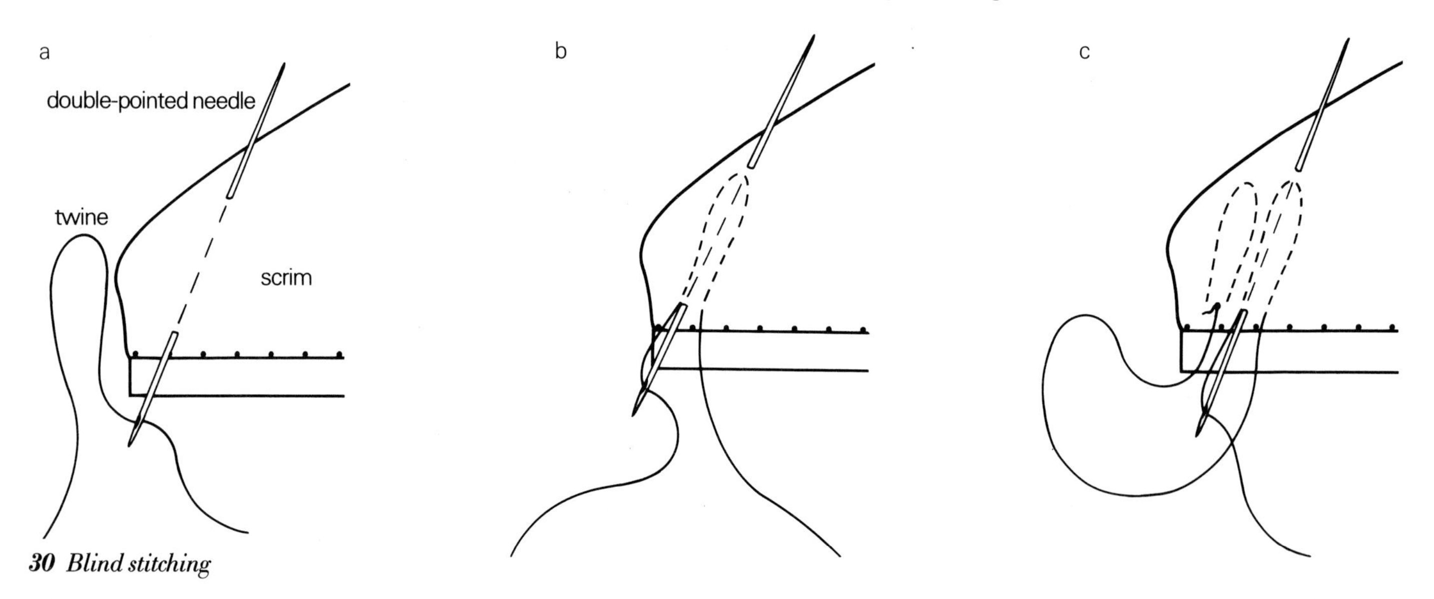

***30** Blind stitching*

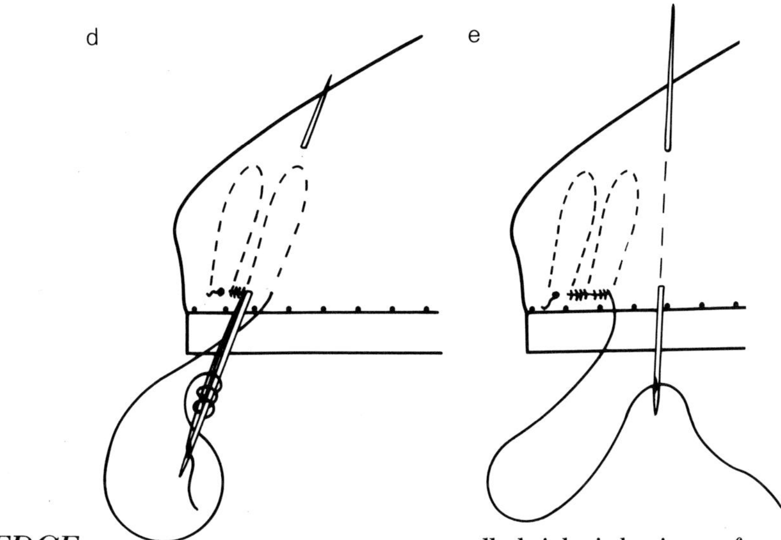

Blind stitching continued

THE STITCHED EDGE

To form the stitched edge, the method is almost the same as the blind stitch with the difference that, instead of leaving the needle in the seat at the top edge, the needle is pulled right out and then placed in the seat about 2 cm (¾ in) to the left, thus forming a stitch. When this is pulled tight it begins to form the stitched edge. Start the stitching about 1.25 cm (½ in) above the blind stitching and come through on the top surface of the seat approximately 8 cm (3 in) from the front edge. The second row of stitching should start about 3 cm (1¼ in) above the first row and on the top surface, the row of

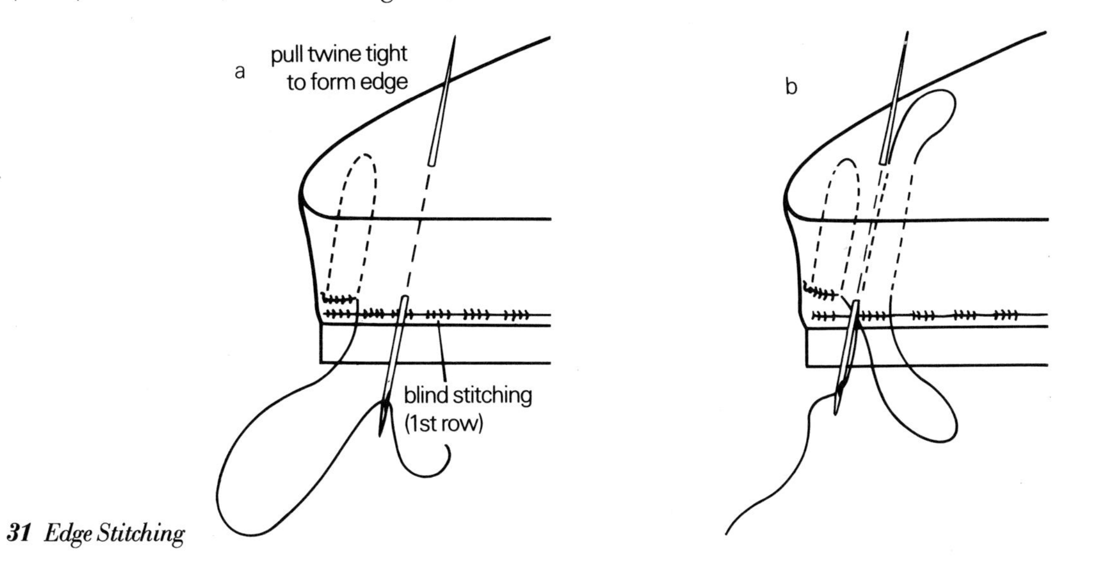

***31** Edge Stitching*

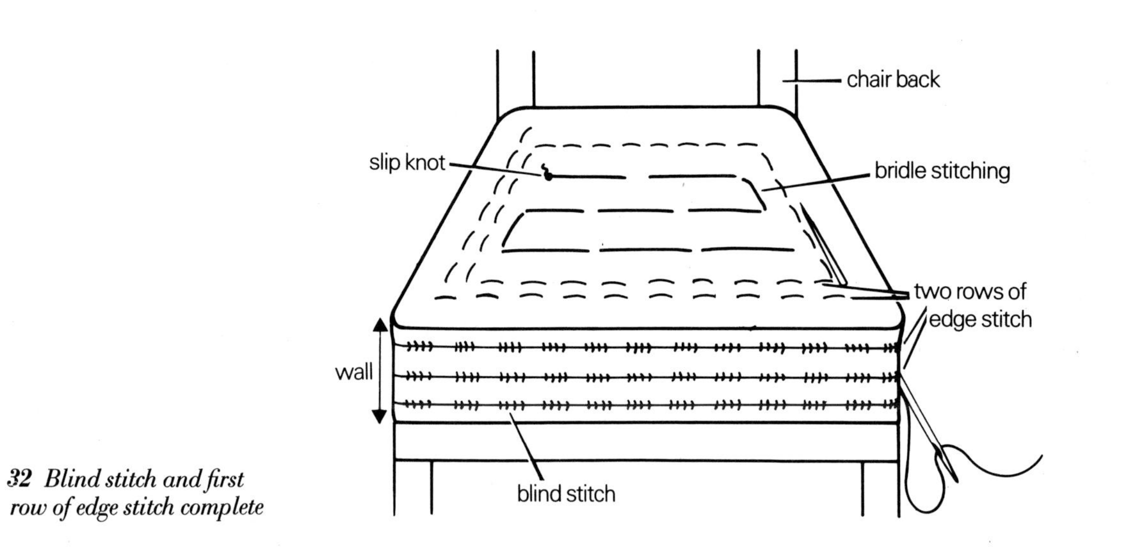

32 Blind stitch and first row of edge stitch complete

Layer of stuffing on overstuff chair

stitches should be about 4 cm (1½ in) inside the first row. Two rows of stitching will normally be sufficient but to make the wall higher, three may be necessary. Finish the stitching all round the edges. The edge should now be very hard and rigid. Proceed with the second stuffing.

Sew bridle stitching across the seat in the same way as for the first stuffing. Proceed to stuff handfuls of hair under the stitching until the whole seat area is evenly covered right to the edge of the seat. Now the seat is ready for covering with calico.

COVERING WITH CALICO

Cut a length of calico to cover the seat and to reach down the sides, front and back. Starting from the middle of the back, place a temporary tack through the calico and into the frame, and pull the calico over towards the front centre. Hammer in a tack to hold it in place, before repeating the process from side to side. (By pushing with one hand and pulling with the other, make the calico as tight as possible.) Working from the centre of each side

'Up to calico' on overstuff chair

Covered and finished overstuff chair

out towards the corners, cut into the back corners and fasten in place with temporary tacks. At the front corners pull down at the centre point and hold with a temporary tack. Then ease the excess fabric into small pleats. An alternative way of finishing the corner is to cut the excess fabric away leaving just sufficient for the raw edges to meet. This is called butting and it gives a square corner.

Once the corner has been completed, the temporary tacks can be tacked home, and the calico trimmed back almost to the edge of the tack line, leaving a raw edge. A layer of wadding should now be placed on the seat, two layers of sheet wadding may be used if it seems thin. This prevents the hair penetrating through to the top cover. Trim the wadding to within 5 cm (2 in) of the frame by pulling between the thumb and fingers. (It must not be cut as this makes an impression right through the top cover.) It is important to leave the wadding short of the frame because when the top cover is pulled over, the padding will be pulled down to the edge. The seat is now ready for its top cover.

HELPFUL TIPS

If the corners of a frame are in bad shape, a piece of buckram or card can be tacked in place. To square a corner, position it under the stitched edge, leaving it shy of the frame at the bottom edge.

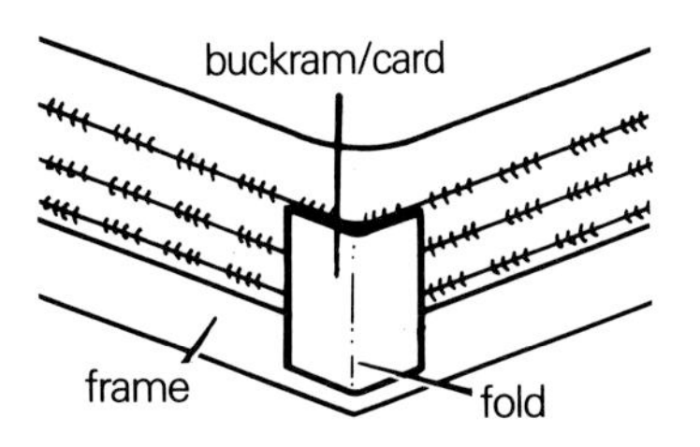

33 *Squaring the corner*

5 RE-SEATING AN EASY CHAIR

The processes used in the re-seating of an easy chair are identical to those used for the overstuff seat, right up to the fitting of the tarpaulin. (Note that cushion seats require level springing and full seats require springing that is 4 cm [1½ in] higher at the centre than it is at the front edge.)

Fit the tarpaulin to the lower rail on the sides and back and to the upper rail on the front. Cut the tarpaulin where it meets the upright rails and turn it back 1.25 cm (½ in). Tack the tarpaulin in place in the same way as for the overstuff chair (page 35). Follow the procedures for sewing the springs to the tarpaulin, and bridle stitch ready for the first stuffing on page 36.

Next, stuff the seat with fibre allowing it to go just under the top rail, and right up to the front edge on the front rail. When the stuffing is complete, place the scrim on the lower rail using temporary tacks, pull the scrim over the stuffing in the front, tuck under and temporary tack in place.

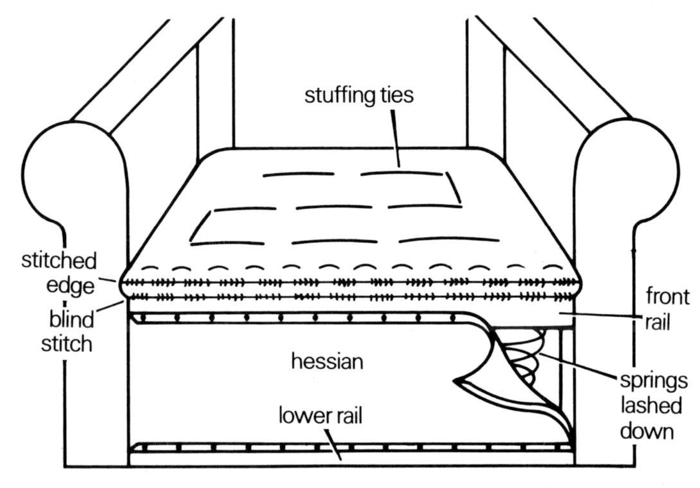

35 Front edge stitched up; hessian almost tacked in place

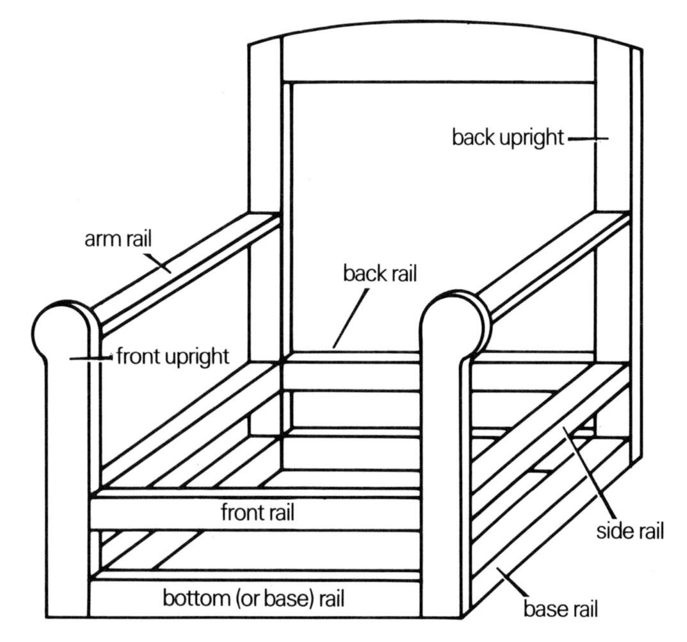

34 Easy chair frame

Stuffing ties should now be sewn right through the seat (page 36). Adjust and tack all the tacks home round the sides and back.

Make sure there is enough stuffing on the front edge. If there is not, add more at this stage by removing the temporary tacks and adding an extra handful of fibre, or more, until the correct effect is achieved. Replace tacks and tack home.

Blind stitch the front edge, regulate the stuffing and then stitch the front edge so that it is very firm and even in depth (pages 38–9).

When the front edge has been completed, cut a length of hessian to fit over the gap between the top and lower rail. Turn the edges back so that the raw edges face front and tack in position (fig. 35).

Bridle stitch the seat in the same way as for the first

stuffing and proceed with the second stuffing. Allow the stuffing to reach just to the frame edge on the side. Cut a length of calico, enough to cover right over the seat area and over the front edge. Tack it to the back rail and to the side rails. Pull the calico over the front edge and tack it onto the front top rail. The edge of the calico must be left raw. Finally, cut the excess away from the corners of the front edge and tack home.

Stitch bridle ties onto the front border, and stuff the whole area with a thin layer of hair. Cover with a length of calico and attach it to either side of the uprights. The seat is now ready to be re-covered (Chapter 13).

Tweed armchair

6 EASY CHAIR WITH SPRUNG BACK, SPRUNG ARMS AND INDEPENDENT SPRUNG FRONT EDGE

This type of chair is one of the most difficult to do, but one of the most comfortable available. Use the best materials that you can afford, because even though they cannot be seen under the cover, this foundation is most important. The use of a good wadding directly beneath the cover not only stops the hair coming through, but also stops the cover from wearing. A cover can wear out just as quickly from the inside, especially if it is a pile fabric which has an abrasive material under it. The abrasive stuffing wears the pile away from its backing and makes the pile fall out.

Independent front edge

There are a number of chairs and settees which have not been stuffed with hair. The variety of stuffings in old chairs ranges from alva (seaweed) to rag flock, wood wool and so on. Stuffings and fillings are being improved and experimented with and, in time, many of the old materials will disappear. (Some are already difficult to obtain.) For this reason, it is important to try some of the new types of stuffing as well as the traditional ones. This does not mean that I recommend substituting the original materials on a Victorian chair for a piece of foam. However, duck down for instance has become so expensive that many people are using a foam substance wrapped in a fibrefill material for seat or back cushions. The effect has the feel of a soft and squashy cushion.

On a clean frame, the arms are attended to first (because they are less accessible once the seat is finished), then comes the seat and finally the back. However, it is not always necessary to re-upholster the entire chair. The seat is the most likely area to require attention and, therefore, this is the step described first.

THE INDEPENDENT SPRUNG EDGE

This type of chair has springs set on the front edge of the frame to give a softer seat. The main part of the seat is webbed, stitched and lashed in exactly the same manner as the overstuff dining chair (Chapter 4). Place the spring canvas over the seat springs allowing enough extra to cover the front springs and to form a gutter between the seat springs and the front edge.

Using 15 cm (6 in) by 8 gauge springs, (four or five are usually sufficient), place the springs level with the

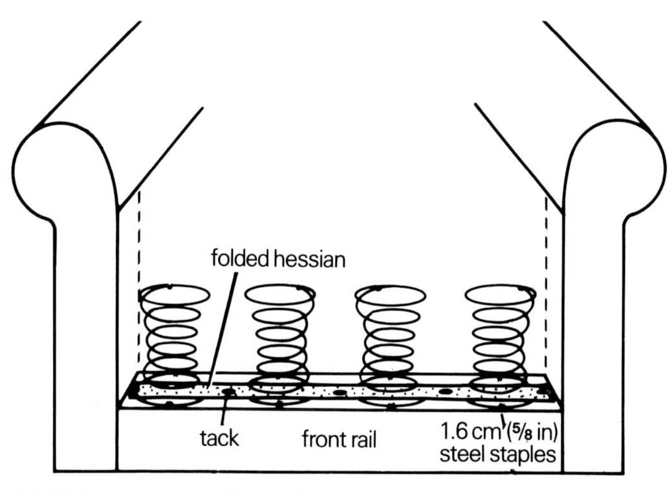

36 Fixing springs on front edge

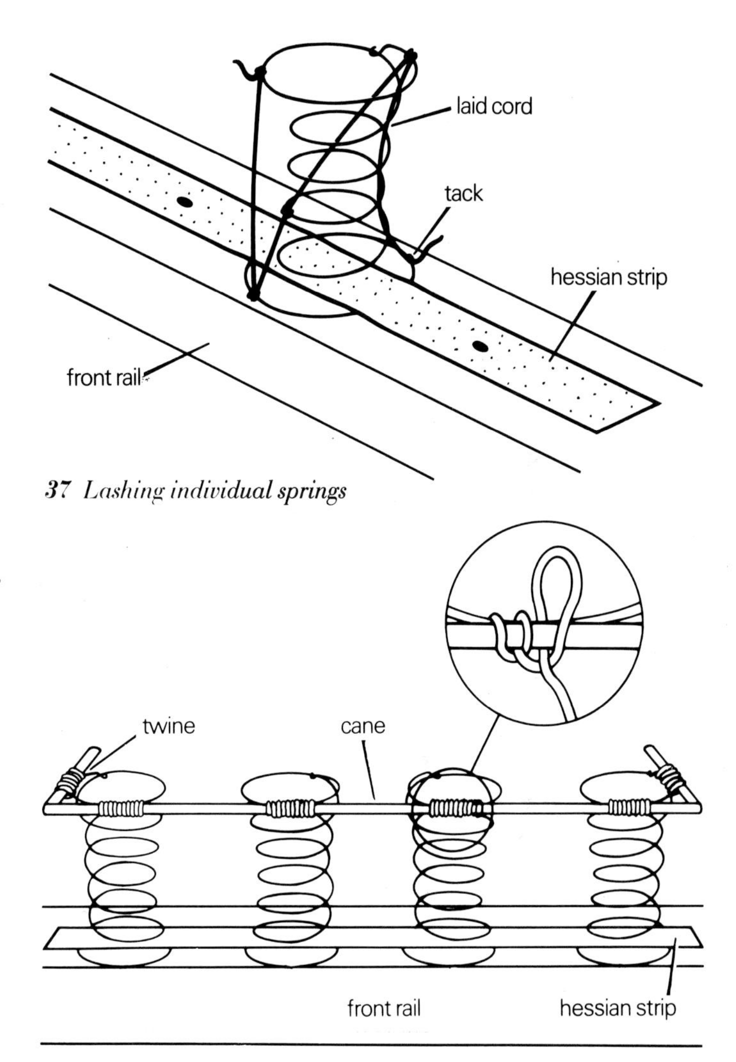

37 Lashing individual springs

38 Cane bent to shape and bound to springs

front edge of the frame. Fix in position using 1.5 cm (⅝ in) steel staples. Lay a double thickness strip of hessian (or webbing folded in half lengthwise to a width of 4 cm [1½ in]) along the length of the front rail so that it passes through the spring lying across the bottom coil. Place a tack in between each spring through the hessian into the front rail and tack home. The hessian prevents the coils from hitting the front rail and making a clattering noise when someone sits down.

Use your hand to compress each spring to a height just below the level of the seat springs. Lash each spring into position using laid cord following this procedure. Fix a temporary 16 mm (⅝ in) imperial tack on the inside of the front rail directly behind one of the springs. Attach a length of laid cord to the rack and hammer home. Take the laid cord up through the spring and knot on the inner side of the middle coil. Take to the inner side of the top coil and knot again. Now bring the laid cord through the spring down to the outer side of the middle coil and knot. Follow down to the bottom coil, knot and then fix a final knot on the outer side of the top coil (fig. 37).

Once the springs have been lashed down, a length of cane must be bent in shape to fit along the front edge and width of the front rail. Sometimes, a heavy gauge wire is used instead of cane. Now bind the cane to the top coil of each spring using a medium-weight twine. (Follow the binding process illustrated in fig. 38.)

Having bound the cane to the springs, the next step is to make a gutter between the seat and the spring edge, so that the front edge remains independent. To do this, tuck the spring canvas that is already attached to the seat down between the seat and front edge. This gutter is held in place by fixing a length of laid cord from the side rail across the gutter and on to the opposite side rail. Loop each end of the laid cord round 16 mm (5⁄8 in) imperial tacks, and tack home. Fold the spring canvas back over the laid cord and at a point between each spring make a hole through the canvas using the regulator. Thread a length of laid cord through the hole and tie with a slip knot, so that the knot holds the laid cord in the gutter firmly together with the canvas. Place two of these ties between each spring, and secure them by tacking them to the top of the front edge.

After completing the gutter ties, pull the spring canvas forward over the spring edge and temporary tack halfway down the front rail to allow room for the turn under. Fold the edge under and tack down. The spring canvas must now be attached to the outer side of the springs by using a medium twine to stitch through the canvas and catch both the top coil and the cane. (See stitched edge on page 39).

Now sew bridle ties over the whole seat area (page 11) and insert stuffing under the ties. Fill in the gutter with stuffing also, until the whole seat has an even layer of hair or fibre across it. At this stage, a length of scrim must be cut to fit right over the seat from the back rail to the front edge leaving enough to tuck under. Fold the scrim under approximately 1.25 cm (1⁄2 in) and temporary tack along the middle of the top side of the back rail. Pull the scrim over the hair or fibre and tack down on the two side rails. Keep the threads of the scrim straight, from front to back and from side to side. Then, starting in the centre of the front edge, fold the scrim under and tuck it beneath the stuffing along the front edge. Use a

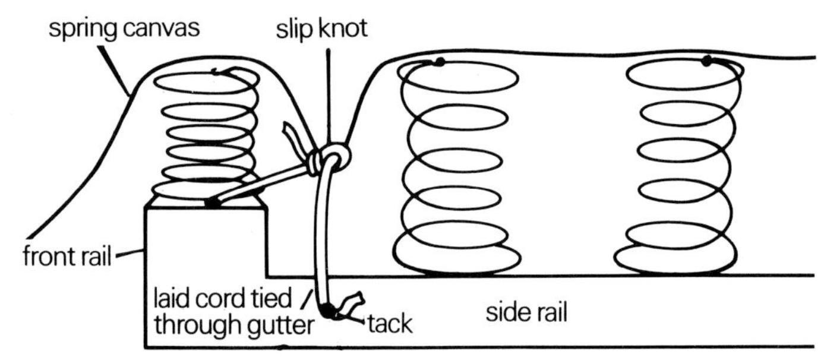

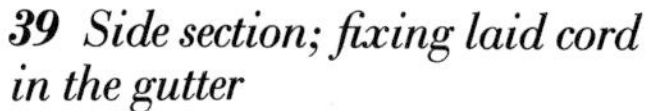
39 Side section; fixing laid cord in the gutter

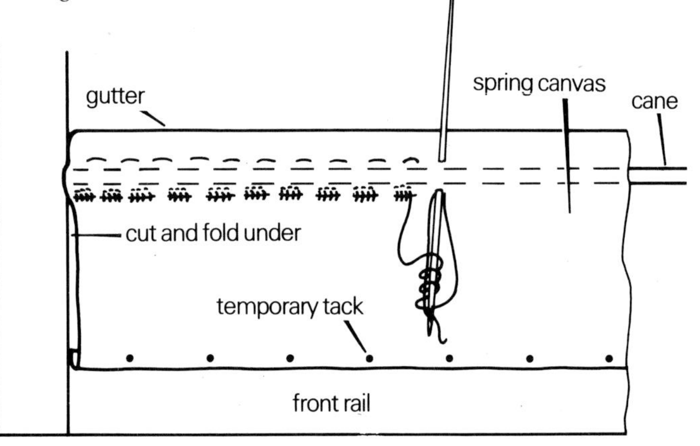

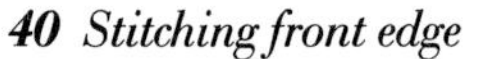
40 Stitching front edge

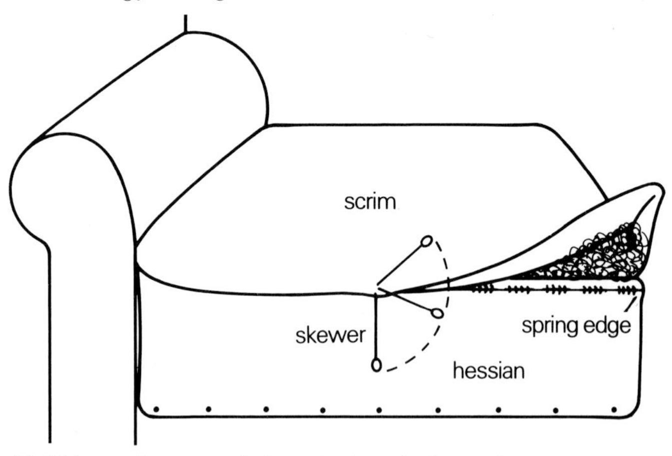

41 Using a skewer, push the scrim into the front edge

skewer to hold it in place. (To use a skewer, push it into the scrim, lever it down, then push it up into place so that it holds firm.)

Having tucked the scrim under the front edge, it must now be secured to the hessian using a blanket stitch. But first, before starting the blanket stitch, sew the stuffing ties through the seat so that you will not be caught out if the skewers need adjustment.

Now blind stitch (pages 38–9) the front edge and then stitch it up with one row of running stitches. Continue to finish in the same manner as for the overstuff chair up to the point where calico is fitted over the front edge. When fitting calico to an independent edge, it cannot be tacked to the frame. Instead, you should follow this procedure. Pull the calico over the edge, ease the fullness on the corners and proceed to stitch right through the calico into the front edge, using a strong twine and a circular needle. The stitch used is a long running stitch. Secure the twine at the beginning and at the end of the border, and cut off excess calico. Pad the front border section and slip stitch down under the lip. Tack the rest of the front edge in the same way as for the overstuff chair (pages 40–1).

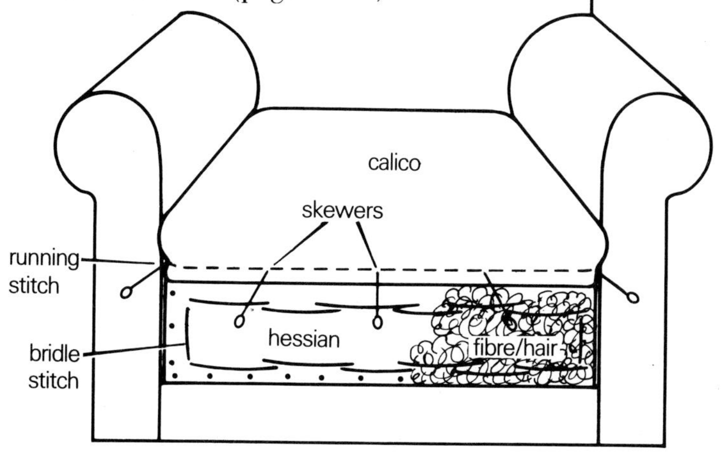

42 Stuffing the front edge

THE INDEPENDENT SPRUNG ARM

To make a sprung arm, first tack two pieces of webbing vertically on to the inside of the frame. The piece nearest the inside back should be folded in half, and placed about 5 cm (2 in) from the frame edge, this gives a line to the inside arm and allows the outer cover to be pulled through at a later stage. The other piece of webbing should be placed approximately half-way along the arm stretching from the top rail to bottom rail.

Before positioning the springs place a strip of folded hessian or a length of webbing, folded in half, along the length of the arm frame and tack down diagonally. This step helps prevent the springs clattering against the frame. After fixing the webbing, place a length of hessian on the frame, and tack home, this is called 'backing up' (fig. 43).

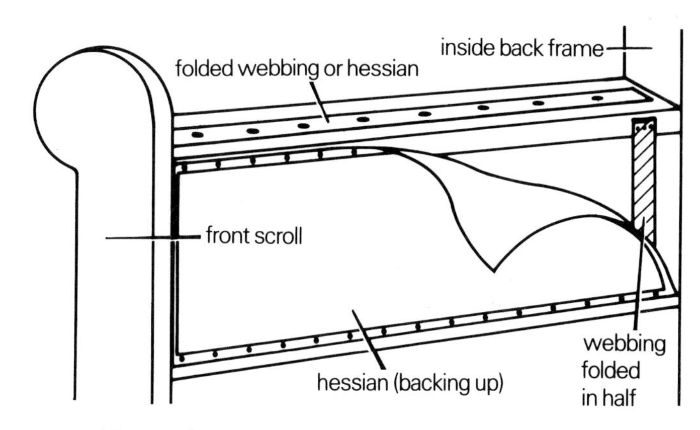

43 Backing up the arm

A much lighter spring is used for the arm (12.5 cm [5 in] by 12 gauge) is sufficient. Staple (using galvanized staples) the springs on the lowest coil of each spring, in line with the front scroll. Usually, five springs are placed along this rail. If the springs are wider than the rail, the lower coil is bent over the edge and stapled down.

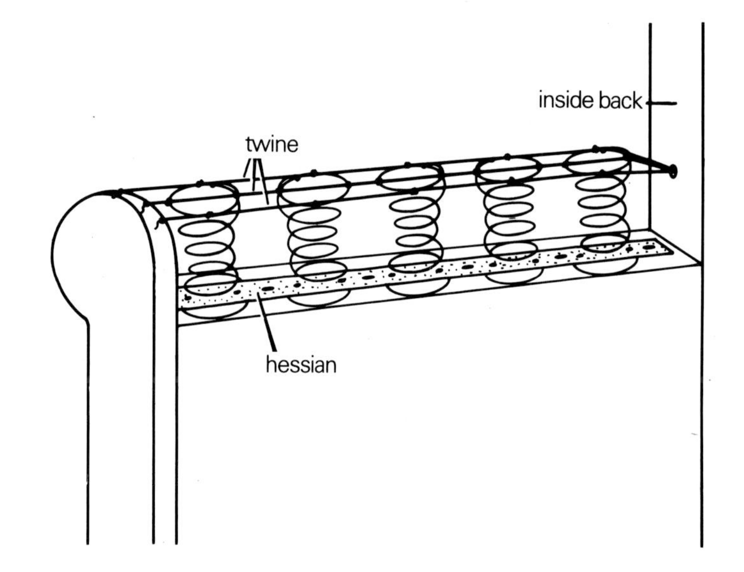

44 Lashing springs

The next stage is to lash the springs with three lines stretching the length of the arm. Starting with the centre line, fix a temporary tack into the inside back upright, loop the twine around it and hammer it home. Draw the twine in a line across the centre of the springs fastening with a knot on each top coil at front and back, and secure around a tack on the front scroll (fig. 44). Use a spring twine (heavy gauge) and tie the knots illustrated on page 32. The spring is not held down very tight and it should be just above the level of the front scroll.

Now cut a length of hessian 8 cm (3 in) longer than the arm and wide enough to cover from the bottom of the inside arm rail over the springs to the bottom outside arm rail, allowing an extra 6 cm (2½ in) for turning. Starting on the inside, temporary tack the hessian along the rail. Then pull the hessian over the top of the springs and temporary tack on the outer side of the rail. Keep the hessian taut by placing a temporary tack in line with the outer lashing both at the scroll and at the back. Adjust the tacks, if necessary, and tack home on the arm rail both sides.

The lines of twine are now completely enclosed in hessian, and must be stitched in place. Using a blanket stitch, put the needle through the hessian catching in the lashing twine which runs along the edge of the springs. Trap the twine as the blanket stitch proceeds, and catch in the edge of each spring as you come to it. Carry out this stitching on each of the outside edges to make a good boxed shape. Now sew in bridle stitches and start to stuff with fibre. The stitching prevents the stuffing from being displaced in wear.

Tuck the hessian under the edge of the scroll, adding extra stuffing if needed. Tack in place. Blind stitch round the edge and then top stitch, using the regulator to keep stuffing even and hard (fig. 46). The position of this stitched edge depends on whether the scroll is on the edge or under the edge. For the under-edge scroll add more stuffing and let the stitched edge stand proud of the frame. For the edge scroll the stuffing stays level with the scroll.

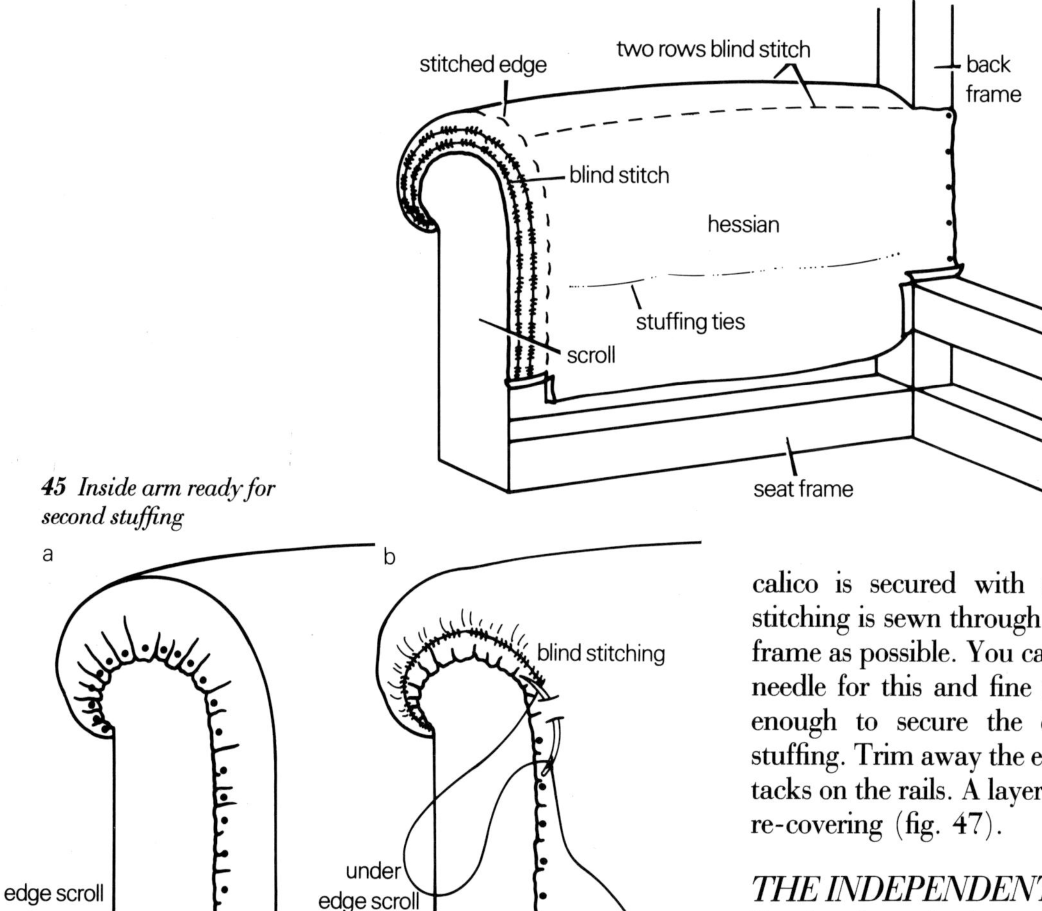

45 Inside arm ready for second stuffing

46 Making edge scroll and under edge scroll

The arm is now bridle stitched and a second stuffing has been added. Cover the whole arm in calico, temporary tacking it at the back, on the arm rail and on the side rail. Draw the calico over the front of the arm. If the chair has an edge scroll the calico can be pleated in and then tacked in place taking care to keep a good outline on the outer edge. On an under-edge scroll, the calico is secured with skewers, and a row of blind stitching is sewn through the stitched edge as close to the frame as possible. You can use either a curved or cording needle for this and fine twine. Pull the twine just hard enough to secure the calico, without disturbing the stuffing. Trim away the excess calico, and drive home the tacks on the rails. A layer of wadding is added just before re-covering (fig. 47).

THE INDEPENDENT SPRUNG BACK

Starting from the bottom rail, evenly space the vertical strips of webbing following the frame line. (The distance between each strip should be approximately the width of a piece of webbing.) Tack in place on the outside of the bottom rail and on the inside of the top rail. Use the web stretcher for this step and tack in a staggered formation (page 26). Weave in four horizontal strips of webbing. Place two of these close together near the bottom rail as this takes the bulk of the wear. Place the remaining two above the arm frame (do not web in between the arm frames as this blocks the passage of the fabric when re-covering). Tack each end of the web strips on to the outside of the back verticals in a staggered formation.

Springs
The method for sewing the springs in place is the same as for the seat. The springs are sewn on from the back of the webbing (fig. 47). A strong gauge spring (15 cm [6 in] × 10 gauge) would be used for the bottom row and a lighter gauge (17 cm [7 in] × 12 gauge) for the two top rows. Nine springs are sufficient for an average-sized chair.

The springs must now be lashed on the front to hold them in place. The three heavy springs at the bottom are lashed from side to side with laid cord in the same way as for the overstuff dining chair (page 34). The remaining springs are tied in place with twine following the pattern shown in fig. 48. Starting at the spring on the top left, fix a tack towards the end of the top rail. Secure the twine around this, then take a twist around the centre coil of the spring and attach the other end to a second tack placed in a position the same distance from the centre of the spring as the first tack. Repeat for the other two springs on the top row. Use the same principle for the second row, except that on the two side springs, fix the first tack to the side rail rather than the top rail.

Now the springs are in position and the back is ready for the spring canvas. From this point the processes for stuffing and stitching the edge are exactly the same as for the overstuff seat (pages 35–40). Once the second stuffing is complete, cover the back with calico and wadding. The back is now ready to re-cover.

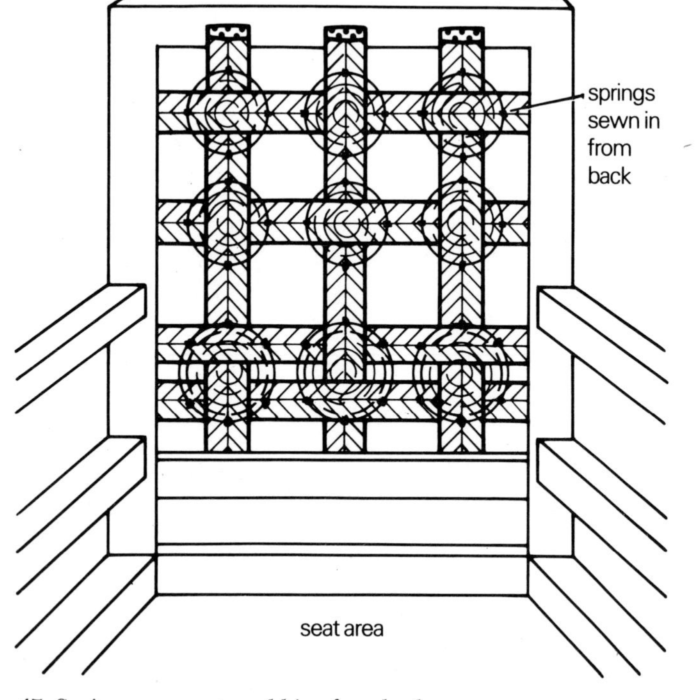

47 Springs sewn on to webbing from back

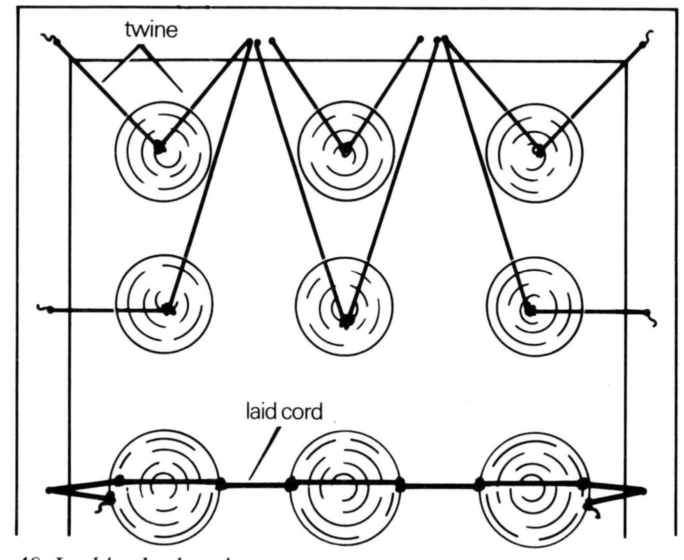

48 Lashing back springs

A collection of furniture covered with traditional fabrics

7 WINGS AND FACINGS

WINGS

With the traditional method of upholstery the wings are 'built up' to the covering stage, whereas with the modern method they are either cut to size in foam or rubberized hair, or simply padded with a layer of linter felt or black felt. If you are following the modern method the padding can be left until you start the final covering.

To build a wing by the traditional method, first cut a length of webbing to fill the gap in the frame. This is placed near to the back, so that the cover may be pulled through past this web (fig. 49). Fold the webbing in half down its length before tacking into place. A length of hessian is then cut and stretched across the opening, turn the edges back and tack to three sides leaving the back loose. Thread the hessian through the gap between the inside wing and inside back (you can sew it to the webbing). If a tack roll is appropriate for the wing, make it now (pages 29–30). Finally, the wing can be filled with fibre and a layer of linter felt following one of two procedures:

1 Bridle stitch the hessian, tease in the fibre under these ties, and cover with scrim. Place a stuffing tie through the wing, and then proceed to make the stitched edge in the same manner as for the overstuff seat (page 39). One blind stitch and one edge stitch will generally be sufficient. Finish the wing with a layer of hair, fibre or linter felt.

2 A slim solid wing simply needs a piece of linter felt laid directly on the hessian of the wing. The final fabric can then be shaped and pulled straight over this padding, and secured in place with tacks.

On some modern chairs where the wing has been glued and screwed on to the chair after the back has been covered, it is very difficult to remove the wing without damage. If this is the case, the inside back should be covered first and then enough fabric should be cut for the wing to allow for back tacking into the frame. Back tack by placing a plastic strip or strip of card on the wrong side of the fabric in line with the hem edge (fig. 50). Make sure that the fabric is kept upright and the pattern runs straight across in line with the inside back. Now tack the backing strip through the fabric and into the frame upright. When this has been completed, the wing can be padded with a layer of linter felt plus a thin layer of wadding. Then cover the wing (page 75).

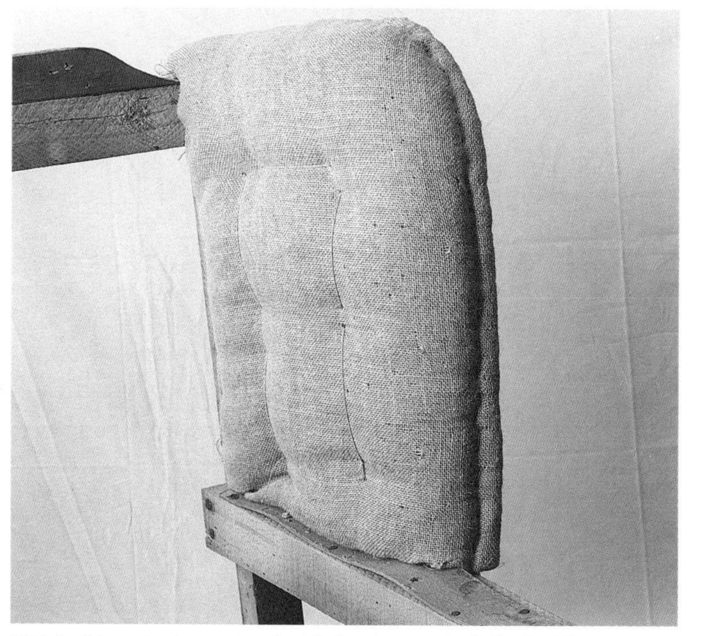

Old-fashioned wing covered with hessian and stitched with bridle ties

49 Opposite right *Tack a folded length of webbing to inside arm*
50 Opposite far right *Fitting fabric using plastic back tack strip*

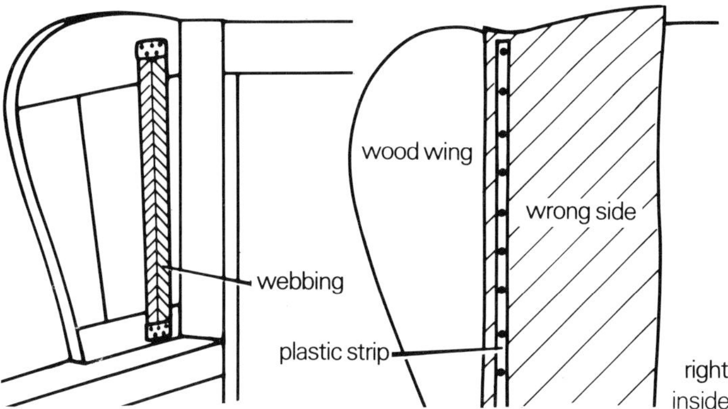

FACINGS

A front facing can be cut from plywood and bolted onto the front of the frame. The bolt hole must be countersunk from the front using a drill. Attach the bolt pad and then apply the final cover. With the exception of the wooden or cardboard facings, most of the scrolls and soft facings are either machined in with the arm cover or they are slipped in place after the arms are finished. In each of these cases they would be padded at the time of covering.

8 CONSTRUCTING A DEEP-BUTTON-BACKED HEADBOARD

A deep-button-backed headboard can be made to any shape required. The headboard here uses a basic method to construct a fairly simply shape. If the shape is too fussy it will detract from the button work.

First measure the width and height required. Draw a shape on a piece of brown paper and place it behind the bed. Raise or lower it until the height looks right, then mark the paper where the top edge of the mattress meets it. This is the point at which padding will begin.

Take a length of 1.25 cm (½ in) chipboard or ply board (for a double headboard use 2 cm (¾ in) chipboard) and use the template to cut the headboard. Measuring from the mark on the template, leave 15 cm (6 in) extra on the lower edge to go down behind the mattress. Now, lay the template on a sheet of 8 cm (3 in) foam and draw round the shape (do not add the extra 15 cm [6 in] this time.) When the shape has been drawn, measure 3 cm (1¼ in) from the line all the way round and draw a second line, this one is to be the cutting line. Cut the foam using a sharp knife. An electric carving knife is very useful for this purpose in the absence of a foam cutter.

The board must now be marked ready to drill holes for the buttons. First measure across the board and mark the middle. Draw a line vertically up through this point. Measure from the 15 cm (6 in) mark to the top of the board, mark halfway and draw a line horizontally forming a cross. Mark the centre with a circle. The headboard can be buttoned in large or small diamonds, depending on the size and depth of the board, and, of course, on personal choice. An average size of 15 cm (6 in) marked on the board makes a diamond of approximately 10 cm (4 in) from outer edge to outer edge. Mark the board in the following manner.

Draw horizontal lines on the board at 8 cm (3 in) intervals. Then mark intervals along each horizontal line. Make the first points at a 8 cm (3 in) distance each side of the centre vertical. Then progress along the horizontal with a point at 15 cm (6 in) intervals. After marking in all along the lines, use a straight edge to draw a diagonal line through the marks from left to right, then from right to left (fig. 52). Continue to draw the lines across. The point at which they cross each other is the point at which the buttons will be positioned. The board is ready to be

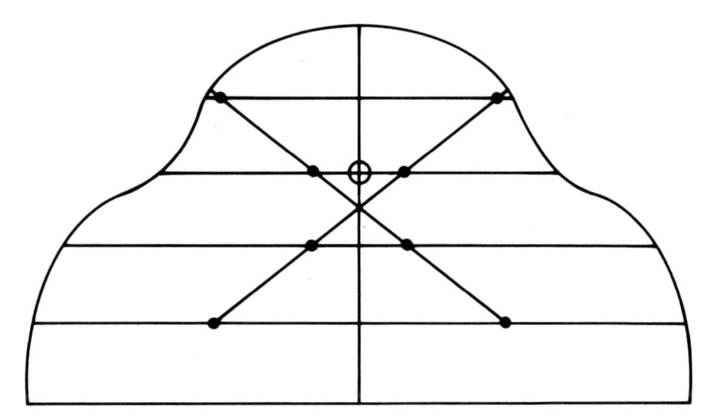

51 Draw the first two diagonals

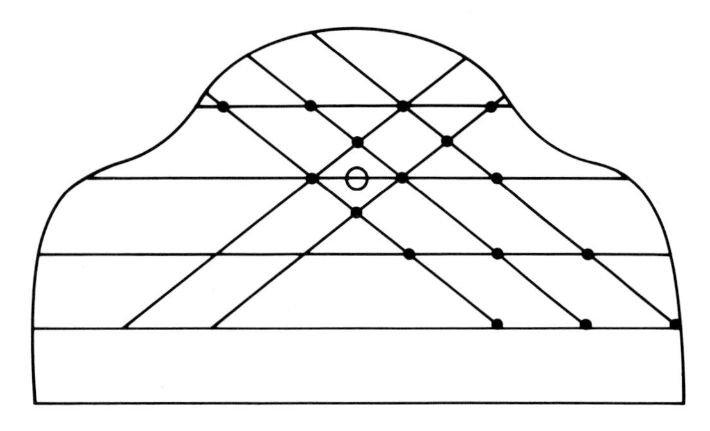

52 Lines marked at regular intervals

drilled as soon as the marking is complete. The drill hole should be large enough to allow a mattress needle and thread through, 3 mm (⅛ in). Drill the holes right through the board, and make sure that they are at the centre of each cross. If the button marks are near the edge, drill to the nearest within 5 cm (2 in) of the edge.

Once the holes are drilled the next stage is to prepare the foam, for good deep effect at least 8 cm (3 in) foam

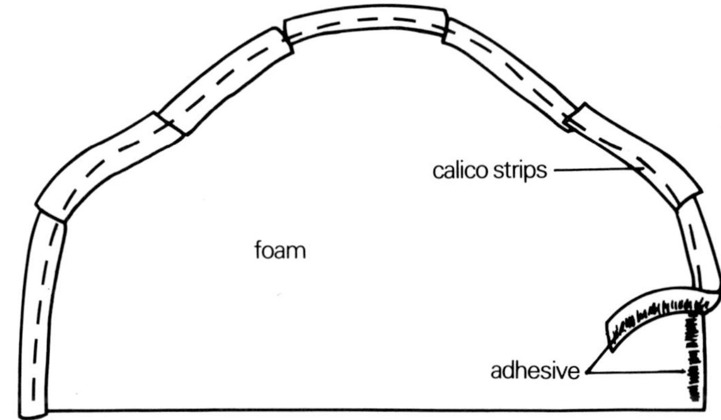

53 Glueing calico strips to foam

should be used. For a small area, however, quite a good effect can be achieved with 5 cm (2 in) foam. Now the 3 cm (1¼ in) margin on the foam must be champhered off to fit the board. To do this cut a line from the outer edge of the foam diagonally across to meet the 3 cm (1¼ in) margin line. Next, cut some strips of calico to approximately 8 cm (3 in) wide. Cut a snip in the edge and tear the calico across so that it does not make a sharp edge under the cover. Arrange the strips around the outer edge of the foam, overlapping on to the foam by approximately half the width of the strip. If the foam is curved in shape, overlap each section (fig. 53) so that the outer edge is covered. Using a good adhesive, spread it across half the width of the calico strip and the same distance in from the outer edge of the foam. Press the two together, and leave to dry.

Centre the top edge and place a temporary tack in the back of the board. Repeat at the centre of the two sides, pulling the calico until the outer edge of the foam covers the outer edge of the board. Temporary tack in position until the foam is lying smoothly. To ease round the corners, gather the calico into small pleats and tack down. If the foam is pulled too hard it will result in a 'girt'. If this happens release the tack from the calico until the girt disappears. When satisfied, tack home and trim the calico off to the tack line, snipping the edge to aid the fit.

With a mattress needle, mark the hole through the foam by pushing the needle through from the back of the board. Where it appears on the foam, make a cross cut, this helps to eliminate resistance when buttoning. The headboard can now be finished with the final covering (page 81).

9 DEEP-BUTTON-BACKED, IRON-FRAME CHAIR

The deep-button-backed chair is usually the one that beginners choose to tackle. My advice is to start on something simple and master the basic stitching first. This type of chair has a wooden base frame, and so the seat can be re-upholstered using the methods described on pages 42–3. This will bring the seat up to the calico stage. The back of the chair, however, is made entirely of iron, therefore everything on this part of the chair has to be hand-stitched in place.

Before deciding if the chair needs re-upholstering or just re-covering, remove the old cover by cutting the button ties and stitching which hold the cover in place, inspect the scrim, the hessian and the stuffing. If the stitched edge is not worn and the back hessian is not torn, then the chair will only need re-covering. Keep the old cover so that the button markings can be used for a guide. (Do not, however, use as a pattern but rather, to measure distances.) Then turn to page 86 for the re-covering procedure. If you decide that the whole chair needs re-upholstering, the first step is to strip it right back to the frame. Save the hair, as this can be teased out and re-used. (Repair the frame at this stage if necessary.)

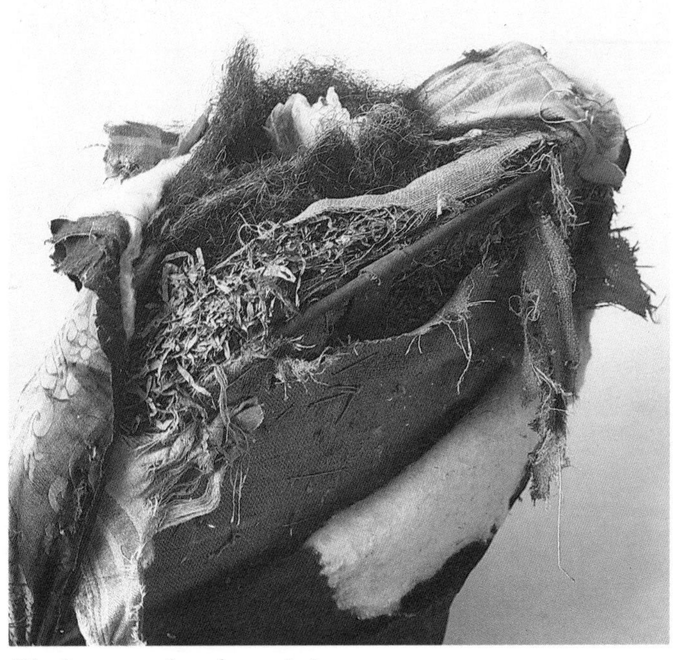

Ripping out an iron-frame chair

Start by cutting strips of hessian or calico approximately 5 cm (2 in) wide. These strips are used to bind the frame which provides a base on which to sew, and also stops the metal from wearing the hessian foundation. The binding should be left raw on the edges, and should overlap on each turn. Secure the binding lengths with a few stitches at each end. The uprights and horizontals should be bound first, then turn to the outer edges of the frame.

After the frame has been bound, cut a length of

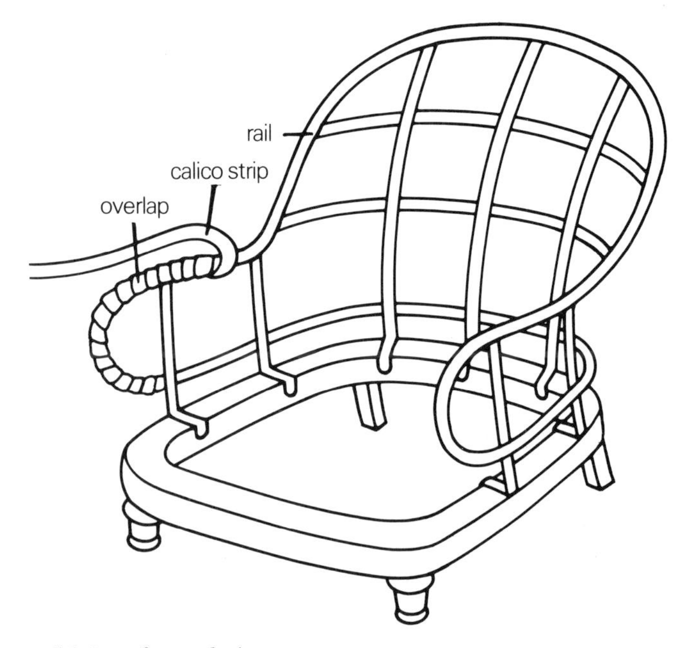

54 Iron-frame chair

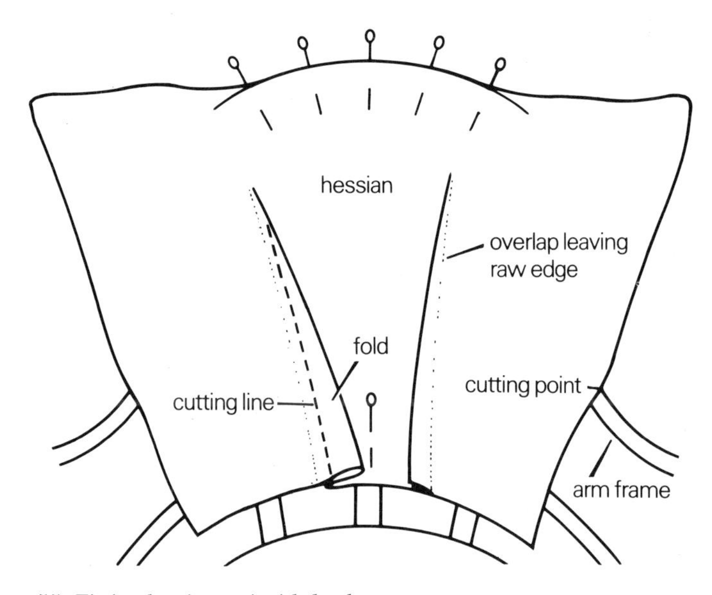

55 Fitting hessian to inside back

hessian sufficient to cover the entire back, with enough allowance, approximately 6 cm (2½ in), to turn over the top and bottom edges. Place the hessian on the front side of the frame (some upholsterers prefer to place it on the outside of the frame), and with the grain of the fabric running upright, turn it right over the top edge until it meets under the frame rail. Secure with skewers, and then repeat along the top edge until the inside back meets the arm uprights. Secure the centre of the hessian to the bottom rail with skewers in the same manner as you secured the top. The hessian will be full at this stage, so to mould it to the shape of the back, two cuts must be made. Starting from the bottom, cut approximately two-thirds up the hessian to cut out the fullness. To bring the hessian round to the back, cut it at the point at which the frame curves toward the arms. Having made the cuts, overlap the edges of hessian so that the piece lies flat. Trim back the excess leaving approximately 5 cm (2 in) under the overlap. Secure the hessian under the bottom rail keeping it taut between top and bottom.

After positioning the hessian on the back, use exactly the same method to cover the arms, overlapping the hessian where the back and arm sections meet. Skewer the hessian in place, and then starting at the lower edge, sew all round the outside edge of the frame. Keep the stitch line close to the frame so that it does not allow any movement, which ultimately causes wear. Use a medium twine and a spring needle to form either a running stitch or a locking stitch (preferably the locking stitch—see fig. 57).

To ensure a firm foundation for the stuffing, a stitched-up edge should be made from the point where the arms meet the seat, all round the top edge of the frame. To make the stitched edge, cut strips of scrim approximately 20 cm (8 in) wide. Fold one edge under

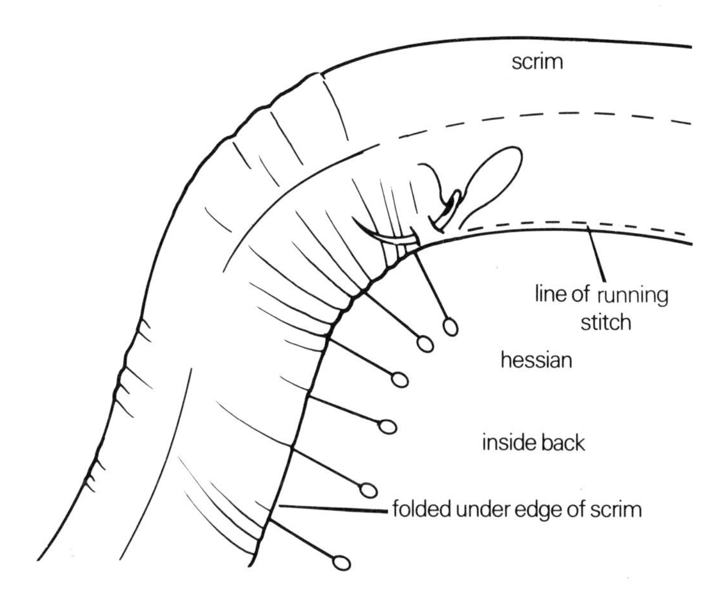

56 Fitting scrim around frame back

1.5 cm (⅝ in). Measure about 8 cm (3 in) down from the top of the frame edge and draw a line following the contour of the frame. Fold the scrim under at this line and stitch all round on the same line. Allow extra on the open curves and ease in on the closed curves, to allow the scrim to fold over the top of the frame without distortion.

Complete the stitching all round, then taking a handful of fibre, pack it into the scrim. Pull the scrim over the back edge of the frame, thus forming a roll over the outer edge. Tuck the ends of the scrim under and secure with skewers just under the frame. Continue to make the roll by adding more fibre. Keep the roll evenly packed and regulate the stuffing at intervals so that no lumps are formed. When the roll is in position, use a double-pointed needle and twine to sew a blind stitch right through the roll on the underside of the metal frame coming out again with the needle over the top of the frame. The blind stitch will secure the scrim to the

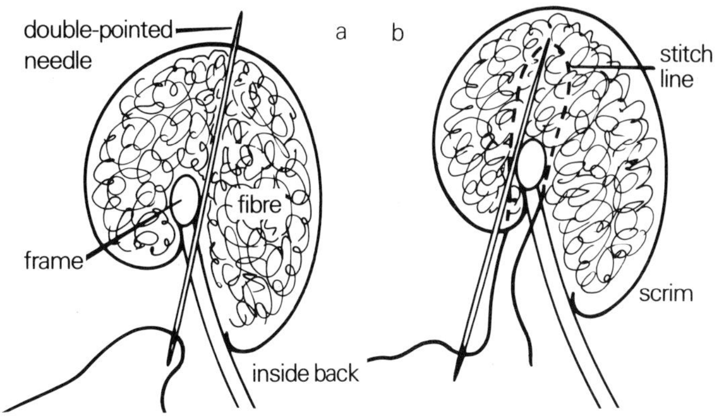

57 Sections showing position of blind stitch

hessian on the outside back during this process.

(When upholstering a wooden frame, spoon back chair, the hessian is tacked to the back edge of the frame and the edge stitched to follow the outline of the frame.)

Once the blind stitch has been completed all round, move on to the stitched edge. Stitch just above the blind stitch on the outside back, keeping the needle to the back edge of the frame. (See stitched edge on page 39.) Once the edge is stitched the next stage is to make a swell in the lower part of the inside back.

Draw a semi-circle measuring approximately 25 cm (10 in) from the bottom frame to the centre of the circle and graduating to nothing where the back joins the arms (fig. 59). Fill this area with bridle stitching. Now cut a length of scrim large enough to cover the area plus an allowance of 15 cm (6 in) all round to enable it to cover the stuffing. Turn the scrim under on the top edge and stitch to the curve of the swell. Stuff fibre under the bridle stitches until the area is firm. Pull the scrim over the swell and under the frame line to the outside back. Cut away the scrim where it is trapped by the upright. From the outside back, sew the scrim on to the foundation hessian using a running stitch.

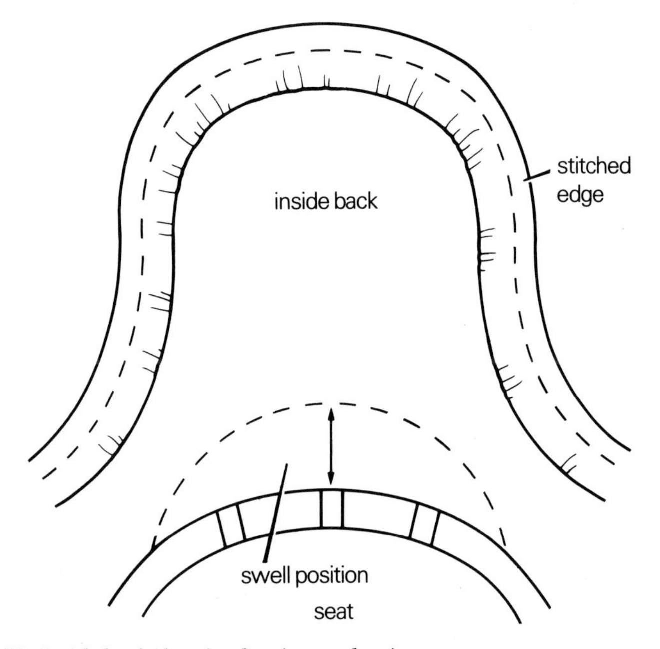

58 Inside back showing hessian and scrim

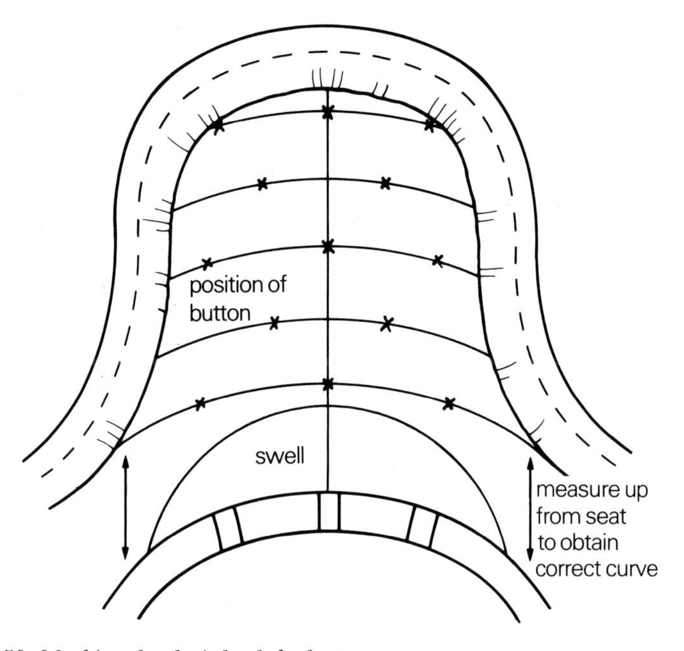

59 Marking the chair back for buttons

Now that the swell is completed, the position of the buttons should be marked. Using a needle and thread, mark from the front side, right through so that they can be seen clearly from the back of the hessian. A pattern of three, two, three is a fairly common one (that is to say, three buttons at the top, two in the centre, then three again and so on). To establish the position of the buttons, draw a vertical line down the centre of the chair back; cross this with another line across the top of the swell, keeping it even by taking the measurement up from the seat. Measure four more lines up from the bottom line, with a distance of 9 cm (3½ in) between each line. (This is an average measurement, it will vary depending on the size of the chair. The number of buttons different chairs require will also vary.)

At this stage, the arms, too, should be marked for buttons. Generally, one button is placed in the centre, and one where the arm meets the back; these are in line with the lowest row of buttons on the back of the chair. Bridle stitch the arms and back, tease the hair and stuff under the ties until it feels firm. Push the regulator through from the back and break open the hair. Add a layer of wadding and then break holes in this layer. At this point, the back and arms may be covered in calico, particularly if the top cover is a fine fabric. Now follow the instructions for top covering (Chapter 17).

Covered iron-frame chair

PART II
COVERING AND RE-COVERING

10 TYPES OF FABRIC FOR COVERING

Ambla: a laminated fabric which has the look of leather, but is much cheaper and also easier to clean.
Brocade: made in silk, cotton and man-made fibres, this fabric has an embroidered look with a sheen on the surface. The designs are usually traditional. It is not recommended for very hard wear.
Brocatelle: a fairly heavy fabric, with a silky look. The design is woven in and looks padded. Made in cotton, silk, man-made fibres or a mixture of both man-made and natural fibre.
Calico: a fine cotton fabric, made in different weights, and used unbleached as under covering.
Chintz: cotton fabric with a heavy glazed surface. Suitable for areas where it will have fairly light wear.
Cirrus: a man-made, leather-look cloth, in a great variety of colours and finishes.
Damask: a self-patterned fabric achieved by reversing the weave on the back to produce a light and shade effect. Available in silk, cotton, rayon and terylene.
Hide: this is usually cow hide which can be dyed to a variety of shades and is very hard-wearing as long as it is not allowed to dry out. Hide food or wax polish will keep the hide supple. It is sold by the square foot.
Linen: linen and linen union are often used for loose covers because of their washing qualities.
Moquette: a looped, pile fabric with loops that can be cut or uncut, or a combination of both. It is very hard-wearing and made in wool, cotton or man-made fibres.
Tapestry: if it is hand-made in wool on a linen backing it will wear for many years. Most tapestry, however, is made by machine, in cotton, wool, and worsted yarn. Many designs are traditional, although modern designs are available.
Tweed: a woven fabric which can be heavy or light-weight. Different effects are achieved by a variety of yarn thickness. Made in wool or mixed with a man-made yarn, it is hard-wearing.
Velour and velvets: a cut pile fabric made in silk, cotton and man-made fibres. (Dralon has become known as a velvet pile fabric, although it is, in fact, the name of a yarn, rather than a type of fabric. When Dralon is made into a velvet pile it can be sponged or dry-cleaned easily.)
Vynide: another leather-look, laminated fabric.
Weave: weaves belong to the 'tweed family' and are generally made in wool or cotton. They are now available with a latex backing and a man-made fibre surface. These fabrics make a very good imitation of tweed or weaves and they can be sponged clean without the water penetrating the stuffing underneath.

11 MEASURING AND ESTIMATING

To estimate the amount of fabric required for covering a piece of furniture the piece must be measured accurately, taking into account the pattern and weave of the fabric and the style of the piece of furniture. With a patterned fabric, the pattern on the arms should run round in line with the inside back and ensure, too, that the pattern is central on the inside back and that this lines up with the pattern on the seat, cushion and front border. When measuring fabric for a buttoned back piece, leave extra large seam allowances to ensure that there will be enough fabric to pull down into each button well (page 81). If the fabric has a pile, this must always run down on the piece of furniture. (After cutting mark the top of each piece with chalk to help you get the fabric the right way up.)

60 *Positioning patterns*

Take a sheet of paper, and write down all the different parts of the piece of furniture and their measurements. This becomes the 'cut' sheet (fig. 61). Measure each length in the direction shown (fig. 62) and using abbreviations write down the length first, then the width of each part of the item of furniture. Make a plan of the piece of fabric by drawing on paper the exact area and shape that each piece will take, roughly to scale. Use this as a guide when cutting the cover. When measuring, add at least 10 cm (4 in) on the tuck-in (the tuck-in is the flap of material which tucks in between the seat and the inside back) and at least 5 cm (2 in) extra on all other pieces. However, there is no need to allow enough margin to stretch to the actual place where it is tacked to the frame. Generally, an extra piece of hessian (called a fly) is sewn on, to make up this length. Flys are used to reduce bulk and also to save fabric. Up to 1 metre (1 yard) can be saved on a chair by using flys in the tuck in.

Chair sizes

	cm length × cm width	inch length × inch width
Inside back	76 × 65	27½ × 25½
Seat	65 × 85	25½ × 33½
Inside arms	52 × 75	20½ × 29½
Outside arms	40 × 80	16 × 32
Front border	25 × 55	10 × 21½
Front scrolls	40 × 18	16 × 7
Back scrolls	30 × 16	12 × 6
Outside back	76 × 56	30 × 22
Cushion	56 × 50	22 × 20
Cushion borders	10 × 56	4 × 22
Piping	50 × width	20 × width

61

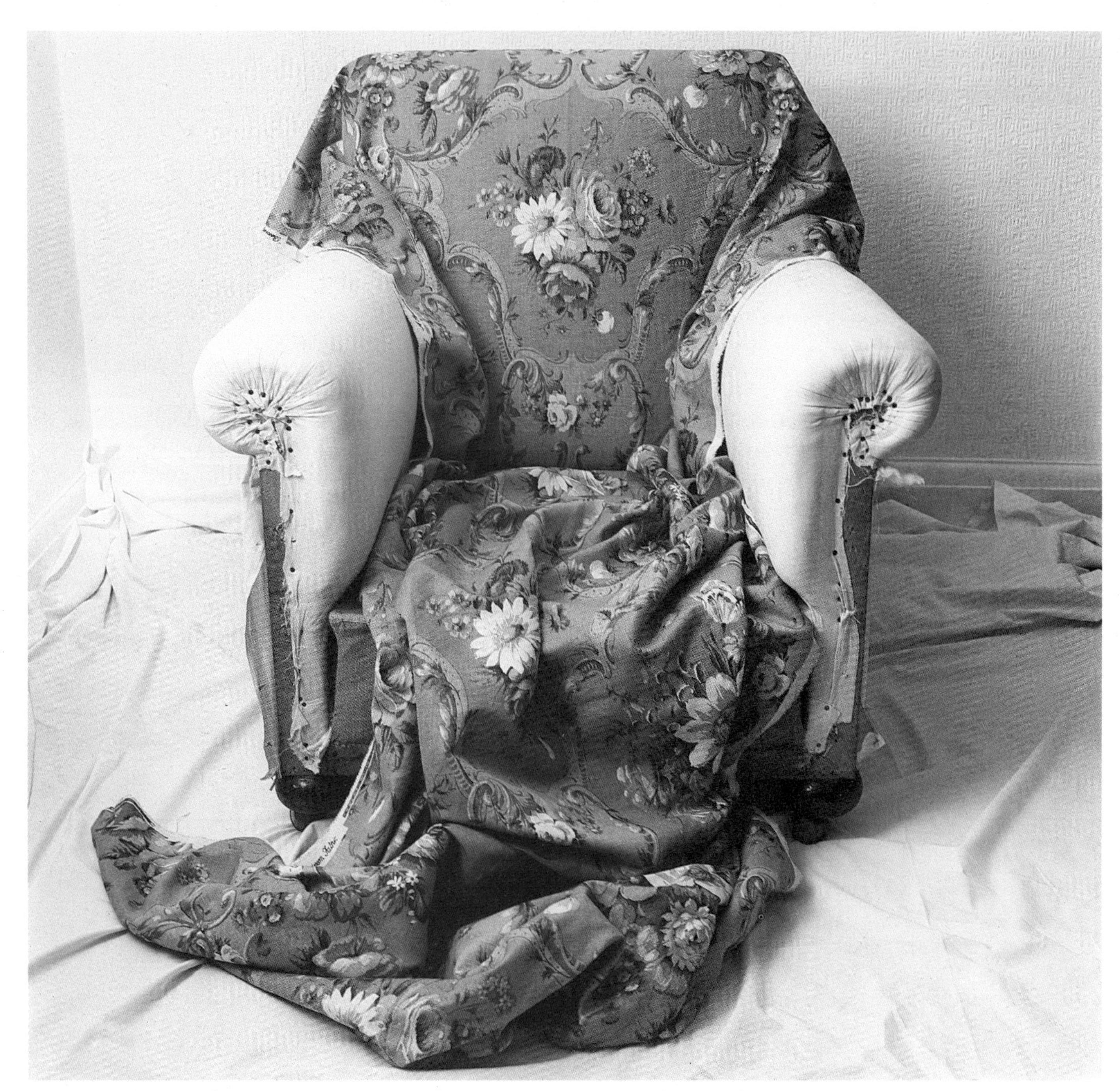

Positioning of patterned cover fabric

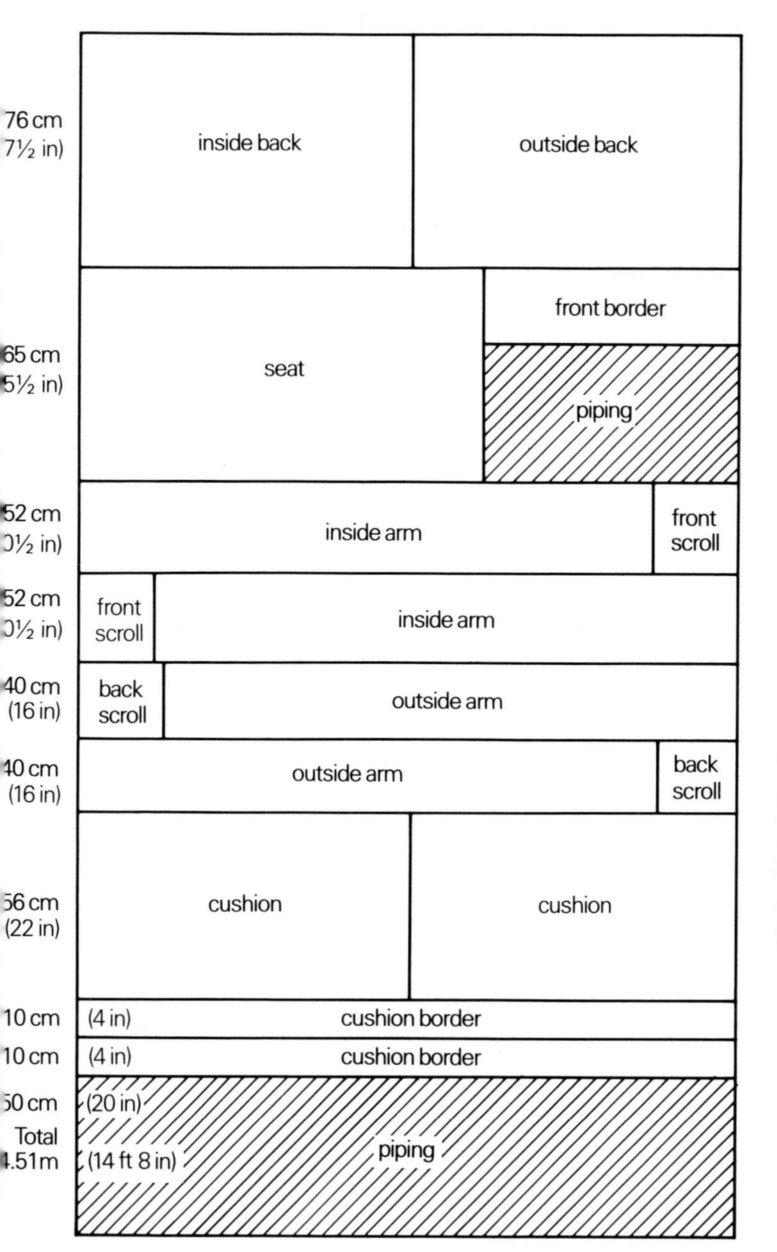

61 Cutting plan for easy chair

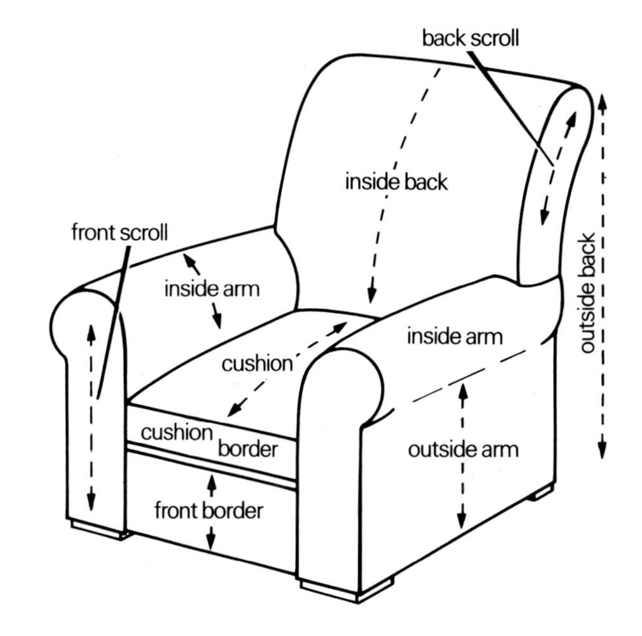

62 Four scroll easy chair

Check that you have allowed for all the pieces. Add the component lengths together to give the overall length of fabric needed for the chair cover. When estimating the length of piping remember that you will need to pipe the front scrolls and back scrolls, front borders, and the top and bottom edge of the seat cushion. Approximately 6.5 metres (6 yards) of piping can be made from 25 cm (10 in) of fabric if it is 122 cm (48½ in) wide.

12 PIPING AND RUCHING

CUTTING AND MAKING PIPING (WELTING)

Piping is used in both upholstery and soft furnishing. It is usually called 'welting' by upholsterers and 'piping' by soft furnishers. To cut and make a length of piping, lay the fabric flat on a table and fold one corner over until it forms a right angle. Cut along the fold, and then from the cut edge, measure strips 3.5 cm (1½ in) wide and cut into lengths. Join each length from corner to corner, with the right sides together to produce one long length. Trim the turnings to 1.25 cm (½ in) and open out flat.

Lay piping cord in the prepared length of piping, and fold over the fabric lengthwise. Using a grooved or a zip foot on the machine, sew along the length keeping the stitching close to the cord, without catching it in. The piping is now ready to stitch to the fabric/cover. Different gauge piping cord is available and the choice must depend on the thickness of the fabric to be welted, and the effect required. As a general principle, a thick fabric requires a thin cord and a fine fabric needs a thick cord. The most popular sizes are '00' and '4'. To join piping in a complete circle (for example, for a cushion top) the following method is used. Lay the two ends of the strip out flat; fold back in a straight line so that the folds meet. Cut across each piece leaving 1.25 cm (½ in) turning from the fold. Take the top corner of one piece and place it to the lower corner of the opposite piece. A to A. Pin across diagonally B to C. Trim off to 13 mm (½ in) and open the seam out flat. Now place the two lengths of cord side by side and cut directly through the centre. The two ends of the cord will now butt together without leaving a gap. Fold the welt over the cord and continue the stitching line.

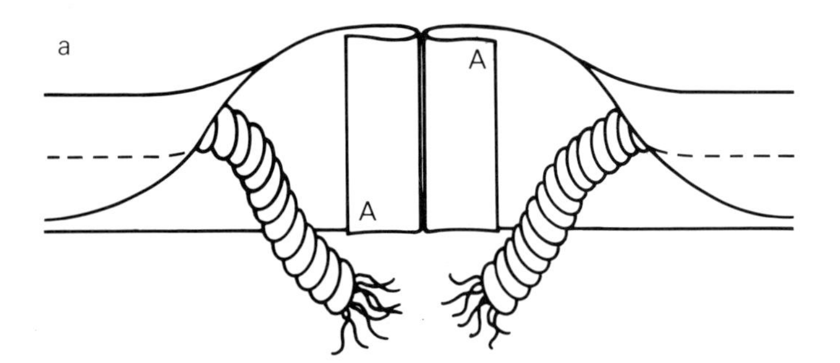

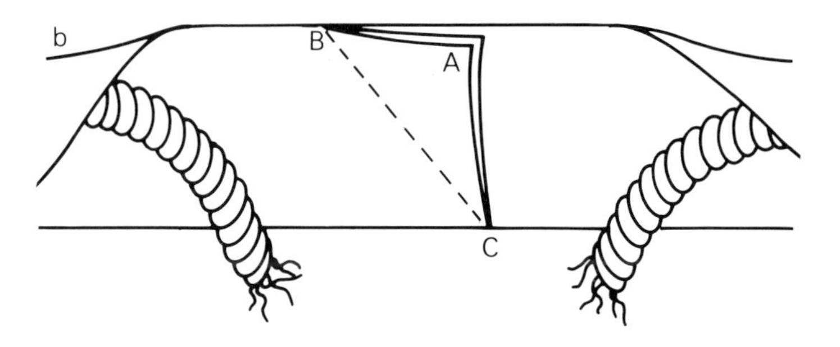

63 Above and right *Joining lengths of piping*

MAKING PIPING BY THE CYLINDER METHOD

This method is the most economical way of using small lengths of fabric; it can be used on any material including pile fabrics. First trim the fabric so that the sides are even. Then fold one corner at an angle of 30° across the width, so that it runs across the grain of the fabric. This allows the piping to stretch. Fold the diagonally opposite corner across the width at exactly the same degree. (To make sure that the angle is the same at both ends, measure from A to B and then make C to D the same length.) Pin corner C 4 cm (1½ in) from the edge of corner A. Join along this line until the other end is

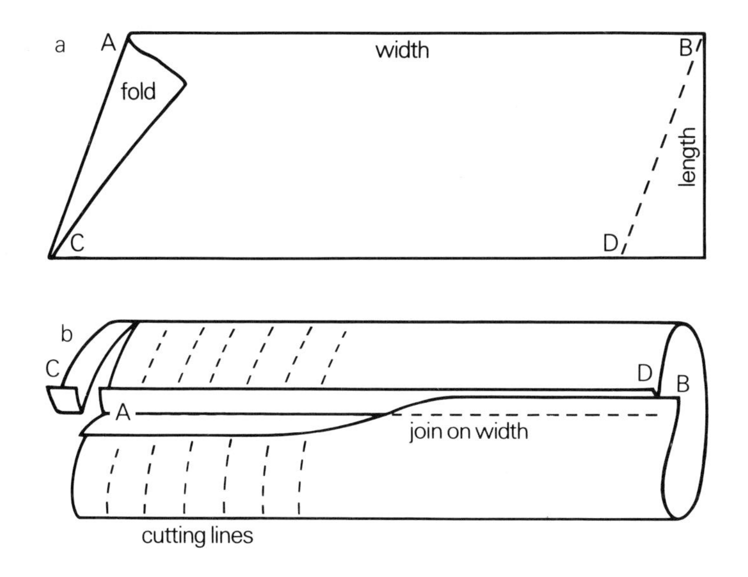

64 Making piping using the cylinder method

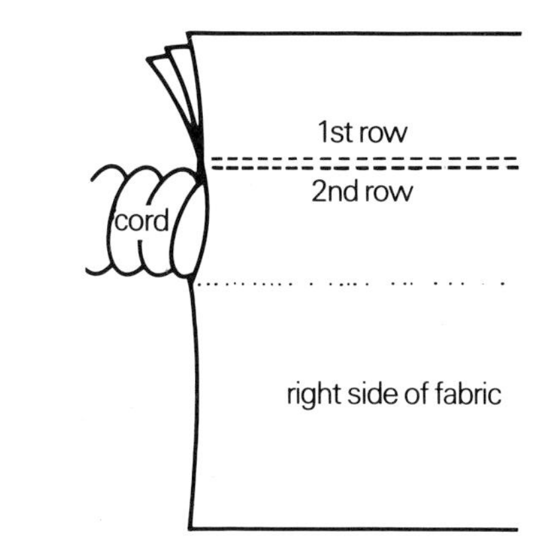

65 Sew piping to first length of fabric

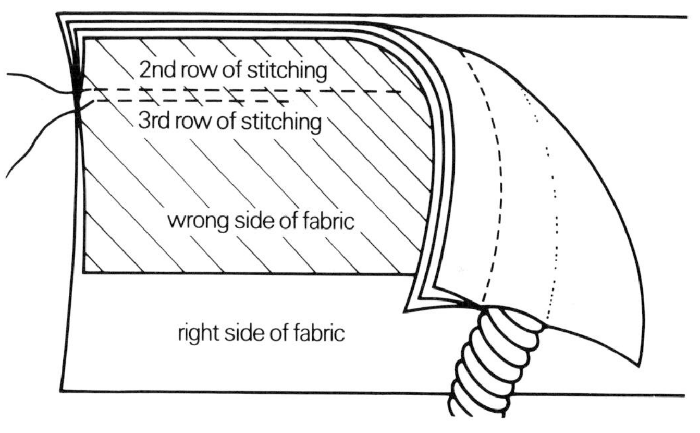

66 Add second piece of fabric to complete piped seam

reached. (At this stage, if the fabric is wide, the cylinder formed by the join may start to twist, this does not matter.) On reaching the opposite end you will find that corner B is 4 cm (1½ in) longer than corner D. Machine sew the join across using a small stitch and press open the seam. Start cutting from corner A in a continuous strip 4 cm (1½ in) wide. The strip is now ready to insert the piping cord.

JOINING PIPING TO THE MAIN FABRIC

Take the lengths of piping and join them together (page 64). With practice the cord can be placed in its outer case and straight on to the fabric. Beginners, however, are advised to make up the piping with the cord inserted before joining it to the fabric. It is most important that the cover is piped well, as wrinkled piping can spoil what might otherwise have been a very good piece of work. Machine stitch the piping to the right side of the first piece of fabric close to the seam line. Place the second piece of fabric (right side against the piping) and stitch a second line. Turn the whole piece to the right side; the cord is now firmly inserted between the two lengths of fabric. If the last row of stitching was close enough to the cord, there should be no stitching visible on the right side.

When approaching a corner during piping, stitch up to the corner and make a cut into the edge of the fabric almost up to the needle. Now, leaving the needle in the corner of the welt, lift the presser foot, turn sharply at the corner, replace the foot and continue stitching. On a curve, snip the piping to help ease it into position.

APPLYING RUCHE (CUT OR UNCUT) TO THE MAIN FABRIC

Ruche can be bought by the metre with either cut or uncut edges. It is available in many colours and varies between 2 and 3 cm (¾ in and 1½ in) in depth. Ruche is joined to the main cover in exactly the same way as the piping welt. Make sure that the fluffy edge lies away from the edge and that the stitching is kept in a straight line. To join the ruche cut 1.25 cm (½ in) longer than the fabric, and lap one piece over the oher. Stitch across both, taking care to keep them in line. Turn the corner at a right angle by easing the ruche so that it is extra full at the corner. Unlike piping, ruche must not be cut on a corner or it will fray badly.

13 SPRUNG EASY CHAIR

The sprung easy chair takes a traditional style of covering and the process begins with the seat. Having cut out the seat fabric so that it stretches at least 6 cm (2½ in) into the tuck-in, cut flys for the outside back and for the two sides which will reach from the fabric to the base rail with a 5 cm (2 in) allowance for turning. (A fly is used on the seat and on the back of a chair in the tuck-in area. Use strong lining, hessian or odd pieces of fabric.) The fly must be folded back 1.25 cm (½ in) before being stitched to the cover so that the threads do not pull away when under pressure. Join the fly along the two sides and the back.

A sprung easy chair does not need a fly which comes right to the front of the cover because it has to be cut away around the chair upright. Nonetheless, you should use a piece of cover fabric for this fly as it is visible at the front edge. Centralize the seat cover on the chair and temporary tack the flys to the back and to the two side base rails. Smooth the cover forward and using skewers attach the seat firmly under the front lip. Smooth the seat out towards the sides, and after cutting round the uprights at the back and sides (fig 68), tack in place.

Stitch right through the cover into the hessian, using a back stitch. Fold the corners under, making sure that they are symmetrical. Place the front border in position using skewers and fold under the top edge. Secure it so that the previous stitch line is covered. Place a length of sheet wadding on to the calico, and pull the cover over the top; temporary tack it to the underside of the base rail. If the front edge is sprung, make a snip just below the top front rail (fig. 68) and temporary tack the raw edge to the front facings on the lower part. Turn in the upper part and pin in line with the edge of the border.

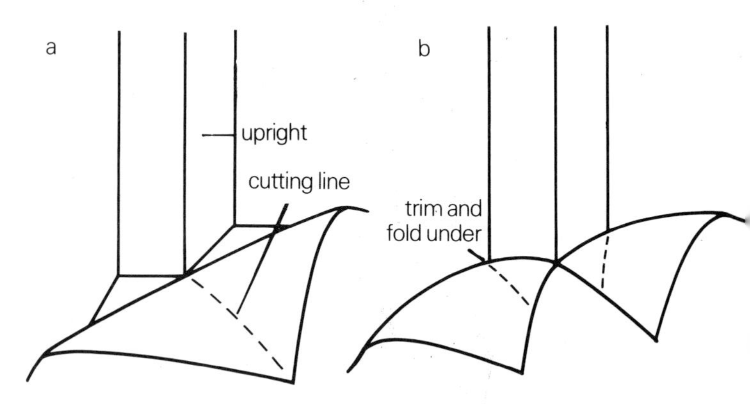

67 Cutting round upright

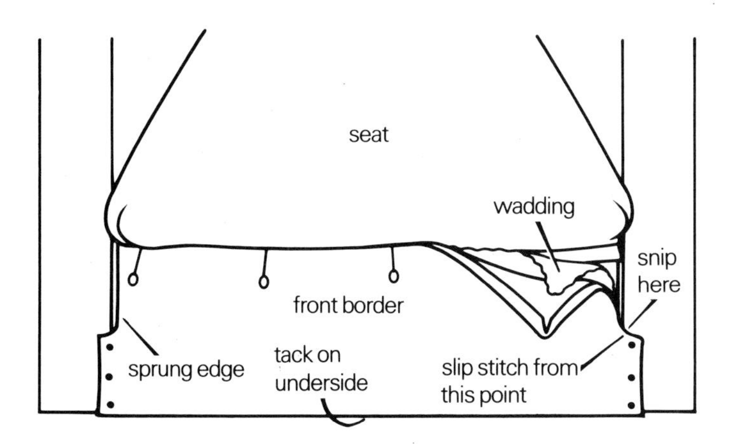

68 Covering front border

On the firm edge tack the raw edge of the front border on to the facing on both sides. Slip stitch along the top edge.

This type of border is corded, but as an alternative, a row of piping can be machined across the top of the front border before attaching it to the chair. The front is stitched on in the same manner, with the piping showing between the seat and border.

THE PLATFORM SEAT

Different styles of chairs obviously need different approaches to covering. A platform seat is unusual in that it has a separate seat cushion. Generally, the platform is covered with a platform cloth that matches the main fabric and the lip (about 15 cm/6 in deep) is covered in the main fabric.

With right sides together sew the front lip to the platform cloth leaving a 1.25 cm (½ in) seam allowance. Take a length of cotton webbing about 3 cm (1¼ in) wide and stitch it by machine to the back edge of the lip where it joins the platform cloth. Stitch right through the seam allowance starting and finishing off firmly. Stitch only the actual width taken up by the seat, not the tuck-in area. The webbing should, however, extend down into the tuck-in so that it may be secured to the frame.

Having sewn the webbing in place, pipe the front border from the point where it meets the scroll or outside arm (depending on the type of chair). Assemble the front border and the lip, and turn the 'right way out'. Place the front lip in position on the seat and check that it fits snugly round the front border. Pull the two lengths of webbing at either side of the lip, and temporary tack them to the bottom rail of the frame. Push the platform cloth in place, and secure with temporary tacks to the sides and back of the frame.

Turn the front border back to expose the webbing; then, using a curved needle and twine, sew right through the webbing, making sure the stitches catch right through to the stuffing.

Place a length of wadding over the lip and front border area of the chair, pull the fabric over the top of this, cutting around the frame upright. Tack in place underneath the frame, making sure that the seam allowances on the piping are turned flat, before tacking home. The chair is now ready for the next process.

THE MODERN SEAT

Covering the lip and front border on a modern chair which has tension springs or rubber webbing seat demands a slightly different approach. This type of seat usually has a platform cloth laid over the tension springs. The cloth can be padded by stitching it to a thin layer of foam or felt. Along the back of the platform cloth, stitch a tube wide enough for a tension spring to pass through. Now attach a piece of the main covering fabric to the front edge of the platform cloth, while at the same time and on the same line, sew to the underside a length of hessian wide enough to stretch over the front lip. Pull the platform cloth forward to the front border of the chair. Bring the hessian forward over the lip and front border,

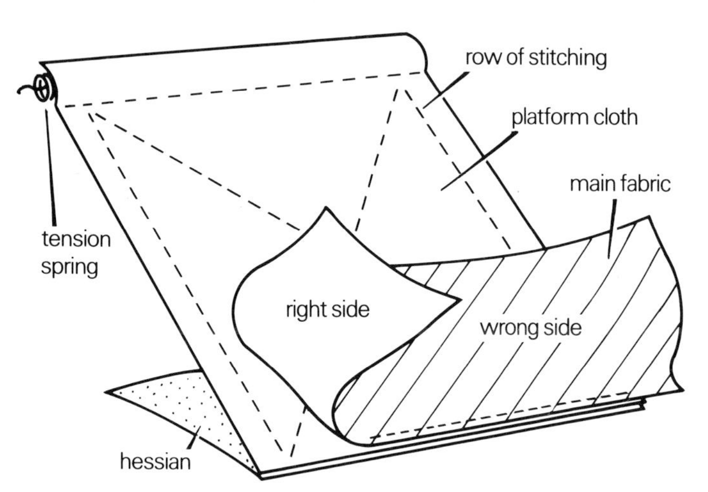

69 Attaching hessian and cover fabric to platform cloth

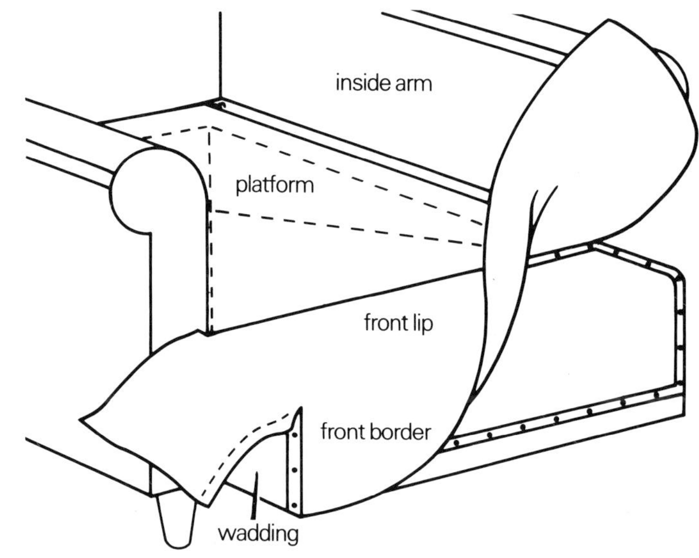

70 Fitting platform cloth

turn the edges under and tack to border frame.

Take a piece of 5 mm (¼ in) foam and fit it over the lip, front border, and down the sides of the front border. Over the foam, place a length of wadding to cover right to the bottom edge of the frame. Pull the main cover over the lip and border, and temporary tack under the frame on the front edge. Turn under the bottom edge of the corner, trimming off the excess fabric back to 1.25 cm (½ in). Turn under the upright edge towards the scroll. Tack the fabric under the frame at the base and then slipstitch the front corner, making a neat finish. Repeat this process on the other side of the chair.

In some cases, a fireside chair with a polished wooden frame will be sprung with tension springs or rubber webbing. The platform can be made in the same way as for the traditional chair, by padding and stitching a length of platform cloth. The size must allow for a slot to be made at both ends for a spring to be slotted through.

In the same way as for the traditional chair, the front edge has a piece of the main fabric stitched to the platform cloth so that the hessian is not visible. The depth of the main fabric should be approximately 20 cm (8 in) to allow for the turn under. Thread tension springs or rubber webbing through the slots, and attach these to the fittings on the sides of the frame.

INSIDE ARMS AND INSIDE BACK

The re-covering process described first is for a traditional chair. Re-covering the arms on a modern chair is slightly different (page 69). Place the fabric for the inside arm in position leaving enough overlap in the front to pleat on to the front facing. Temporary tack under the arm at the front, and, keeping the pattern or grain of the fabric horizontal, pull the cover towards the back and temporary tack in place (fig. 73). Push the cover through between the rails of the arm and seat and temporary tack to the base rail. When satisfied that the arm is in the correct position, cut round the front upright from the

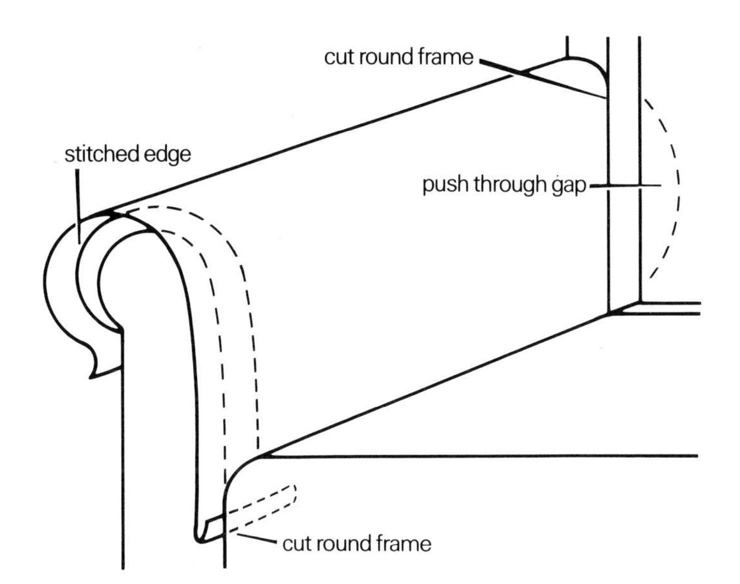

71 Covering inside arm

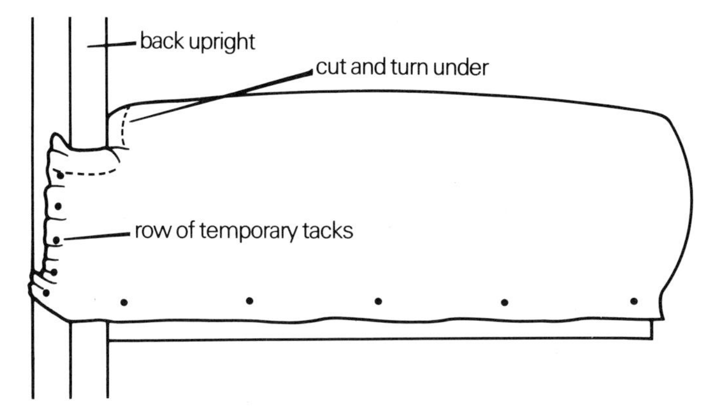

72 Fitting cover fabric around upright

point where it will not tuck away. Push the spring edge down to find this point. Trim back to 1.25 cm (½ in) and turn under. Pull the rest of the cover right through under the rail and temporary tack in place.

Cut the cover at the back rail, push through between the web and the rail leaving free at this stage. Cut the fabric into the frame at the top of the arm allowing the fabric to spread round to the back. Temporary tack to the back upright. Keep the fabric taut between the back and front and temporary tack to the rail. Using a strong twine fasten one end to a tack placed at the bottom of the facing and then run a row of stitches along the edge of the fabric, pull as you sew until they are tight. Place a temporary tack in the corner of the facing where the straight edge becomes curved, wind the twine around it and tack home. Even the gathers out round the scroll and tack in place using 13 mm (½ in) gimp pins keeping to the line of the scroll. Cut off the twine, and trim the edges back to the tack line. Leave the arms at this stage and start on the inside back.

Place the cover on the back keeping the pattern central. Hold it in place with skewers along the top of the outside back, push the cover through the lower back rail and position a temporary tack in the centre of the rail.

ARMS ON A MODERN CHAIR

Start re-covering the arms of a modern chair once the inside back has reached the stage described in the last section. On a modern chair, the inside and outside arms are piped and then sewn ready to use in one piece. The cover must be cut and pinned to fit the contour of the arm leaving extra length on the cloth to enable the cover to be pulled on. The excess is cut away after the cover has been tacked in place. Back up the outside arms and place wadding over inside and outside arm before placing on the sewn cover. The inside of the arm must be cut into the frame first. When this is all in place, tack home. Pull the outside arm into place and tack home on the underside of the frame and down the outside back upright.

Working on the inside back, now push the cover in at

the point where the inside arm and inside back meet. Mark this line with chalk and mark also the point where the frame joins at the base of the arms and back, as the fabric has to be cut away at this point to allow free passage round the frame. Trim the fabric back to within 1.25 cm (½ in) of the marking, and remove the cover from the chair.

Cut strips of the main fabric to use as a collar for the inside back. Then cut strips of hessian for flys to fit on the lower edge. The collar can be piped if the style of chair is a bordered back (characteristic of the sprung-back armchair), otherwise it is joined as a plain seam. The collar ensures a good fit and enables the fabric to spread out and follow the contour of the arms, thus preventing the fabric from splitting. Having stitched the flys in place and joined the collars to the back, place the fabric on the chair again lining up the pattern if any, with the seat. Secure at the bottom edge by temporary tacking into the base rail at a point in the centre of the fabric. Check that the layer of wadding is smooth, then tack the fabric to the back of the top rail, so that the cover is pulled over the top edge. Place a tack on either side of the upright rails, again pulling the fabric right through to the back.

Push the collars through the opening between the inside arm and inside back and after making sure that they are smoothly in position tack in place on to the uprights. The inside arms that were left untacked can now be pulled through and tacked in place on to the uprights.

By pushing the inside back cover with one hand and pulling with the other hand, smooth from the centres out towards the corners and temporary tack in place. Cut into the frame on the lower rail and, leaving a 2.5 cm (1 in) turning, fold under, round the frame. Pull down and tack in position. Fold the fly over so that the tacks are through the double fabric, this will prevent the fly from fraying out if any strain is put on it. Continue to

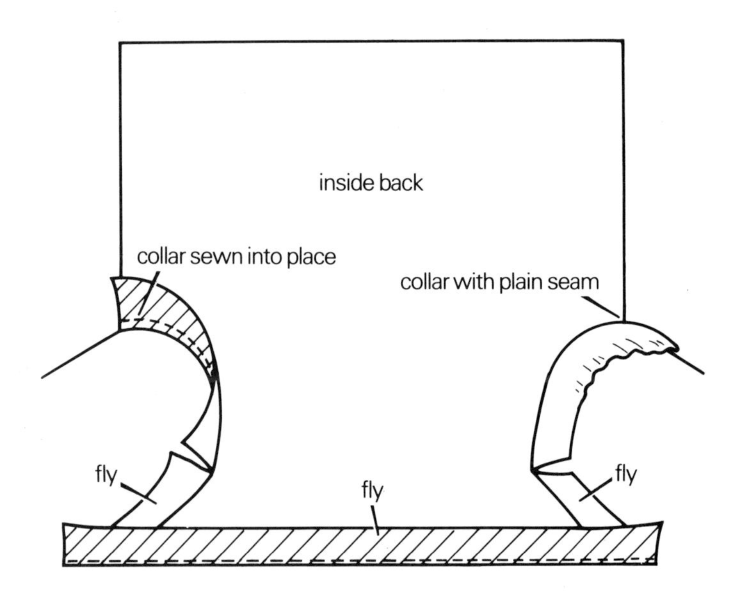

73 Sew collars and flys to inside back

tack all round until the top corners are reached. If the corner is square then smooth the fabric from along the back and up from the sides until it meets at the corner in a dart. Cut along this dart leaving 2.5 cm (1 in) to turn under. On a round corner two darts from front to back will be needed if the back is deep. On a shallow back, however, the fabric can be eased over the edge of the back without any pleats or darts on the front surface.

After the darts or pleats have been placed in original position, check that the pattern is still central, and that it is running round in line with the inside arms. When this has been checked, the tacks can be hammered home, and any excess fabric may be cut off. The next step is to place the outside pieces in position. On a firm back chair with padded arms, there is no need for a collar. Place the fabric on the chair and temporary tack in position on the bottom rail, on the top of the outside back and on the sides of the outside back. When the fabric is in position, start to push the fabric through the gap between the inside arms and inside back. The cover must be cut at the points at which its free passage is restricted by the frame.

At this stage back up the outside arms with hessian. Place a length of sheet wadding over this whole area, before applying the cover fabric.

OUTSIDE ARMS

On a traditional chair, the next step is to cover the outside arm. (This will already have been covered on a modern chair.) Starting with the outside arm, leave an allowance of at least 2.5 cm (1 in) proud of the front scroll at its widest point. Line the fabric up so that the pattern or grain of the fabric is running parallel with the floor and temporary tack to hold in place. Fold back the fabric where it meets the inside arm on the rail, mark along this line by folding with the thumb or marking with chalk.

Cut a length of back tacking strip (buckram or cardboard can be used) to the length of the arm less 1.25 cm (½ in) at each end. Lay the fabric back over the arm and line up the mark under the inside arm. Place the strip as hard against the inside arm as it will go and then tack along the strip making sure the line of the fabric remains in place. Trim off excess fabric and then place the sheet wadding so that it covers the tacks. Pull the fabric back down and secure under the base frame with a few temporary tacks. Secure the fabric on the front scroll and outside back in the same manner. Fill in with tacks and tack home.

SCROLLS

Cut out the scrolls to shape by taking a template on a piece of card. Follow the line of the frame on the outer edge and the line just inside the stitched edge on the inner edge.

Cut the fabric 1.25 cm (½ in) larger than the template all round, keeping the pattern or grain lines upright. Turn the edges over the template and press down with your thumb, hard enough to make a crease line. Remove the template and place a layer of wadding in its place. Using skewers, place the padded scroll in place with the edges turned under. Temporary tack on the underside at the base of the frame and then slip stitch in position all round the scroll. This type of scroll would be corded to match the front border. Start and finish the cording on the underside of the base frame. However, if the front border is piped, the scroll may be piped before stitching in position on the chair.

If the scroll is finished right to the edge, proceed as follows. Pin the fabric in position on the inside arm, following the outer edge where it dips inwards under the outside arm. The fabric must be left with a 4 cm (1½ in) turning, while the remaining layers should be trimmed

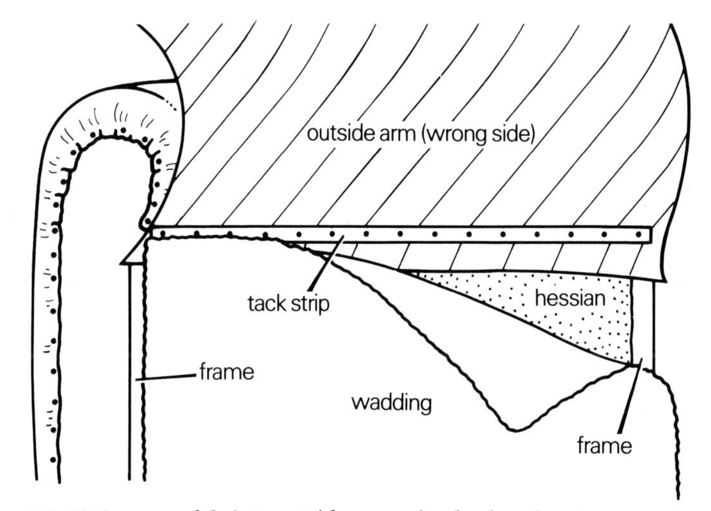

74 Fitting cover fabric to outside arm using back tack strip

back to 1.25 cm (½ in), and notched to match the inside arm. Starting from the bottom, the piping can then be stitched around the facing up to the point at which it meets the outside arm. Leave a length of piping hanging from this point, sufficient to tack along the length of the outside arm.

Using the machine, join the facings to the inside arm, up to the underside of the arm. The arm is pulled over and fixed at this point, when this has been done. Pull the excess fabric at the side of the facing round to the outside arm and tack down. Tack the piping down the edge finishing just under the edge of the base frame. The outside arm is now back tacked in place and where it meets the front facing it is slip stitched, catching in the piping and the front facing. At the point where the front border meets the front facing, the piping must be tucked under and slip stitched over the front border.

On an overstuff scroll, the facing would be cut to the inner shape; allowing 1.25 cm (½ in) turning, it is then padded with wadding and fixed in position with skewers. It can be piped round the edges or corded. Slip stitch in place using a waxed thread and a cording needle (fig. 76).

Some types of facing are made from wood. With these, the facing is padded with a layer of wadding after a fixing bolt has been placed through the wood. The fabric is then placed on the facing and pulled over the edges so that it can be stapled or glued to the wood. 5 mm (¼ in) tacks may be used if the wood is of sufficient thickness. Fit the facing into position on the front of the arm, and then finish the outside arm. This type of facing is usual on leather-covered chairs and can be finished with close nailing. Generally, it is best to follow the style of the original trimming, but depending on the fabric used, the appearance of a chair can be enhanced by the choice of a different type of trimming.

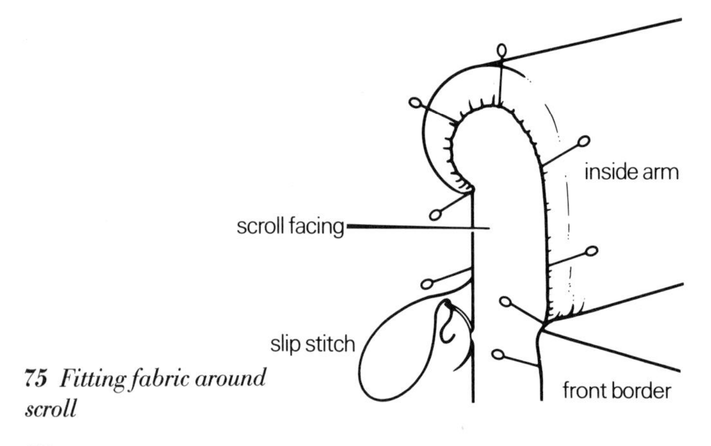

75 Fitting fabric around scroll

The outside back is the next section to be covered. Start by backing up with a length of hessian or calico in the same way as for the outside arms. Place a length of wadding to fit over this and back tack the outside back along the top edge of the frame keeping just below the frame line. Pull the fabric over the wadding, temporary tack on the underside of the base, turn in the sides, and slip stitch in place using a cording needle. Tack home the tacks in the base, and trim off the surplus fabric.

Turn the chair completely upside down and if the chair has castors fitted directly to the frame, lever them out from their sockets. Cut a length of 213 g (7½ oz) hessian or black linette to fit the base allowing an extra 1.5 cm (⅝ in) all round. Turn the fabric under and starting from the four centre points at the front, back and sides, tack 8 cm (3 in) just inside the frame edge. Work from the centres towards the legs.

Cut into the legs at a right angle, turn under and tack home (the tacks should be placed at intervals of approximately 3.5 cm [1½ in]). Now refit the castors. Starting directly above the centre of the castor socket, make a series of cuts in the hessian (or black linette) from the centre to the side of the socket. Turn under and tack down, then replace the castor.

Turn the chair the right way up, check that all the

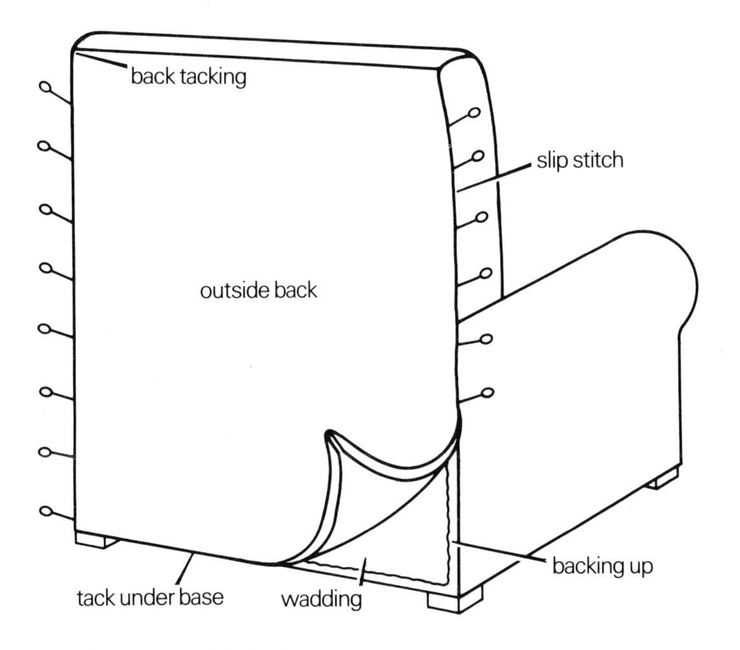

76 Covering outside back

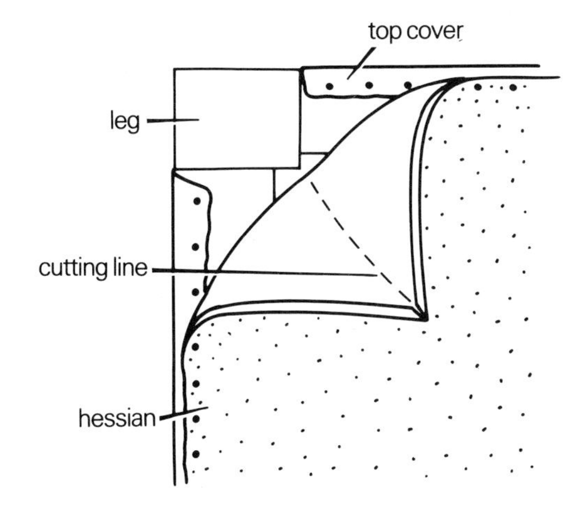

77 Fitting hessian around leg

threads have been cut off and finished tidily. Brush off any surplus fluff or dust using a pad made of the same fabric. If it is a pile cloth, finish by brushing the pile down towards the ground. A fringe can be sewn on at this stage if required (page 89), in every other respect the chair is ready for use.

FLUTING

Fluting is sometimes worked on the inside back of a chair. It has an attractive effect and adds extra padding. To make up a piece of fluting, cut a length of hessian to fit the back with an extra allowance of 20 cm (8 in) all round to allow for take-up. Starting in the centre draw a vertical line. Then mark off more vertical lines down the fabric at intervals of 10 cm (4 in). This width can be varied according to taste. Mark the main fabric in the same way on the wrong side allowing an extra 5 cm (2 in) for each strip to allow for padding and stitching.

In a factory or large workshop, the padding would be pre-covered in long lengths which could be slid into place with a tool. The padding is usually linter felt which is liable to break up if it is pushed into a tube and result in a lumpy mess. Nowadays, as fluting is a 'one-off', I suggest using the following method. Start on the left-hand side with the hessian laying flat. Crease down all

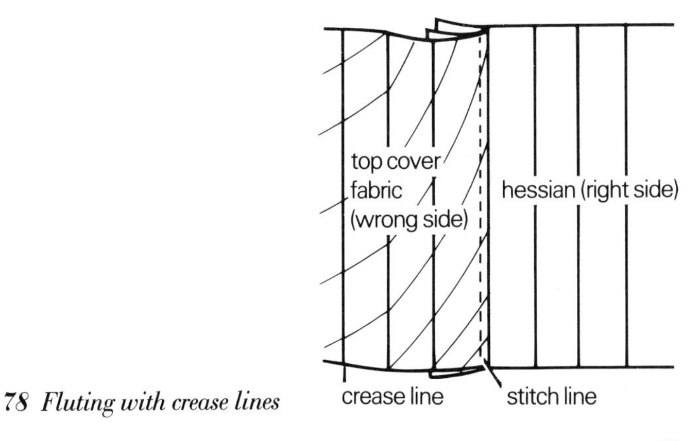

78 Fluting with crease lines

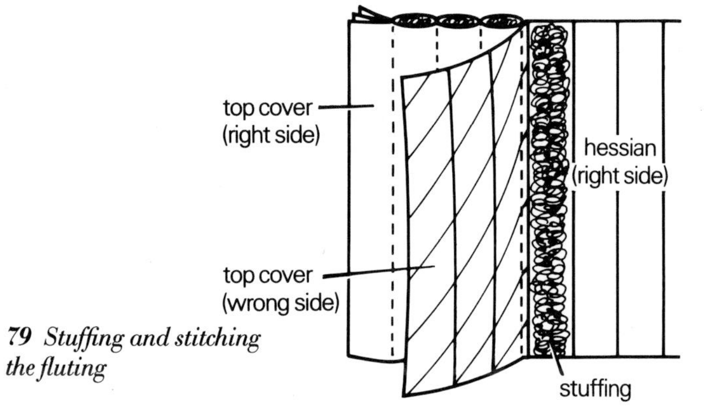

79 Stuffing and stitching the fluting

the lines on the main fabric using the wrong side of a ruler. Lay the first crease on the first mark on the hessian, and fold back, taking a small turning approxi-ately 1.25 cm (½ in) stitch line from top to bottom (fig. 79). Take a length of linter felt and lay it on the hessian (use enough linter felt to fill the pad out tight). Then stitch the fabric down the crease line on to the hessian in the same manner as the first line (fig. 80). Continue across until all lines are sewn and padded. The fluting is now ready to use as a normal length of fabric to re-cover the chair back or seat as the case may be. Pad the outside flutes before tacking home.

High back chair

14 WINGS

There are many different types of wings and methods of covering them differ accordingly. However, this basic method of covering used for an overstuff wing with a stitched edge, can be adapted to suit most traditional types. Place a length of wadding over the wing, trimming back to the edge by tearing with the fingers. The piece of fabric already cut should measure from the widest points both ways with an allowance of 5 cm (2 in) extra on each measurement. Place the fabric for the inside wing with the grain running vertically, and secure with a few temporary tacks to hold it in place. Push the excess fabric through the space between the frame, two cuts must be made to accommodate the frame. Cut right to the frame, so that the fabric will spread round towards the outside back. Trim back to within 1.25 mm (½ in) of the cuts and turn the fabric under. Temporary tack over the back edge.

Push the fabric down to meet the inside arm and make a cut, to allow the fabric to spread. Trim back to 1.25 cm (½ in) and fold under. Secure with skewers ready to be slip stitched. Ease the fabric round the outside of the wing, making two pleats where the excess fabric meets at the widest part of the curve. Tack round the outside wing approximately 3 cm (1¼ in) from the edge. Pull the fabric, calico and hessian through to the back upright and tack in place. Slip stitch round the lower edge of the wing.

Now 'back up' the outside wing with a length of hessian. Tack the hessian over the hollow section attaching it to the frame below the part where the fabric has already been tacked. Cover the whole outside wing area with wadding, trimming it off at the outer edge. Place a length of fabric over the wing and trim to shape, allowing a 2 cm (¾ in) turn under all round. Tack the fabric in place along the back edge on the outside back. Turn under the edges on the remainder of the fabric, fix with skewers just shy of the edge and slip stitch in place. Leave the lower edge free to tuck under the inside arm.

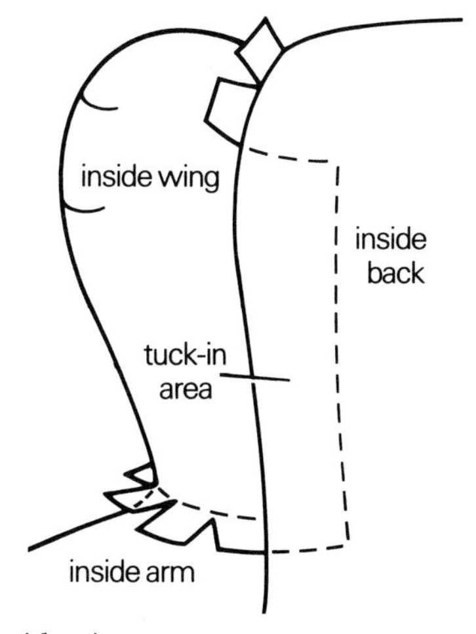

80 Covering inside wing

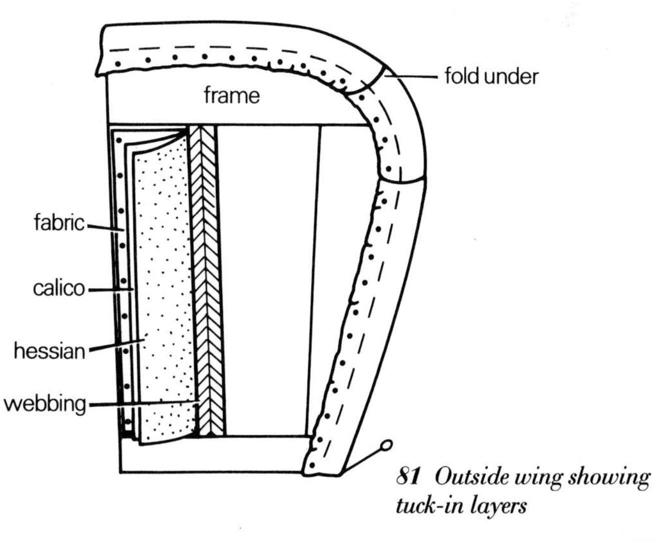

81 Outside wing showing tuck-in layers

The wing may have a piping between the inside and outside wing. This should be tacked on after the inside wings have been finished and before the outside wings have been started. It starts at the lower edge of the wing, goes round the outside wing, across the outside back and finishes at the base of the opposite wing. The outsides are then skewered in place and slip stitched catching the piping and securing it in place between the inner and outer wings.

RE-COVERING A MODERN WING CHAIR

Modern chairs often have flat wings which means that the inside wing and the outside wing can be joined before fitting. Trim down to allow 1.25 mm (½ in) turn under then machine together. Piping can be inserted at this stage if required. (Cut notches in the seam allowance so that they may be matched with machining to prevent any twisting.) Now, lay padding (linter felt or foam) on to the wing of the chair and fit the wing covering. Pull the complete wing on over the padding and cut the inside wing in exactly the same way as before (page 75). Tack in place. Pull the outside wing towards the outside back and secure to the upright. Leave the bottom edge of the wing free, so that the outside arm will cover the raw edge. This bottom edge will be secured when the outside arm is back tacked in place.

15 CUSHIONS

CUTTING AND MAKING A DOWN OR FEATHER CUSHION PAD

Use a fabric called downproof cambric for these cushion pads. Make sure the seams are waxed after sewing, to prevent the down penetrating them. Use a piece of beeswax to rub along the sewing line. (A second row of stitching on the edge of the turning is an extra safeguard.) To make a flat cushion pad, measure the downproof cambric to the size you require the cushion to be. Cut two pieces leaving seam allowances of 1.25 cm (½ in) each side, then add an extra 2 cm (¾ in) all round. Lay out the two pieces with right sides together and machine round the edge, leaving the 1.25 cm (½ in) seam allowance. Start machining all round leaving a gap large enough to allow the case to be filled (about half the length of one side).

Make a second row of stitching along the outer edge and wax the stitching lines. Turn the cover right side out and fill with down or feathers. Turn the edges of the opening inside and top stitch along the edge. Wax the stitches. A good guideline when filling a cushion is to ensure that the corners are well filled and that the centre is convex in shape. When pressed in the middle, the pad should feel spongy; if it resists light pressure, it is overfilled.

CUTTING AND MAKING A BORDERED CUSHION WITH PARTITIONS

The advantage of adding inner walls to a bordered cushion is that the filling remains evenly distributed. Measure the cushion pad to be covered along the length, width and border depth. Add 2.5 cm (1 in) to each measurement for seam allowance. Then add an extra 2.5 cm (1 in) all round and cut. (Cut the border length in two pieces.) In addition, cut an extra border length to use as partition walls.

After cutting, lay the top and underside of the cushion with wrong sides up and mark with a pencil two lines

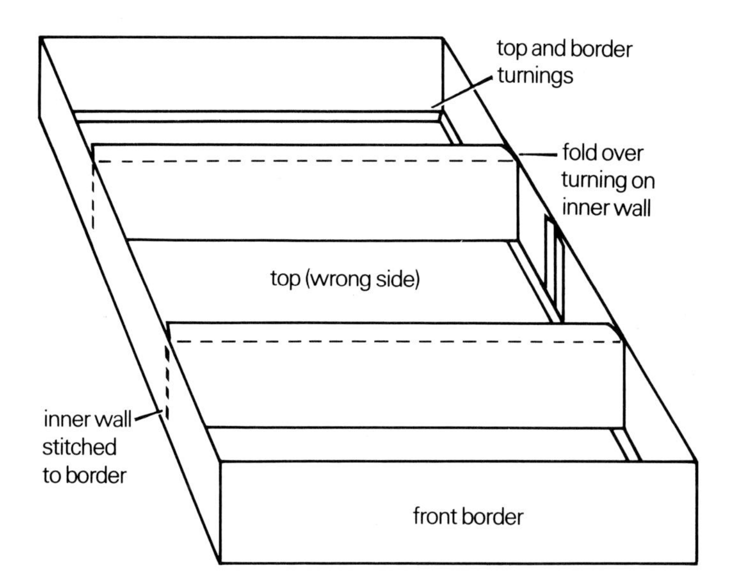

82 Bordered cushion pad showing inner walls

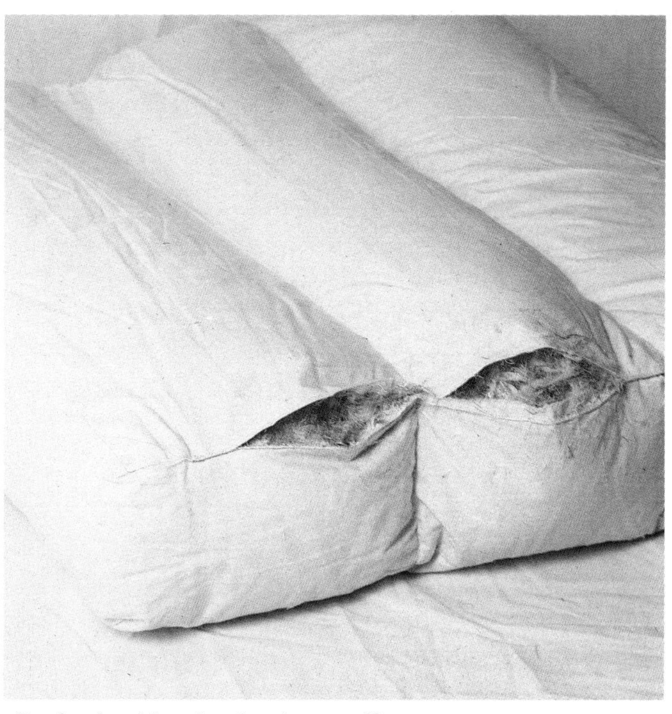

Bordered cushion showing down stuffing

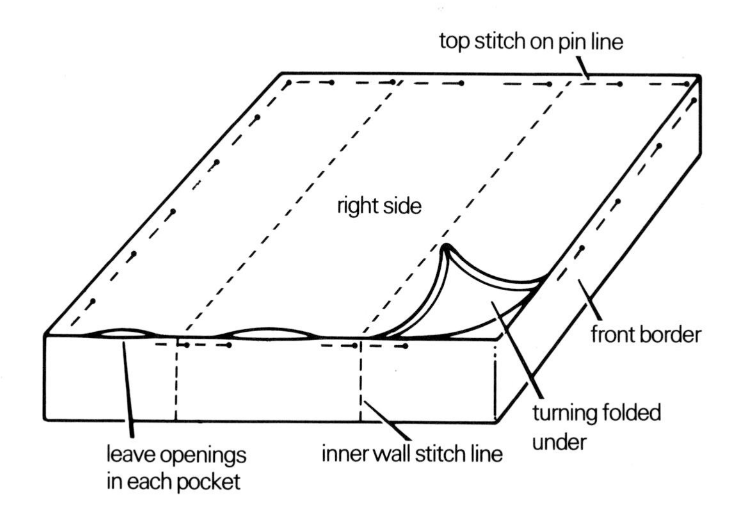

83 Stitching underside of cushion to inner walls

across the width, dividing each piece of fabric into thirds. Machine sew together and mark the two side borders to line up with the marks on the cushion. Cut the extra length of border into walls to fit the size of the cushion width. Fold over the 1.5 cm (5⁄8 in) seam allowance on the partition walls. Stitch the walls to the wrong side of the top side of the cushion, leaving the seam allowances unstitched. With right sides together, join the border to the top section. Take care not to catch the partition walls at this stage. Turn right side out. Stitch the partition walls upright to the side borders along the markings. Stop the stitching at the seam allowance. Fold over the seam allowance.

Place the underside fabric flat and match the inner walls to the pencil marks across the width. Stitch across, starting at the front, or first, inner wall, to prevent the seam allowance being inaccessible. After stitching the walls in place, the border edges and underside edges must be turned in and joined. Pin the two edges together all the way round the cushion leaving a gap in each section so that they can be filled with down.

Fill the individual sections, and test to see if they are evenly filled. First check that the corners are well filled and that the centre of each section is slightly convex. When pressed in the middle, the pad should feel spongy; if it resists light pressure, it is overfilled. After filling, fold in the edges of each gap and continue the top stitch to close the cushion.

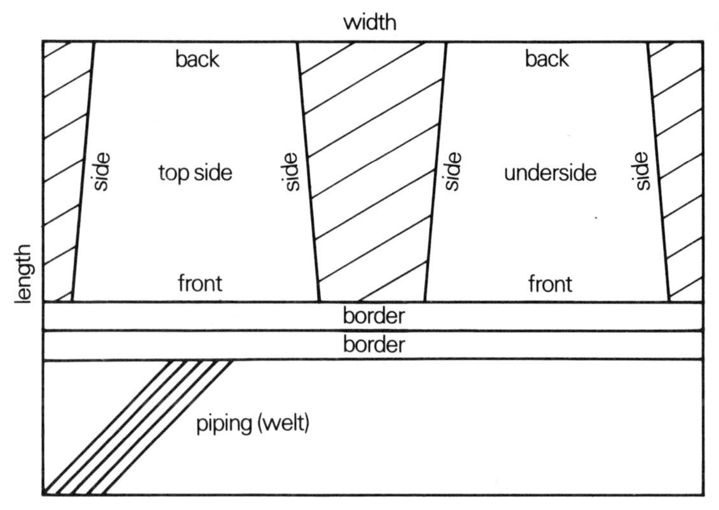

84 Cutting plan for bordered seat cushion

CUTTING AND MAKING A BORDERED CUSHION WITHOUT PARTITIONS

Measure the cushion to be covered and cut out the pieces as described on page 76 (leaving out the extra fabric required for partition walls). When cutting a seat or back cushion, make sure that the pattern runs in line with the back and front border.

Cut out all the pieces before attempting to assemble the cushion. With right sides together, lay the centre of one piece of border against the centre front on the top side. Check that the pattern on the border runs down in line with the top side of the cushion. Pin the two border pieces round the cushion. Join together the ends of the border and, leaving a seam allowance, cut off any surplus. Cut a notch in the centre of the back and border seam. Unpin the border and flatten the seams on the side joins.

Make up a length of piping, and, starting at the notch at the back of the top side, pipe the top all round joining the piping when it meets at the back. Repeat on the underside of the cushion.

Before assembling decide how much opening to leave unstitched. For a down or foam cushion, leave the length of the back of the cushion on the underside, but for a firm cushion it will be necessary to leave the cushion open halfway down each side as well as across the back of the underside. Starting at the notch, assemble the cushion by laying the top side on to the border (with right sides together), and stitching closer to the piping than previously. After stitching the two together, place the underside in position on the border, and line the corners up so that they are upright. Cut a notch in the seam allowance of each corner. Match up these notches as the cushion is stitched to prevent the cushion border being twisted on the finished article.

Make a second line of stitching nearer the piping on the part which is to be left open. This will keep the piping at an even thickness. Turn the cover right side out, fold the cushion pad in half, and push the front right into the corners. Turn the piping down towards the border as the pad is fitted in, to encourage the piping to stand up and make a good straight line.

With foam cushions, the front edge should be secured to stop the pad rolling round inside. Take two strips of

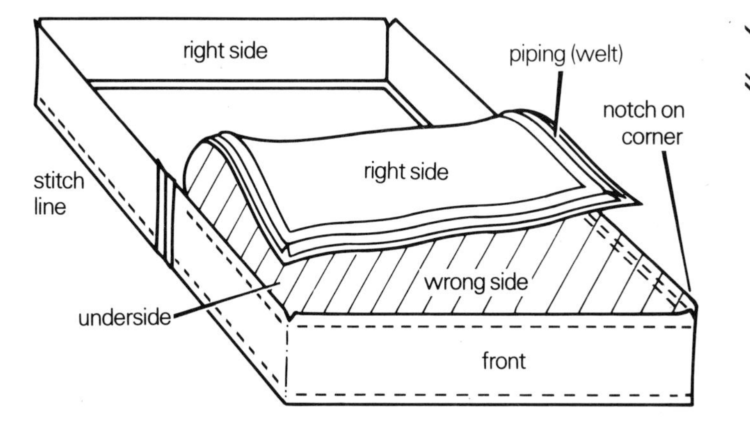

85 Cushion assembled with opening on underside

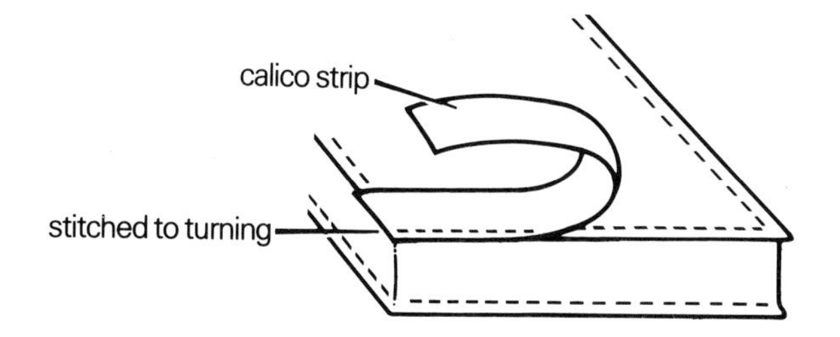

86 Attaching calico strip

calico, approximately 8 cm (3 in) wide and long enough to fit the cushion front. Machine the two strips on to the seam allowances on the front top side and front underside of the cushion cover. When the two strips have been stitched in place, spread adhesive on to both the strip and foam interior. (There are many adhesives on the market these days, each with a special purpose. Read the intructions to make sure the type being used is the right one for the purpose.) Stick the calico strips to the foam, making sure the foam is pushed right up against the front border. When the adhesive is dry, push the

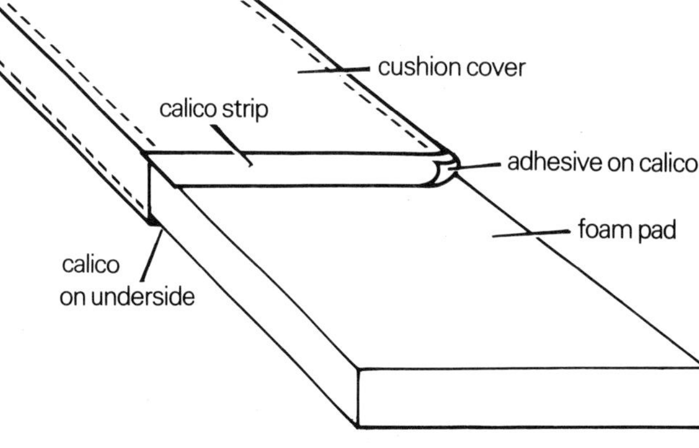

87 Fitting foam pad into cover

foam pad into the cover as you turn the cover right side out. To close the cover, pin the opening together, fold in the raw edges and slip stitch with a linen thread or twine.

CUTTING AND MAKING A GATHERED CORNER CUSHION

A gathered corner cushion can be used as a back cushion, instead of the bordered type. Although it is piped as a flat cushion it does retain the depth on the corners, which makes it as thick as a bordered cushion.

To cut out, measure the inside pad, and add 1.25 cm (½ in) turning each side. Cut the top of the cushion, making sure that the pattern is central (if the fabric is plain, cut to the thread). At this stage cut a square shape only. Cut the underside of the cushion in exactly the same way as the top, matching the pattern so that the cushions may be reversed individually. When both pieces have been cut, with the wrong sides together, lay them flat on the table. Measure 8 cm (3 in) in from each corner, and strike a line across to each mark. This measurement will be approximately 10 cm (4 in). Repeat this process at each corner, and then cut across each line.

The measurement given is for an average thickness cushion of 8 cm (3 in). For a deeper one, increase the measurement, so that the corner is cut out wider. Do *not* cut too much away as the more that is cut from the corner, the smaller the circumference of the cushion will be. The corner should now be pleated and pinned in position, either with four pleats or two, this is a matter of choice. Make sure the pleats face in towards each other, on the right side of the cushion (see fig. 88).

The measurement across the corner should now be 3 cm (1¼ in). This is the turning allowance and it applies whatever the measurement cut across the corner. It must be pleated in so that the pleats meet in the centre. Leave the pins in position, and continue to pleat the remaining corners on the top and the underside of the cushion. Now make up the piping and apply it to the cushion top, starting on the lower edge, halfway along.

Pipe the cushion as shown in fig. 85. When you reach the corner, make sure the pleats are lying flat and do not get caught up underneath. Follow the line of the outer edge of the fabric, taking care to leave the correct seam allowance (1.25 cm [½ in]). The stitching line should be slightly rounded at the corners. Join the ends of the piping together and, placing the right sides together, assemble the cushion. Leave a gap in the lower edge of the cover large enough for the cushion pad to be inserted. Before stitching the cushion together, sew an extra line close to the piping along the gap (page 78). This makes sure that the piping is the same thickness all round.

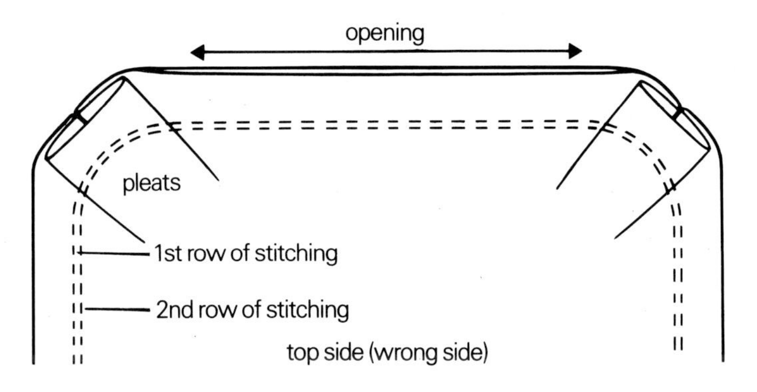

88 Inside of gathered corner cushion

Fold the cushion pad in half and push it through the opening into the cover. Push the pad well into the corners and turn in the raw edges. Slip stitch the opening together with a linen thread.

DEEP-BUTTON-BACKED HEADBOARD

To estimate the length of fabric you will need to cover the headboard, measure the widest part of the board, allow 10 cm (4 in) extra each side to turn round the back, and then add 5 cm (2 in) for every diamond. This total will constitute the width required. Measure the length in the same manner but exclude the unmarked base as this is covered separately.

Cut out the piece of fabric, leaving it square (do not trim it to shape). Mark the centre of the fabric with a cross (to find this use the method on page 54). The diamonds must be marked larger than they are on the board. On a board where the buttons are marked at 15 cm (6 in) intervals an extra 3 cm (1¼ in) will generally be sufficient. If, however, the board has been marked with different sized diamonds, place a piece of foam on the board between two measured button marks and, using a tape, measure over the foam from mark to mark. This will give the exact width required on fabric, for that diamond.

Mark the fabric on its wrong side in the same way as for the board, but using the new measurement. If you are using a pile fabric, the pile must run downwards, so mark the top. If the fabric is not wide enough to cover the entire width of the board, then it must be joined and this is called van dykeing. The seam follows the line of the pleats so that it is invisible when buttoned.

Van dykeing

To van dyke, machine stitch the two pieces together allowing one length to overlap the other by at least the width of half a diamond. Mark the whole piece of extra fabric with the button positions, keeping the marks in line. Pin the pleating lines right through the two pieces of fabric, then with a piece of chalk mark a curved line

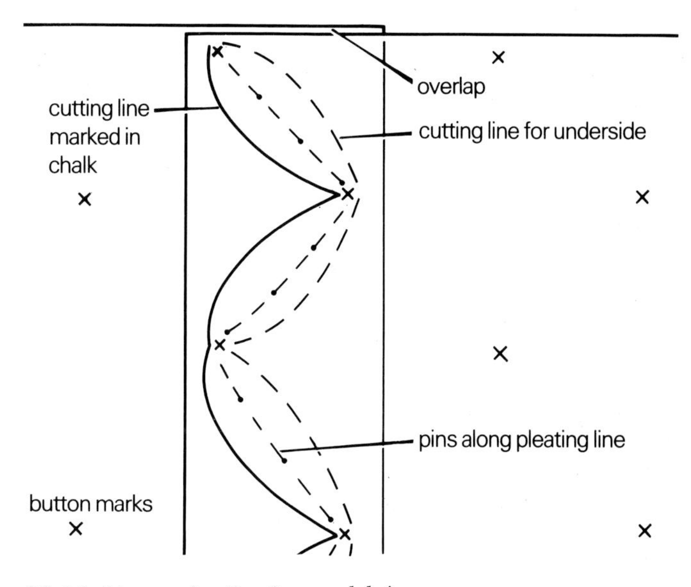

89 Marking cutting line for van dykeing

from the button mark to the button mark below, the widest part of the curve being about 2 cm (¾ in) graduating to about 3 mm (⅛ in) from the button mark.

After cutting the top piece of fabric turn the whole thing over and cut the underside as marked in fig. 90. Turn the pieces so that the two right sides are now together and place a pin through the two pieces right on the button mark. The outer curve of one side fits to the inner curve on the other side. Pin in place and machine stitch fairly close to the edge. Machine the two pieces together, stitching right to the button mark. Snip through the turning right to the button mark. This stitching must be accurate otherwise the pleating line will not be straight, if it is not cut in far enough at the buttons the pleat line will drag. Turn right side out. The piece of fabric is now ready to be used for buttoning.

Place a sheet of wadding, skin side up, on the foam,

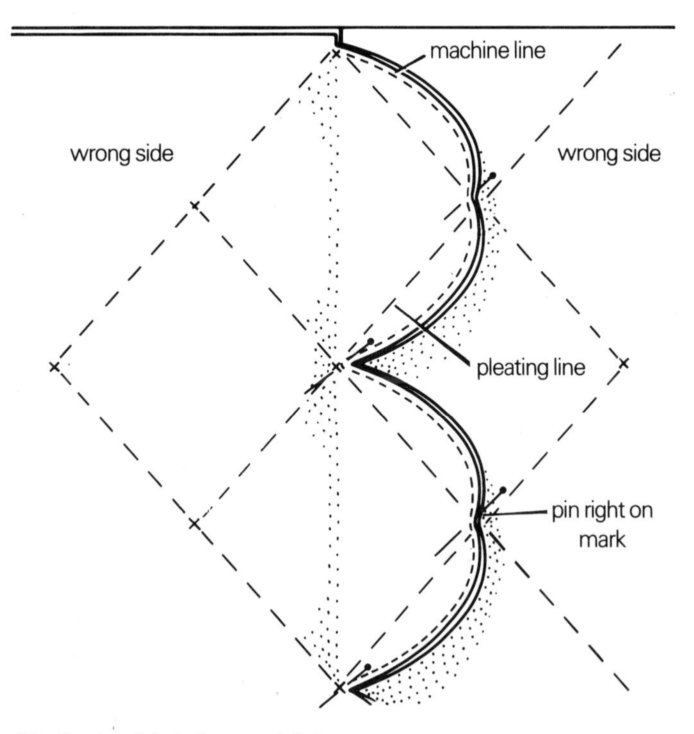

90 Cutting fabric for van dykeing

Deep-button-backed headboard

extending it well over the edges. Place the fabric over the wadding and cut lengths of button twine approximately 30 cm (12 in) long and put to the side. Take a long mattress needle (unthreaded) and push it eye first through the drilled centre mark on the back of the board. Take the fabric in one hand and find the centre button mark; push the needle through right on the mark far enough to allow you to thread the eye with a length of twine. Thread one end of the twine through the eye, thread the button on and then thread the remaining end of twine back through the eye. Pull through to the back. Place a tack just to the side of the hole on the back of the headboard. Wind one end of the twine round it and then hammer home. Place a second tack half-way in to the board and pull the other end of the twine taut, at the same time push the button from the right side until it reaches the board, to take some of the strain. When the button is right home, wind the end of the twine round the tack and tack home. Repeat this until all the buttons are in place. Work away from the centre completing each diamond as you work. Use the flat end of the regulator to turn the pleats so that they are facing down.

When all the buttoning has been completed, pull the excess fabric round to the back of the board. Reduce the fullness by pleating the fabric and secure with temporary tacks at the back. The pleats do not always run off in line with the button work, particularly if the edges are shaped. Try to clean out any curves and then pleat the excess that forms into downward facing folds, making these balance on each side of the headboard. When you have arranged the pleats to your satisfaction, tack down the fabric on the back of the board and trim it back to the tack line.

When the back has been tacked in place, begin work on the bottom edge of the headboard. The foam should be cut with a sharp knife from each of the buttons on the bottom row down to the bottom edge. The fabric is then pulled tight so that it falls into the cut and thus forms a straight pleat. Tack the fabric home just below the marked line on the board. To finish this part of the board, cut a length of fabric to cover the remaining area on the board. Cut it wide enough to allow you to turn it round to the back and deep enough to go under the bottom edge to be tacked to the back. (Generally, about 10 cm [4 in] extra on all sides is sufficient.) If the fabric has to be joined to make up the width, make two joins each side of the central width. Using a length of buckram or webbing, back tack the fabric along the bottom pleats in a straight line (page 52). Place a length of wadding over the board, pull the fabric over and tack to the back of the board. Trim excess fabric up to the tack line.

Use a length of lining fabric to cover the back. Cut it to size, allowing 5 cm (2 in) extra all round for turning under. But first, lay a length of wadding on the board tearing it to shape using your fingers. Lay the lining on top and, using skewers, pin it in place. Slip stitch all round the edge. Alternatively, you could tack or staple the lining to the back of the headboard. Now the headboard is ready to be fitted either with screws, if it is to be attached to the wall, or with legs, if it is to be fitted to the back of a divan base. When you make the screw holes, use a bradawl to pierce the lining fabric before screwing in, otherwise the screw turns the fabric and tears it. Turn to the front and, using the flat end of the regulator to tuck under the folds, straighten all the pleats.

Float buttoning

Float buttoning is used on headboards, chairs and cushions. It is not only decorative but also useful for keeping the stuffing in place. The buttons are not pulled right down tight to the backing, instead, they are allowed to 'float', making only a shallow indentation on the front surface.

When float buttoning, the actual buttoning is done after the front fabric is backed in place, and no allowance is made for pleating. The twine should be tightened only enough to hold the button firmly in place; the degree of indentation is a matter of choice. The twine will be pulled through to the back and, depending on the type of backing, will either be tacked home or tied round a washer.

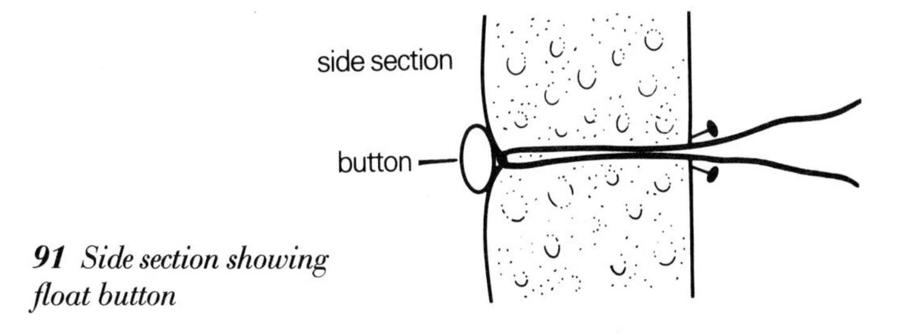

91 *Side section showing float button*

A cushion is sometimes float buttoned both sides. To do this, instead of fastening the twine around a tack or washer, you secure it to another button. Tie the button on, make a slip knot and pull the two buttons towards each other. Lock the knot and cut off the ends of twine.

MAKING A BORDER-EDGED HEADBOARD

This type of headboard can be made using foam for the centre pad, and linter felt for the outer edge. (See deep-button-backed headboard on page 54). Cut the piece of board to shape, and then mark a line 10 cm (4 in) in from the edge, round the top and both sides. Draw another line 15 cm (6 in) up from the bottom edge;

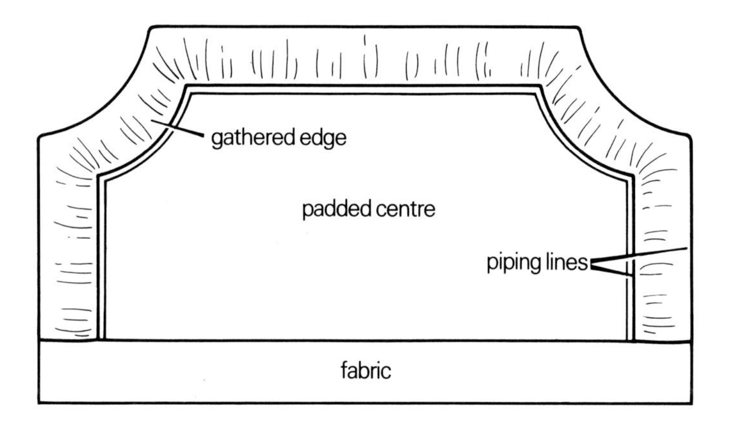

92 Finished board showing gathered edge

below this line the board is only slightly padded as this part goes behind the bed base and mattress. Cut a length of 5 cm (2 in) foam to fit the space between the lines. Add 3 cm (1¼ in) all round (see deep-button-backed headboard on page 54).

Chamfer the edge and stick strips of calico on the edges (fig. 53). Using staples or 10 mm (⅜ in) tacks, fix the edge of the foam directly to the marked line all round. Cover the foam with a layer of wadding, then place a length of fabric over the foam covered area, overlapping by approximately 1.25 cm (½ in). Tack or staple the fabric to the line marked all round. Trim away excess fabric and calico strips. Make up a length of piping (in the same or contrasting colour fabric), to go down the two sides and along the top edge twice. Now tack the piping to the board with the raw edges facing towards the outside edge. The piping should follow a line right round the edge of the foam, except for the bottom edge. When the piping reaches the corner, make a snip to prevent puckering.

Once the piping has been tacked in place the next step is the gathered edge. Measure the area to be covered on the outside edge of the board and double the measurement; this should give you sufficient fullness in the gathers. Cut strips of fabric (across the width of the fabric) so that the pattern will be upright along the top to match the centre pad. The width of each strip should be 15 cm (6 in), this will allow room for the turnings and the padding. Now, machine the strips together to make one long length. Make a mark half-way along and at each quarter. Mark the board in the same way on both the inner and outer edge. This helps by providing a guideline to the amount of gathering required in each quarter and the marks also help keep the gathers upright along the top and horizontal on the sides. Put a line of 1.25 cm (½ in) stitches along the edges of the fabric strip. Using a strong thread, stop and start again at each

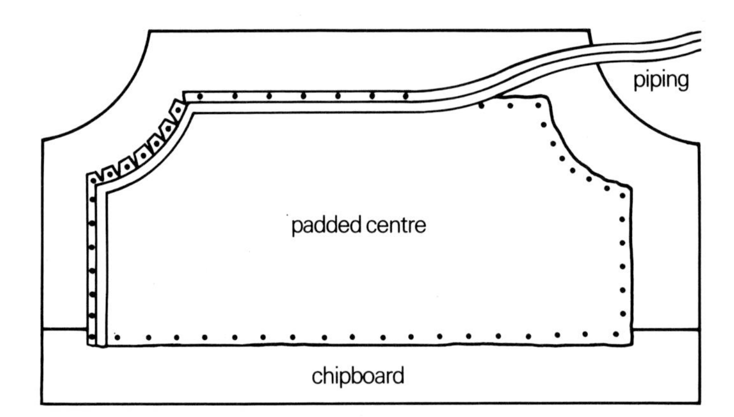

93 Fixing piping around padded centre

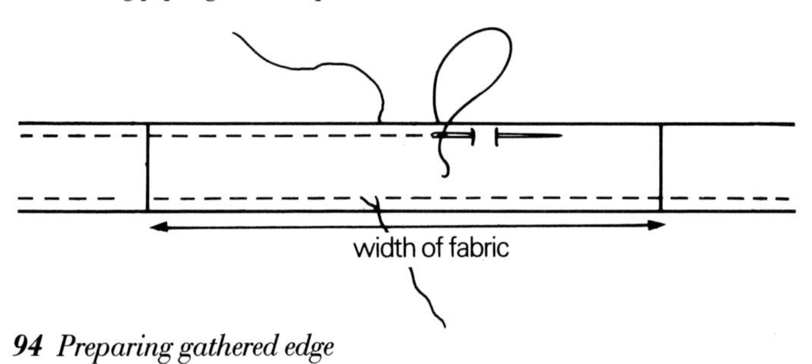

94 Preparing gathered edge

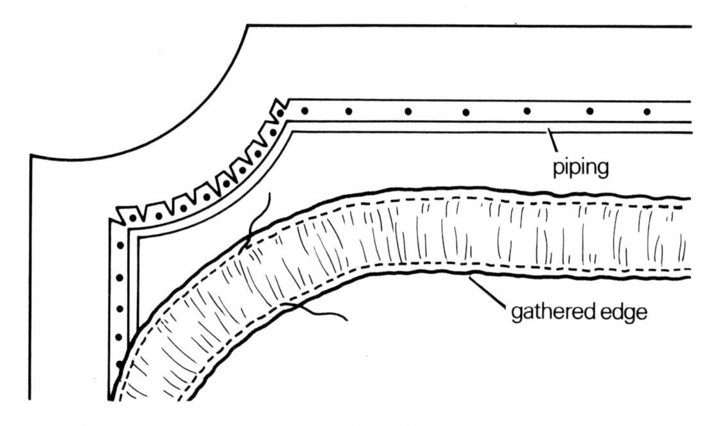

95 Placing gathered edge around padded centre

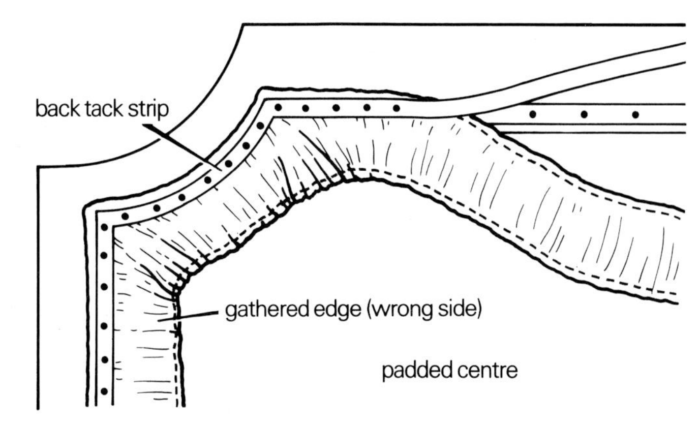

96 Tacking on gathered edge using back tack strip

quarter mark. Gather both edges so that the outer edge fits the board, then start on the first section on the side of the board. Lay the gathered strip right side down against the piped edge. Use a length of back tack strip or a strip of buckram tack close to the piped edge so that the gathers are caught against the piping. When you reach the corner of the inner edge, the gathers must be tacked closer together. This allows enough gathering to cover the extra length of the outer edge. Without this allowance, you will find that you have a flat area without gathers when you fit the outer edge.

Continue all round the board, finishing just below the line marked at the base. Once the inner part has been tacked home, place a length of linter felt on the unpadded edge of the board. (Polyester can be used instead of linter felt if you wish; in fact, if the fabric is light in colour polyester would be better.) Pad the edge so that it has a rounded appearance. Pull the gathered fabric over the padding and then temporary tack over the back edge.

When all the gathers are in position, tack home. Now, take the other length of piping and tack it all around the back edge of the board, starting at the base line. Keep the piping level, allowing it to stand just proud of the edge all round. Once the piping is complete, the next step is to pad the lower edge (page 83). Finally, finish the outside back in the same way as for the buttoned headboard (page 83).

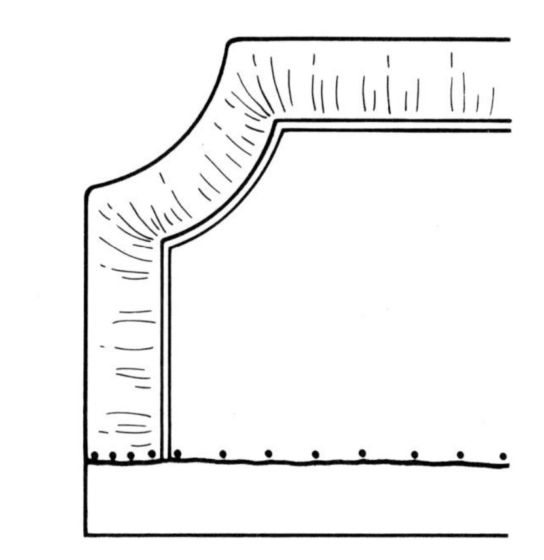

97 Completed headboard

Variations to a headboard can be made by deep buttoning or float buttoning the centre section. The suitability of these techniques will depend principally on the kind of fabric being used.

17 DEEP-BUTTON-BACKED CHAIR

Once the chair has been upholstered 'up to calico' or, alternatively, once it has had its outer cover removed, it is ready for re-covering.

First, using a cut sheet (page 61), cut out all the lengths of fabric required. Remember to allow for the extra taken up in buttoning (page 81). Mark all the pieces on the back with chalk for identification. The buttons should be made professionally; your local upholsterer or sewing shop will probably be able to do this. A 1.25 cm (½ in) button needs approximately 4 cm (1½ in) square of fabric. The metal shank buttons are widely used as they are stronger than the fabric-backed button.

I prefer to cover the seat of the chair first but it is a matter of choice. Place the cover square on the seat after positioning a sheet of wadding over the calico. Fix three temporary tacks in the back rail, pull the cover forward, and place three tacks in the underside of the rail at the front. Repeat from side to side, pushing the cover down between the back and seat rails. The cover will have to be cut round the uprights at this stage to allow the fabric to pass freely. Make sure the cover is placed correctly before cutting in to the uprights.

Pull the cover through between the seat and inside back and temporary tack it down on to the back rail. Smooth the cover forward and tack under the front rail. As the front of a seat has rounded corners, the excess fabric will have to be eased in along the bottom edge of the front. This can be done in two ways, either by bringing two pleats together at the centre of the leg, or by gathering a series of small pleats at the top of the chair leg.

If the leg is set back from the front of the frame, then tack the fabric right underneath. If it is level with the front then the fabric is tacked on to the face as low as possible and later cut away flush and covered with gimp. Once the front is finished, tack home all round the back and sides and trim off any excess fabric.

Now place the correct piece of fabric square on the arm, leaving enough turnings all round. Place a button in the centre of the arm, going right through the fabric in the same manner as for the back (page 87). Tighten sufficiently to hold the fabric in place. Smooth the fabric up over the arm and secure with skewers underneath the stitched edge. Allow the fabric to form a pleat in a vertical line with the button, over the arm. Fix with a skewer and let the pleat continue from the button down into the tuck-in. Secure with a temporary tack to the base rail. Cut round the uprights and push the remainder of the fabric down through the tuck-in, temporary tack in place.

To finish around the front of the arm, wrap the fabric round the front forming pleats with the excess (face the pleats down towards the seat). Fix in place with skewers. Tighten up the button, tack home the tacks, snip the fabric round the curve where the inside back and arm meet so that it lies flat and then proceed to sew the cover to the underside of the arm right through the hessian (figs. 98–99).

The next stage is to mark up the fabric ready for buttoning the back. Measure and draw a vertical line down the centre of the fabric (because the fabric now has to stretch over the stuffing an extra allowance must be made to accommodate this). When measuring this, use a tape measure and push it right to the back hessian over the stuffing and to the nearest marked button on the hessian. This will give you the allowance needed. An average chair will need 2.5 cm (1 in) extra on the vertical and 2 cm (¾ in) on the horizontal. Mark out the measurements on the back of the fabric with a small cross at each button spacing. The markings are only used as a guide. A good deal depends on the way the fabric handles (i.e., if it stretches or folds well) and also on the fact that the lower buttons may be moved further away to allow for the curve. Most upholsterers 'feel' the buttons in, which is a skill learned by experience. Most beginners would be well advised to take a great deal of trouble in marking out as accurately as possible. If the chair has only to be re-covered, you can use the old cover as a guideline. Do not, however, cut a pattern from the old cover, as it will be much too small without the chair allowances left for stitching. It is very much better to re-cut a new cover to fit the chair rather than to try to make a chair fit a cover.

Once the fabric is marked out, cut a length of buttoning twine approximately 45 cm (18 in) long. Using a 25 cm (10 in) double-pointed needle, start to button the back. I prefer to tie off at the back of the chair, but if you prefer to tie off at the front then just reverse the following process, it will give the same result.

Starting with the mark nearest the centre, and working from the outside back, push the eye of the needle through the mark right through to where the hair and wadding is parted. Find the corresponding mark on the piece of fabric and push the needle through from the wrong side. Thread the button on the twine and then thread both ends of twine through the eye of the needle. Pull the needle back through the chair, and tie an upholsterers slip knot in the twine. Roll up a small length of calico approximately 5 cm (2 in) wide until it makes a tube, and use this as a washer. Place the washer in between the back hessian and the knot, then pull the knot up until it grips the washer. Do not tighten up fully at this stage as the pleats formed in the front have to be manipulated into position. Working in this manner, form one diamond at a time. The excess material between the buttons should be folded under so that each pleat formed

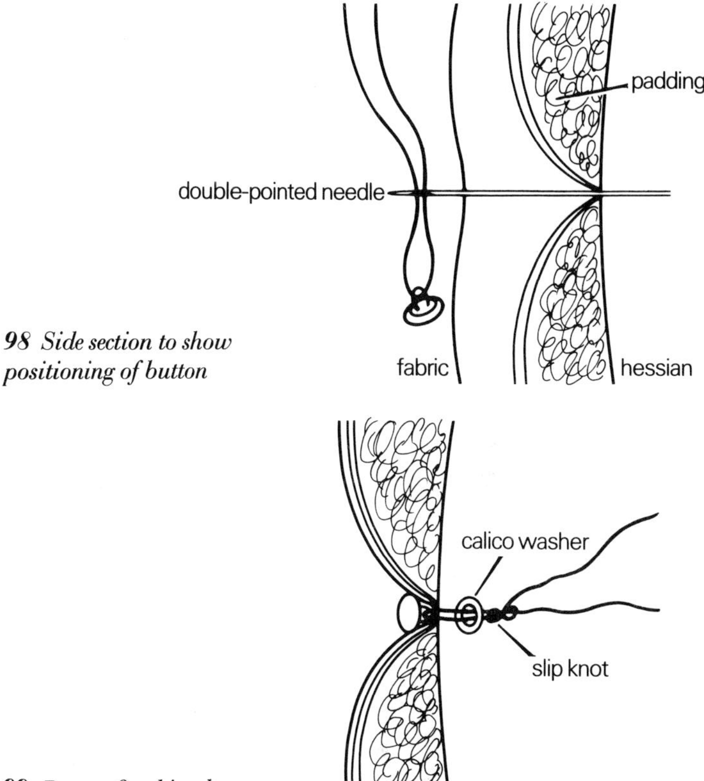

98 Side section to show positioning of button

99 Button fixed in place

is facing downwards. (This stops dust settling and also follows the way of the pile if this type of fabric is used.)

Using the spade end of the regulator, tuck the excess fabric under between each button keeping the fabric fairly taut between two buttons. The buttons will, of course, tighten down when the knots are tightened at the back of the hessian. Keep the padding even underneath each pad that is formed between the buttons and add more hair if necessary underneath the wadding. Continue to place all the buttons, and when they are even and the folds are all lying flat, tighten up the knots at the back. Check once more that they are even and fasten off by locking each slip knot with a single knot.

Fold the excess fabric into pleats, starting from the centre back and working towards the seat. Try to get each side balanced by manipulating the folds. When they are correct, skewer them in place on the underside of the top rail and sew all round. Overlap the inside back over the inside arm, snip to accommodate the curve and turn back under to make a fold. Place a button in position right on the fold line. The cover is now ready to be sewn all round (fig. 100).

Having sewn all round the outer part of the chair, break off a length of linter felt sufficient to cover the outside back and arm area, trim to shape with the fingers

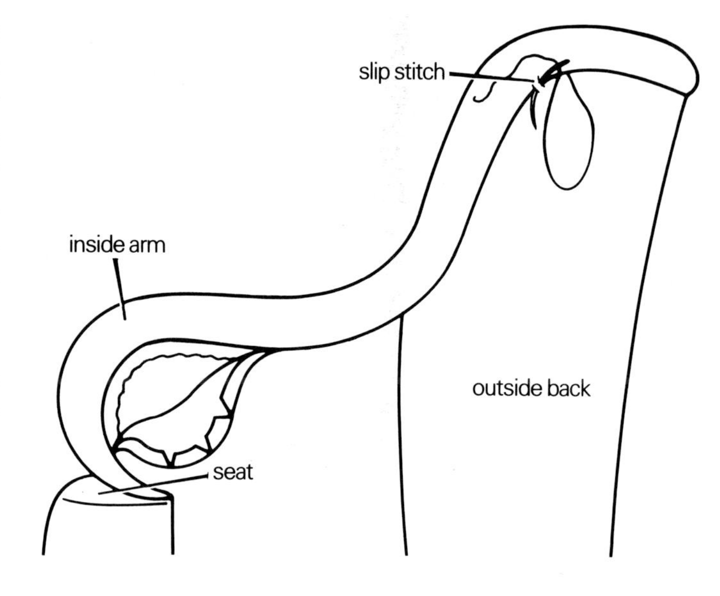

101 Fitting outside cover

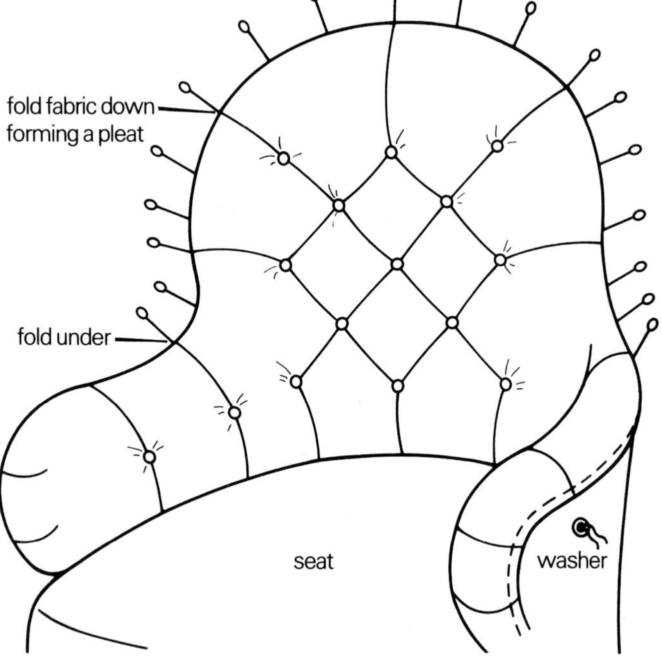

100 Arranging folds in fabric

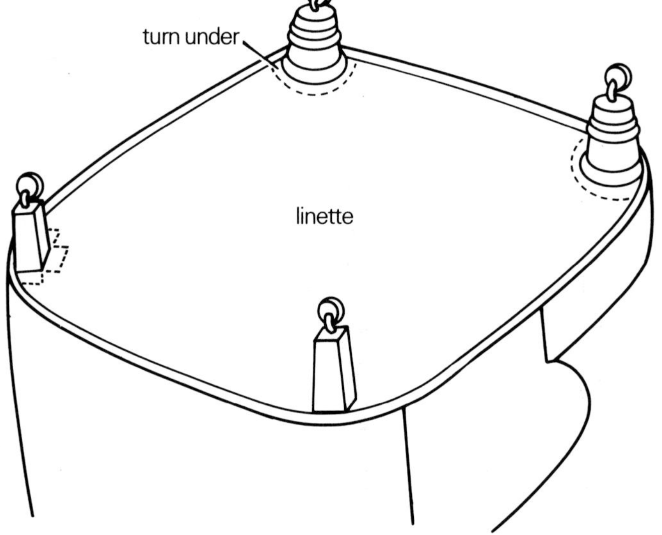

102 Fitting linette around legs

and place it on the outside back. Make sure it covers the stitch line. Take the outside arm fabric and place in position, trim back to shape leaving approximately 2 cm (¾ in) turnings. Turn this allowance under and skewer the cover in place, just under the edge of the rail. Pull the cover down and attach it under the wooden base rail, tacking at intervals of 4 cm (1½ in). Stitch the outside arm in place, using slipping thread and a slip stitch. Repeat the process to fit on the outside back. At the point at which the back meets the outside arm, trim away excess fabric and turn under; slip stitch in place (fig. 101).

Turn the chair upside down, to finish the underneath. Tack home all temporary tacks on the underneath of the frame. Cut a length of black linette to fit the base of the chair, turn the edge under and tack it to the bottom of the frame, thus covering all the raw edges. Cut round the legs to obtain a tidy fit, turn under the raw edge and tack home (fig. 102). If extra width is needed across the inside back (of a settee, for example) the fabric can be van dyked (page 81). However, if the piece has a curved back, it is not necessary to make the join by machine sewing. Instead, overlap on the folds leaving the raw edges tucked out of sight.

18 TRIMMINGS AND FINISHES

Chairs do not necessarily need trimming, but most chairs upholstered in the traditional manner come from an era when trimming was popular. Piping and ruche is applied during the re-covering process, but the trimmings and finishes which follow are all applied when re-covering is complete.

GIMP

Gimp is a type of braid that is used to conceal tacks at the edge of a show wood chair. It is usually .75 cm to 1.50 cm (⅜ to ⅝ in) wide, and is available in a number of designs and colours. To fix gimp, either use gimp pins which match the gimp in colour, or glue it using a good quality adhesive. If an adhesive is used, make sure it is designed for fabric before purchasing it. Scroll gimp is usually fixed with gimp pins as it has an uneven edge.

FRINGE

Fringe is usually applied at the base of a chair or as extra decoration along arms. It is best sewn on as this makes it stronger, although it is sometimes glued on in the same manner as the gimp. Most fringes used for trimming bases have a heading above the fringe, and this is the part that is sewn. The fringe should be positioned so that it hangs just clear of the carpet.

BRAIDING

Braiding is used to outline shape on inside backs, headboards, etc. Braid is usually wider and flatter than gimp and comes in a variety of designs. Mark the section to be braided with chalk and pin the braid in place. In an area which takes a good deal of wear, it is best machined in place on the fabric before re-covering. If, however, the area will receive light treatment, the braid can be hand-stitched in place after the article has been covered.

CORDING

Cording is generally used to cover a seam or to outline pleats, and can often be found on the chair edges and around scrolls. Cord usually consists of three lengths of silk-covered cord, twisted to form a rope. The ends will unravel easily so before cutting always bind the ends.

CLOSE NAILING

Close nailing is an effective type of finish, particularly on hide chairs. Antique nails are generally used and they can be bought in different finishes and diameters. The chair is covered and trimmed right to the rebate or the finished edge, and then the nails are hammered in place in an absolutely accurate line. When hammering in the nails it is advisable to wrap a piece of soft leather or a piece of fabric round the hammer head, as this stops the nails from being bruised.

A selection of gimps and braids

CURTAINS AND BLINDS

INTRODUCTION

Many people remark that they do not know where to begin when it comes to making curtains. They are presented with so many choices. Which fabric and what colour? Which track or pole and where to position it? What style of curtains and heading, and how much fabric will be needed?

The answers to these questions depend partly on your budget, and partly on your requirements as curtains have many purposes: insulation, shade from sunlight, privacy, aesthetic appeal, and on occasions to obscure an unwelcome view.

Windows are essential to let in light and air, but unfortunately they also let out vital heat. Lined and interlined curtains help to overcome the problem of heat loss, and exlude draughts. Interlined curtains, as the name suggests, have a layer of thick, soft, fluffy fabric between the outer curtain and the lining. The thicker and more dense the curtains, the less draughts will be able to penetrate, and any air that is trapped between the layers will act as insulation. Where circumstances permit, it is possible to use several window treatments at one window; a blind in the reveal, and a pair of curtains on the wall outside the reveal. There are many thermal linings available and although they are more expensive they will eventually pay for themselves by savings on heating. Another way of cutting down on draughts is to take the curtains beyond the sides of the window, then take the outer edges of the curtain back to the wall when the track projects into the room. Floor-length curtains certainly give a warm feel to a room, but it is not advisable to fit them over radiators, thereby cutting out heat and possibly damaging the fabric as well.

Sunlight is always welcome, but it can make a south-facing room very warm in summer and it can fade fabric and shorten the life of curtains. Light-coloured linings will reflect a certain amount of sunlight and give some protection to curtain fabric, but they can cut out too much light if the curtains are drawn during daylight. Louvre drapes (vertical slatted fabric blinds) or Venetian blinds, which are making a come-back, are a better solution. They are marvellous at deflecting the sunlight while still allowing a certain amount of light into a room, and at the same time they protect inner curtains.

The need for privacy will depend upon the situation of your home. If it is in a secluded position you may feel there is no need for further privacy. Side-dress curtains that are not operational could be used for appearance with perhaps a sheer, which would soften the window, particularly at night. However, in built-up areas where houses are more likely to be overlooked you may wish to cover your windows during daytime without losing too much light. One of the following suggestions may solve the problem: a roller blind of transparent fabric; a café curtain which covers the lower half of the window permanently, leaving the top half uncovered; a Venetian blind; louvre drapes, or a sheer. Alternatively, use curtains with a heading fixed in a closed position across the window opening, and draw the curtains away from the middle of the window, tying them back to let in just enough light to suit your purpose.

Although many people consider window treatments as functional, there are others who regard them as an important decorative feature and derive great pleasure from their appearance. They not only soften the hard outline of the windows, but also contribute to the ambience of a room by way of their colour, texture and style.

Part I provides the background information, on interior design and basic curtain-making techniques, to help you decide on your requirements. Parts II and III give step-by-step instructions on how to make different types of curtains and blinds, from simple unlined curtains to the more complex swags and tails.

Currently we are enjoying an exciting revival of some of the more elaborate and 'romantic' window treatments of the past, such as festoon blinds, pelmets, valances and swags and tails. We also have a tremendous variety of fabrics to suit every conceivable décor, purpose, design and price range. The combination of these styles with beautiful fabrics, together with the constant stream of ideas from advertising and the media, should enable us to express some of the creativity that is within us by being a little more adventurous with our window treatments.

PART I

1 *INTERIOR DECORATION*

COLOURS, TEXTURES AND PATTERNS

Curtains and blinds can form a focal point in a room, and should not only harmonize with the overall interior décor but also enhance it. The success of your scheme will ultimately depend on the harmony and proportion of your colours and furnishings in relation to the size of your room.

Style and colour are a matter of personal taste. Colours, textures and patterns affect everyone differently so there are no hard and fast rules, but there are some guidelines that will help you with your choice.

Colour can affect mood and create atmosphere. Blues and greens, for example, are considered to be cool and restful; yellow is thought of as sunny and gay; while red, orange and tans are associated with warmth, as are peach and apricot.

At the outset, think about the type of feeling you want to create in the room—whether formal or informal, restful, lively, elegant or cottagey. The room itself may suggest a character, particularly if it is in an old period house. The main colour in your scheme should reflect this mood. Restrict this colour to large areas such as walls, carpet or curtaining and build up from here, introducing one or two further colours or tones of one shade, and adding interest with patterns and texture.

Texture affects colour. A colour will seem brighter on a smooth, hard surface and more muted and darker on a rough, softer surface. Texture provides contrast in a room, and adds further interest and another dimension.

Patterns can be fun and some people are very adept at mixing them successfully. If you are uncertain about a particular balance, keep to plain colours and introduce just one pattern into the room. Alternatively, use co-ordinated patterns which have been designed to blend together. Bear in mind that large patterns are eye-catching and can be very dominant. And if too many patterns are used together, they will detract attention from each other, thus losing impact. A beautiful design is worth making into a feature, so take care that the overall effect is not too fussy and muddled. When mixing prints, make sure that they have colours in common, or tone well together. The size of a pattern is important, too, particularly in relation to where it is to be used. A large-patterned fabric may be very successful for a full-length pair of curtains but totally overpowering on a short pair at a small window.

Finally, before deciding on a style for your window, stand back and take another look at its size in relation to the rest of the room. Decide whether the room would benefit by altering the proportions of the window, which can easily be achieved by clever positioning of the curtain track. A window can be made to appear larger by fixing the track above the window reveal, at ceiling height if necessary, and extending it beyond the sides of the window. This will give the curtains a larger expanse and create a striking splash of colour. In a small room, however, this could make the room appear even smaller. It is a question of whether the size of the room can take the increased proportions.

CHOOSING A STYLE FOR YOUR WINDOW

Having decided upon the type of atmosphere you want to create with colour, texture and patterns, and having considered proportions, you are now ready to choose a style for your window. Remember that your window is quite likely to be unique.

First consider the alternatives open to you. Conventional curtains are just one option. These can be short or long and with one of several headings. Floor-length curtains, generally, will add sophistication and, with a crisp, hand pinch pleated heading, will suit a formal background. Pencil pleats or a frilled, gathered heading on short-length curtains blend well with an informal, more relaxed atmosphere. Decorative trimmings can be added to emphasize a particular feeling. Braids following the outline of curtains give a formal, traditional appearance. Contrasting binding on the leading edges of curtains (those that come to the centre) will give a sharp definition and a smart finish.

Frills suggest informality and would complement curtains with a channelled, gathered or pencil pleat heading and look most appropriate in a pretty, feminine bedroom or a cottagey kitchen/breakfast room. A frill with the edges bound in a contrasting or toning colour adds a further individual touch, making the curtains a little more special. Café curtains, which traditionally only cover the lower half of the window, offer a very simple solution to privacy and are ideal in kitchens which face onto a busy road. They can be teamed up with an additional pair of short curtains hanging above them which would be drawn at night, thus giving a tiered effect. They can be made even more attractive by the addition of frills or a scalloped heading.

Your choice of curtain track or pole should also complement your style, from an elegant brass pole for a traditional setting to a more modern, unobtrusive track. Pelmets and valances can further emphasize a particular style, as well as hiding any unsightly tracks. The defined outline of a hard pelmet suits formal surroundings whereas a frilled valance will soften the overall appearance of windows, particularly when teamed with curtains that have frilled leading edges. A hard pelmet can be softened, if necessary, by adding a flowing shape such as a scallop to its lower edge.

For a touch of real extravagance, a swag and tail would give a rich and sumptuous finish to curtains in an elegant, formal setting.

Curtains that are draped back and held in position with tie bands can give a completely different appearance to those that hang down straight. They can be held back with stiffened, shaped bands, strips of fabric or ribbons, or with thick, coloured cords with tassels. Another alternative is to drape fabric back over specially designed hold-back hooks in brass or chrome. The higher up the curtains are tied back, the more light you will admit, but by fixing the tie band lower down you obtain a fuller drape in the fabric.

In some cases a blind may be more appropriate, used either on its own or combined with curtains. Roller blinds offer a good deal of scope through colour and fabric combinations, from floral patterns to bold geometric prints. An individual finishing touch can come from your choice of shaped hemline, which could be angular, castellated or scalloped. These blinds are particularly practical in kitchens and bathrooms, being easy to clean.

Venetian blinds are often thought of as being suitable for kitchens but the atmosphere here is inevitably hot and sticky and the slats quickly become grimy. They are then very tedious to clean. Venetian blinds are better suited to a study or workroom where a simple, practical treatment is needed, and where they can be easily dusted over. Their most important asset is the way in which they can deflect light.

Where a tailored, modern and unfussy line is required Roman blinds would be ideal. When these are pulled up they form into defined horizontal pleats which lie on top of each other to look like a soft, layered pelmet.

In complete contrast, ruched or festoon blinds are both pretty and feminine, and can be lavish and opulent, depending on the fabric used and their surroundings. The fabric of ruched blinds is permanently gathered up in rows along its length, forming a ruffled scalloped appearance over the whole surface of the blind. When the blind is drawn up the scallops become even fuller. A festoon blind, on the other hand, hangs like a curtain when it is down but it has vertical rows of rings on the back through which cord is threaded. As it is drawn up, swags appear between the rows of rings, forming a scalloped hemline. These blinds give a beautiful soft line to a window and the scalloped hemline can be further enhanced with a frill.

2 *WINDOW SHAPES*

It is not possible to describe a suitable treatment for every type of window and there is no such thing as a standard window, since two identical windows located in a different position on a wall may need quite a different treatment. I will, therefore, concentrate on a few problem shapes and situations.

The first point to consider with any window is light. By dressing a narrow window with curtains inside the reveal you will cut out light during the day as there is no additional space in which they can be stacked back. This also applies to festoon, ruched and Roman blinds when fitted inside the window reveal. It is advisable in these circumstances, and in other such situations where light is particularly important, to fit your curtains outside the reveal and extend the track beyond the sides to allow for this stack back, and in the case of blinds to fit the batten above the reveal. The wider the curtains, or longer the blind, the more space needed to accommodate them. In the case of a small pair of curtains, a minimum of 15 cm (6 in) each side should be allowed, increasing progressively with the size of the curtains.

The strategic placing of the track or pole is the solution to many of the problems surrounding window-dressing.

Tall narrow windows can be made into a feature by keeping the treatment simple and fitting a roller or Roman blind within the window embrasure in order to preserve its outline. This type of window would not be suitable for a festoon or ruched blind, however, unless there was enough width for a minimum of two scallops. Alternatively, it would have to be fitted outside the window reveal.

To change the window's shape, you can create width by extending the curtain fixture beyond the sides of the window and placing it as close as possible to the architrave at the top of the window. Fabrics with horizontal patterns will also give the impression of width, and curtains that are draped back will help to break the vertical line that would otherwise be formed by curtains which hang straight down at the sides. A pelmet or valance would also help to reduce height provided it is fixed as close as possible to the top of the architrave, thereby covering the top part of the glass.

Multiple windows are marvellous for creating a bright and airy room but the effect could become over-fussy if the windows are treated individually, particularly if they are of different sizes. The windows can be unified by placing just one track above all the windows on one wall, giving the illusion of one large window when the curtains are closed. During daylight hours the curtains could be arranged either drawn back to either side of the track, or covering the walls between the windows.

In a room where there are windows on different walls, aim to fix the curtain fitments at the same height to create a unified appearance.

A single corner window presents the problem of where to allow the curtain to hang during daylight. The obvious answer is to draw it back to the side away from the corner, but this can create an unbalanced appearance. An attractive arrangement where light permits is to have one curtain with a heading fixed in a closed position and tie the curtain fairly tightly in the centre of the window with bows. Another alternative would be to fit a blind within the window reveal.

Where there is a window on either side of a corner, again the aim is to unify them. The choice would be whether to draw one pair of curtains to stack back on the walls beside the windows, thus exposing the corner, or to have two separate pairs of curtains that draw from the centre of each window and thereby cover the corner area with fabric. This may cut out a certain amount of light, but as there are two windows in one corner, the room has light coming in from two directions and is probably lighter than average anyway.

A shallow and wide window is not the best proportioned, and is often placed high on a wall. Privacy may not be a consideration, in which case the simplest treatment may be a sheer to soften the window outline; or, for a more cosy feeling at night, combine it with a roller blind. If you want to improve the window's proportions, use a café curtain and place the curtain rod just above the sill level, allowing the curtain fabric (which should be opaque) to cover the wall below to a suitable level. (The window must be above eye-level so that the sill is not visible.) The curtain will create the illusion of a deeper window. You could add a smaller top tier of curtains which could be drawn at night should you want complete privacy.

Windows that pivot from a central point are frequently fitted in modern flats for ease of cleaning. The fitments will need to be placed well above and beyond the sides of the window to give maximum freedom of movement. Sheers would present a problem at this type of window unless they are fixed onto the top and bottom of the pivoting window-frame on rods or wire.

Dormer windows, fitted into alcoves in the roof, are difficult to treat because there is little or no space into which the curtains can be drawn back. Most blinds other than a roller blind will screen out too much light. One straightforward solution for sash windows is to allow minimum fullness in the curtains themselves and tie them back tightly during daytime. A small, shallow valance approximately 15 cm (6 in) deep, with more fullness than the curtains, would enhance the window's appearance and would make very little difference to the light in the room.

Another alternative would be to have cross-over sheers, which present a soft, pretty appearance. On inward-opening casement windows attach sheers, fitted at the top and bottom on wire, and draw in the centre of each curtain with ribbon tied into bows.

Bay windows present the same problem as corner windows: where do the curtains hang during daylight hours? One pair of curtains drawn back to the two outer corners of the bay will look attractive, but they will cut down the light from the side windows. One solution for a large bay is to make one large pair of curtains to fit across the front window and allow it to be free standing, that is, do not fix its outer edges to the corners. Make another pair of curtains, one for each side window. During the day, position the large pair at the middle of the main window and draw in the centre of each curtain with tie bands to form two attractive drapes. Tie the side curtains back to the walls adjacent to the side windows.

Bay windows also lend themselves to blinds of all types. Ruched or festoons could add style to the setting. Roman blinds would suit a squarish bay and could be teamed with a pair of full-length draw curtains fitted across the flat wall in front of the bay, or with dress curtains standing at the sides of the bay.

Bow windows are a natural asset to any room and should be highlighted. They are not difficult to deal with, thanks to the many tracks on the market which can be bent to fit the shape. Floor-length curtains which hug the curve present a beautiful flow of fabric, and can be drawn back to the sides of the window to expose the sweeping curve during the daytime. A valance following the outline of the windows can offer another pleasing effect. If there is a window seat, curtains should hang to sill level. Or a pair of full-length curtains could be hung from a pole across the wall in front of the bow, framing the windows by day and closing off the alcove at night.

Arched windows are one of the most elegant forms of window, and any treatment which hides the beauty of the classical shape seems like sacrilege. They do pose difficulties in dressing, however, and in some instances there is no alternative but to hang draw curtains from a track or rod placed above the arch.

Shaped curtains fitted to arched windows cannot be operational. The heading must be fixed to the arch, and the curtains are draped back and held open with tie bands. This treatment gives a lovely shape both day and night. It is also possible to use festoon or ruched blinds at this type of window, but they would only draw up satisfactorily as far as the level at the bottom of the arch. For a very simple treatment, dress only the rectangular section below the arch, leaving the top uncovered.

Doors that swing inwards present the problem of curtain fabric interfering with the operation of the doors. One of the most practical treatments with a glass-panelled door, but not necessarily the most attractive, is to anchor sheer fabric to the top and bottom of the glass panel. A roller-blind covering the glass area is an alternative. However, both these methods would be greatly improved by adding full-length curtains at the sides where space allows. These could be hung from a decorative pole, perhaps set well above and extending beyond the sides of the door, to enable the curtains to be drawn well back.

3 FABRICS

SELECTING FABRICS

The choice of a suitable fabric can be daunting because there is such a wide variety of fabrics on the market today. The different combinations of colour, beautiful designs, textures, fibres and weaves all add up to a vast range of fabrics from which to choose and at enormously varying prices. Ultimately, however, the fabric you select

For this unusual pelmet the design of the fabric has been cleverly used in creating the geometric pattern. The curtains hang very straight to emphasize the striped pattern of the material and give the window a square outline.

for your window treatment should not only complement your chosen style with its visual appearance but it must also suit its purpose. It would be inappropriate to pick a cotton repp, for example, which is a thick, firm fabric for a feminine style with frills. This style requires a soft flowing material such as a lightweight cotton seersucker. Conversely a loosely woven fabric would not be successful for a Roman blind, which requires a firm, stable fabric.

Apart from the visual appearance of curtain fabric, and suitability for its purpose, the other important characteristic to consider is its drapability. Soft, weighty fabrics tend to fall easily into gentle folds; an obvious example is cotton velvet which is both soft, supple and heavy. Every fabric handles differently, and the only way to find out how it is likely to drape when made up into curtains is to hold up a large sample and study how it hangs.

It is always advisable to buy furnishing fabrics rather than dress materials as they come in wider widths and are usually of a more suitable weight. Widths vary from 120 cm (48 in), 130 cm (51 in), 137 cm (54 in), 140 cm (55 in) and 150 cm (59 in). Make a note of the width of your chosen fabric as you will need this information when you come to estimate the amount of fabric needed.

TYPES OF FIBRE

In order to recognize the different characteristics of individual fabrics it is helpful to know a little about the raw materials used (i.e., fibre content) and the weave and various finishes which may be applied to it, as it is the combination of these factors that affect its appearance, how it handles and its performance. Time spent examining and handling fabric for yourself is time well spent as there is no substitute for experience.

Yarns are made from either natural or man-made fibres, and the quality of fabric will ultimately depend upon the type of raw materials used and how the yarn was manufactured into cloth.

Natural fibres are derived from vegetable or animal sources and provide cotton, linen, silk and wool.

Cotton is strong, hard-wearing, easy to handle and relatively inexpensive. It is prone to shrinking and should be pre-shrunk during the manufacture to make it a good buy. It creases easily in its natural form but often has a crease-resistant finish applied to it.

Linen is one of the oldest fibres known and is even stronger than cotton, but it creases badly unless treated with the appropriate finish. It has the advantage of staying clean longer than most other fabrics. Its main use in furnishing fabrics is as linen union, a hard-wearing fabric. Although curtains are sometimes made up in this fabric it is not always satisfactory as it can be rather stiff.

Wool is warm and soft. It has good insulating qualities, and is used in furnishing fabrics mixed with other fibres.

Silk, although it is considered a delicate fabric, is in fact very strong, but it is adversely affected by sunlight. Silk curtains should therefore be lined to give some protection. Some silk fabrics will drape beautifully while others have a light, crisp appearance.

Man-made fibres were first developed to imitate natural ones, and ultimately to keep pace with the growing demand for fabrics, as it is not possible to produce enough from natural sources alone. Many new qualities were introduced into these man-made fibres that could not be obtained from their natural counterparts. Many of the best fabrics are made by using a combination of man-made and natural fibres.

Man-made fibres can be split into two groups, those that are derived from natural sources but have been transformed by chemical treatment, and those that are made totally from chemical sources and are therefore synthetic.

The first group consists of rayon and acetate.

Rayon is frequently blended with other fibres and used extensively in furnishing fabrics. It is soft, and handles and drapes well.

Acetate fibres are blended with other fibres to produce silk-like fabrics that are soft, drape well, and have a rich, lustrous appearance. Many dupions, brocades and moirés have a high acetate content, and all are suitable for curtains. Too much heat during ironing will damage fibres and they should never be damped down during ironing otherwise the fabric will be permanently spoilt with a watermark.

Among the synthetic fibres used in furnishing fabrics are nylon, polyester and acrylic.

Nylon made a great impact on the textile industry when it was first discovered. Fabrics produced from this fibre are fine, strong and hard-wearing can be washed frequently without the shape and size altering, and can be drip dried. They requires very little ironing and an iron that is too hot will melt the fabric. Nylon is crease-resistant and is often mixed with other fibres to give them this quality plus extra strength. One disadvantage, however, is that it acquires static electricity, causing it to pick up dirt easily. Nylon is damaged by sunlight so is not the best fabric to use for curtains.

Polyester has become one of the most successful of the man-made fibres. It is hard-wearing, crease-resistant, easy to wash and quick drying. It is frequently mixed with other fibres, particularly cotton, to impart improved life and easy-care qualities. It is suitable for curtaining as it is not harmed by sunlight.

Acrylic fibres are made into fabric which is soft and warm, and consequently has similar characteristics to wool. It is most commonly woven into textured or pile fabrics and it has an advantage over wool in that when washed correctly (without too much heat) it will retain its shape, drip dry and need little ironing. It drapes beautifully and is consequently most suitable for curtains, with the added advantage that it is not affected by sunlight. It can be blended with other fibres too. Loosely-woven textured varieties are often made up into a heavier type of unlined sheer curtain.

Modyacrylic fibres have many of the same qualities as acrylic. In addition, they are flame-resistant, making them most suitable for furnishing fabrics.

TYPES OF FABRIC

It is impossible to list all the fabrics that would be suitable for window treatments, as the range is constantly growing. Fabrics are not always given a particular name but are often referred to just by the fibre content, e.g., cotton or polyester print. The table describes the standard types of fabric.

Bolton twill A firm, hard-wearing fabric. Should be lined to reduce light penetration.

Brocade A heavy fabric with patterns woven in a jacquard weave. Produced in a variety of yarns. Drapes well.

Buckram A loosely-woven plain weave, impregnated with glue to stiffen. Used for pelmets and in a finer quality for curtain headings. It is not washable.

Bump A fluffy, blanket type fabric, made of plain weave and used as a curtain interlining and to soften pelmets.

Casement A closely-woven plain weave fabric. Drapes well. Usually produced in plain colours.

Chintz A finely-woven stiffish cloth with a glazed finish. Usually printed with highly coloured patterns. If the glaze is produced chemically it will be permanent, otherwise it is liable to wash out.

Cretonne A finely-woven plain fabric. Often printed with patterns with a shadowy outline.

Damask Similar to brocade but traditionally of one colour. Contrasting tones are achieved by a woven matt pattern on a satin-weave background.

In this large, awkward bay window the curtains have been attractively arranged to break up the window but still let in plenty of light.

Domette A fine, plain-weave type of flannelette, with a soft fluffy surface. Used as interlining. It is made of cotton alone or mixed with wool.

Dupion A plain weave, often with a slub surface and with a satin backing. Made mainly of man-made fibres such as viscose, acetate or blends.

Folkweave A loosely-woven cotton fabric, using coarse yarn, often with stripes. It has a rustic appearance.

Gingham A lightweight fabric woven with coloured yarns in stripes or checks.

Moiré A finish applied to the fabric to give it a watermarked appearance. It is used on cotton, silk and man-made fabrics.

Plush A fabric with a long pile, often made of wool or synthetic yarns in the pile and with a cotton ground.

Repp A firm fabric with a heavy weft thread forming a ribbed surface, usually made of cotton, or cotton and wool mixture.

Sateen A strong lightweight satin weave used for linings, and as curtaining with an added print. Mainly made of cotton with a shiny surface on one side where the weft threads lie on the surface.

Taffeta A crisp, plain-weave fabric with a sheen and a slight rib running across it. Fairly stiff.

Tapestry Only fine qualities are suitable for curtains. A woven fabric with an embroidered appearance made of cotton or wool, or mixtures.

Velvet A closely-woven fabric with a short-cut pile on one side. Made in numerous yarns, silk being the most luxurious and expensive. Cotton velvet makes excellent curtains.

LININGS

Lining provides essential protection for the main curtain fabric against exposure to sunlight, dust and dirt.

Cotton sateen is the most widely used lining fabric as it is strong and drapes well, and its shiny outer surface helps to resist dust. It is manufactured in various qualities and widths. It can be bought undyed, bleached or dyed in a variety of colours. Black or dark-coloured linings help to reduce the light penetration into a room but should only be used with an appropriately coloured outer fabric in order not to spoil the appearance of the curtains.

Plain-weave polyester and cotton fabrics are also used as linings. Although the latter may be slightly cheaper than sateen, it may not have the same draping quality.

Thermal linings with a soft, fluffy coating on the inside provide excellent insulation although some do have a rather unattractive rubber-like appearance on the outside. One type of insulating lining has a coating of aluminium on the reverse side which not only provides protection from heat loss in winter but also prevents excessive heat build-up in a room during summer by deflecting the sun's rays. It is also more dense than a normal lining and is thus able to cut out more light.

AFTERCARE

Fabrics are expensive, but they will last for years and give great pleasure provided they are looked after in the proper manner. If large curtains are vacuumed in situ with a hand attachment, this will keep the fabric fresh and prevent a build-up of dust, reducing the need for frequent cleaning. Ruched and festoon blinds will benefit from this attention, as they tend to be dust traps.

Check the care label on the bale of fabric when you are buying it. It is important that the instructions are followed carefully in view of the many different types of fibres and finishes used in modern fabrics. Ask for advice if no cleaning instructions are available.

Curtains that have linings sewn in will require dry cleaning in order to reduce the risk of lining and curtain fabric shrinking at different rates.

Any curtains with stiffened buckram headings should be dry cleaned.

4 CURTAIN HARDWARE

Curtain hardware has come a long way since the days of the narrow brass rod and rings. There is now a large range of fixtures and fittings from which to choose. It is of paramount importance that you select a type that will take the weight of your curtains; after all, the main purpose of tracks and poles is to act as a means of support. You will also want to choose a type that will suit your special needs, for example, you may require it to bend round a bay, and you will need to consider whether a pre-corded version is necessary. (Corded fitments enable curtains to be drawn without handling or soiling the fabric.) In addition you will need to decide whether you want a type that will act as a further embellishment of your scheme or one that blends insignificantly into the background in order not to detract attention from the curtains themselves. Finally, remember when buying your curtain fixture to allow extra length to enable your curtains to be drawn back beyond the sides of the window, where possible.

TRACKS AND POLES

Tracks are made from either plastic, aluminium, steel or brass, and in general those made of metal are stronger. They can be coated with a white, gold, silver or brass finish, either plain or decorative. Some can be fitted with finials, most can be fitted into the wall or ceiling and are usually bought complete with all the necessary fixtures and fittings. A selection is shown in fig. 1.

There are several plastic tracks available, varying in strength, which are suitable for straight runs and which can also be bent successfully round bays. Some have gliders which slot into grooves on the back of the track. Others have all-in-one hook gliders which clip onto the face of the track and eliminate the use of separate curtain hooks. These hook gliders also have a small hole in their

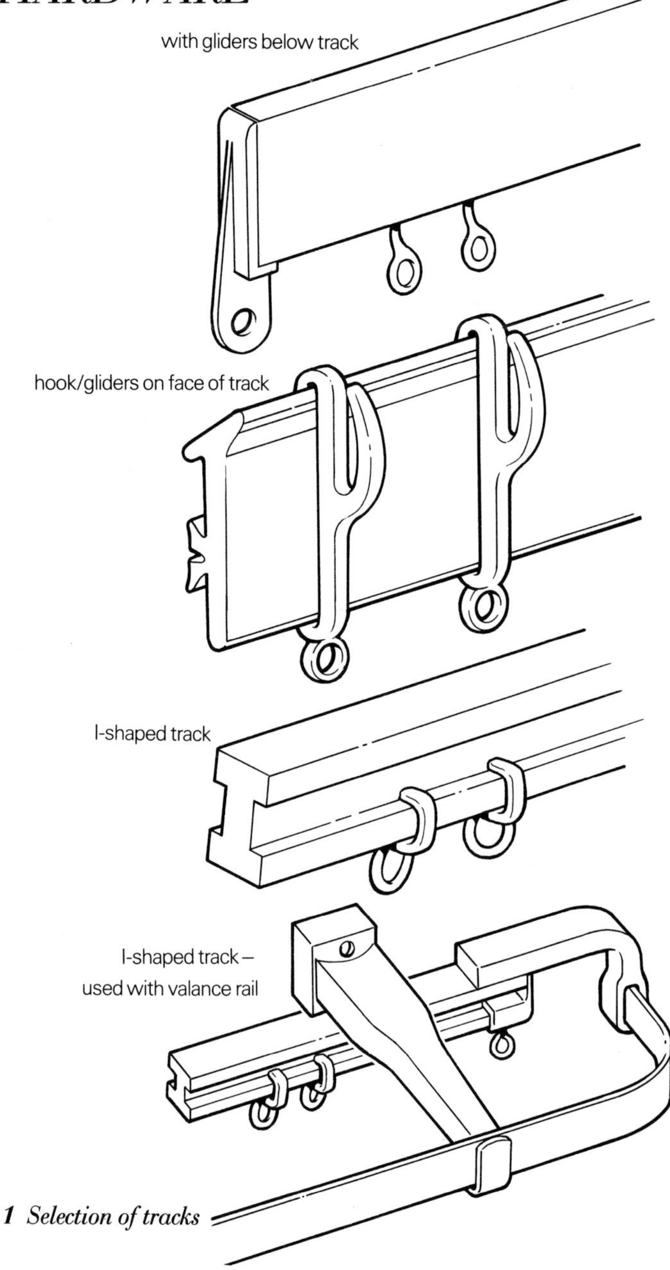

1 Selection of tracks

base which is positioned below the track from which a separate lining can be hung. Optional cording sets with overlap arm are available which enable the curtains to overlap at the centre when closed. However, these sets are mainly for use on straight runs.

Tracks which are cut to measure are essential for the more awkward fitting situations. These strong steel tracks can be cut to length by a supplier, pre-bent to fit an awkward bay, and have the additional advantage of being ready corded.

Steel telescopic or extendible tracks are a good investment because of their adaptable length, making fitting easier, but they are suitable only for straight runs.

The conventional 'I' shaped track made of brass with wheeled runners and rings is now also available in a lightweight plastic version. The former is more suitable for use with heavyweight curtains, but the latter will operate more silently. These tracks can be fitted round bays with the optional use of a cording set, and can be fitted with a valance rail.

Although tracks are now less unsightly, you may still feel they need to be covered with a pelmet or valance. A decorative pole could be the alternative; there is a tremendous range from which to choose, but they are all only suitable for straight runs.

Wooden poles suit an informal, unsophisticated atmosphere, and the untreated type could be painted or stained to suit your décor. They are generally made of a hardwood called ramin with a natural, mahogany or walnut finish, and are available in lengths up to 300 cm (10 ft) with diameters of 25, 30 and 35 mm (1 in, 1⅛ in, 1⅜ in). They are generally supplied with deep projecting wall brackets, up to 88 mm (3½ in), which makes them ideal for placing over radiators or projecting window sills. However, with some varieties it is possible to buy short-reach brackets or recess brackets, if preferred. On wide spans it is essential to use enough support brackets to prevent the pole from bending under the weight of the curtains.

The traditional brass pole will add a touch of classical elegance to a room. These are available in all manner of finishes from bright brass to antique gold and antique brass. The choice of finials ranges from sculptured pineapples and lanterns to simple ball-ends.

Some are manufactured from steel and give the illusion of the classical style but have simulated half-rings that run smoothly on nylon gliders in the back of the pole. These tracks are also extendible and can be purchased in two diameters, 25 mm (1 in) and 35 mm (1⅜ in) and span up to 609 cm (20 ft) although some of the narrower types only span up to 381 cm (12 ft 6 in). In addition they are internally corded with the bonus of an overlap facility.

Narrow rods are intended for use with café curtains and can be purchased with rings and special clasps which simply grip the top of the curtain, eliminating the use of curtain hooks.

Slim-line tension rods, which are telescopic, are used to carry net curtains neatly without any fixing brackets, but they can only be used within a window reveal as they spring out to grip the sides.

ACCESSORIES

There are many useful accessories available which will give curtains a professional finish. They include brackets which enable two separate tracks to be used together (or a pole and a track) giving good clearance between the two sets of curtains. Extension brackets project the track out to avoid protruding window sills and radiators. Recess brackets enable a pole to be used within a window reveal and replace end finials.

Cording sets incorporating overlap arms are available to fit certain straight tracks as an optional extra. An alternative to a cording set is a draw rod, which is a simpler and cheaper method of operating curtains without handling them. It is a slim wooden rod which slips into the first ring of each curtain on the leading edge and, when not being used, hangs out of sight.

Fabric and corded tie bands need to be attached to hooks, and these are available in a range of designs. Curtains can also be elegantly draped back over specially designed curtain-holders.

Essential technical hardware used in making up curtains includes a variety of curtain hooks of varying strengths, made of plastic or metal, which can be sewn on, slotted into pockets on special tapes, or pinned into hand headings.

Weights will improve the hang of curtains. They can be bought either as small, round discs, which are sewn into the corners of curtain hems, or in strip form, to be inserted along the whole length of the hemline. This is sold by the metre in three weights—light, medium and heavyweight.

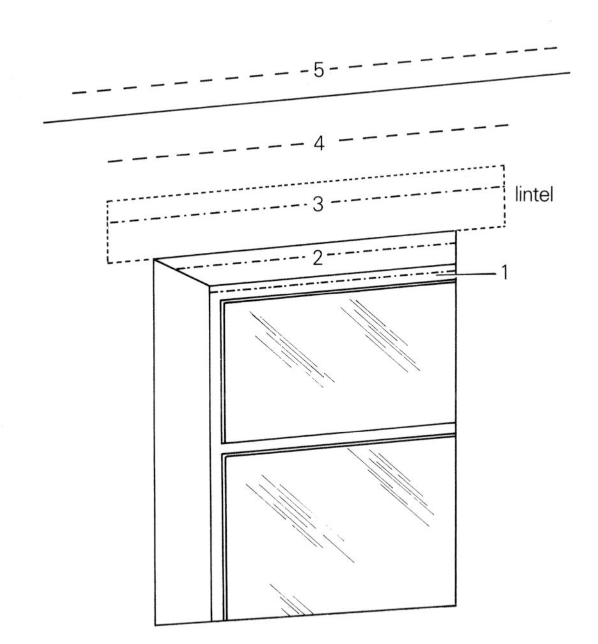

2 Fixing points

INSTALLATION

Whatever hardware you choose, it is essential that it is securely fixed, and it is worth thinking about the actual fixing point at your initial planning stage. There are several options open to you (fig. 2): 1. window frame; 2. ceiling of window reveal; 3. wall just above window; 4. higher on wall above the window; 5. ceiling.

Fixing into wood is the easiest method, therefore fitting to the window frame should not present any problem provided the depth of the frame is deep enough to take the track brackets. Make pilot holes, then insert screws.

Positions 2 and 3 could be the most difficult if there is a concrete lintel above the window, as this will involve drilling into concrete. In this instance, it may be easier to fit a batten into the actual concrete, which will require fewer holes. The track or pole could then be screwed into the batten.

Higher above the window there may be brickwork, in which case a batten may again be the easiest method to use. Its only disadvantage is that it will project the curtain fixture further into the room and when the curtains are open the batten will be visible. The resulting space from the end of the track or pole back to the wall is known as the 'return' and can look rather unattractive unless covered with fabric. Attach a screw-eye into the end of the batten near to the wall into which the end curtain hook can be slotted.

When fixing into the ceiling, you should ensure that you screw direcly into the joists. If these are not in the right position for your track, you can make fixings with special plasterboard plugs, but you should then avoid hanging heavy curtains.

In modern timber-frame houses, it is possible that you

could be fixing into the timber frame itself and/or plasterboard above the window reveal. In this case, screws fixed into the timber will be quite satisfactory, but plasterboard plugs (cavity fix) should be used in between.

Finally, tracks and poles will benefit from regular attention as dust and dirt will impair their performance. Some tracks are treated with silicone to ensure smooth running, so an occasional polish with a silicone-based spray will help to keep them in good operational order.

5 EQUIPMENT

Prior to making any curtains or blinds, make sure you are properly equipped. There is nothing more irritating than to start a job, and find halfway through that you do not have a vital piece of equipment.

Your most important piece of equipment will be a *sewing-machine*, and you should of course know exactly how it works. Ensure, too, that you always have a selection of spare needles ranging from fine to heavy (70–100). You should change your needle regularly, and not only when it is blunt or broken. Different fabrics require different thread and size of needle. Always practise on a sample of fabric first to find the right combination. One of the most common reasons for a machine not stitching correctly is using a blunt needle or an incorrect size of needle for the fabric and thread.

A large pair of *cutting scissors* are essential. They should be kept in a sharp condition, otherwise they will be no use at all. Bent-handled shears are best of all, as the blades rest flat on the cutting surface.

A *small pair of scissors*, about 15 cm (6 in) long are useful for trimming or unpicking. Embroidery scissors are excellent for this as they have pointed blades.

A *seam ripper* is useful, but should be used with caution to avoid cutting fabric.

Pinking shears are not essential but can be useful. They cut a zig-zag edge to prevent fraying. Never use these scissors to cut paper as this will blunt them.

An *iron*, preferably a steam one, will be needed. The base of the iron should be kept clean. A pressing cloth prevents fabrics from becoming shiny.

A well-padded *ironing-board* is necessary, but when ironing big curtains, a large flat surface is more suitable, softened with several layers of cloth.

A metal *tape-measure* of a good length is essential for measuring your window. A good quality tape-measure that will not stretch is necessary for general sewing use. It should have both metric and imperial markings.

A *padded weight* is useful, approximately 15 cm (6 in) square by 5 cm (2 in) deep, to hold fabric firmly in position and prevent it slipping. To make one, fill a cardboard box with sand or other heavy material. Seal the box with tape, then pad and cover it, attaching a handle across the top.

Tailor's chalk is needed for marking the fabric.

Pins Sharp dressmaker's or glass-headed pins are best. Never use rusty pins as they will mark the fabric.

Have a selection of hand-sewing *needles* to hand, in assorted sizes (1 coarsest–10 finest).

Thread Cotton thread is available in different deniers: 50 for lightweight fabric, and 40 for medium to heavyweight. Synthetic thread is very strong and should be used with synthetic or stretch fabric as it has more elasticity. It is essential to use the correct thread to obtain perfect stitching.

6 HEADING STYLES

The style of heading should enhance the fabric and complement the décor of the room. With the easy-to-use tapes that are available, decorative headings need not present any difficulties to the inexperienced needle-woman. A pencil pleat tape, which produces a deep, stiffened upright heading, will create an overall gathered effect below it. Pinch and cartridge pleats, however, form distinct folds in the curtain fabric below the heading, enabling the fabric to drape beautifully. For the more experienced needlewoman, hand-pleated deep headings can give the great satisfaction of creating beautiful curtains with a professional finish.

It is important to decide on the heading style before estimating and buying the fabric, as the heading will determine (i) how much fullness is needed in the curtains, and (ii) the necessary heading allowance, that is the amount of fabric needed to make up the heading. The heading allowance should be added to the finished length measurement.

TAPED HEADINGS

Most deep tapes have two or three rows of pockets, making them adjustable for use with all types of track or pole. The top row is used with a pole, or slotted onto combined hook/gliders to prevent the heading from standing well above the track. The lower rows are used with conventional gliders (which hang below the track) so that the heading will cover the face of the track. The deepest headings, approx. 14 cm (5½ in), are used with particularly long curtains to give a better proportion and are sold in two varieties—one for use with a track, the other with a pole.

When applying any tape, always position the free ends of the draw cords, which are used to pull up the heading, to the outside edge of the curtain (i.e., the edge furthest away from the centre). After pulling up the curtain to the desired width, tie the cords neatly but do not cut them off. The heading can then be released for cleaning at a later date.

Standard gathered heading tape

This tape is approximately 2.5 cm (1 in) wide and is available in several colours. A new type is on the market which will produce small groups of narrow pleats in addition to a standard gather, simply by pulling up an alternative set of cords. By placing the tape 2.5 cm (1 in) below the top of the curtains a good-sized frill will form when the tape is drawn up. This heading is generally used with a track. The depth of the frill can be increased in order to conceal a track by positioning the tape further away from the top of the curtain. However, deep frills tend to become floppy and fall forward unless they are slightly stiffened. This tape will achieve a satisfactory curtain fullness with a minimum of one and a half times the track length using a thick fabric, but double fullness is preferable, particularly with lightweight fabrics.

A heading allowance of 4 cm (1½ in) should be added to your finished length to make a 2.5 cm (1 in) frill.

(To apply this tape, see pages 127–8).

Pencil pleat tape

This deep tape is available in several depths, 6 cm, 7.5 cm and 14 cm (2¾ in, 3 in and 5½ in), to suit all sizes of curtains. It needs fabric fullness of two and a quarter to two and a half times the track length, depending on the thickness of the fabric. The thinner the fabric the more fullness is required. It will need a heading allowance of only 1.5 cm (½ in).

A channelled heading with frill above. The curtains drape well and are drawn back to create a pretty outline.

Pinch pleat tape

This tape produces tall, elegantly fanned pleats, with flat spaces between them, by drawing up cords. It is a quick and easy method of achieving triple pleats. It is available in three depths to suit all lengths of curtain. Generally, it requires fabric fullness of exactly twice the track length, depending on the variety. It needs the same heading allowance as pencil pleat tape—1.5 cm (½ in).

The tape should be applied so that the pleats and spaces are symmetrical on both curtains of a pair. It is not a gathered heading. The size of the pleats and spaces are predetermined and cannot be altered. In certain instances, the length of your particular track may not coincide with a balanced pleating arrangement because of the pre-determined size of the pleats, thereby leaving a larger than usual space at one side of your curtain. However, this can be overcome by stitching a small pleat by hand to improve the balance.

Apply this tape as for pencil pleat, bearing in mind the manufacturer's instructions.

Cartridge pleat tape

This tape produces full rounded pleats with well balanced spaces between them. It is 9 cm (3½ in) deep and needs fabric fullness of twice the length of the curtain fixture. The heading allowance is only 1.5 cm (½ in). These pleats are also of a predetermined size and therefore any adjustment is limited, as with pinch pleat tape. It should be treated in the same way as pinch pleat tape. The roundness of the pleat is improved by filling it with a little wadding or a tube of curtain buckram.

FRILLED CHANNELLED HEADING

This is the simplest form of heading to achieve without the use of a tape. The frill is obtained by sewing a channel through a double thickness of fabric below the top of the curtain. Through this a rod, pole or wire can be inserted. The fabric fullness is then gathered along the curtain fixture, creating a frill above it. As mentioned in Chapter 1 this type of curtain heading is fixed and cannot be opened, but the fabric can be draped back and held with tie bands. It is most suitable for lightweight curtains, nets and café curtains, and requires a fullness of twice the length of the curtain fixture, but this is adjustable. Less fullness is needed with thicker fabrics. The depth of the frill is also variable, as with a taped frilled heading. A heading allowance of 7.5 cm (3 in) is needed to fit over a 19 mm (¾ in) diameter rod with a 2.5 cm (1 in) frill above.

HAND-PLEATED HEADINGS

The superior results of these headings more than justify the extra time involved in making them. A professional finish is achieved in part by showing a minimum amount of stitching on the right side of the fabric.

All these headings should be stiffened. Pinch pleats are best stiffened with curtain buckram, but with most other types, strips of firm dressmaker's interfacing are quite satisfactory. Curtain buckram is available in several depths, 10 cm, 12.5 cm and 15 cm (4 in, 5 in and 6 in) and in two varieties—iron-on and standard.

Hand pinch pleat

A hand pinch pleat heading, producing sharp, crisp pleats, is far superior to a taped version. It can be pleated up to the exact length of your particular curtain fixture by adjusting the amount of fabric in each pleat and the spaces between them.

This heading is normally applied to lined curtains and is stiffened with curtain buckram.

The amount of fabric fullness required is variable and although a minimum of twice the length of the curtain fixture is satisfactory, two and a quarter to two and a half times fullness is preferable to achieve a well-balanced, attractive pleating arrangement. A minimum heading allowance of 2 cm (¾ in) plus the depth of the curtain buckram, should be added to the finished curtain length.

Several points should be borne in mind when planning your pleats:

Each curtain of a pair should have the same number of pleats.

A space of 10 cm (4 in) to 12 cm (4¾ in) between the pleats gives an attractive arrangement, but this is variable in order to arrive at the desired finished width of curtain. It is important to remember that the amount of fabric left unpleated (i.e., the total of all the spaces) must equal the length of your track (plus returns and overlap arm where applicable).

Where the curtains are to cover returns, locate one pleat at each end of the curtain fixture and leave a flat space at the outside edge of the curtain to cover the return.

When curtains are to butt together, plan to have a half space at each leading edge. When using an overlap arm, leave enough space to correspond to the size of the fitment. One complete space on each curtain is sufficient.

Finally, do not let the following calculations and precise measurements deter you. It is possible to juggle the pleating and spacing arrangements within reason, putting more or less fabric into the pleats and spaces to achieve your desired result.

To calculate the pleats-and-spacing arrangement, work on the basis of one curtain. When dealing with a pair, divide the track length in half and use this measurement when referring to track length.

Pleats As a guide start by allowing four pleats to one fabric width of 120 cm (48 in), adjusting up as necessary, particularly with wider fabric, to arrive at an attractive balance of pleats and spacing.

Subtract the track length (including return and overlap arm where applicable) from the total width of the finished flat curtain. The remainder is the amount of fabric which will be fitted into the pleats. To ascertain the amount of fabric in each pleat, divide this remaining fabric by the number of proposed pleats, using the guide above.

Spaces To establish the size of the spaces in between the pleats:

(i) *With a half space at each side of the curtain* Divide the track length by the proposed number of pleats (fig. 3a);

or (ii) *When covering an overlap and return* Divide the track length, excluding the amount needed to cover the overlap and return, by one less than the proposed number of pleats (fig. 3b).

For instructions on making up this heading refer to PART II Interlined Curtains.

Cartridge and goblet pleat headings

These headings need a minimum fullness of twice the track length and calculations should be treated in the same way as for pinch pleat heading, but allowing for more pleats ('tubes') of a smaller size and closer spacing. A good arrangement is to allow about 10 cm (4 in) each for a 'tube' and space in between, but vary this in order to arrive at your track length. A cartridge pleat heading is **made up in the same way as pinch pleats (page 110), but** the bases of the small tubes (pleats) are not pinched up but left rounded by filling with a soft stuffing such as wadding. A goblet heading (fig. 4) is made in the same way, but use a firm dressmaker's interfacing rather than curtain buckram, as the base of each tube is randomly pinched in (as opposed to pleated in) and held in position with a few hand stitches. The heading allowance is the same as for pinch pleats

Box pleat headings

This heading is quite extravagant on fabric and needs

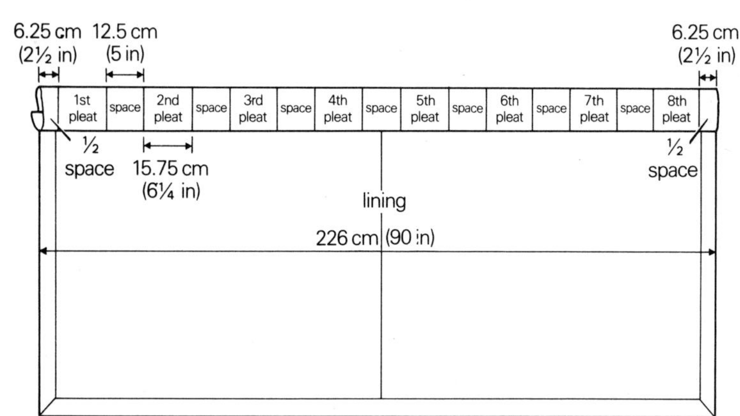

3 Pinch pleat arrangements: **a** above *with a half space at each side;* **b** right *allowing for an overlap and return*

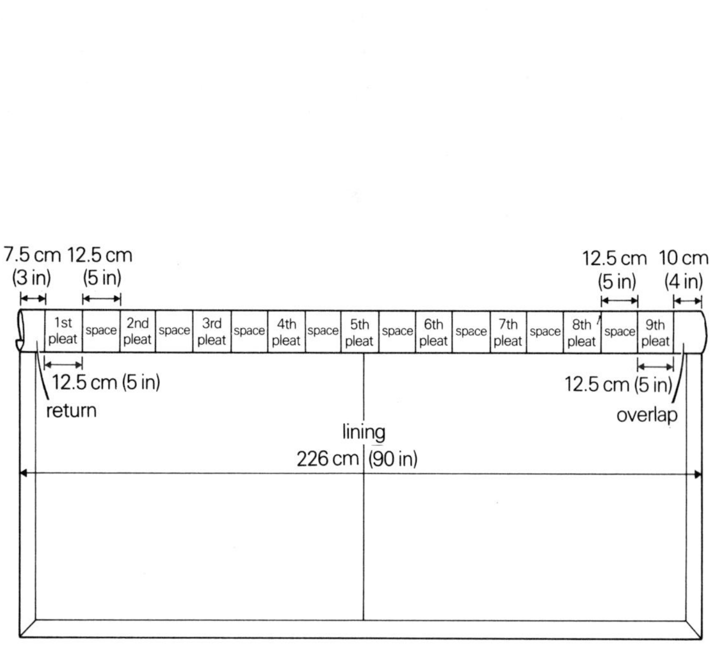

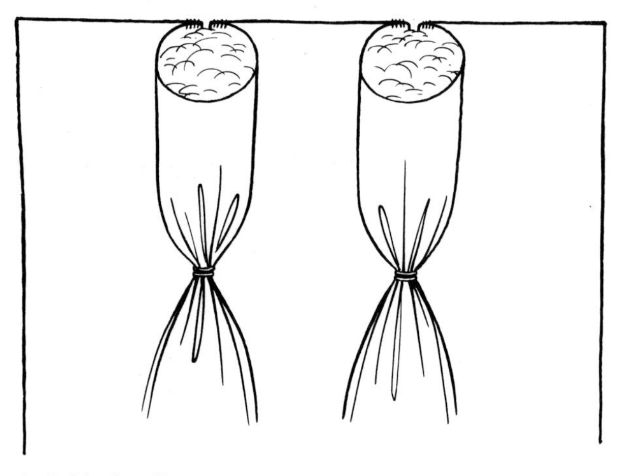

4 Goblet heading

fullness of three times the track length for true box pleats which butt up against each other. The pleats can be spaced out if preferred, needing approximately two and a half times fullness. The heading should be planned in a similar way as for pinch pleats. When planning the spacing, once again bear in mind that the total of spaces and/or the back of each pleat must equal the track length.

The size of the pleat is a matter of choice. A flattened pleat with a width of 6 cm (2⅜ in) uses 12 cm (4¾ in) of fabric plus a further 6 cm (2⅜ in) for the space behind it (fig. 5). Plan to have a flat space at either side of the curtain beyond the outer pleats for any returns.

You will need the same heading allowance as for pinch pleats if it is to be made up as a curtain heading, but for making a valance you will need only 1.5 cm (½ in) for the heading allowance.

Hand pinch pleated curtains hanging on a rod. They reflect the elegant, classic style of the room.

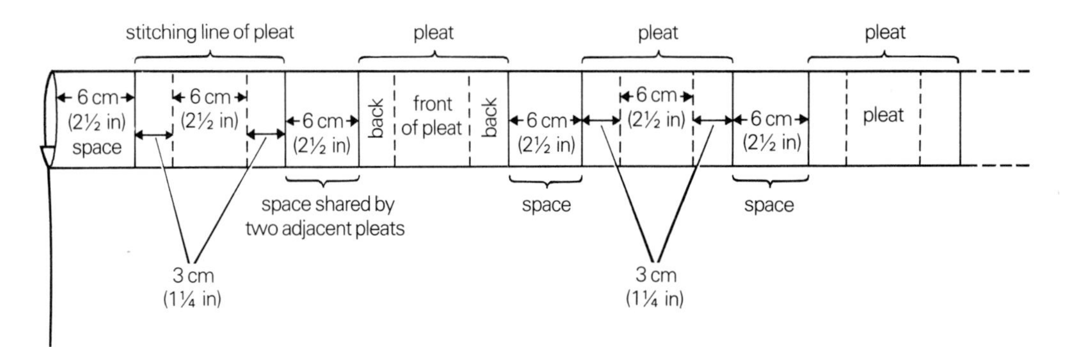

5 Box pleat arrangement

Scalloped headings

Scalloped headings are normally used on short café curtains and are hung below a narrow rod from rings. When the spaces between the scallops are left plain, it needs very little fabric fullness. One and a quarter fullness will enable the curtain to lie reasonably flat across the window. With pinch pleats between the scallops, a minimum of twice the pole length is necessary.

A heading allowance of 2 cm (¾ in) plus the depth of your stiffening is needed. The stiffening should be approximately 3 cm (1¼ in) deeper than one scallop.

Plain scallops Decide on the width of the scallops and the proposed width of the spaces between them. Divide the finished curtain width by the width of one scallop and space, to give the number of scallops. Add one to this figure to give the total number of spaces, bearing in mind that one extra space will be needed to balance the heading at the sides. Adjust the size of the spaces fractionally, if necessary, so that the total of scallops and spaces equals the width of the finished curtain.

Example Pole length 90 cm (36 in).

Using one and a quarter fullness, i.e., one width of 120 cm (48 in) wide fabric with finished curtain width of 112 cm (44 in).

Using scallop width 9 cm (3½ in) and space of 4 cm (1½ in) = 13 cm (5 in)

Divide curtain width 112 cm (44 in) by 13 (5 in)

Makes 8 scallops of 9 cm (3½ in), using 72 cm (28 in) of fabric

9 spaces of 4 cm (1½ in), using 36 cm (15½ in) of fabric

Total width—108 cm (41½ in).

Adjust by fractionally increasing size of a few spaces.

Pinch pleats between scallops This heading uses extra fullness in the spaces between the scallops. It is calculated in a similar way to ordinary pinch pleats in that the total measurement of unpleated fabric, i.e., scallops and spaces, must equal the pole length.

You will need a pleat and space at each end of the heading for balance.

Decide on the width of the scallops and allow approximately 4 cm (1½ in) per space, (which will be divided either side of each pleat when making up). Divide the pole length by the width of one scallop and space, to give the number of scallops. Add one.

To calculate the amount of fabric that is left for the pleats, deduct the pole length from the finished fabric width, and divide the result by the number of spaces.

Example (fig. 6) Pole length 105 cm (41½ in). Using two and a quarter fullness, two widths of 120 cm (48 in) wide fabric will be needed, to give a finished

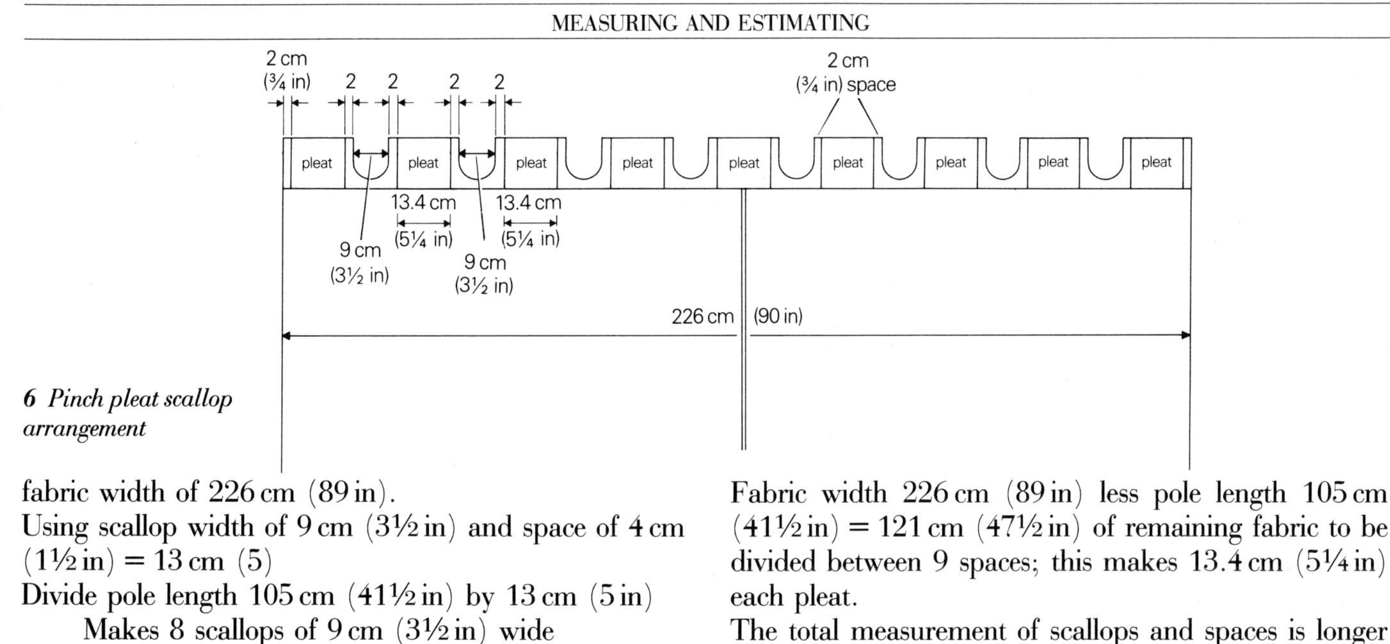

6 Pinch pleat scallop arrangement

fabric width of 226 cm (89 in).
Using scallop width of 9 cm (3½ in) and space of 4 cm (1½ in) = 13 cm (5)
Divide pole length 105 cm (41½ in) by 13 cm (5 in)
Makes 8 scallops of 9 cm (3½ in) wide
9 spaces of 4 cm (1½ in) wide
Total width—108 cm (41½ in).

Fabric width 226 cm (89 in) less pole length 105 cm (41½ in) = 121 cm (47½ in) of remaining fabric to be divided between 9 spaces; this makes 13.4 cm (5¼ in) each pleat.
The total measurement of scallops and spaces is longer than the pole length, but this can be lost by increasing the size of one or two pleats.

7 *MEASURING AND ESTIMATING*

It is advisable to fix your track first, as it may be necessary to alter its planned position. You may decide, also, to fix a batten, in which case your track or pole will project further into the room, increasing the size of the return. Remember that unless you are fitting within a window reveal, your track should, where possible, extend beyond the sides of the window to enable the curtain to stand free of the window during daylight. The larger the curtains, the more space is required.

MEASURING

Before starting to measure, it is necessary to establish the depth of the heading, i.e., from the suspension point to the top of the curtain (fig. 7a and b). With deep-taped headings, the depth is calculated from the appropriate row of pockets to the top of the tape. With a frilled gathered heading, the depth of heading will vary according to the depth of the frill. With other hand headings, you need to decide where your curtain hooks should be positioned in order that the heading will cover the track. It may be worth making a sample heading with a little spare fabric and fitting it to the track with appropriate hooks in order to ascertain the depth needed. This point is not relevant to a pole, where the heading will hang below the suspension point (fig. 7c).

You should also decide on the length of the curtains

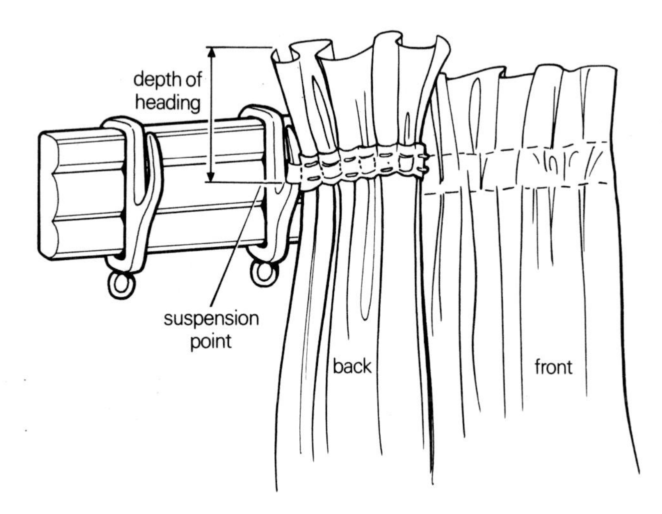

7a Depth of heading and suspension point

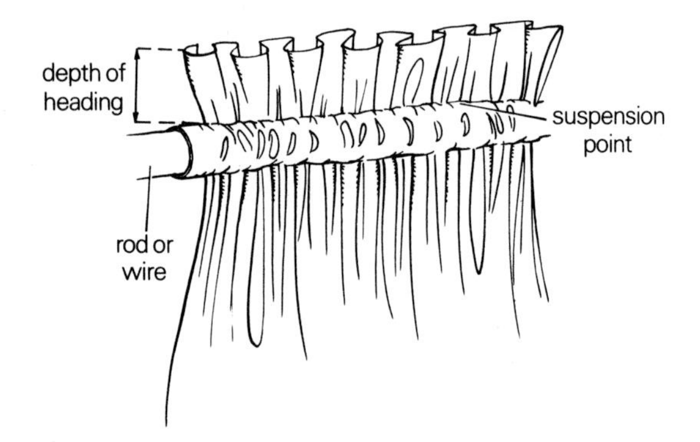

7b Channelled heading

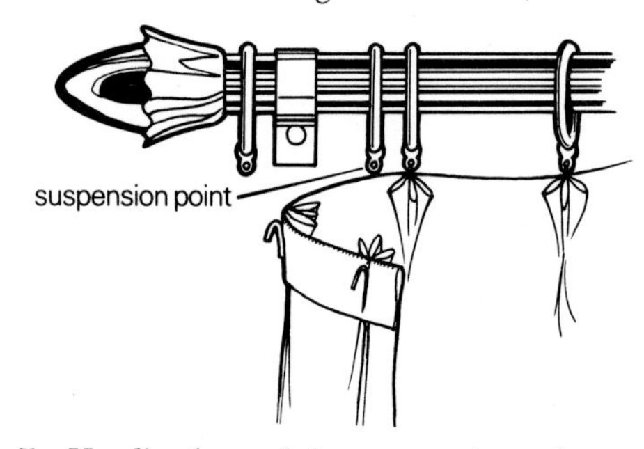

7c Heading hangs below suspension point

(fig. 8): (a) to sill, (b) just below sill, or (c) to floor. Bear in mind that in positions (a) and (c) the curtains should skirt the sill or floor to prevent undue wear and avoid soiling the hemline. Therefore, deduct a fraction from your finished length measurement unless the curtains are to act as draught excluders.

Finally, always use a metal or wooden rule for measuring as tape-measures tend to stretch and therefore are not accurate.

There are two measurements needed in order to calculate your fabric:

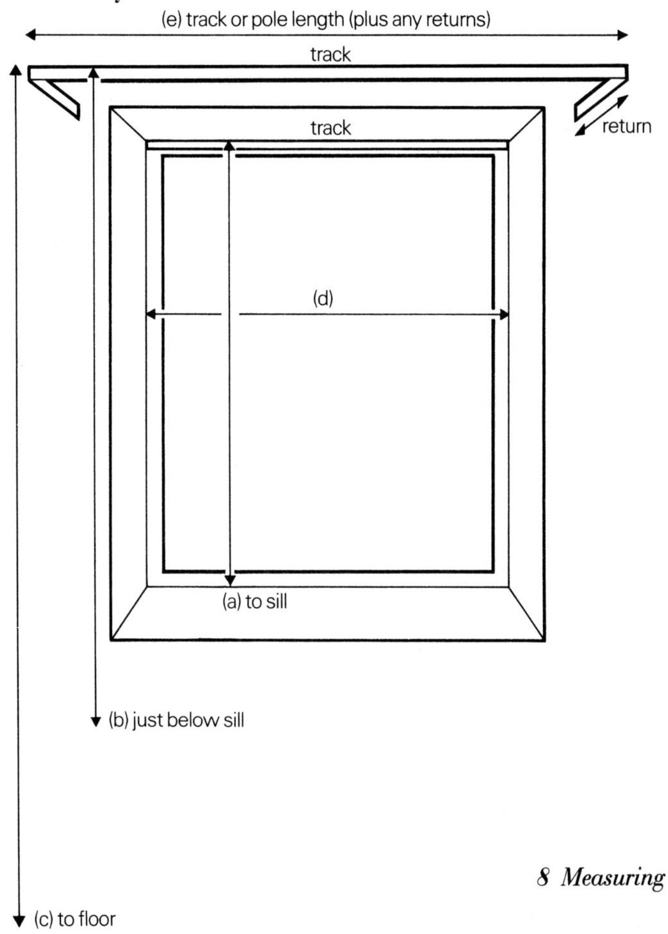

8 Measuring

Width Measure the track or pole length, excluding any finials. Add to this measurement the depth of any return(s) plus an extra 10/15 cm (4/5 in) if you have an overlap arm attached to your fitment.

Length (a) Pole—Measure from the point where your curtain will be suspended, to your chosen length.

(b) Track, rod or wire—Measure as above but *add* the depth of your chosen heading.

Measurement (a) or (b) will be your *finished length* (less an allowance for skirting the sill or floor where appropriate). Add between 20–30 cm (8–10 in) to this finished length for a double hem and a heading allowance. This final figure is your *cutting length*.

NB A double 7.5 cm (3 in) hem is usual. It improves the hang of curtains, and allows for shrinkage and alterations.

ESTIMATING FABRIC

In order to estimate the amount of fabric needed, you need both the measurements you have taken and a note of the width and pattern repeat of your chosen fabric.

(*1*) Multiply the total track length including return(s) and overlap by the fullness needed for your chosen heading.

(*2*) Divide this by the width of the fabric to give the number of widths of fabric required. Round off to the nearest full width, bearing in mind that although most headings are adjustable (excluding pinch and cartridge tapes), by rounding down you risk the curtains looking skimped.

(*3a*) *For plain fabrics* Multiply the number of widths by the cutting length for your total fabric requirement.

(*3b*) *For patterned fabrics* Extra fabric will be needed for matching patterns. Where there is a small pattern repeat the quickest and simplest method is to allow one full pattern repeat per width after the first width. However, when using fabric with a large pattern repeat this can prove wasteful, so your fabric requirement should be calculated as follows:

For large pattern repeats Divide your cutting length by the size of the pattern repeat and round up to a whole number. This is the number of pattern repeats needed per drop. Multiply the number of widths by the number of pattern repeats per drop to give the total number of pattern repeats required. Multiply the total number of pattern repeats by the size of the repeat to give your total fabric requirement.

Two-part staggered patterns Calculate as above, but allow one further half pattern repeat when making a pair of curtains with more than one width in each curtain, and when complete pattern repeats are needed for each drop (fig. 9).

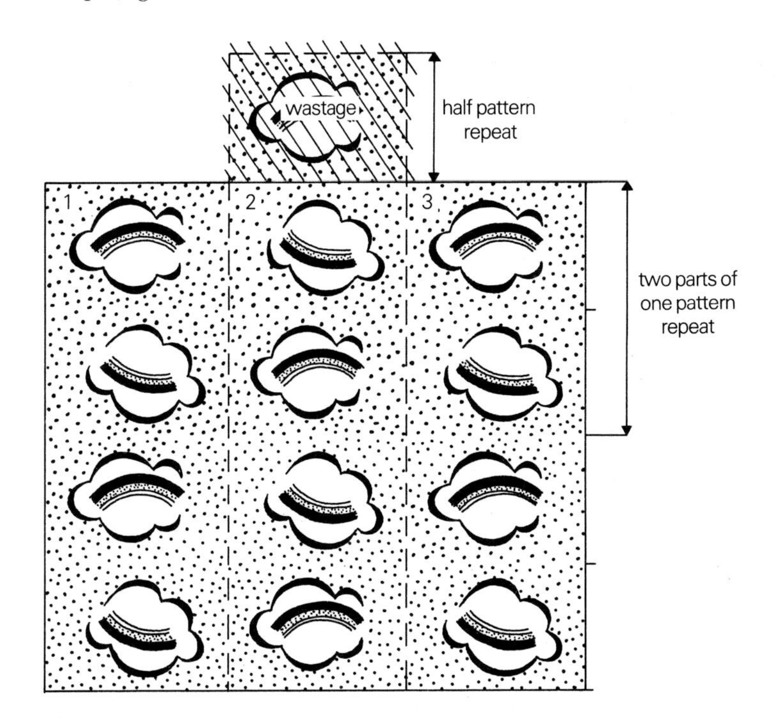

9 Two part staggered patterns

Any wastage from matching patterns could be used to make tie bands and cushions.

You will need the same amount of lining as outer curtain fabric, less allowance for pattern matching.

You will also need curtain heading tape or stiffening to equal the total width of your fabric. Allow a little extra for pinch pleat tape in order to balance your pleats.

When interlining curtains, you will need the same number of widths of fabric as your outer curtain, but no allowance for patterns, hems or headings is necessary.

As a guide to the number of curtain hooks you will need, allow about 4 hooks per 30 cm (12 in) on gathered headings. On pleated headings you will need one hook for every pleat and one at each side of the curtain.

Finally, you will need matching thread, plus a weight for the base of every seam and one at each corner. If you use weights in strip form you will need enough to fit the width of your hemline.

8 *CUTTING OUT AND HANDLING FABRICS*

Look at your fabric carefully before starting to cut out, as there are several points to observe. Give yourself plenty of room, particularly when dealing with floor-length curtains. Work on the floor if necessary.

Strictly speaking all fabrics should be cut on the straight grain. True straight grain occurs when the weft (crosswise) and warp (lengthwise) threads are at right angles to each other. This is easier to see by placing the fabric on a large rectangular table with the selvedge level with the long edge of the table. The fabric will be on grain if its width is square with the end of the table. On some fabrics it may be possible to pull a weft thread from the fabric leaving a guideline along which to cut. Problems occur on some printed fabrics when the pattern has been printed off grain. With a small print, follow the design instead of the weave so that the curtain looks right visually. A slight deviation from the grain will not affect the hang of your curtains. In bad cases, however, with large patterns, by following the pattern your curtain could be so off grain as to adversely affect its drape. On the other hand by following the grain your pattern could be on a definite slant, which would be very irritating. Unfortunately, the problem increases with multiple-width curtains. Either strike a balance between the pattern and grain or, if the problem is very bad, return the fabric before cutting.

Plain fabrics

With some plain fabrics, all drops will need to be cut in the same direction in order to match a pronounced woven design, or to ensure that fabrics with a high sheen catch the light evenly. Taffeta, pile fabrics and some dupions fall into the latter category. There are no rules as to which direction the drops should be cut. Velvets with the pile running upwards can become dust traps but some people prefer the darker, richer colour that results. With the pile running down, the colour tends to be lighter, shows fewer pressure marks, and can be brushed more easily with a downward stroke.

Patterned fabrics

It is obvious, with many patterns, in which direction the pattern should run, but others may need careful scrutiny if the top is not indicated on the selvedge of the fabric. Unbalanced stripes also have to be cut in one direction. With large patterns, aim to place the hemline at the base of a complete pattern.

Curtains with a pencil heading, caught back with tie bands, combined with a festoon blind. The combination of pole and frills creates a pretty cottagey look.

Matching patterns

With patterned fabric, the design must line up across the whole width of the curtain. To match the pattern, turn in the side of one width of fabric and line up the pattern with the width to which it will be joined. Pin, then sliptack the two pieces together from the right side (fig. 10), making sure that the pattern does not move out of line.

Machine the seam from the wrong side over the tacking. Remove tacking and cut off the selvedge. Press seam open.

Cutting

Measure and mark off the cutting length with pins or chalk before cutting, and mark the fabric to indicate the direction of the top, where necessary. To prevent excessive fraying cut out using sharp pinking shears.

HANDLING DELICATE FABRICS

A little extra care than normal is needed when handling such fabrics as velvet, silks and fine transparent fabrics, including nets. Test a small sample of fabric for stitching, pressing and general handling prior to making up in order to obtain results free from puckering and slipping.

Velvet

Pin as little as possible as pins tend to leave marks. When pinning use needles, which are finer, and place them across the seam. Then firmly tack the seam, leaving the needles in place, to hold the layers together. The top layer of fabric tends to slip over the bottom layer while under the pressure foot, so carefully machine the seam over the needles and tacking, following the direction of the nap (i.e., the direction in which the pile is lying).

Velvet drapes beautifully, so it is acceptable to use a single mitred hem, which will lie flatter, particularly as it cannot be pressed. In this instance, you must finish off the raw edge of the hem either by overcasting or, for a really professional finish, by binding it with a fine bias binding.

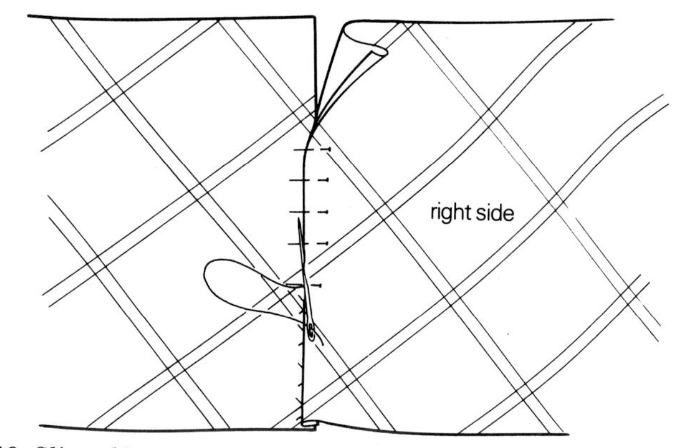

***10** Sliptacking*

Pressing is difficult with pile fabrics. It is advisable not to press the seams at all unless you have a needle board (a length of canvas covered with fine, shallow wires into which the pile side of the fabric is pressed). It is possible to use a spare piece of velvet as a substitute so that the pile of the fabric you are working on sinks into the pile of the spare piece underneath. The point of the iron should then be applied very gently to the seam only. I cannot emphasize enough the amount of care needed in this process, so if you are in any doubt about the outcome, do not attempt it. Newly hung velvet may show creases and pressure marks but as the pile and lustre returns these will drop out.

Fine fabrics

These include silks, transparent fabrics and nets. Use very sharp, fine pins (or needles), and very sharp scissors when handling these lightweight materials to prevent snagging the fine threads and puckering the fabric. Try to keep the fabric absolutely flat when cutting out. Use a padded weight to anchor the fabric to the table to prevent it slipping. Place the pins across seams. Fine fabrics are more easily stitched when tacked to tissue paper, which can be torn away afterwards. Use fine thread; silk thread with silk fabrics, and synthetic thread with synthetic fabrics. Transparent fabrics require neat seams as they can be seen from the right side. Narrow french, or mock french, seams should be used, or a narrow plain seam with the seam allowances finished off together with a zig-zag stitch. Make double hems where extra weight is needed and provided it looks right visually. Alternatively, make a narrow double-stitched hem (page 126).

9 *BASIC SEWING TECHNIQUES*

Whatever you plan to make, the contents of this chapter will be useful. It is worth remembering that 'practice makes perfect'. Once you have made yourself familiar with the basic sewing processes, you will then be able to cope with any of the projects in this book.

STITCHES

Basting (tacking) is a temporary stitch used to hold layers of fabric together (fig. 11).

Drawstitch is used to join two folded edges together (fig 12).

Hemming is used to hold a folded edge against another layer of fabric (fig. 13).

Herringbone stitch is generally used to hold a single turned edge securely in position against a single layer of fabric (fig. 14).

Lockstitch is used to loosely hold linings to curtains and is like a long loose blanket stitch. It is worked from between the curtain and the lining (fig. 15).

Overcast (oversewing) is used to neaten raw edges to prevent them from fraying (fig. 16).

Serging is used to hold a single turning in place on the sides of the curtains. It is like a large hemming stitch and must not show on the right side (fig. 17).

Slipstitch should be invisible from both sides and is used to hold a folded edge in place (fig. 18).

Stabstitch is a tiny, almost invisible stitch, and is used to attach trimming to materials (fig. 19).

Seams

For the inexperienced, it is advisable to pin and tack before permanently hand or machine stitching seams.

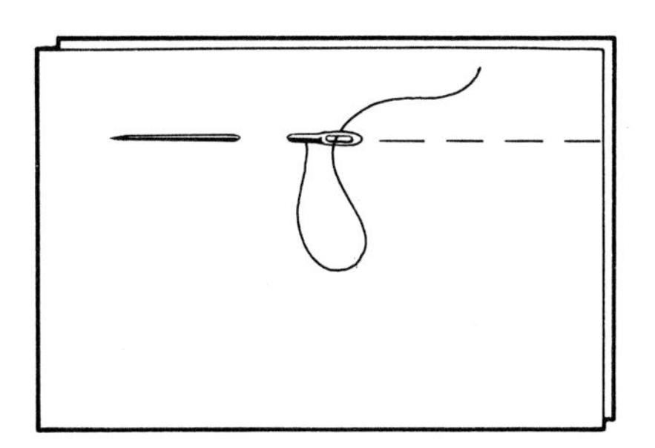

11 *Tacking*

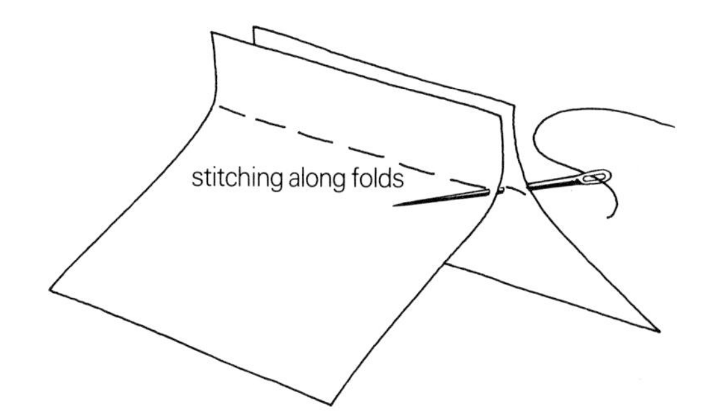

12 *Drawstitch*

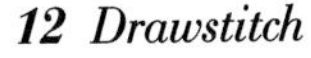

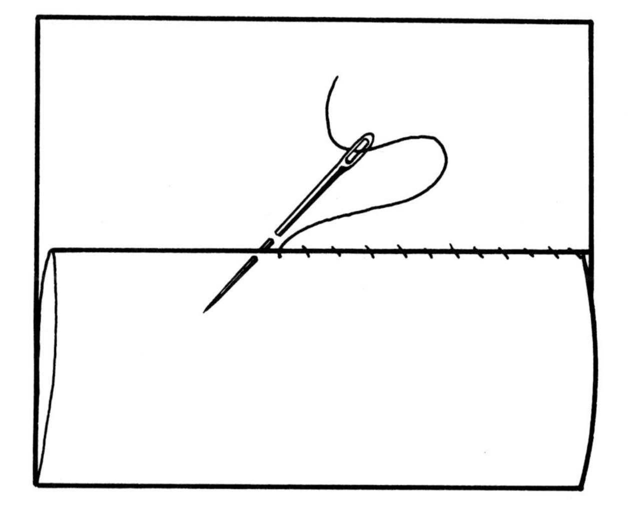

13 Hemming

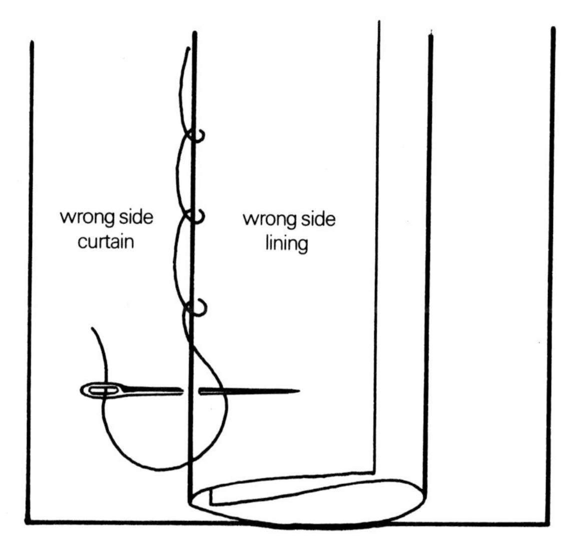

15 Lockstitch

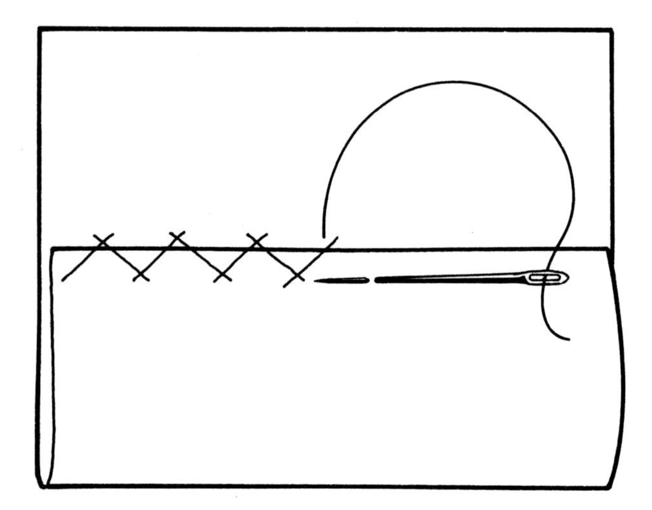

14 Herringbone

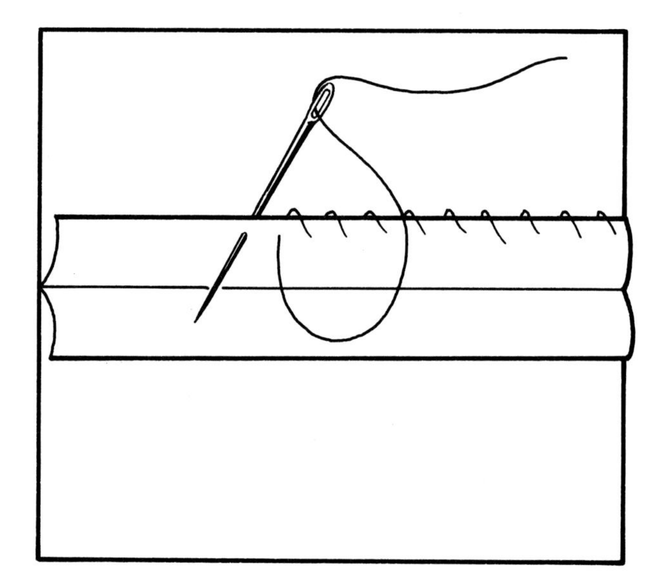

16 Overcast

Roller blinds are well suited to a modern room.

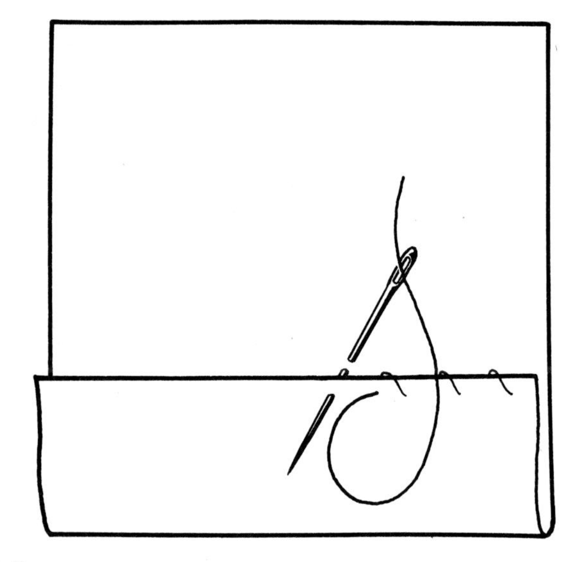

17 Serge

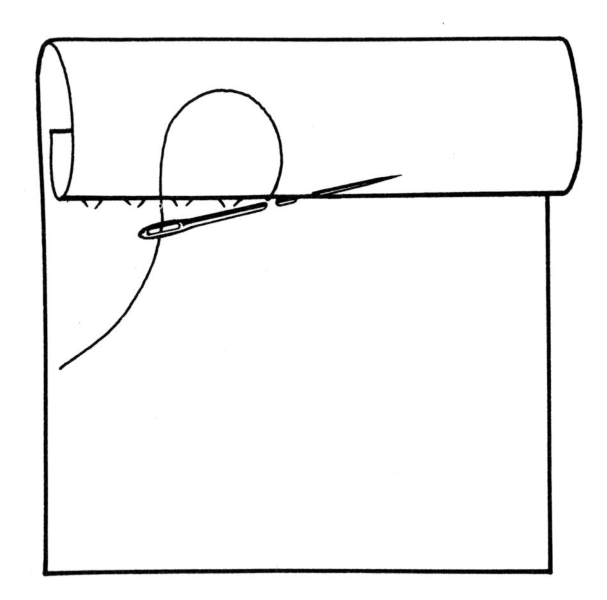

18 Slipstitch

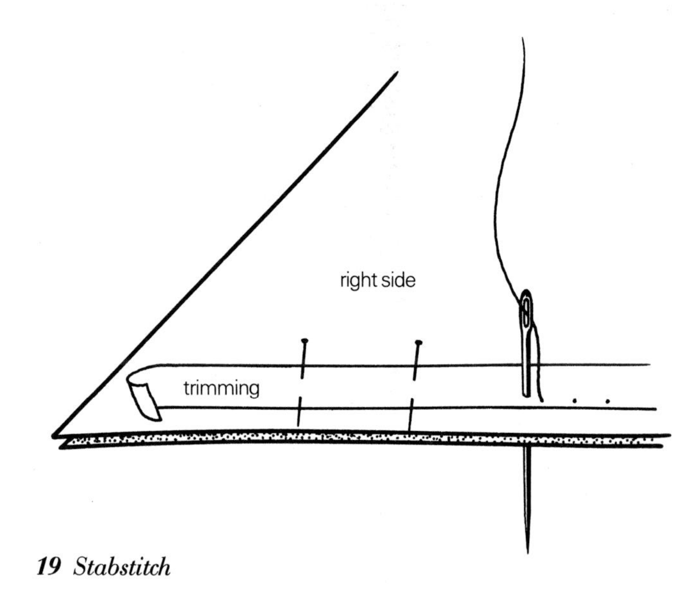

19 Stabstitch

Plain open seam is inconspicuous from the right side and is the most widely used, with an average-sized seam allowance of 1.5 cm (⅝ in). To make a plain seam, place two pieces of fabric together with right sides facing and with raw edges level. Pin on the seamline, 1.5 cm (⅝ in) in from the raw edges, with pins placed at right angles to the seam. Less fabric is taken up when they are placed at this angle, preventing the seamline from reducing and puckering. Tack the seamline and remove pins (fig. 20), then machine. To press the seam, first press the seam allowances together on the wrong side to embed the stitches in the fabric, then press the seam open. The seam allowances should be neatened, when not covered by a lining, with a machine zig-zag over the raw edges, or by overcasting.

The seam allowances of the following seams are self-neatened by enclosing them in the seam itself, and are therefore useful when making unlined curtains.

Flat fell seam is a neat, strong seam. Stitch a plain

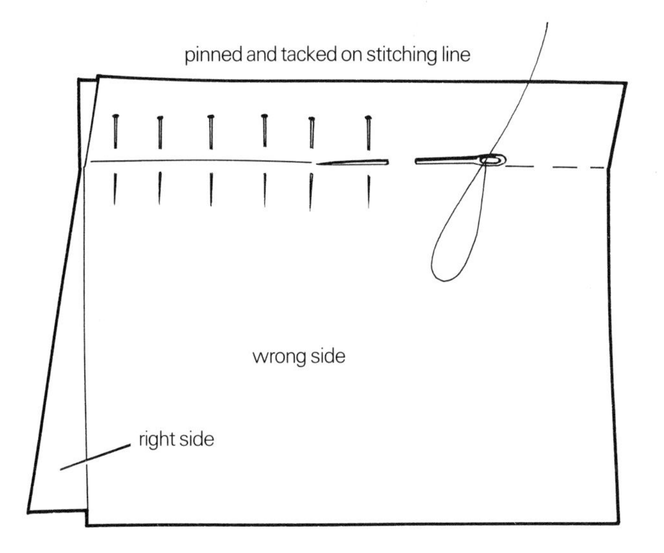

20 Plain open seam

seam on the wrong side of the fabric. Press the seam allowance to one side. Trim the under seam allowance to 3 mm (⅛ in). Turn under the raw edge of the top seam allowance and tack in place over the trimmed edge. Topstitch close to fold. Alternatively, to prevent any stitching being seen from the right side, slipstitch the top edge in place (fig. 21).

French seam is used on lightweight, sheer fabrics where a strong, narrow seam is required. No stitching is visible from the right side. With wrong sides facing, stitch 6 mm (¼ in) from the seamline within the seam allowance. Press seam allowances together. Trim seam to 3 mm (⅛ in). Turn right sides together; fold and press on the stitching line. Stitch another row of stitches on the seamline to enclose the raw edges (fig. 22).

It is not possible to match a large defined pattern in the normal way (page 120) with this seam as the first row of stitching is carried out with wrong sides facing. It would therefore be easier to restrict this seam to plain fabrics or those with a small overall design.

Mock French seam is a type of french seam which is quicker to achieve. Stitch a plain seam with right sides together. Turn in the raw edges of both seam allowances towards each other and match the folded edges. Stitch the turned edges close to the fold (fig. 23).

HEMS

As mentioned earlier, curtains should have good-sized hems. Mitres are folded at the corners of hems to distribute the bulk of fabric evenly and neatly. Never cut off the excess fabric across the corner or you will not be able to let the curtain down.

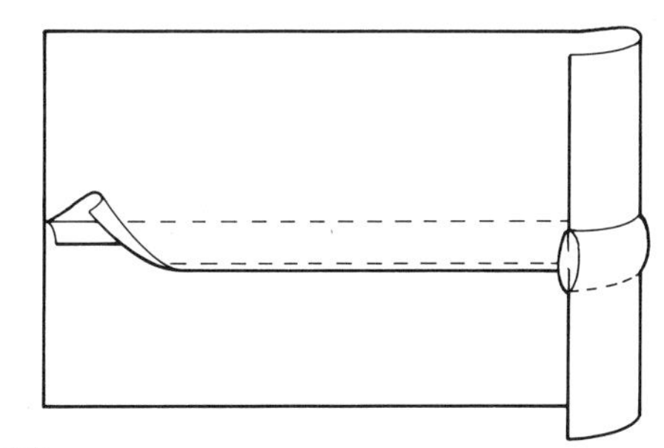

21 Flat fell seam

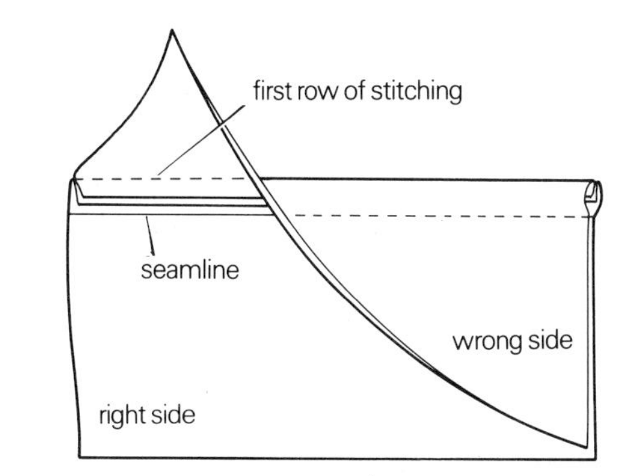

22 French seam

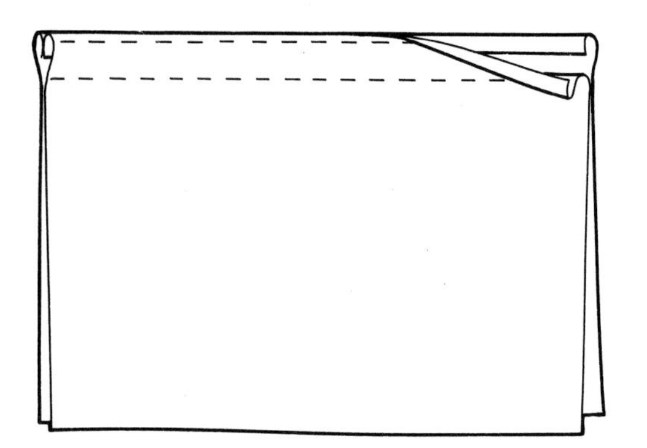

23 *Mock French seam*

Double plain hem with mitred corner is used with all lined curtains (fig. 24). A finished hem of 7.5 cm (3 in) is generally sufficient. To make this hem, turn and press approximately 4 cm (1½ in) to the wrong side along each side of the curtain and press; then open out. Turn up 15 cm (6 in) hem allowance and press to mark the hemline. Turn it back down again to reveal the corner between the creased hemline and sides. Fold the fabric diagonally through the corner of the hemline and sides of curtain. Turn in the sides again and make the first 7.5 cm (3 in) fold in the hem. Then make a second 7.5 cm (3 in) turning so that the diagonal folds meet. Pin in place and stitch the folds of the mitre with a drawstitch and hem or slipstitch the remainder of the hem.

Narrow double-stitched hem is suitable for fine lightweight fabrics to finish off single-sided frills. Machine 5 mm (¼ in) away from the raw edge with small stitches. Turn under 5 mm (¼ in) to the wrong side on machined line. Then turn 5 mm (¼ in) again. Machine in position.

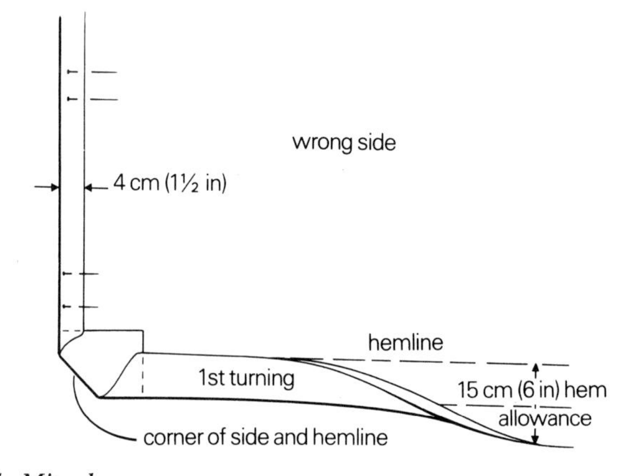

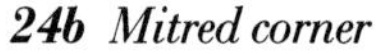

24b *Mitred corner*

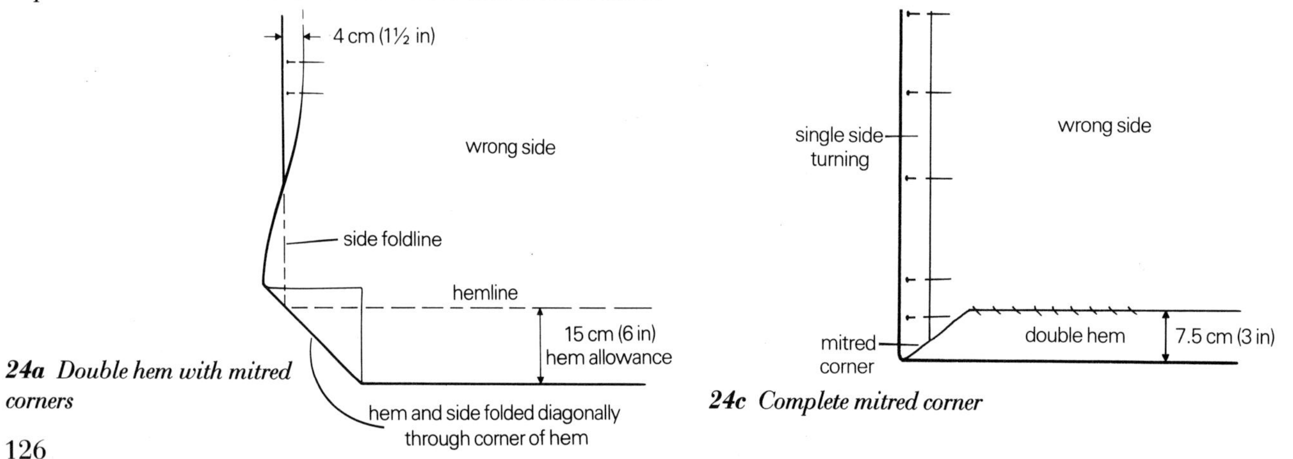

24a *Double hem with mitred corners*

24c *Complete mitred corner*

PART II

10 UNLINED CURTAINS

With gathered taped heading and a detachable lining.

Unlined curtains are ideal when made up in easy-care fabrics which can be laundered frequently, making them perfect for kitchens or bathrooms. Reversible fabrics are good where no lining is used at all, making the curtains as attractive from the outside as inside. A detachable lining which can be removed and washed separately need not use the same fullness as the outer curtain; one and a half times the track length can be sufficient. A special lining tape is available which has two flaps of tape running along one edge, between which the top of the lining is sandwiched.

MAKING UP

(Refer to Chapter 6, 7 and 8.)

Cut out the required number of drops, matching the pattern where appropriate. Cut off the selvedges completely to remove the tension along these tight edges. This will prevent the seam from tightening up with the result that it could be shorter than the surrounding fabric. Join the widths together, matching any pattern, with a mock **French or flat fell seam (page 125). Press seam. Place any** half or part widths to the outer edges of the curtain, when making a pair, so that you have a left and a right hand curtain.

Sides Make a double 2 cm (¾ in) turning to the wrong side along each side of the curtains. Pin and tack to hold in position. The width of the side hems can be varied to suit the thickness of fabric. Either machine these side hems, or slipstitch by hand.

Hems Turn up, then pin a double 7.5 cm (3 in) hem (a double 5 cm (2 in) hem is sufficient for short length curtains). Stitch a weight inside the hem at each corner and at the base of each seam. Tack hem, then slipstitch. Drawstitch the sides of the hem together.

Heading

Lay the curtains out flat. Measure up from the hemline and mark the finished length of the curtains, either by tacking across the width of the fabric, or with a row of pins on the right side. Turn the 4 cm (1½ in) heading allowance to the wrong side along the tacked line indicating the top edge of the curtains. Pin and tack to hold. Cut a length of standard gathering tape approximately 8 cm (3 in) longer than the width of the finished curtain. Pull out 4 cm (1½ in) of cord from one end and knot. Trim the tape to within 1 cm (⅜ in) of knot, then turn it under. Position this end at the leading edge, pinning the tape over the raw edge of the turned down heading allowance, and leaving 2.5 cm (1 in) above it (fig. 25). At the other end of the tape pull out 4 cm (1½ in) of cords and leave free for gathering up later. Trim the tape to 1 cm (⅜ in), turn under then pin and tack it to the outside edge of the curtain. Machine the tape close to its edge, avoiding the cords, stitching along

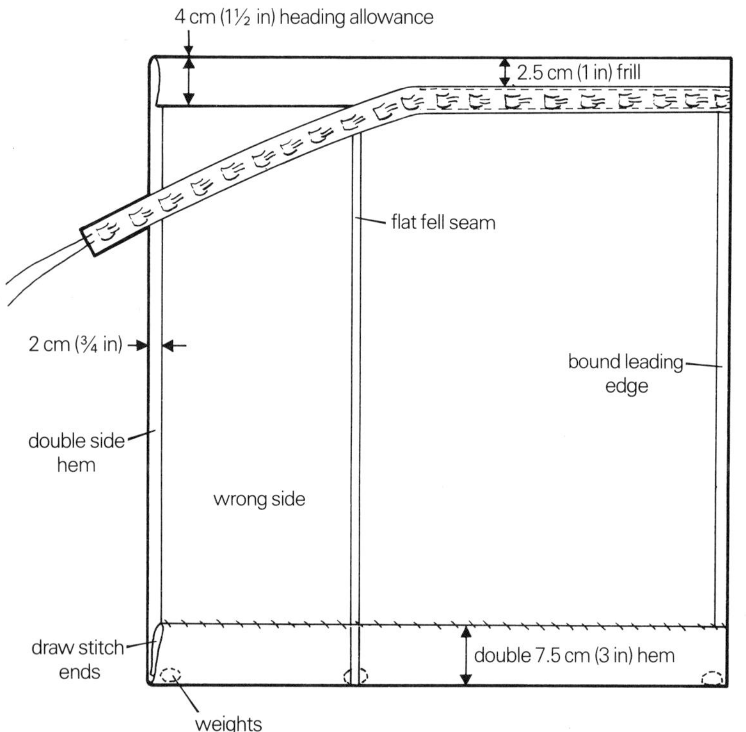

25 Left: Unlined curtain with standard heading tape

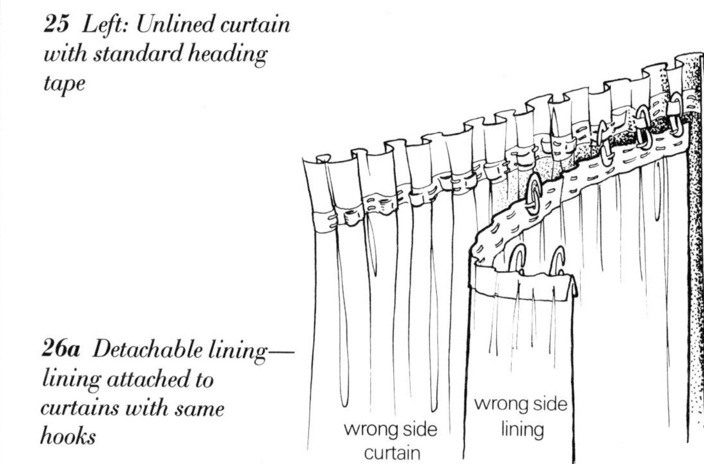

26a Detachable lining—lining attached to curtains with same hooks

the top and bottom in the same direction. Pull up the tape, tying the cords neatly, and spread the gathers evenly.

DETACHABLE LINING

This lining can be fitted to the outer curtain by hanging it from the same curtain hooks (fig. 26a), or from the base of the glider on a track with combined hook/gliders (fig. 26b). When fitting as in fig. 26a, cut the lining to the finished length of the curtain, less 2.5 cm (1 in) to clear the hemline, less a further 4 cm (1½ in) for the depth of the heading, but include a double hem allowance. When fitting as in fig. 26b deduct a further 2.5 cm (1 in) to allow for the distance between the hook of the glider and the top of the lining.

Make up the lining in the same way as the curtains, but machine all hems. Cut a length of lining tape approximately 8 cm (3 in) longer than the finished width of the lining. Pull out 4 cm (1½ in) of cords from one

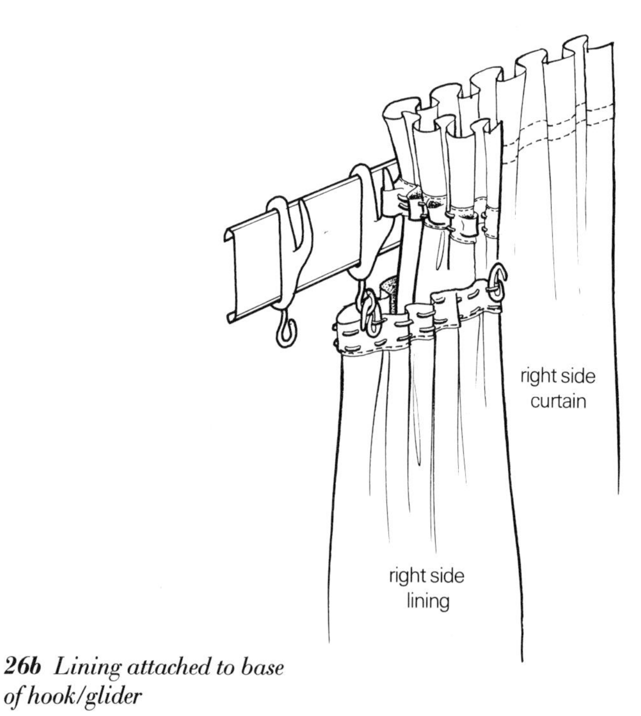

26b Lining attached to base of hook/glider

end and knot them together. Trim 2 cm (¾ in) from the tape. Position this end to the leading edges of the lining. Repeat at the other end but leave the cords free. Sandwich the top of the lining between the two layers of the tape, turning the ends over twice to bring them level with the sides of the lining (fig. 27). Pin and tack the tape in position. Machine along the bottom edge of the tape, trapping the lining, and across the ends to neaten them off.

Pull up the lining to fit the size of the outer curtain and insert the curtain hooks, first into the lining tape then into the standard tape on the curtains to hang them on a conventional track. In the case of fig. 26b, slot the curtain hook on the lining into the hole at the base of the hook/glider.

The sides of the lining can be temporarily hand stitched to the sides of the curtain, if desired.

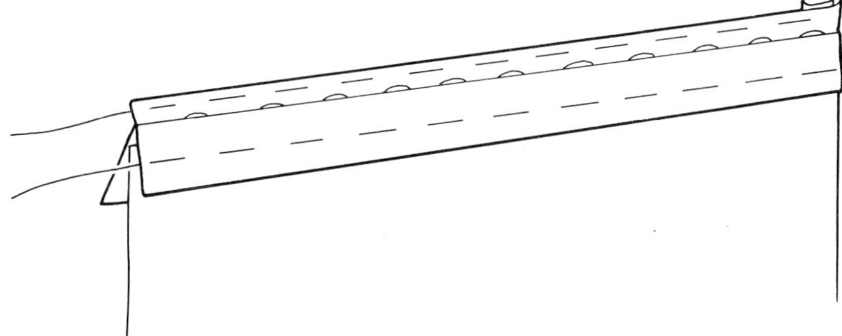

27 Lining sandwiched between two flaps of lining tape

11 LINED CURTAINS

With deep taped heading.

A lining not only protects the curtain fabric from sunlight but when sewn in as opposed to being detachable, it also improves the hang of the curtains. Coloured lining looks attractive from the outside and can also be displayed in the room during daytime as a contrast to the curtains by draping the curtains back in tie bands and turning the leading edges into the room.

MAKING UP

(Refer to Chapter 6, 7 and 8.)

Cut out the required number of drops of curtain fabric, matching the pattern where appropriate. Join the widths with a plain seam, placing any part widths to the outer edges of the curtains. It is acceptable to snip the selvedges approximately every 10 cm (4 in) to release the tension on a plain seam. Press the seams open.

Mark the hemline on the curtain fabric by turning up the 15 cm (6 in) hem allowance to the wrong side, and press. Lay the curtains out flat and measure up from the creased hemline to mark the finished length of the curtains (top edge) with a row of tacking stitches across the width of the curtain.

Sides

Make a single 4 cm (1½ in) turning to the wrong sides on each side of the curtains. Pin turning, then hold it in place with a large herringbone stitch or serging, (page 33) stopping approximately 25 cm (10 in) from the bottom edge in order to complete mitred corners.

Hem

Turn up and pin a double 7.5 cm (3 in) hem on creased hemline, folding mitres at each corner (page 38). Stitch weights in the hem at the base of each seam and at each corner. Complete the hem by slipstitching.

Complete herringbone stitching at the lower part of side seams, above the mitres.

Lining

Cut the lining as for the outer fabric and join the widths together in the same way. Turn up and pin a double 7.5 cm (3 in) hem, then machine it in place.

Lay the curtain out flat with wrong side uppermost. Lay the lining on top with wrong sides facing and with its hemline 2.5 cm (1 in) above the curtain hemline.

Turn the sides of the lining back and lockstitch (page 33) lining to the wrong side of the curtain from top to bottom on all seams, and along the middle of each width (fig. 28). Smooth the lining out flat again, then turn in the sides of the lining and pin it to the curtains, leaving a 2.5 cm (1 in) margin of curtain fabric showing at each side. While the curtain is laid out flat, pin and tack the lining to the curtain along the marked top edge of the curtain. Slipstitch the lining in place along the sides and continue round the hemline for approximately 2.5 cm (1 in).

Attaching a deep heading tape

Lay the curtains out flat with lining sides uppermost. Trim the lining to the same level as the curtain at the top. Turn the 1.5 cm (½ in) heading allowance to the wrong side on marked top edge of curtain. Pin and tack in place.

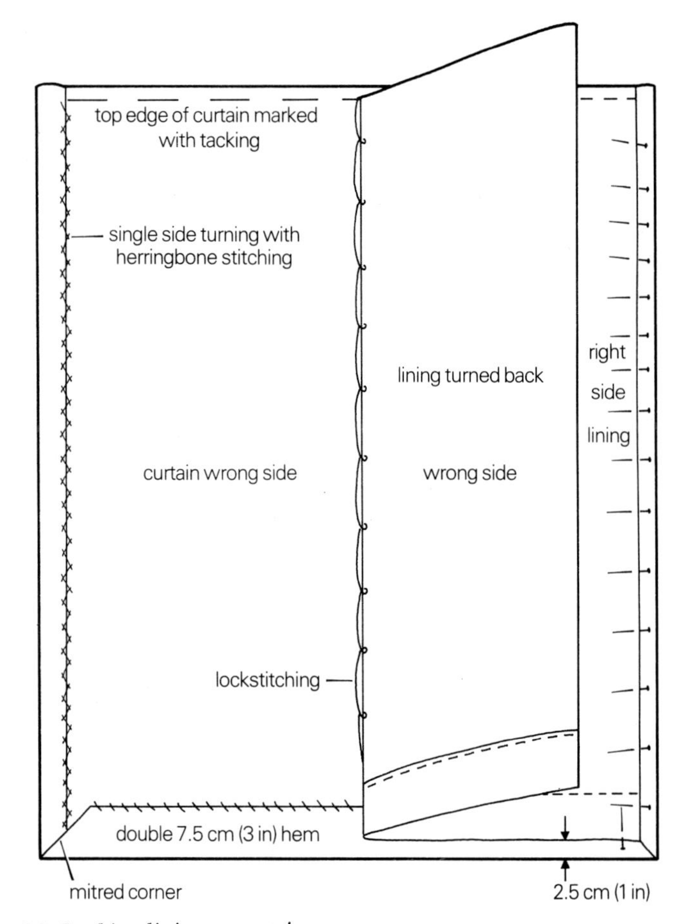

28 Locking lining to curtains

Cut a length of tape approximately 8 cm (3 in) longer than the finished width of the curtain. Pull out approximately 4 cm (1½ in) of cord from each end. (It may be necessary to pick these out with a pin on pinch pleat and cartridge tapes if you are not cutting between the pleats.) Tie knots in the cords at one end, and if using pencil pleat tape trim the tape only to within 1.5 cm (½ in) of knot. Place this end to the leading edges of the curtains, turning in the ends of the tape. With pinch and cartridge pleat tape you will need to balance your end spaces to make your pleating symmetrical on both curtains. You will, therefore, have to vary the amount of tape turned under. Pin the tape to the curtain over the heading allowance, fractionally down from the top of the curtain (fig. 29). Turn in the other end of the tape, leaving the cords free for pulling up. Pin, then machine the tape in place, making sure you stitch the top and bottom row in the same direction.

Pull up the tape to fit the track; tie the cords neatly and insert curtain hooks.

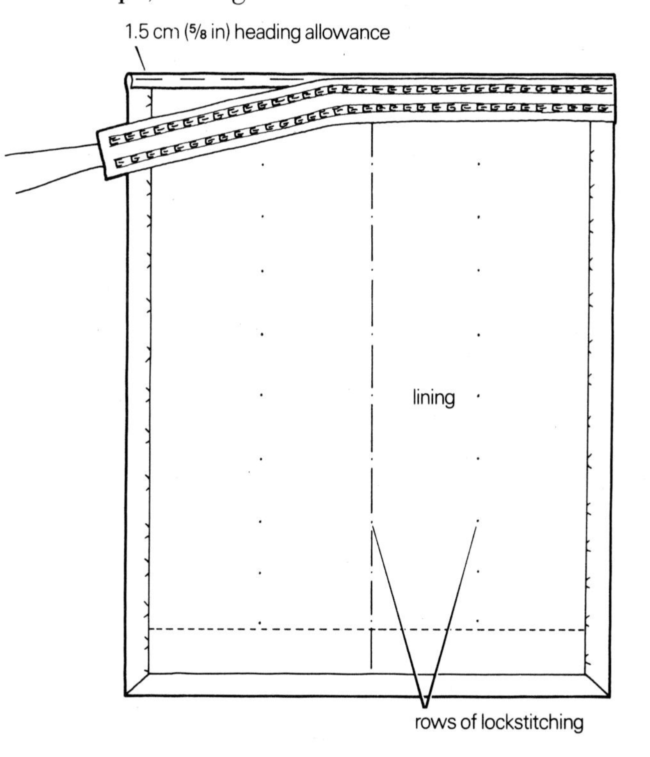

***29** Attaching deep heading tape*

12 *INTERLINED CURTAINS*

With hand pinch pleat heading.

These curtains make excellent draught excluders and give extra insulation. Interlining will add years to the life of your curtains and you are likely to tire of them well before they wear out. The stiffness of a hand pleated heading will help to keep the heading crisp and firm, giving a truly professional finish. Curtains are normally interlined with bump, but other soft fabrics can be used.

MAKING UP

(Refer to Chapter 6, 7 and 8.)

This method gives a less bulky finish to the hem. If a thick, weighty hem is preferred, however, interlining can be cut to the exact size of the outer curtain, excluding the heading allowance, but you will need slightly more fabric to allow for a hem allowance. Once the interlining has been locked in, the two layers of fabric can be treated as one and made up in the same way.

Cut out the required number of drops of curtain fabric and lining to your cutting length as calculated, and join matching the pattern where appropriate, as with lined curtains. Turn up and pin a double 7.5 cm (3 in) hem on the lining and machine it in place.

Cut out the same number of widths of interlining to the finished curtain length. To keep the seams as flat as possible, join the widths by overlapping the selvedges by approximately 1.5 cm (½ in) then zig-zag two rows of stitching, each row catching a raw edge (fig. 30).

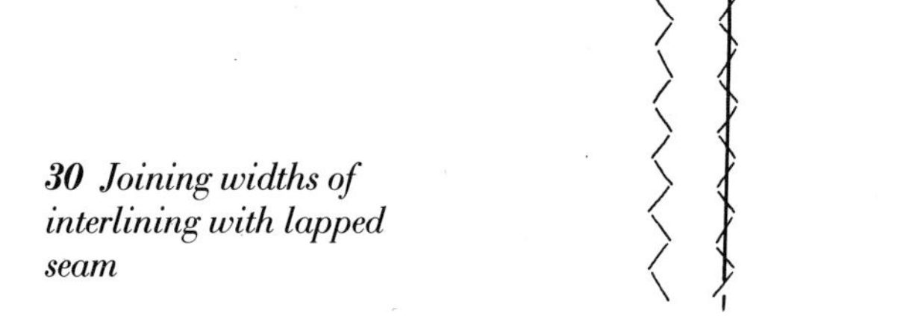

***30** Joining widths of interlining with lapped seam*

Mark the hemline and finished top edge of the curtains as with lined curtains. Also mark the finished side edges by turning in 6 cm (2½ in) to the wrong side and press. Open out all turnings after pressing.

Attaching interlining

Lay curtain fabric out flat with wrong side uppermost. Lay the interlining on top with the raw edges of interlining level with the marked hemline and top edge of the curtains (fig. 31). Fold the interlining back and lockstitch it to the wrong side of the curtains in the same way as for the lining in Lined Curtains, but stitch two vertical rows for each width of fabric at equal distances apart and along all seams. Smooth the interlining back and tack the outer edges of bump to the sides of the curtain all around.

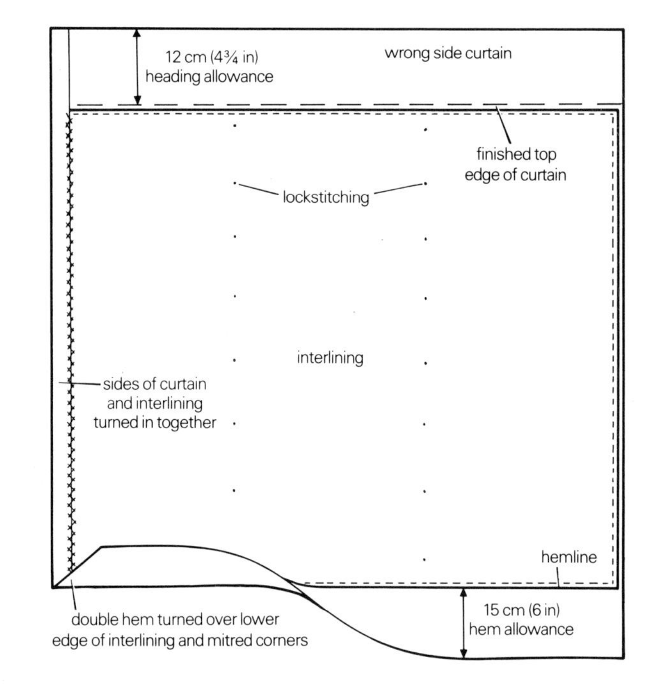

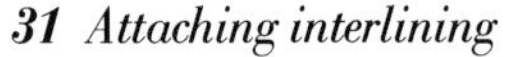

***31** Attaching interlining*

Sides and hem

Finish off the sides by turning them in to the wrong side on the creaselines, with the interlining. Take the curtain hem allowance over the cut edge of interlining, and complete the sides and hem with mitred corners (page 126).

Lining

Lay the curtain out flat with the interlining uppermost and apply the hemmed lining to it in the same way as for Lined Curtains, but lockstitching along the same lines as the interlining and along all seams.

Hand pinch pleat heading

Cut a length of 10 cm (4 in) deep curtain buckram to the finished width of the curtain. Lay the curtain out flat with the lining uppermost. Place the buckram over the heading allowance with its lower edge level with the marked top edge of the curtain. Turn the top 2 cm (3/4 in) of curtain and lining over the top edge of the buckram, then tack and machine it in place close to the folded edge (fig. 32). Turn the buckram down to the wrong side on the marked top edge of the curtain and tack it in place.

Plan your pleating arrangement as on page 110–111. On the wrong side of the heading, mark your calculated pleats and spaces with tailor's chalk, or with rows of pins on the right side (fig. 33). Fold each pleat by bringing the marked sides of each pleat together on the wrong side. Tack each pleat in place on the right side, from top to bottom of buckram. When all the pleats have been tacked, check the finished curtain width and adjust as necessary, bearing in mind that the total finished width of both curtains must equal the track length. Machine the pleats over the tacking, using a reverse machine stitch to start and finish the stitching, for security. Remove the tacking. At the sides of the curtain, machine a double row of stitching, 5 mm (1/4 in) apart, along the depth of the heading.

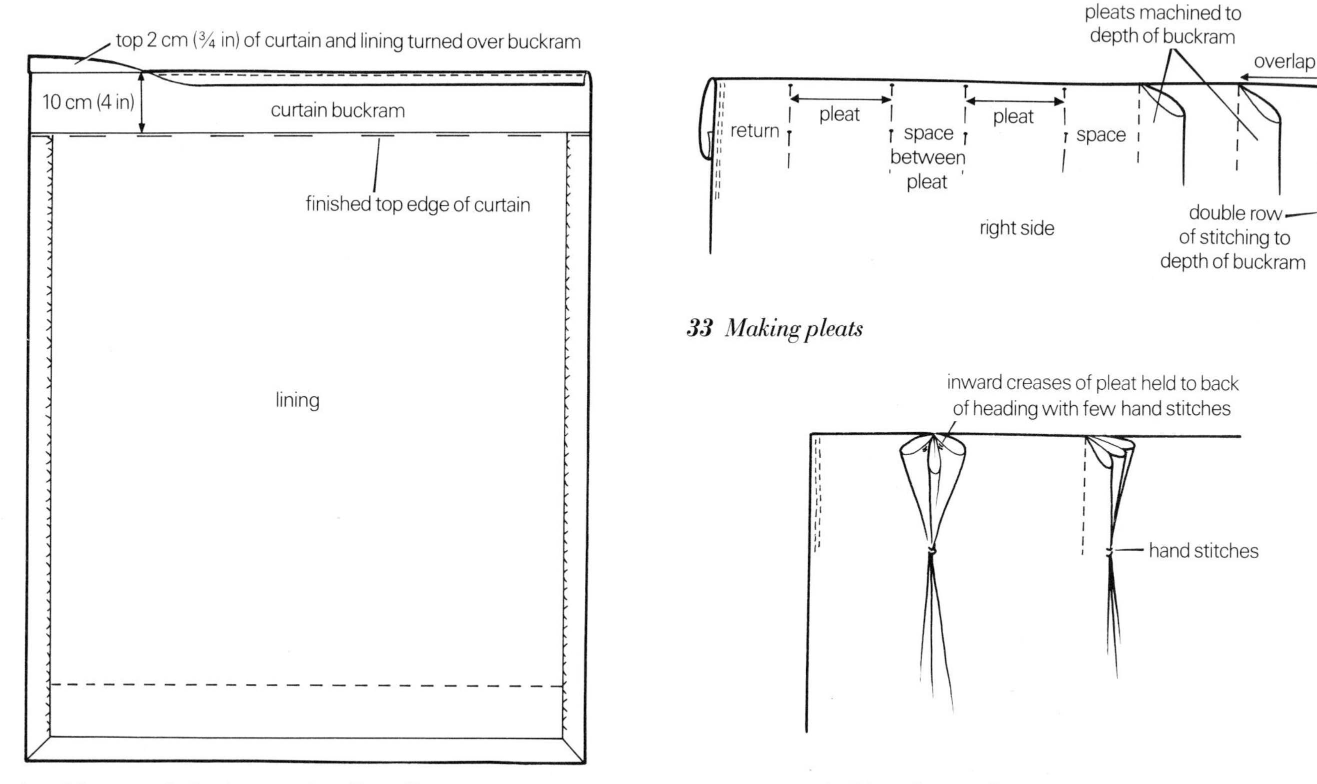

32 *Attaching curtain buckram to heading allowance*

33 *Making pleats*

34 *Pleat pinched into three sections*

Forming the pinch pleats Hold the centre of the single pleat and press it towards the stitching line behind, to form three separate pleats of equal size. Hold the pleats in place by oversewing a few hand stitches at the base of each pleat (fig. 34). Also hold the inward creases of the pleat to the back of the heading with a few hand stitches at the top of the pleat. Insert pin hooks at the appropriate depth into the back of each pleat, taking care not to break the thread, and at each side of the curtain.

Hanging
Hang the curtains by inserting one curtain hook into each glider on track or pole and draw the curtains back into an open position. If fitting to a track pull the spaces between the pleats forward, but if fitting to a pole, gently push the spaces back. Position the folds in the fabric which form below each pleat by running your fingers down the length of the curtain. The drape of the fabric will improve if the curtain is left like this for a while.

13 CAFÉ CURTAINS

A café curtain is an ideal way of giving privacy if you are overlooked, or for blocking out an unwanted view, as this type of curtain covers the lower half of the window permanently, leaving the top half uncovered.

It is normally unlined and made as one short curtain rather than as a pair. It can have one of several headings; a frilled channelled heading can be fitted onto a narrow rod or it can hang below a rod from rings with a plain or pinch pleated scalloped heading. It could be teamed with an additional short pair of curtains hung from the top of the window to create a tiered effect. These could be drawn to give further privacy at night.

TO MAKE A CAFÉ CURTAIN WITH PLAIN SCALLOPED HEADING

(Refer to Chapters 6, 7 and 8.)
Allow for a double 5 cm (2 in) hem. You will also need strips of iron-on dressmaker's interfacing to stiffen the heading to equal the finished width of your curtain fabric by the depth of the scallop plus 3 cm (1¼ in).

Firstly, you will need to make a card template for your scallops in order to mark them off accurately. Draw a circle with a diameter equal to the width of your scallop, then draw a horizontal line across the diameter. At each end of the line draw a vertical line upwards to equal the radius of the circle. Then join the top of these two vertical lines with another horizontal line (fig. 35). If you would like deeper scallops, extend the length of the two vertical lines to suit. Cut round the outline.

Cut the required number of widths of fabric and join them as for unlined curtains (page 127). Cut strips of interfacing to equal the width of the curtain fabric less the

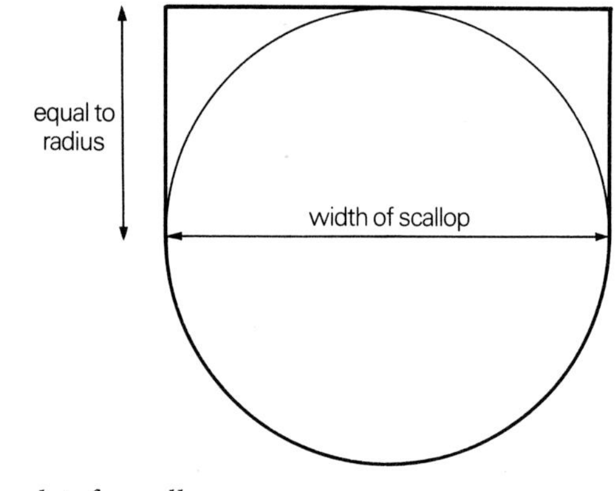

35 Template for scallop

side hems, by the depth of the scallop plus 3 cm (1¼ in). Turn in the 4 cm (1½ in) side hem allowance and press it to mark. Open out. Mark the finished top edge of the curtain by measuring down the depth of the heading allowance (interfacing plus 2 cm (¾ in)) and tack a line across the curtain at this depth. Iron the interfacing to the wrong side of the heading allowance, with its lower edge level with the marked top of the curtain and its ends touching the creaseline of the sides. Turn the top 2 cm (¾ in) down over the interfacing, then pin and machine it in place (fig. 36). Fold the sides, hem in place and treat as for Unlined Curtains, but making a double 5 cm (2 in) hem.

Turn the heading allowance to the right side on marked top edge of curtain and pin in position temporarily. This heading allowance also acts as a facing. Mark the position of the scallops with chalk on the interfacing, using the template. Tack round the marked scallops, through the facing and curtain, then machine. Trim the fabric away inside the scallops, cutting close to the stitching line and notching out the seam allowance round the curves (fig. 37). Turn the facing to the wrong side and press. Drawstitch the ends of the facing and curtain together along the sides.

TO MAKE A SCALLOPED PINCH-PLEATED HEADING

(Refer to Chapter 6, 7 and 8)

Complete the curtains in the same way as above, having left larger spaces between the scallops for pleating, as calculated. On the wrong side of the heading (facing), mark the position of the pleats as planned, remembering that the total measurement of all the scallops plus the spaces either side of each pleat must equal the length of the pole (fig. 6, page 27). Make up the pinch pleats as Interlined Curtains, leaving a tiny space on either side of the pleats (fig. 38).

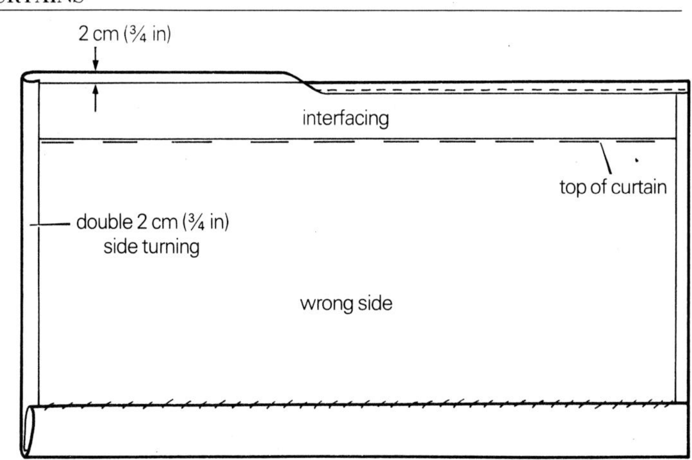

36 Interfacing on wrong side of heading allowance

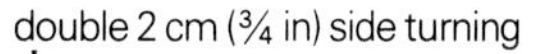

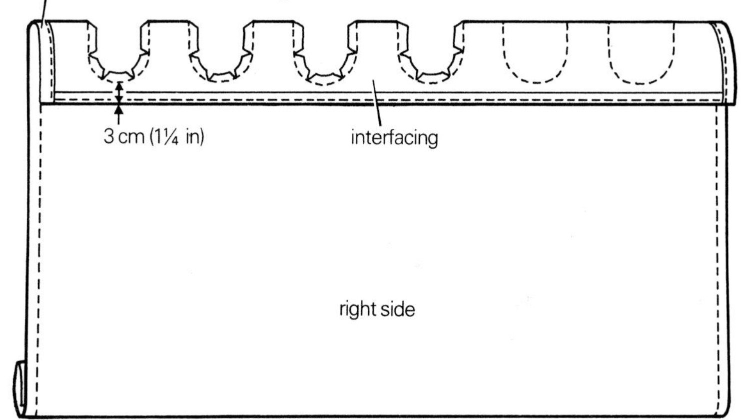

37 Facing (heading allowance) turned to right side: scallops marked, stitched and cut out

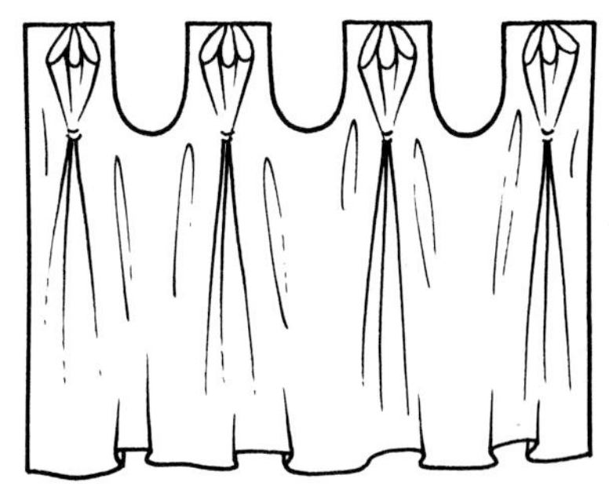

38 Finished pinch pleat scallop

14 PELMETS

A fabric-covered pelmet can give a neat finish to the top of curtains, and at the same time conceal any unattractive tracks. A shaped edge will soften its general appearance and, trimmed with braid or fringing, it will suit a traditional, formal setting. Its success depends largely on its proportions to the accompanying curtains and surroundings. A deep pelmet in a room with a low ceiling can have a heavy effect, increasing the problem. A depth of between one-sixth and one-eighth of the overall curtain length will give a good proportion, but this will depend upon individual shapes of windows and should vary accordingly.

Pelmet buckram, available in 90 cm (36 in) and 45 cm (18 in) widths, is used to stiffen the fabric cover. It is impregnated with glue, and fabric can be ironed on when dampened. The stiffened cover is fitted to a pelmet board—like a three-sided shelf—to give it support. The board can be made up in 25 mm (1 in) thick softwood to a length fractionally longer than the curtain track, to allow access to fix the track and hang the curtains (fig. 39). The depth of the shelf from the wall should be a minimum of 10 cm (4 in) to allow room for the track and bulk of fabric when the curtains are drawn back. The frame can be fitted to the wall outside the window reveal with a number of angle brackets spaced evenly along its length. The curtain track is fitted either to the underside of the board towards the back, or to the wall. The stiffened cover can be fitted to the board either with touch-and-close fastener; or with drawing pins inserted through pockets on webbing tape, stitched to the back; or tacked directly onto the board with steel tacks, provided the tacks are covered with braid.

A selection of designs is shown in fig. 40. When choosing a shape, consider any pattern on your fabric and select a shape to blend with the design. Try to avoid angular prints on a pelmet with a highly curved edge, as the designs could conflict. Any pattern on the accompanying curtains should unite with that on the pelmet.

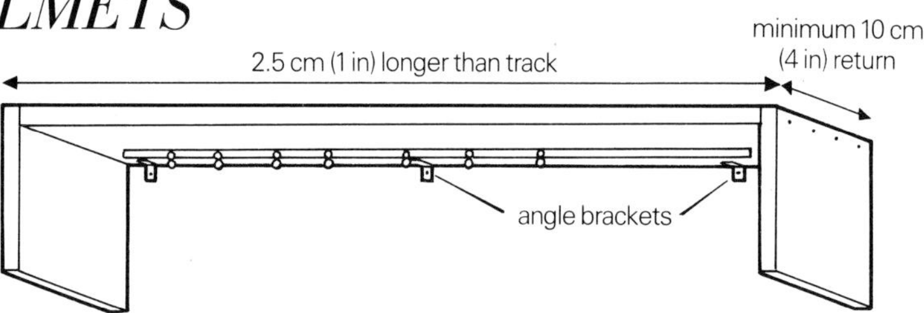

39 Pelmet board with track fitted to underside towards back

It is advisable to make a paper pattern for all shaped pelmets. Measure the front edge of the pelmet board plus the two returns. You will need a strip of paper to equal this length by at least the desired depth of your pelmet. Fold the paper in half, and taking the fold as the centre of the pelmet, mark the position of the return on the opposite end. Draw half the pattern between the fold of paper and the beginning of the return, leaving the latter plain. Cut round the design through the double thickness of paper. Open out the pattern and place it in position at the window to check its proportions.

For a scalloped design, after deciding upon the number of scallops needed, divide the paper into the same number of equal sections, excluding the returns. Make a template of the scallop (see Café Curtains, page 134) or use an appropriately sized plate, to mark them off accurately.

To calculate your fabric requirements, you will need a strip(s) of outer fabric and lining to equal the length and depth of your pattern, plus a 2.5 cm (1 in) turning allowance all round, plus extra for matching a pattern. You will need pelmet buckram and bump to equal the exact size of your pattern. For fixing your pelmet, allow

The pattern of the fabric has been used to create an unusual pelmet design.

either enough touch-and-close fastener, or 4 cm (1½ in) deep webbing tape to fit the length of the board plus two returns. For trimming, allow enough braid to go round the pelmet outline, or fringing for the bottom line of pelmet only.

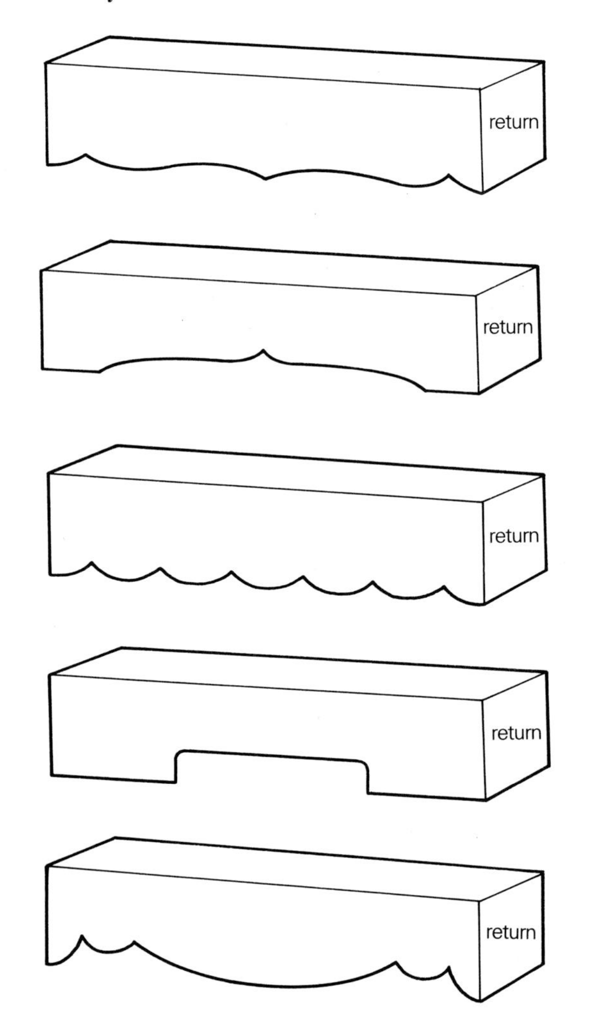

40 Selection of pelmet shapes

MAKING UP

Cut out the buckram and bump to the exact pattern size. Iron pattern to the buckram for ease, and cut with sharp scissors. Cut out the pelmet fabric and lining to the pattern shape with a 2.5 cm (1 in) allowance all round. If your pelmet is wider than one width of fabric, and to avoid an obvious central seam, you should make joins on the pelmet fabric and lining either side of a central panel, with a plain seam pressed open, and match any pattern. Join widths of bump, if necessary, with an overlapped seam (see page 132).

Dampen the edges on one side of the buckram, lay the bump on top, and press (not iron) with a damp cloth and warm iron to adhere.

Reinforce the turning line of the pelmet fabric and lining, 2.5 cm (1 in) in from raw edge, on inward corners, such as between scallops, with a row of small machine stitches.

Lay the pelmet fabric out flat with wrong sides uppermost. Then lay buckram on top, with bump sandwiched in between and with a 2.5 cm (1 in) border of fabric showing all round. Dampen the edge of the buckram and bring the turning allowance of pelmet fabric over, and press with an iron to bond together, snipping the allowance to the reinforcement stitching on inward corners, and around all other curves to allow the fabric to spread. Notch out fabric on inner curves to reduce bulk and enable the fabric to lie flat. Remove tacking.

Stabstitch braid to the outline of the pelmet on right side at this stage, but stitch fringing to the lower edge of the pelmet when the pelmet has been completed, or fix with fabric adhesive.

Depending on your method of fixing, *either:* pin and machine the soft side of touch-and-close fastener to the right side of the lining along the top, 2.5 cm (1 in) in from the cut edge; *or* pin a length of webbing tape in the same position turning in the ends of the tape. Machine down the ends and along the lower edge; then stitch vertically every 8 cm (3 in) to form pockets in the tape (fig. 41).

Pin the lining to the pelmet with wrong sides facing, turning in the allowance after snipping and notching out as on the pelmet fabric (fig. 41). Slipstitch in position. In order that the method of fixing is secured to the pelmet buckram and not only to the lining, hand stitch, with a strong needle and thread, along the previous machine stitching on the tape, catching the buckram but not allowing the stitches to show on the right side.

Finally, to attach the pelmet to the board, either attach the firm side of the touch-and-close fastener to the top edge of the board with steel tacks, if using the first method above, or place a strong drawing pin through each pocket on the tape and into the top edge of the board, bending the returns round the ends of the board.

NB When using pile fabrics which cannot be ironed in the same way, cut the bump 2.5 cm (1 in) larger than the buckram all round. Then apply the interlining to the buckram by pressing the bump turning allowance to the back, as with the pelmet fabric described above. Then serge (page 122) the turning allowance of the outer fabric to the turning of the interlining on the back of the pelmet and through the buckram, making sure no stitches show on the right side.

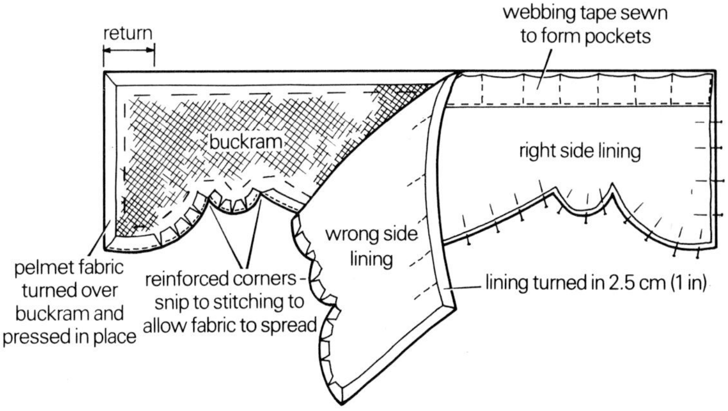

***41** Buckram covered with face fabric and lining*

15 VALANCES

A soft, pretty valance will give a feminine, romantic finish to the top of curtains, and at the same time hide those unattractive fixtures and fittings. They can be gathered or pleated with most headings, provided the depth of the heading is in proportion to the depth of the valance. Individual touches can be added by shaping the hemline, or by binding the top and bottom edges with fabric in a contrasting or toning colour. They should be lined and/or interlined to match accompanying curtains.

The depth of the valance should be in proportion to the accompanying curtains, as with a pelmet. Here again, allow one-sixth to one-eighth of the overall curtain length, but bear in mind individual window shapes.

Valances can be fitted in one of several ways. There are a few tracks available which combine with a valance rail (page 104). Valance or curtain hooks, inserted into the heading, are then simply hooked over the rail. Alternatively, a 25 mm (1 in) thick wooden shelf can be fitted inside or outside a window reveal with angle brackets, into which staples or screw-eyes can be fixed along the front edge and returns. These metal loops should be spaced to correspond with the curtain hooks on the heading (fig. 42).

To estimate your fabric and lining requirements, you will need to measure the length of the valance rail, or shelf, plus returns. Decide upon the depth of the valance and calculate as for curtains (page 117), but add only 4 cm (1½ in) for a single hem plus 1.5 cm (⅝ in) heading allowance.

You will also need curtain heading tape or stiffening of your choice (Chapter 6) to the length of your valance strip, plus enough valance or curtain hooks to space approximately every 7.5 cm (3 in) along a gathered heading, or one for each pleat on a pleated heading, and one for each end.

TO MAKE A LINED BOX-PLEATED VALANCE

Cut the required number of widths of fabric and join them to make one long strip with a plain open seam and matching any pattern. Press seam open. Repeat for the lining, but cut each width 2.5 cm (1 in) shorter. After joining the lining widths, trim the sides so that the total width is 10 cm (4 in) less than the total width of valance.

Turn a single 4 cm (1½ in) turning to the wrong side on the valance sides and hem, mitring the corners (page 38). Press, then open out. Pin a length of curtain buckram or strips of softer stiffening to the wrong side across the whole width of the valance between the creasemark of the sides, and positioned 1.5 cm (½ in) down from the cut top edge. Tack in place all round, or iron on, according to the type of stiffening used. Turn the top 1.5 cm (½ in) heading allowance down over the stiffening and tack in place. Turn in the sides on the creaselines, over the ends of the stiffening. Serge (page 121), or herringbone, the sides in place, above the mitred corner (fig. 43).

Turn 1.5 cm (½ in) to the wrong side along the sides and top edge of the lining and press. With right sides facing, pin the hem of the valance to the bottom of the lining, taking a 1.5 cm (½ in) seam between the diagonal lines of the mitre (fig. 24). Turn lining to the wrong side by folding the valance up on the creased hemline, re-folding the mitres so that 2.5 cm (1 in) of valance fabric shows below the lining, and the top edges are level. Pin sides of lining to sides of valance, leaving a 2.5 cm (1 in) margin of valance fabric showing. Slip-stitch lining and mitres in place. Pin top edges of valance and lining together and drawstitch the folded edges together.

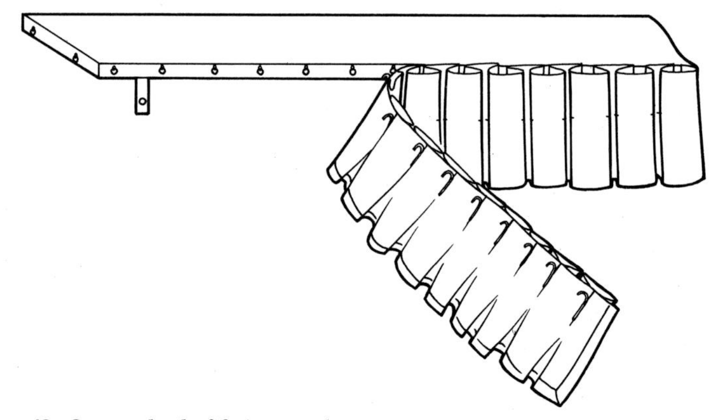

42 One method of fixing a valance

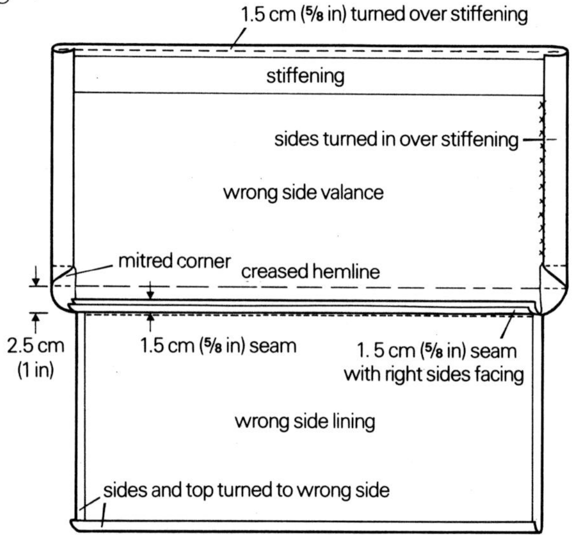

43 Attaching lining to hem of valance

An original style of valance, fitted to a pelmet board. The sides have been pleated up and the fabric caught up in the centre to form two swags.

Box pleats

On the wrong side, mark off your pleats and spaces with tailors chalk, as calculated on page 133, fig. 33, to the depth of stiffening, leaving a space between the pleats if preferred. Draw solid lines on either side of each pleat, indicating those that will be stitched together, and tack through the heading to indicate the fold lines of each pleat. Pin and tack the pleats on the right side from top of valance to bottom of stiffening, by bringing the solid lines together on the wrong side as with pinch pleats (fig. 33). When all the pleats have been tacked in place, check that the finished width equals the length of the valance rail. Machine over tacking, then remove tacking. Press each pleat flat on the tacked fold lines. Catch both top corners of each pleat to the heading behind with a few hand stitches and also at the base of the stiffening, to hold in position (fig. 44). Insert a curtain pin hook into the back of each pleat and at sides.

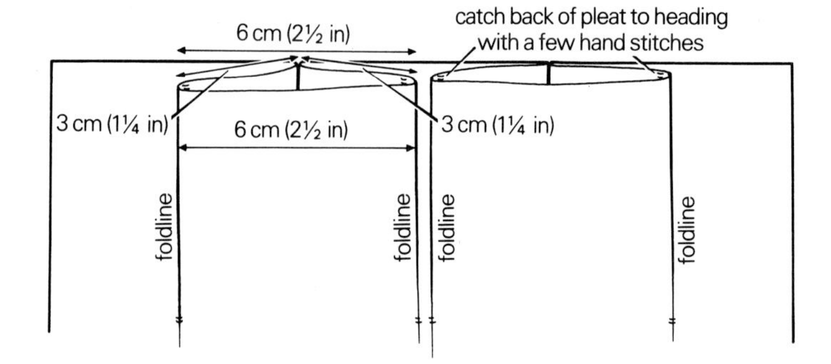

***44** Box pleats*

16 SWAGS AND TAILS

Swags and tails are an elegant form of heading which suit a large room with a classical, formal décor. They will add a sumptuous air to your curtains, particularly when made up in soft, supple fabrics which drape beautifully. Lining the tails with fabric of a contrasting colour will show on the graduated ends, and edging the whole creation with a braid or fringe trimming will add a splendid finish.

They are normally made by professionals in a workroom, and depend on a skill in handling and arranging fabric to achieve the best possible folds and drape in the fabric. There is no reason why these should not be made in the home provided the design is kept to a simple one for a first attempt.

Many of these headings are cut on the bias to improve the drape of the fabric, but this requires more skill to achieve and is also more extravagant on fabric. Several swags can be positioned across a large window, but do not attempt this until you are more experienced.

It is well worth experimenting with a cheap soft fabric, such as mull. You can then use the result as your cutting pattern and to estimate your fabric and lining requirements.

Avoid velvet, as it is difficult to handle. Large-patterned fabrics will loose their appeal when combined in a complex swag, and should certainly be avoided for bias-cut swags. The latter should be made up in plain fabrics or those with a small overall design.

The restrained style of this swag and tails is in keeping with the simple décor of the bedroom.

Swags and tails are an elaborate form of valance and as such should be in proportion to their accompanying curtains. As a guide, the depth of the swag and inner edges of the tails should be approximately one sixth the overall curtain length, but the outer edge of the tails should be at least twice this depth. They are normally pinned to a pelmet board in the same way as a pelmet, through pocketed webbing tape, hand stitched to the back. They can be basted more easily directly along the front edge of the board with steel tacks, provided the tacks are covered with braid, but then it cannot be removed.

To make a pattern for a swag, cut a width(s) of mull to equal the length of the front of the board, by approximately twice the proposed finished depth. Join the widths if necessary, to form a rectangle. For a fuller swag, add approximately 4 in. (10 cm.) to either side of the bottom edge of the rectangle, then cut a diagonal line between each bottom corner and the top corners of the swag. The steeper the diagonal line the tighter the folds will be in the swag (fig. 45). Using drawing pins, attach the top edge to the pelmet board. Fold each side of the rectangle into four or five pleats, and pin them side by side along the top edge of the board so that each pleat falls into a soft fold across the swag, forming a gentle curve (fig. 46).

The tails should fold round the returns at the corners of the pelmet board and should extend round the front to at least cover the pinned pleats of the swag. Cut a shape as suggested in fig. 47, bearing in mind the points

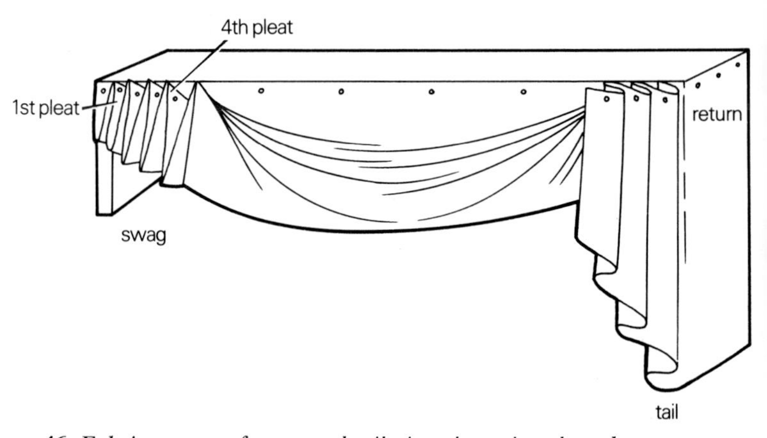

46 Fabric pattern of swag and tail pinned to pelmet board

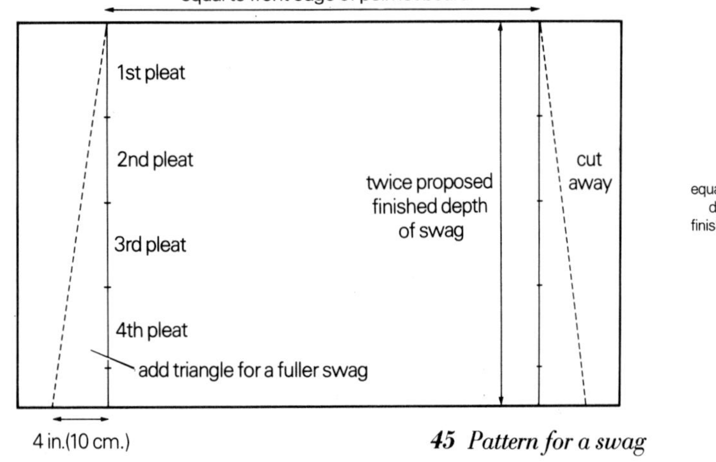

45 Pattern for a swag

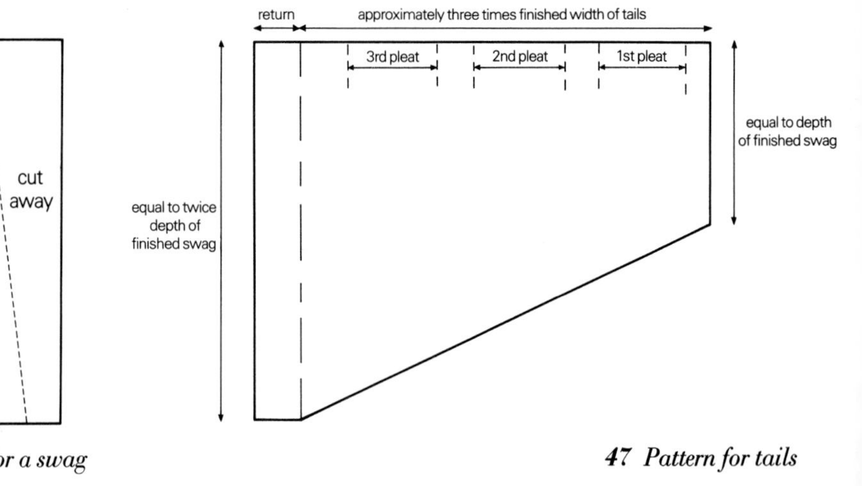

47 Pattern for tails

mentioned above concerning their size. The diagonal line forms the jabot effect. Experiment to get the right proportions and then pin the top edge of the tails into the required number of pleats (two or three), leaving the returns flat. Pin the top of the pleats to the pelmet board over the ends of the swag (fig. 46). Check the whole effect and adapt as necessary.

Remove the pattern from the pelmet board, carefully keeping the pleats folded in order to mark their position with chalk or basting thread before removing the pins.

MAKING UP

Cut out the fabric and lining using the pattern pieces with a ½ in. (1.5 cm.) seam allowance all round. If you need to join widths of fabric for the swag, do so either side of a central panel, as with a pelmet (page 138) and match any patterns. Remember to cut a left- and a right-hand tail. Mark the positions of the pleats with basting stitches.

Swag

With right sides facing, pin and baste the swag to the lining on the stitching line, 1.5 cm (½ in) in from the raw edge, leaving an opening along the top edge to turn it through. Stitch, then trim the seam. Turn right side out and press. Drawstitch to close opening. Stitch braid or fringing to the right side on the lower edge. Fold the sides into the pleats and bring them to lay side by side along the top edge of the swag, pinning and handstitching them securely in position, as previously planned. Stitch braid to the top edge of the swag between the pleats.

Handstitch a length of webbing to the top edge of the lining as for Pelmets (page 138) and pin the swag to the board in the same way.

Tails

With right sides facing, pin and baste the tails to the lining, on the stitching line, leaving an opening to turn through. Machine, then turn right sides out. Press. Drawstitch the opening. Pin the pleats as previously planned and hand stitch securely in position, close to top edge. Stitch braid to the outline of the pleats, covering stitching along top edge. Attach webbing tape to the top edge of tails on the lining side, in the same way as for the swag. Pin them over the pleated ends of the swag, through the pocketed webbing tape on the back.

17 ARCHED WINDOWS

These windows are very elegant and it is well worth taking the trouble to highlight them by shaping the top of the curtains to fit the curve. Curtains for arched windows cannot be fitted onto a conventional track, nor can they be operational in the sense that they can be drawn. The heading must be in a fixed position and fitted to a thin batten which is bent and fixed to the ceiling of the curve. Screw-eyes can be fitted into the front of the batten, equally spaced apart, from which the curtain can be suspended. The curtains can then be draped back and held with tie backs, to form a beautiful outline to the window. The simplest heading to use with this style is a gathered frill as any deep, stiffened pleated heading would be difficult to position around the curve satisfactorily.

TO MAKE A PAIR OF LINED CURTAINS WITH A SHALLOW CURVED TOP

To measure your window, treat it as two sections: the curved area and the rectangular section below it.

Measure and note the lengths at positions halfway (AE) and a quarter of the way across the window (FH) plus the outer edge (CI), as shown in fig. 48, and add the depth of heading. For very wide windows, take further length measurements in between these. The more measurements you take, the more accurately you can plot the curve (fig. 49). Take width measurement CD.

To estimate your fabric and lining requirements, use the width of the rectangle (CD), instead of a track length, to calculate the fabric width, allowing double fullness. Treat the centre of the window AE as your length measurement (including depth of heading) and calculate as normal (page 117) adding hem and heading allowances. You will need to cut all fabric drops to the total length measurement as at the centre of the window. For your heading-tape quantity, you will need to plot the curve as below and double the measurement.

Cut and join the widths of fabric, as for Lined Curtains (page 41), then shape the top of the two curtains in one operation as follows:

Lay the two curtains out flat on top of each other with right sides facing, and bear in mind that one curtain as laid out represents half the window (fig. 49). Mark the hemline with chalk and take one side as the centre leading edge (AE), then measure up along AE from hemline to mark the finished length. Next, mark the finished length from hemline, taken at a quarter of the way across the window (FH), at a position halfway across the fabric. Then mark finished length on the outer edge of the fabric (CI). Continue to mark further finished length measurements across the fabric, if extra measurements were taken, to correspond with the same point across the window.

Draw a line with chalk to connect these points to form the top curve. Add heading allowance by drawing a line parallel to the curve 4 cm (1½ in) away. Cut out on this line through double thickness of fabric. Make up as for Lined Curtains but with a standard gathered heading, as follows:

Heading: Turn 4 cm (1½ in) heading allowance to the wrong side and tack down. The inner edge of the turning will be slightly larger than the curtain it rests against, so it will be necessary to make tucks periodically along the edge so that the turning will lie flat. Add standard tape as in Unlined Curtains. Pull up heading to fit the curve.

For a deep, steep curve it is probably easier and more accurate to take a pattern of half the arch, and spread this to fit the curtain fabric width, as follows:

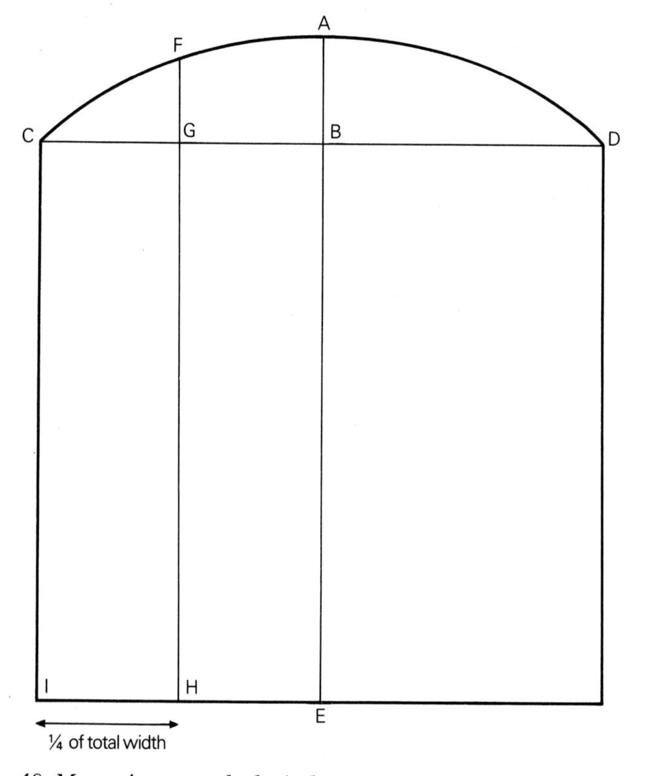

48 Measuring an arched window

TO MAKE A PAIR OF LINED CURTAINS WITH DEEP ARCH

To make a pattern, mask half of the arch with paper and draw round the outline. Remove the pattern and trim round the outline. Then take an additional length measurement along BE.

Calculate fabric requirements, cut out and join widths as for curtains with shallow curved top, and lay curtains out flat in the same manner. Take one side as the centre leading edge. Mark the hemline with chalk, then measure up and mark off length BE on the leading edge and across the fabric width, to form line CB.

It is now necessary to spread your half pattern to fit the width of the curtain fabric as shown in fig. 50b. Cut the pattern from the curved edge to bottom edge at regular intervals (fig. 50a) and place the bottom edge of each strip on the marked line (CB). Spread and space each strip at an equal distance apart, lining up edge AB with the centre leading edge of the curtains. The wider the window the more slashes you should make. Join the highest point of each strip with a chalk line to form a curve. Remove the pattern and add a heading allowance, then continue as for the previous curtains with a shallow curve.

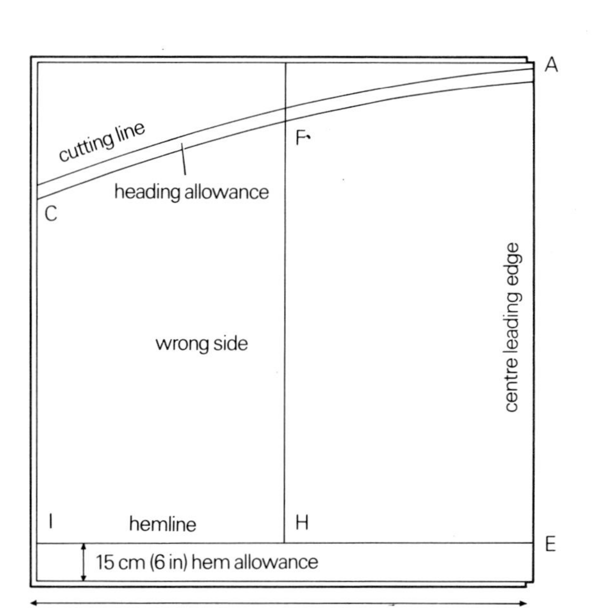

49 *Cutting out and plotting curve on double layer of fabric*

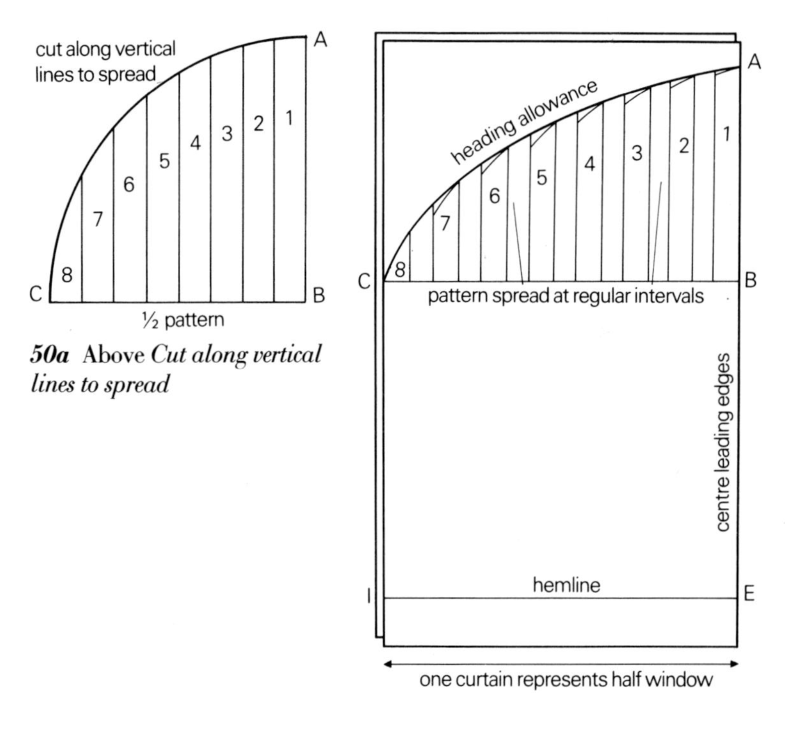

50a Above *Cut along vertical lines to spread*

50b Above right *Cutting out using a pattern for a deep curve, on a double layer of fabric*

18 TIE BANDS

Tie bands hold curtains away from a window or door, allowing the fabric to fall in an attractive drape, while at the same time letting as much light as possible into a room. There are many different styles—stiff, shaped bands blend well with a traditional, formal setting and give a very professional finish. Bows can be tied in satin ribbon or in matching or contrasting fabric. Cords with tassels are available in a good range of colours and thickness and suit heavyweight curtains. Tie bands need to be attached to a tie-back hook.

To establish the size of the tie band, loop a tape measure round the drawn-back curtains; adjust it until the fabric drapes attractively, and note the length of the loop. For bows, add a minimum of 1.50 m (59 in) to this measurement to tie a reasonable sized bow.

STIFF, SHAPED TIE BANDS

It is best to make a paper pattern of your shaped band. Use the half pattern below and enlarge it on dressmaker's graph paper. You will need graph paper to the proposed length of the band. Fold it in half and use the folded edge as the centre of the band. Draw your shape, using the guide and adapting it as necessary to suit your shape and length. Cut round the outline through the double thickness of paper and open out.

For a pair of tie bands you will need approximately 40 cm (16 in) of outer fabric and lining, (use the wastage between pattern repeats for both outer fabric and lining where possible); pelmet buckram 45 cm (18 in) wide to the length of the band; approximately 30 cm (12 in) bump to soften the buckram; two tie-back hooks and two small rings.

Iron the pattern temporarily on to dampened buckram and cut round the outline. Cut out the bump to the exact size of buckram. Cut outer fabric and lining out

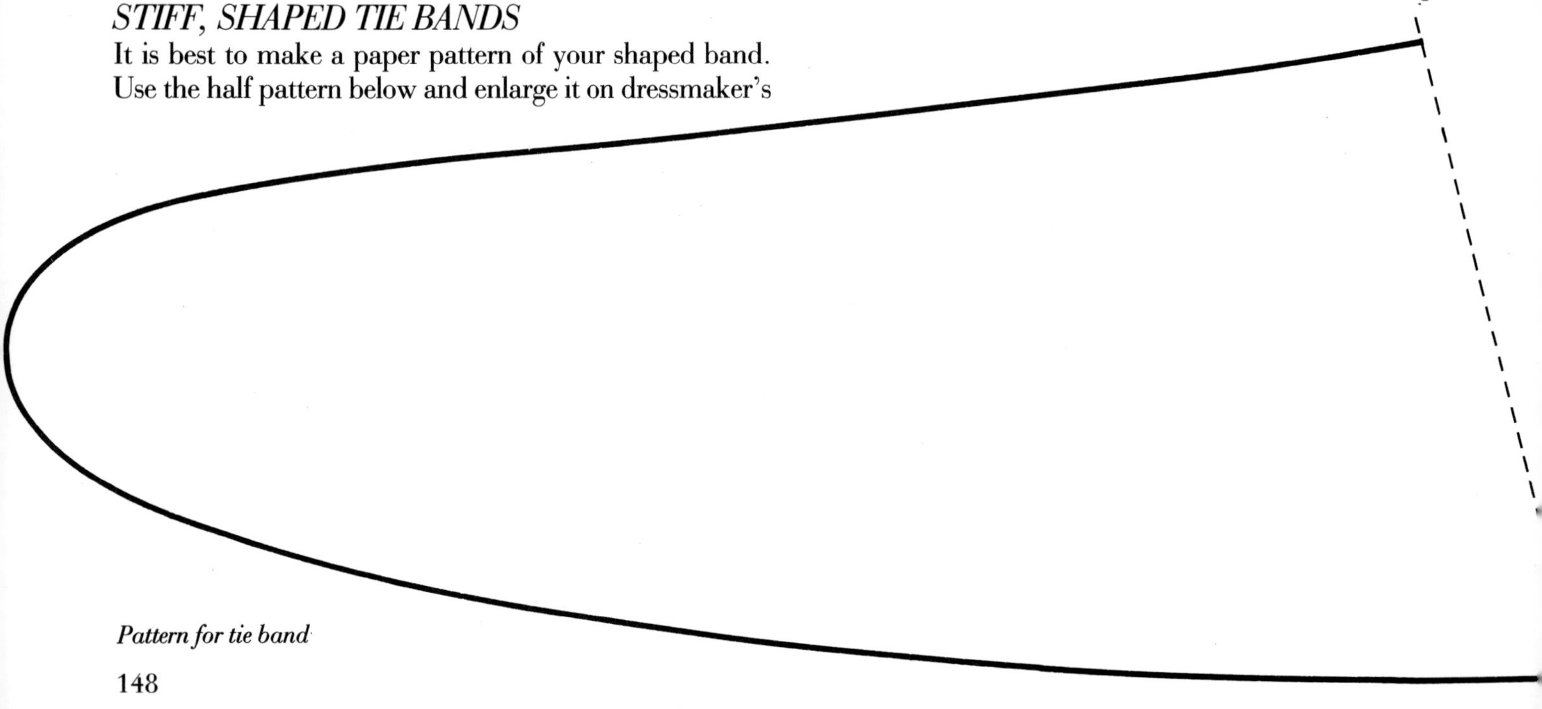

Pattern for tie band

with a 1.5 cm (½ in) seam allowance. Lay bump on one side of the dampened buckram and press to bond the layers together. Lay out the outer fabric flat with the wrong side up and lay buckram on top with the bump sandwiched in between. Dampen the edge of the buckram, bring over the seam allowance of the band and press it on to the dampened edge, notching out excess fabric on inward curves.

Press seam allowance to the wrong side on the lining and notch out in the same way. Pin the lining to the wrong side of the band and slipstitch in place. Sew a ring at either end, on lining side.

FABRIC BOW

Cut strips of fabric to the length measurement described earlier by double the finished width, plus 1 cm (⅜ in) for seam allowances. Join the strips with a plain seam and fold in half lengthways with right sides facing. Machine long edges together with a 5 mm (¼ in) seam allowance, leaving an opening for turning through and stitching diagonal ends. Turn right side out and press. Drawstitch to close opening. Sew a ring in the centre of the band to slip on to a cup hook.

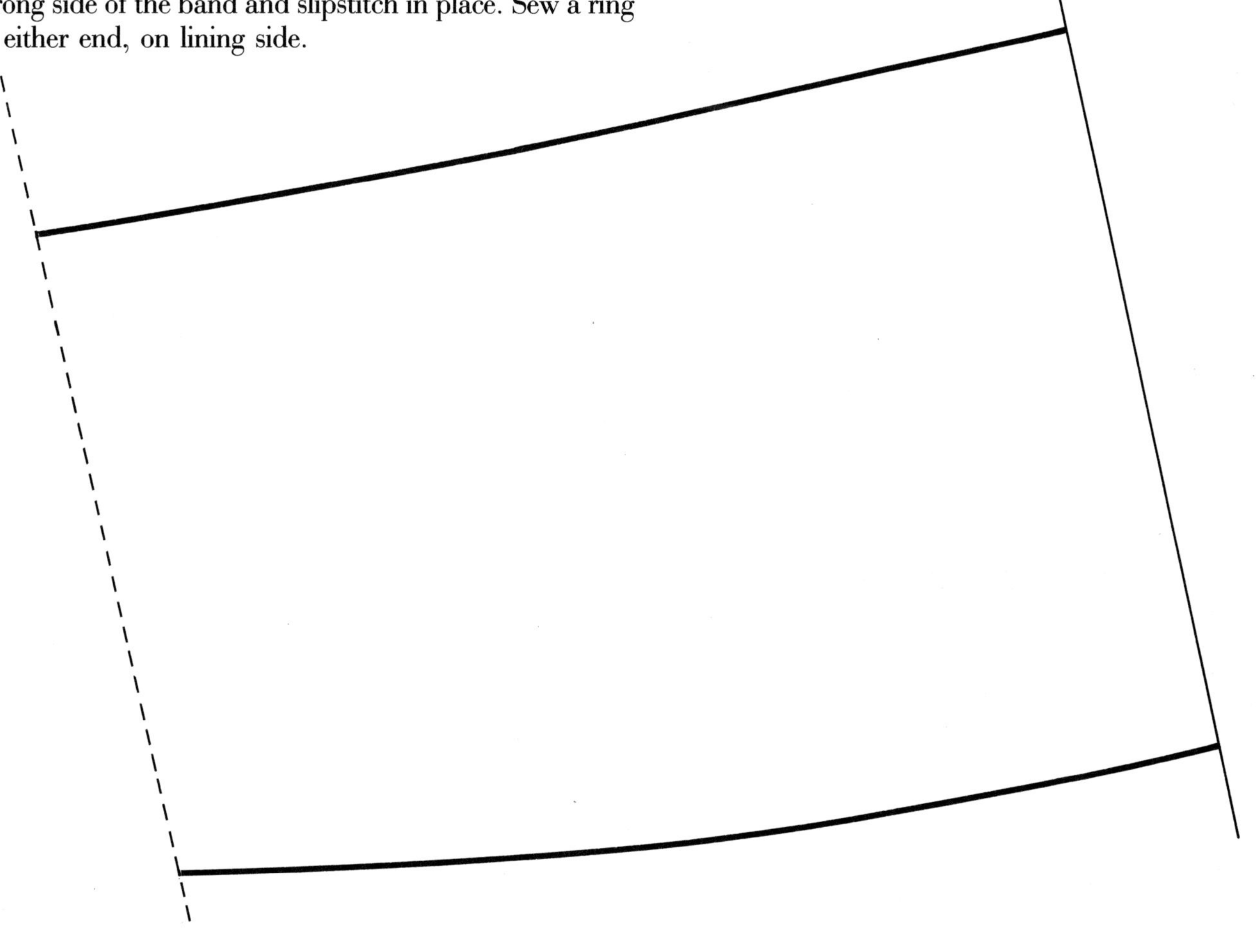

PART III

19 ROLLER BLINDS

These blinds not only offer a practical window treatment for kitchens and bathrooms, but can also look attractive in a sitting-room or bedroom when combined with curtains and made up in co-ordinated or matching fabric. Shaped hemlines are just one way to add a decorative touch. Plain fabrics can be decorated, for instance, with appliqué, or rows of contrasting ribbon. Certain fabrics will take a hand-painted design, using acrylic fabric paints. It is always advisable, however, to test your decorative technique on the fabric.

Ready stiffened and spongeable fabrics especially made for roller blinds can be bought by the metre, and have the additional advantage of being available in widths up to 175 cm (69 in), making joins unnecessary except on the widest of windows. Other fabrics should be closely woven, firm and colourfast, and must be stiffened either with an aerosol spray applied to both sides of the fabric, or by dipping into a liquid stiffening solution. It is advisable to stiffen the fabric before cutting to shape when using the latter method to allow for any possible shrinkage. Thick, textured fabrics are unsuitable as they do not take the stiffening well and also produce too much bulk around the roller. Seams are unsatisfactory on a blind as they too will cause an unattractive bulge on the roller. Where a join is necessary, it is better to glue overlapped edges together with a narrow 1 cm (3⁄8 in) overlap. Alternatively, there is one kit on the market which includes narrow double-sided tape for this purpose. In many ways, however, it would be far more satisfactory to make two smaller blinds to hang side by side.

A roller blind is the simplest type of blind to make and there are several types of kit available to aid the task. All kits have accompanying instructions which should be followed carefully.

MEASURING AND ESTIMATING

Measure your window before buying your kit and fabric, using a metal rule. If fitting your blind inside a window recess you will need to measure the full recess width and depth. If fixing outside the recess, you will need to add a minimum of 10 cm (4 in) to the width of the reveal to prevent light seeping through at the sides of the blind. Your length should allow for whatever overlap you require at the top and bottom of the window.

Kits are available to fit window widths up to 245 cm (8 ft) and if the size of your window falls between sizes, buy the next size up and cut it to size according to the manufacturer's instructions.

You will need fabric fractionally wider than the measured width, by the measured length plus a minimum of 20 cm (8 in) to allow enough fabric to cover

The use of several smaller blinds at a large window, or in a bay, provides freedom to adjust the natural lighting, and creates visual interest.

the roller when pulled down, and to form a channel for a lath. For a blind with a shaped hemline, a further allowance should be added for facing the shaped edge; allow a depth of between 8 and 15 cm (3–6 in) for this depending on the depth of the edging below the lath.

TO MAKE A ROLLER BLIND WITH STRAIGHT HEMLINE

Accuracy in measuring and cutting out is essential. Mount the supporting brackets first, according to the manufacturer's instructions. Then measure the exact distance between the slot on one bracket and the round hole on the other. Cut the roller to this measurement less 3 mm (⅛ in) to allow for the end cap. Fix the end cap with the round pin over the cut end.

If using liquid stiffening solution, first stiffen the fabric, having ironed out any creases. The fabric must be cut with right-angled corners. Measure and mark the fabric to the length of the measurements taken, plus allowances for covering roller and lath. Mark the width of the blind 1.2 cm (⅜ in) less than the cut roller length with two parallel chalk lines, remembering that these lines must be square to the top and bottom marked edges. Centre any pattern. If your fabric is likely to fray, it is advisable to machine a row of zig-zag stitches inside the marked side lines and up against them. Cut out the blind with sharp scissors on the marked lines and/or against the zig-zag stitching.

Hemline

Lay the blind out flat with wrong side uppermost and form the lath channel by turning 1 cm (⅜ in) up to the wrong side along the bottom edge, then turn up a further 4 cm (1½ in). Machine in place. If your fabric is very stiff, make one 4 cm turning and zig-zag stitch over the raw edge or glue in place. Apply any trimming with glue.

Finishing off

Stitch on any surface decoration before spraying the blind. Finally apply any braid trim with glue.

To finish off all blinds, attach the blind fabric to the roller according to the manufacturer's instructions. Insert pulling cord through the cord holder and screw it to the centre of the lath on the wrong side. Insert roller into supporting brackets and adjust the tension according to the manufacturer's instructions.

20 ROMAN BLINDS

A Roman blind offers a smart, clean-cut finish to a window, with its pleats forming a soft layered pelmet when the blind is raised. These blinds are not suitable for very shallow windows as there would be insufficient depth of fabric to form into pleats. On wider windows, two smaller blinds side by side may be better.

There are two methods of making these blinds; Method 1 gives a professional finish using narrow wooden laths, which are slotted into channels in the lining to keep the pleats defined and neatly layered; Method 2 is simpler, using vertical rows of tape and rings, and creates a softer, less rigid line which is more suitable for use at a small window.

The blinds can be fitted on to a wooden batten with touch-and-close fastener for easy removal, and are operated by pulling up cords which pass through rings on the back of the blind, then through screw-eyes on the underside of the batten.

They are easy and inexpensive to make as they require only enough outer fabric to cover the actual window opening, or your desired size, plus a little extra lining when making up as Method 1. It is essential to use closely woven, firm fabric of good quality which is on grain. It is also important to measure and cut fabric accurately to ensure that the pleats not only lie squarely on top of each other when the blind is pulled up but also to ensure that the blind hangs squarely when down. Problems occur particularly when the fabric is printed off grain and the pleats follow a horizontal design on the fabric. This could result in the blind and pleats falling at an angle to the window.

METHOD 1

Measuring and estimating materials
For fitting inside a reveal, measure the window width and length. If fitting outside, extend the blind width by at least 5 cm (2 in) either side, and add to the length measurement sufficient for whatever overlap you require at top and bottom of the window.

Planning
To calculate the number and size of the pleats, the blind length is divided horizontally into sections which form the pleats. These sections should be twice the depth of a bottom pelmet, on top of which all the pleats lie. The depth of the bottom section is also approximately equal to the depth of the 'pelmet' which forms from the layered pleats when the blind is raised. To ensure that all the pleats lie at one level when the blind is raised, the top pleat section should be slightly deeper than those below it in order to cover the front of the batten and to allow for the depth of lath and rings which accumulate at the top of the blind when it is raised. Add approximately 8 cm (3⅛ in) to the top pleat section for this purpose.

Example: Overall length 132 cm (52 in)—Bottom pelmet 14 cm (5½ in); three pleat sections of 28 cm (11 in); top pleat 34 cm (13½ in). Bear in mind that all sections must add up to the overall length measurement.

Materials
Outer fabric to the measurements taken plus 3 cm (1¼ in) for top and bottom turnings (plus a further 7.5 cm (3 in) to enable the top of the blind to lie over the heading batten if fitting outside the window reveal). To the width measurement add 6 cm (2⅜ in) for side turnings.

Lining To the finished width measurement by length measurement plus an extra 7 cm (2¾ in) for each lath channel positioned at the base of each pleat (exclude channel at the base of the blind); plus 3 cm (1¼ in) for top and bottom turnings.

A *softwood batten* 50 mm × 25 mm (2 in × 1 in) to the finished width, plus angle brackets to fix it in position, and three large screw-eyes.

Laths: 25 mm × 5 mm (1 in × ¼ in) by the width of the blind less 20 mm (¾ in); you will need one for the base of the blind and one for each channel.

Plastic rings: allow two for each channel except the bottom one.

Nylon cord: To calculate the amount, add together the width of the blind plus four times the length.

Touch-and-close fastener to the width of the finished blind, plus a cleat to hold the cord.

Matching *thread*.

Making up
Cut the blind fabric with side, top and bottom turnings. Turn 3 cm (1¼ in) to the wrong side on each side edge and herringbone stitch in place.

Lining
Having decided on the number of pleats required, cut the lining as mentioned under *Materials*, above. Pin 1 cm

(⅜ in) to the wrong side along the sides and machine in place. On the right side, mark the stitching lines of the channels with a faint chalk-line (fig. 51). To form the channels above bottom pelmet, bring the pairs of stitching lines together and pin with the wrong sides facing; this will form the channels on the right side of the lining (fig. 52). Tack, then machine along these lines.

Attaching lining to blind

Join the lining to the blind at hemline by placing it centrally over the blind fabric with right sides facing and bottom raw edges level. Pin, tack, then machine along the seamline. 1.5 cm (⅝ in) in from raw edge. Trim seam allowance to 5 mm (¼ in). Turn right side out and press the hemline.

Lay the blind out flat with lining uppermost. Make sure the lining is lying perfectly flat and smooth against blind fabric and square to it. Then pin the lining to the outer fabric across the full width of the blind, starting 3.5 cm (1⅜ in) up from the bottom edge to form the lower channel at the base of the blind. Then pin the lining to the blind as close as possible to each stitching line forming the channels, across the full blind width. Tack, then machine in place, ensuring that the stitching lines are perfectly horizontal and parallel to each other, and make sure you have not caught any of the channel fabric in the stitching. Pin the sides of the lining to the blind, excluding the ends of the channels, then slipstitch (fig. 53).

Finishing off

Turn 1.5 cm (⅝ in) of blind fabric and lining to the wrong side along the top edge. Pin, tack then machine

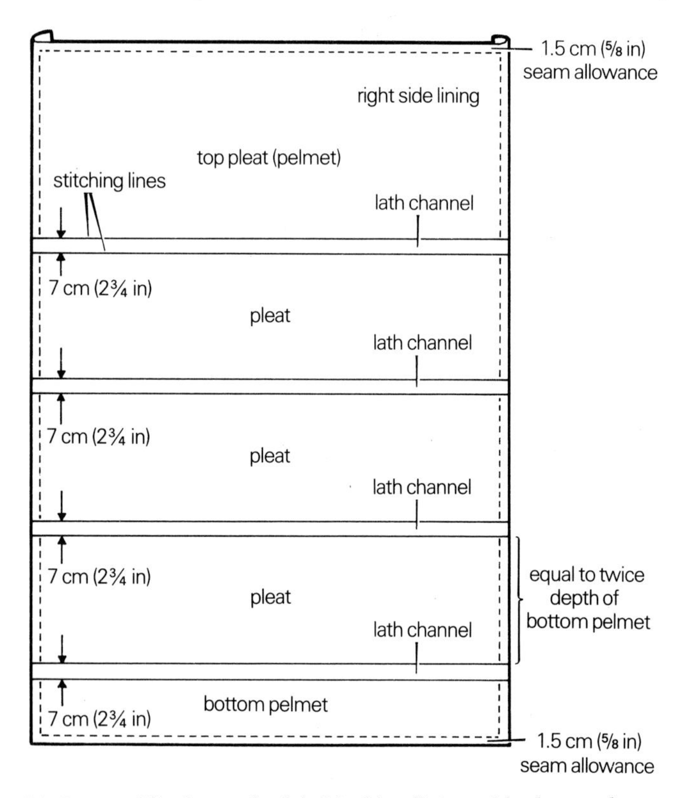

***51** Roman blind—method 1; Marking lining with pleat and channel sections*

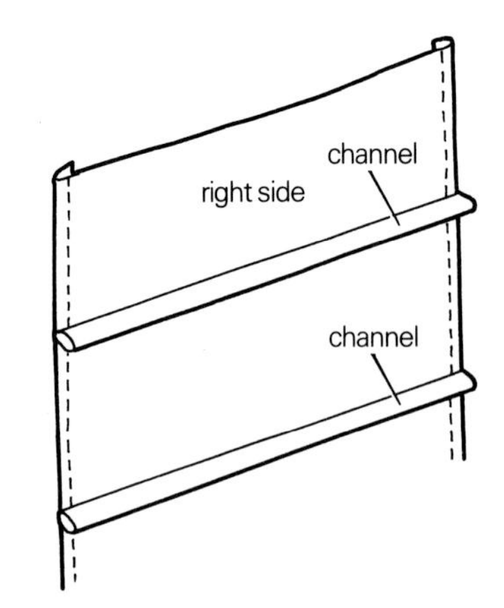

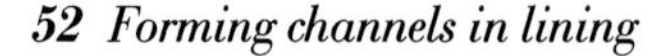

***52** Forming channels in lining*

the soft side of touch-and-close fastener over the raw edges.

Insert a lath into each channel, then slipstitch the ends together. Stitch two rings to each channel, except the bottom one, approximately 10 cm (4 in) in from the sides.

To cord the blind, cut one length of cord approximately twice the length of the blind, and another to the same length plus the blind width. Decide from which side you wish to operate the blind. Tie a length of cord to each of the lowest rings, placing the shortest length nearest the operational side.

Optional: Neatly cover the batten by wrapping fabric round, folding in the ends and holding in place with steel tacks.

Attach the remaining side of touch-and-close fastener to the front edge of the batten with steel tacks or along the top back edge of batten if fitting outside a reveal. Screw two screw-eyes to the underside of the batten to correspond with the two rows of vertical rings, and a third one close to the end of the batten on the operational side.

Fix the batten in place with angle brackets, then attach the blind with touch-and-close fastener. Thread cord up through rings and corresponding screw-eyes and out to the operational side. Tie cords together close to the outer screw-eye.

Screw cleat in position at the side of the window and pull up the blind. Wind the excess cord round the cleat to hold in open position (fig. 54).

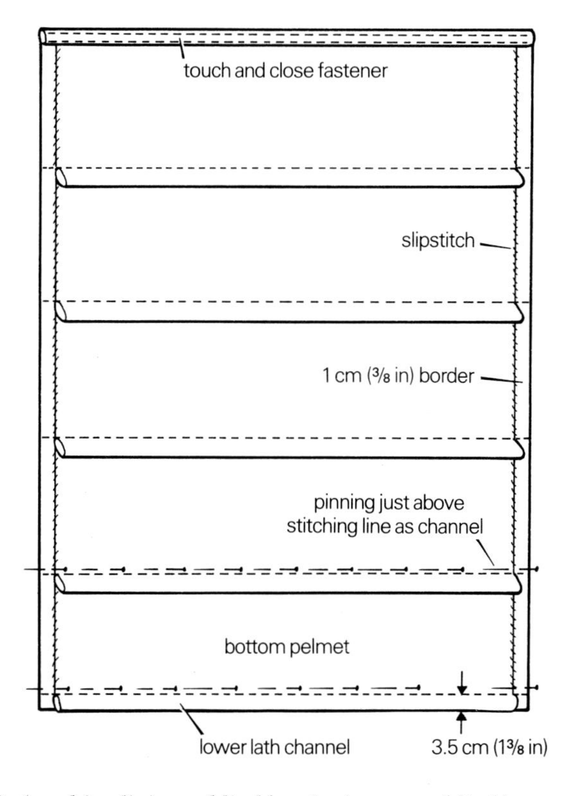

***53** Attaching lining to blind by pinning across blind in same position as channels*

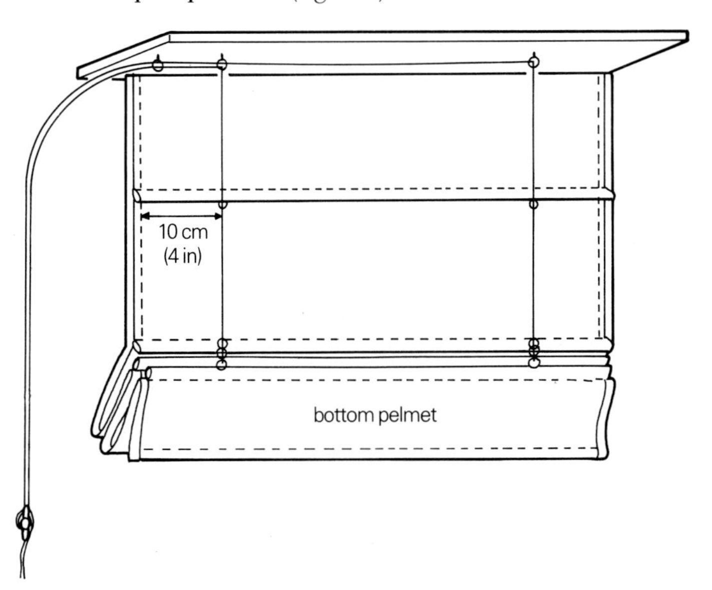

***54** Blind fixed to batten and cords threaded to operational side*

METHOD 2

This version has vertical rows of tapes spaced evenly across the back of the blind. Rings are attached along these tapes to form horizontal rows of rings. The pleats are formed by pulling on cords which are attached to the lower row of rings at the lath position above the bottom pelmet, and which pass up through the rings. The distance between the horizontal rows of rings should be twice the depth of the bottom pelmet to make a pleat the same size as the pelmet. On small windows, using fine fabric, as little as 10 cm (4 in) could be allocated to make a 5 cm (2 in) pleat and pelmet, but on larger windows allow between 15 and 20 cm (6 and 8 in) for a 7.5 cm (3 in) and 10 cm (4 in) pleat respectively. Measure and plan as Method 1.

NB Straight seam tape can be used instead of pocketed tape, but you will then need to sew on rings individually.

Materials

Blind *fabric* and *lining* to the width and length measurements, plus an additional 3 cm (1¼ in) on width and length for turnings.

Narrow *pocketed tape* to make vertical rows approximately 30 cm (12 in) apart (gathering tape is suitable but ignore the draw cords).

Split rings enough to position along each vertical row of tape, and spaced according to the size of the finished pleat (e.g., every 20 cm (8 in) for a 10 cm (4 in) pleat).

Nylon cord to equal the length of each vertical row of tape plus enough to thread across the top of the blind and out to one side, and then down one side.

Touch-and-close fastener to the width of the finished blind.

A *softwood batten* as Method 1, plus a screw-eye for every vertical row of tape. One *lath*, as Method 1. One *cleat*. Matching *thread*.

Making up

Cut the fabric and lining to the measurements plus turnings. With right sides facing, pin and tack the lining to the outer fabric on the seamline, 1.5 cm (⅝ in) in from the raw edge, along the side and bottom edge. Trim seams and cut diagonally across corners. Turn right side out and press.

Lay blind out flat with lining uppermost, and mark the position of the lath channel by measuring up from the hemline to a distance equal to the depth of the bottom pelmet. Draw a second line parallel to the first, 3 cm (1¼ in) away. Tack, then machine the lining to the outer fabric along these marked lines to form lath channel. Unpick stitching along one side between channel stitching to insert lath at a later stage.

At the top of the blind, turn 1.5 cm (⅝ in) to the wrong side and pin and tack the soft side of the touch-and-close fastener over the raw edge. Machine.

Mark the vertical lines for the tapes across the width of the blind at equal distances apart, approximately every 30 cm (12 in), the first and last rows starting and ending 1.5 cm (½ in) in from the sides of the blind. Cut the appropriate number of lengths of tape to the length measurement of the blind from the lath channel. Pin, and tack the tape over the marked lines, turning cut edge under at the top and bottom. Machine along both edges of the tape through the lining and the outer fabric.

Insert split rings along each tape, spacing them at an equal distance spart, at a distance to equal twice the depth of the bottom pelmet starting at lath channel. They should also align horizontally across the blind (fig. 55).

Insert the lath into the channel and slipstitch the end.

Decide from which side you wish to operate the blind. Cut a length of cord for each vertical tape, twice its length plus the distance from tape to the operational side of the blind. Tie a cord to each bottom ring and thread it up through the rings on each tape.

The clean lines of these Roman blinds fit in well with the sharp, uncluttered décor and furnishing.

Cover the batten and attach the opposite side of touch-and-close fastener, as Method 1. Insert screw-eyes to the underside of the batten to correspond with each row of tape.

Attach the blind to the batten and thread each cord through its corresponding screw-eye, then out to the operational side, passing through each screw-eye it passes. Tie the cords together and fix cleat in position.

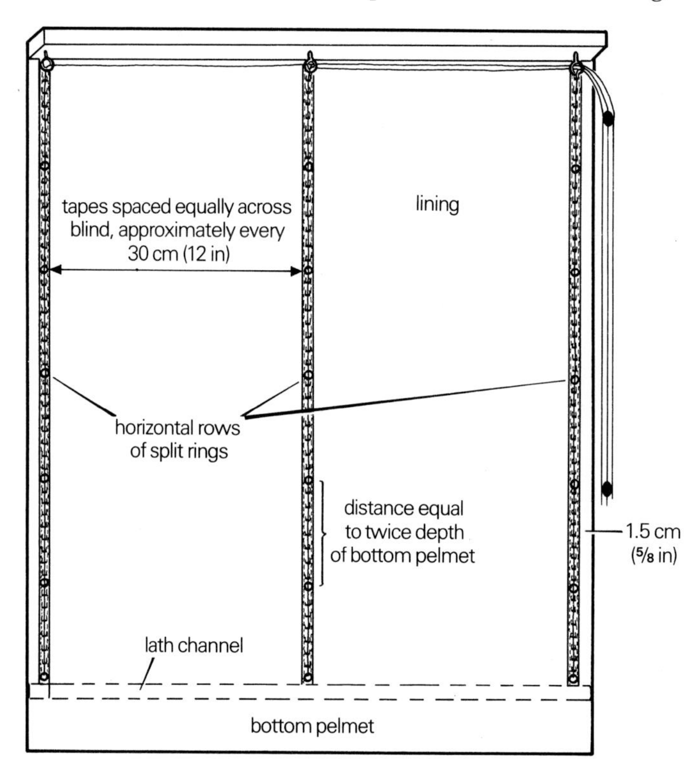

55 Roman blind—method 2

21 *FESTOON BLINDS*

These pretty blinds give a soft, flamboyant appearance and form a scalloped hemline when drawn up. Frills can be added to the hemline and sides to further enhance their feminine appeal. Made up in lightweight fabrics, either soft or crisp, each will offer a pleasing but different effect. The former will allow the scallops to drape in folds, while the latter will create fuller, puffed scallops.

The blind can be fitted inside or outside a window reveal, and is attached to a batten and operates in a similar way to Roman Blinds, Method 2, with cords threaded through vertical rows of rings on the back of the blind (fig. 55, above). They can have a gathered or

A festoon blind used inside the window reveal gives a neat, tailored look that suits the restrained style of the room.

pencil pleated heading, which gives the fullness to the blind to create the festoons. Generally, they need fullness of two to two and a quarter times the batten length (the fuller the fabric the deeper the festoons). They look like curtains when they are down but are made slightly longer than the window length to allow for the scalloped hemline to fall at sill level. They can be lined or unlined; have rings which are handsewn in position or split rings which slot into pocketed tape. The latter method will show the stitching securing the tapes on the right side.

MEASURING AND ESTIMATING MATERIALS

Measure the width of the window opening if fitting inside the reveal, or to your desired width if fitting outside. You will need a batten to this width. For the length, measure from the top of the batten position (inside or outside reveal) to the sill. Add to this measurement 6 cm (2½ in) for hem and heading allowance, and a minimum of 20 cm (8 in) which allows the scalloped hemline to form at sill level when the blind is down, by pulling up the cords fractionally.

To estimate your fabric requirements, multiply the batten length by the desired fullness, two to two and a quarter times, then calculate as for curtains (page 29), adding extra for matching any pattern. If it is necessary to round up to the next width of fabric do not automatically include the extra fullness in the blind. Adding too much fullness to the blind will make the swags heavy and droopy. Use full and half widths in the main, and use any wastage for frills and covering the batten.

TO MAKE AN UNLINED FESTOON BLIND

with pocketed tape and split rings

Planning

You will need to establish the size and number of scallops across the blind in order to calculate the amount of tape needed. The width of an average sized scallop on a finished blind is approximately 30 cm (12 in). Bearing this in mind, divide the batten length into equal sized scallops, and add one to the number of scallops to give the number of vertical rows of tape needed; e.g., three scallops will need four rows of tape. These tapes are spaced across the total width of the fabric at an equal distance apart, bearing in mind that the distance between them will be two to two and a quarter times the finished scallop width, depending on the fullness you allowed. If possible, plan to cover any seams with a row of tape.

Example Batten length 90 cm (36 in) using double fullness (180 cm/6 ft), i.e., 1½ widths of 120 cm (48 in) wide fabric:

Makes 3 scallops each 30 cm (12 in) wide 4 rows of tape spaced 60 cm (24 in) apart (fig. 56).

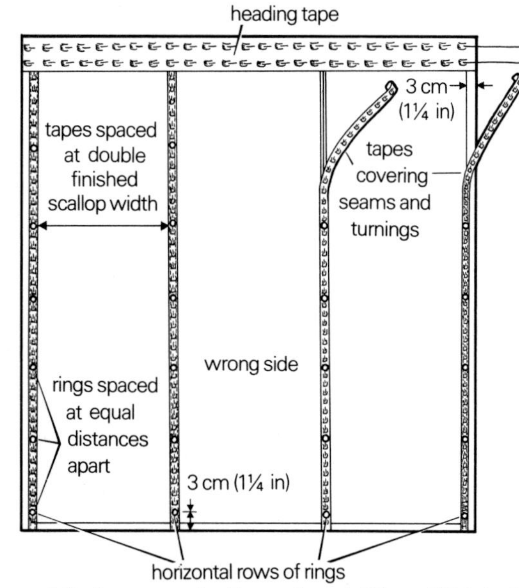

***56** Festoon blind—example: Batten length 90 cm (36 in); 1½ widths of fabric. Double fullness. Finished scallop width 30 cm (12 in)*

A festoon blind with pencil heading fitted inside the reveal gives a fresh, country look to this kitchen.

Materials

In addition to the blind fabric, as calculated above, you will need:

Pocketed *curtain tape* 1.7 cm (5/8 in) wide to equal the length of the blind for every row as calculated. Enough *split rings* to insert every 20 cm (8 in) along each row of tape. Curtain *heading tape* to total width of fabric. *Curtain hooks. Nylon cord* for each vertical row of tape, plus enough to thread across the top of the blind to one side and down side of blind. Matching *thread. Softwood batten* and *angle brackets* as for Roman Blind. Large *screw-eyes* for every vertical row of tape *Cleat. Staples* or small *screw-eyes* to space approximately every 6 cm (2½ in) along the front of the batten.

Making up

Cut the required number of widths of fabric and join them, matching any pattern, with a 1 cm (3/8 in) plain seam if they are to be covered by tape. Otherwise make a narrow french or mock french seam.

Turn 3 cm (1¼ in) to the wrong side along the side edges and tack in place. Make a narrow double-stitched hem (page 38) along the hemline.

Apply the heading tape of your choice (see Lined or Unlined Curtains).

Mark the position of the vertical tapes by folding the width of the blind into as many equal sections as the number of scallops and press lightly to form creaselines (fig. 57). Cut the required number of tapes to the length

2-2.5 cm (3/4-1 in)
finished width of scallop

57 Blind folded into as many equal sections as the number of scallops and pressed to mark crease lines for tapes

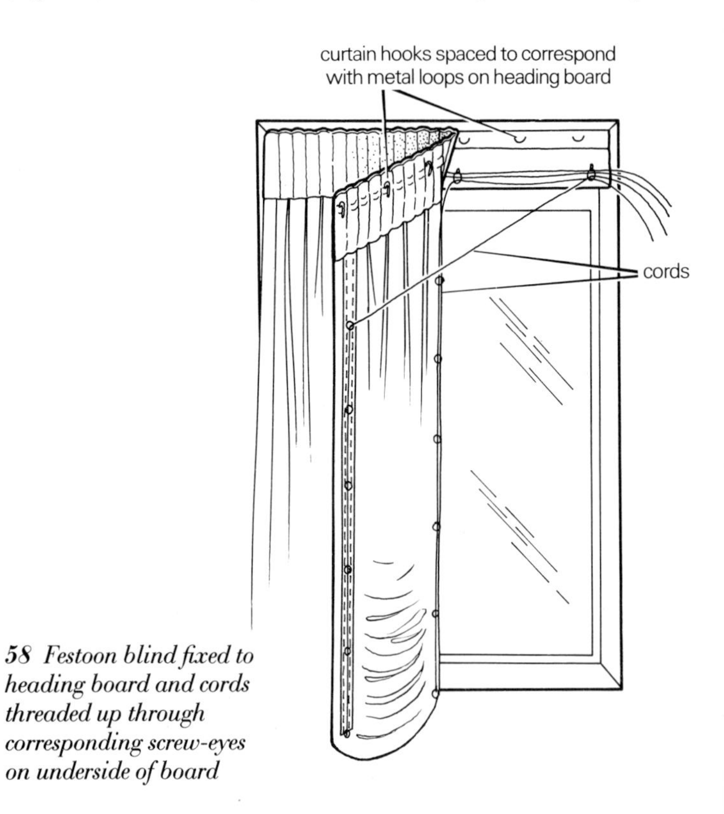

58 Festoon blind fixed to heading board and cords threaded up through corresponding screw-eyes on underside of board

of the blind fabric. Pin and tack them over the creaseline on the wrong side. Position the outer tapes over the raw edges of side turnings. Turn under the cut ends of tape at the top and bottom. Machine the tape along both edges.

Insert split rings along each tape at equal distances apart, approximately every 20 cm (8 in), starting 5 cm (2 in) up from the hem, and finishing about 15 cm (6 in) from the heading tape. Make sure the rings align horizontally across the blind.

Draw up the heading tape to fit the batten. Scallops should now be of equal size and measure their planned finished width. Insert the curtain hooks into heading tape every 6 cm (2½ in).

Neatly cover the batten as for a Roman Blind. Attach large screw-eyes to the underside to correspond with the rows of tape. Hammer large staples halfway in to form loops, or attach screw-eyes along the front edge of the batten spaced every 6 cm (2½ in).

Decide from which side you wish to operate the blind, then cut and attach lengths of cord as for Roman Blind, Method 2. Attach the blind to the batten by inserting a curtain hook into each loop of staple, or screw-eye (fig. 58). Thread the cords through the screw-eyes on the underside of the batten as for Roman Blind, Method 2 (fig. 55). Fix cleat in position, then pull cord to raise the blind, winding the excess round the cleat.

22 RUCHED BLINDS

A ruched blind with its ruffled, scalloped surface, may give the impression of using an excessive amount of fabric, but in fact it can take about the same as a festoon blind, as very little fullness is needed across its width. The effect is achieved by gathering additional fabric along the length of the blind. The amount of extra length can vary enormously to suit the type of fabric chosen and the desired finished effect. The finer the fabric used, the more length should be allowed. Soft lightweight fabrics which gather well are most suitable. Thick fabrics, particularly when used in conjunction with too much fullness, will create heavy swags which are liable to droop. These blinds are normally unlined and are often made up in sheer fabrics which are left down permanently.

Additional surface decoration is unnecessary other than, perhaps, a frill on the hemline to echo the side frill which automatically forms when the blind is gathered up along the tapes.

They are made and operated in a similar way to festoon blinds but often using more closely spaced vertical rows of gathering tape, and when drawn up the blind has an even fuller effect. No heading tape is necessary and the blinds are attached to a heading batten with touch-and-close fastener. By using narrow curtain tape to gather up the blind length (as opposed to permanent gathering stitches) the fullness can be released for cleaning. A covered lath is fitted across the back of the blind just above the scalloped hemline to keep the blind in shape (except with sheers).

TO MAKE A RUCHED BLIND WITH FRILLED HEMLINE

Measure the window width and length as for Festoon Blinds.

Width Multiply the batten length by one and a quarter to one and a half times fullness and add 6 cm (2½ in) for side turnings. Divide the result by the width of your chosen fabric to give the number of fabric widths. If it is necessary to round up to the next full width, do not automatically include all the extra fabric width in the blind as this will make the scallops deep and heavy. Use any wastage from the width for a frill and/or covering the batten and lath. Bear in mind that it is possible to make this type of blind without any fullness in the width, but with the resulting effect of tight rows of ruching and only a slight scallop on the hemline. Only use the maximum fullness when using the minimum extra length.

Length You will need to multiply the *measured length* by between one and a half to three times, depending on the weight of your fabric, to give your *cutting length*.

Fabric Requirements To calculate your blind fabric requirements, multiply the number of widths by the *cutting length*. Allow extra for matching a pattern. If there is no wastage on the width of fabric, you will also need extra for a frill and for covering a batten and lath. For a double-sided frill, you will need enough strips of fabric to equal twice the width of the blind fabric by twice the desired depth of frill, plus 4 cm (1½ in) for seam allowances.

Scallops The width of a finished scallop can be between 25–30 cm (10–12 in), depending on your fabric. Bearing this in mind, calculate the size and number of scallops, and rows of tape needed, as for Festoon Blinds. The tapes are spaced across the fabric in the same way, i.e., an equal distance apart, but spaced, in this instance, so that the distance between them will be one and a quarter to one and a half times the finished scallop width. Plan to cover any seams where this is possible.

To calculate the amount of gathering tape (1.7 cm ⅝ in wide) needed, multiply the number of rows of tape by the fabric cutting length and add 6 cm (2½ in) for each row for finishing off the tape.

Additional materials

In addition to the blind fabric and tape, you will need:

Enough *split rings* to insert along each tape at approximately 20–25 cm (8–10 in) intervals, after the blind has been gathered up to its finished length. The distance between the rings will vary according to the thickness and fullness of the fabric chosen, but they must be spaced at regular intervals. *Touch-and-close fastener* to the length of the batten. Matching *thread; nylon cord, softwood batten, angle brackets* and large *screw-eyes* as for Festoon Blinds. One *lath* as for Roman Blind. *Cleat.*

Making up

Cut out the required number of widths of fabric to the length calculated, and join them as for Festoon Blind.

Turn 3 cm (1¼ in) to the wrong side along the sides and tack down.

Divide the hem line into four equal sections and mark with a pin.

Making the double-sided frill

Cut strips of fabric as calculated and join the strips with right sides together to form one long strip using a plain seam. Press seam open. Fold and press the strip in half lengthways with wrong sides facing.

Divide the frill into four and mark these sections. Machine one row of stitching on the seamline of the frill, 2 cm (¾ in) in from the raw edge, using long stitches and loose tension. Break the thread periodically to make small sections which will ease gathering up later.

Machine a second row of stitching 5 mm (¼ in) away from the first within the seam allowance, breaking the thread at the same position as on the first row (fig. 59). Pull the bobbin threads so that each quarter section of the frill equals a quarter section of the width of the hem.

Pin the prepared frill to the hem line with right sides facing and raw edges level, matching up the quarter

Ruched blinds have a full, pretty appearance.

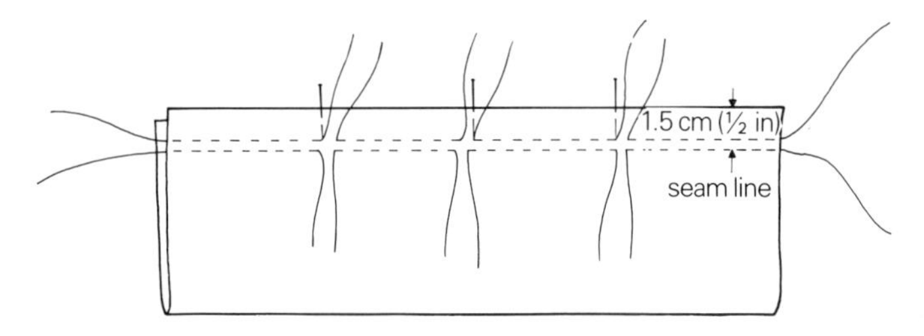

59 Machine gathering

sections. Distribute the gathers evenly and tack, then machine frill in place on seamline 2 cm (¾ in) in from raw edge. Finish off seam allowance with a self-bound finish.

Trim seam allowance of gathered frill only to a scant 5 mm (¼ in) (fig. 60a). Then turn in 5 mm (¼ in) on the seam allowance of the blind and fold the turning over the trimmed seam allowance of frill (fig. 60b). Pin, then slipstitch the binding to the machine stitching line.

At the top of the blind, turn 2 cm (¾ in) to the wrong side and sew two rows of temporary gathering stitches within this allowance by hand or machine.

Mark the position of the vertical rows of tape as for Festoon Blind. Lay the blind out flat with wrong side uppermost. Cut the required number of tapes, to the fabric cutting length plus 6 cm (2½ in) for finishing off. At one end of each tape, remove 4 cm (1½ in) of cord and knot the ends together. Trim the tape to 1.5 cm (½ in). Position this end over the frill seam allowance on hemline, turning under the knot and cut end. Pin the vertical rows of tape over the creaselines and sides as for Festoon Blind, but at the opposite end of the tapes, remove 4 cm (1½ in) of cord, trim tape to 1.5 cm (½ in) leaving the cord free for pulling up at a later stage. Turn under the cut end, finishing the top of each tape 2 cm (¾ in) down from the top of the blind. Tack, then machine the tapes in place along both edges (fig. 61). Pull up the gathering stitches along the top of the blind until the blind width measures the length of the batten and spread the gathers evenly so that the scallops are of equal width. Pin the soft side of touch-and-close fastener to the wrong side of the top of the blind, covering the raw edge of the top turning. Pin, then machine in place. Remove the temporary gathering stitches.

Pull up the draw cords on each vertical row of tape until each tape measures the finished blind length. Spread the gathers evenly. Tie the cords neatly at the top of each tape. Insert split rings at regular intervals starting approximately 3 cm (1¼ in) up from the bottom of the

60a Self-bound seam finish

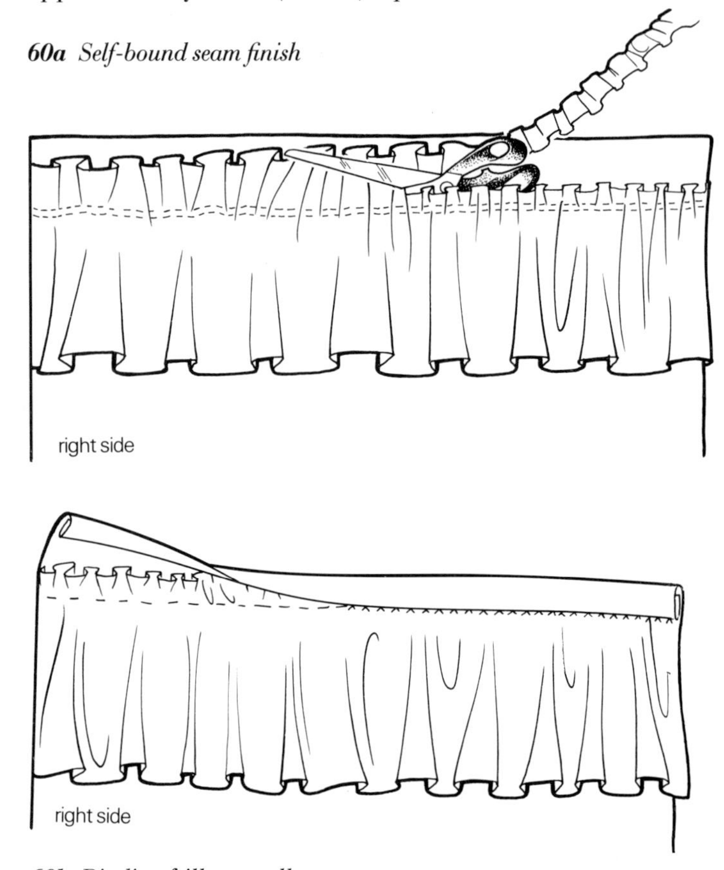

60b Binding frill seam allowance

tape and spacing them between 20–25 cm (8–10 in) apart, ensuring that they align horizontally across the blind.

Cover the lath by making a casing. Cut a strip of fabric to the finished width of the blind by 10 cm (4 in) wide. Turn 1 cm (3/8 in) to the wrong side on two long edges and one short edge, then fold strip in half lengthways with wrong sides together. Topstitch sides together close to folded edges. Insert lath, then finish the casing by turning in the ends and drawstitching to close. Attach the lath with a few hand stitches to the wrong side of the blind, to the base of each tape, making sure that the width between each tape is equal and measures the finished width of the scallops as planned. This will draw the blind to the finished width at the hemline and scallops will form below the lath (fig. 62).

Attach the cords and finish off the blind as for Roman Blinds, Method 2.

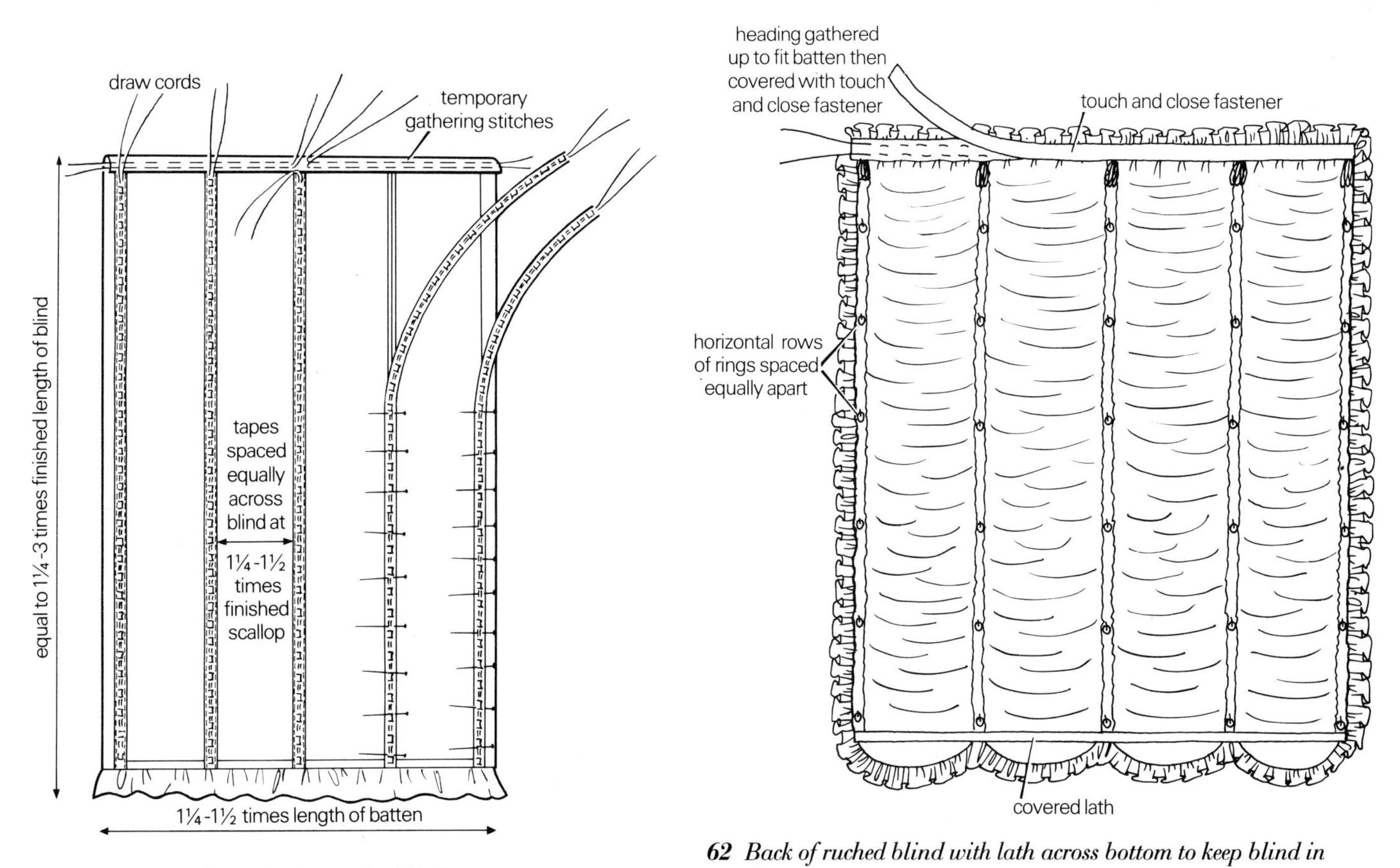

61 *Attaching tapes for gathering up the blind*

62 *Back of ruched blind with lath across bottom to keep blind in shape*

These eye-catching bolster cushions, which have been made to look like crackers, contrast with the plain bed cover

PART I

1 *THE PERSONAL TOUCH*

The most important aspect of furnishing a home is that you should feel entirely comfortable with the end result. Magazines and books may inspire you to re-think your ideas but however you choose to furnish a room it should reflect your personality.

Although cushions and covers are considered to be the finishing touches to a room, they can become the focal point and their importance should not be overlooked. A plain sofa can be transformed by the addition of several brightly-coloured cushions. A rather worn suite can be brought right up to date with a loose cover in a stunning modern print.

Today, when so much of our furniture is mass produced, you can run the risk of living in a home that is identical to those of your friends and neighbours. Sewing your own cushions and covers can give your home that personal touch which makes all the difference.

CREATING THE RIGHT EFFECT

One of the first decisions to be made about furnishing a room is knowing the type of image you want to create. You might like to keep in mind the period of your house and whether you want to furnish it accordingly. A stone cottage is the perfect setting for floral prints in pretty colours; a modern flat, with its stark interior, would be complemented by simple modern furniture using strong geometric shapes and contrasting colours, such as black and white. Alternatively, you may opt for the challenge of creating a rustic country look in a modern flat or use simple stark furniture in your cottage. It is important to make a decision about the type of image you want and then to follow it through in all your rooms so that the decor blends together.

Having decided on the look you want to create you need to study the furniture you intend to cover. Does it have a stark severe line, or is the shape very round? Do you want to emphasize or disguise the shape? A simple stripe or bold geometric pattern will accentuate and complement the lines of a modern chair, and an intricate floral print can exaggerate the comfort of an over-stuffed sofa.

Another point worth considering is whether you need to use your furnishings to create an illusion. This is particularly relevant if you have a room that is especially low or narrow – striped fabrics can most effectively create an illusion of extra height or width.

COLOUR

Selecting fabrics can be very challenging. With such a wealth of colours, prints and textures to choose from it is quite easy for a state of panic to set in and then you can end up buying a 'total-look', from a shop which has co-ordinated wallpaper, with fabrics, paints, borders, china and every conceivable accessory. But shopping this way really takes the fun and excitement out of decorating a room. As a result you may well tire of the whole effect rather quickly.

The first major decision about colour is knowing the colour theme you intend to work with. It is very tempting to play safe and simply work with soft pastel shades, thus creating a rather dull and insipid setting. However, if your property is not over large you may consider having a basic colour used to a greater or lesser extent in every room. This creates an integrated colour scheme and a feeling of harmony and continuity. Remember that doors are often left open when one room is connected to another, so it is important to consider the colour schemes of neighbouring rooms in relation to the one you are currently furnishing. It is helpful to collect a scrap-book of design ideas and colour themes that you particularly like, storing them for future reference if need be. The main priority is to develop a very broad approach to colour and not be limited by those you feel safe with.

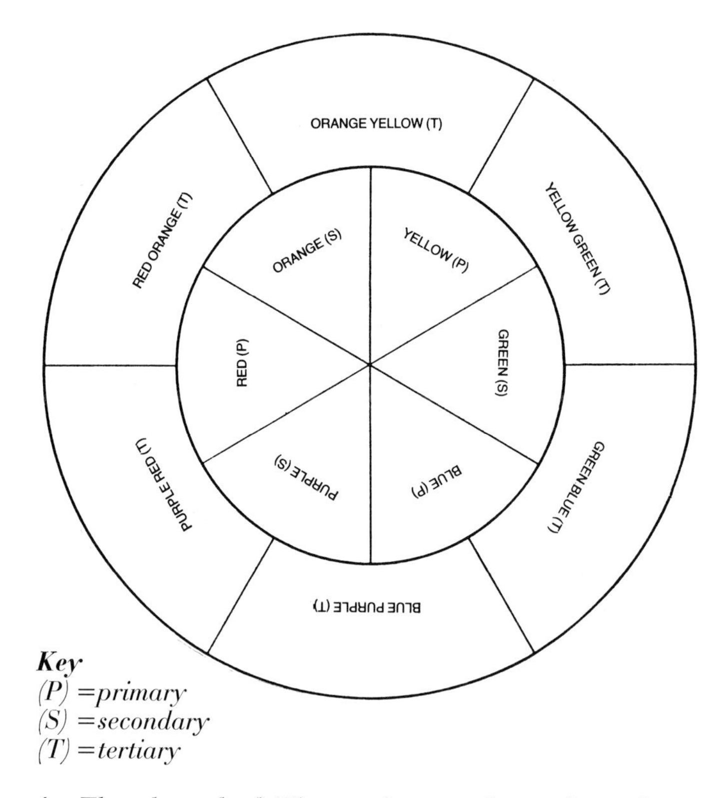

1 *The colour wheel. When a primary and secondary colour are mixed a tertiary colour is produced*

The colour wheel

Knowing which colours complement each other can be discovered by referring to the colour wheel (fig. 1). Essentially there are three basic colours, red, yellow and blue, from which all other colours come. Mixing these primary colours together creates secondary colours, e.g. blue and red making violet. Complementary colours are achieved by matching the secondary colour with the primary colour that has not been used to make it, so that violet would be complementary with yellow. Complementary colours provide the greatest degree of contrast. The remaining colours in the wheel are made up of equal parts of a primary colour and its closest secondary. Neighbouring colours such as violet and pink can be used for a more subtle effect. You might like to paint in the colours on a colour wheel, cut them into sections and, by laying them on top of each other, see how they react with one another. The more you experiment with colours the more knowledge you will gain, and this in turn creates confidence.

Neutral colours are black and white in the most extreme form, but can also include off-white, most of the browns, from beige to dark brown plus camel, also shades of grey, ranging from light silver through to charcoal.

Creating a mood

By working with certain colours you can create a definite mood in a room. In order to create a very cool atmosphere you can use shades of blue plus colours such as off-white, cream, sand, grey and light brown. To create a warm, welcoming room you need to think in terms of colours with yellow or gold properties, or a profusion of rich reds and deep blues. In creating a room with strong colour contrasts you can make a very lively and exciting atmosphere, choosing opposites such as red and green, blue and yellow or black and orange. You may like to take the effect of contrasting things a step further by placing the round curvy lines of flowers, either dried or fresh, alongside a geometrically shaped vase or light fitting. If a contrasting colour scheme is too bold for you, you may prefer to achieve a more integrated look by working with shapes and designs that can be blended together and colour combinations that are gentle and more subtle. Creating a quieter atmosphere may seem simple but success is judged by being able to combine various subtle prints together, without the finished room looking insipid and boring.

Having decided the colours you intend to use for your flooring, walls and ceiling try to keep a small colour swatch of each handy. Keep the swatches with you whenever you are shopping, so that if something catches your eye you can tell immediately whether it will add or detract from your chosen colour theme.

Try to avoid making the mistake of buying something simply because it looks good in someone else's home, or because it has been reduced in price. Bringing a book of swatches home is the most satisfactory way of selecting fabric, so that you are able to judge how the cloth looks away from the shop environment.

Light

By working with swatches of fabric at home you can judge how the cloth reacts to the light in the room you are furnishing. You may have a room with high ceilings that create a feeling of spaciousness and plenty of daylight. Alternatively, you may be limited to a dark narrow room. Colourwise, dark colours tend to make a room appear smaller while light ones create an illusion of extra space. A room that offers plenty of daylight has few drawbacks and you have the opportunity to combine a large number of different prints together. With a small room you need to decide whether you think it would be better to introduce lots of light bright prints to make it appear larger or whether by using rich warm colours you could create a very cosy setting.

Printed or plain?

The size of a room determines the quantity of printed or plain fabrics that you can use. In a small room too many prints can look very muddled, whereas just two or three set against a plain background will look stunning. With large rooms avoid using too many plain colours or the end result will be uninteresting and monotonous.

It is possible to assemble a variety of prints together in close proximity, provided they have at least one colour common to all of them. This might be a soft romantic floral design in different patterns but linked by the colour pink, blue or green. Alternatively, you might like to work with solid,

This delightful chair has a deep frill gathered onto the welt, contrasting white piping and white ribbon ties to secure the cover

bright, primary colours where perhaps a rich red or gold is incorporated on each of the prints you have chosen. If you are planning to bring a group of prints together, always work with swatches first, not by memory, so that you can be sure that all the prints will blend together.

A more harmonious effect is achieved by keeping patterns and furniture in scale with the size of the room. If you want to draw attention to a particular item of furniture, such as a favourite chair or sofa, you might consider using a dominant colour so that your eye is immediately drawn to that particular area of the room. Equally if you want to disguise another area avoid using a busy bright pattern. Choose instead a colour theme that will blend with your surrounding walls and carpet.

2 *FABRICS & FILLINGS*

FABRIC

Before selecting fabric consider the function of the room you are furnishing. In the kitchen, for example, use an easy-care fabric that can be thrown into a washing machine if food or drinks get spilt on it. You will need to bear this in mind, too, when choosing cushions and covers for dining areas. Washable fabrics are also more suitable for children's rooms where sticky hands are liable to wander over furnishings. If you have a young family and/or pets it is worth considering using *only* washable fabrics, so that you can feel more relaxed when youngsters or animals invade a newly-furnished room.

The swing ticket on the end of a roll of fabric will describe its particular properties. By studying it, you will discover the width of the fabric, washing or cleaning instructions and the fibre content. If you are unable to find a ticket or require more information, ask to speak to the department manager. It is never worth simply guessing whether a fabric is washable or not. A cloth that has been designed to be dry-cleaned only can be ruined by washing and many hours of careful work will be wasted.

Another point worth considering is whether plain light-coloured fabrics are advisable if you have an active family. Soft, subtle shades might look very attractive but a busy print or darker shade will disguise marks and stains more easily. Consider also just how much wear-and-tear your cushions or covers are likely to receive. Floor cushions and loose covers will require heavy-duty fabrics, whereas cushions and throwover covers, used for purely decorative purposes, can be made from delicate cloths such as satin or lace.

For a professional finish you will need to match patterns on a printed fabric which has a large motif, especially for loose covers and you will need to buy more material if you are using a cloth with a large pattern repeat rather than one which is plain or has an overall pattern.

It is not just colour and patterns that make fabric interesting – the texture of cloth is just as important. Consider whether you want to sit on something smooth and silky or would you prefer a natural, warmer-looking cloth which is perhaps rougher. For added interest it can be fun combining fabrics with different textures. Note that shiny fabrics tend to reflect light whereas rough coarse ones will absorb it affecting your overall scheme.

Your choice of texture might also be determined by other features in your room. Study the room and decide whether you want to echo or contrast with existing surfaces such as a rough brick fireplace, a shaggy rug or a glossy ceiling.

By studying fabrics with different textures you can begin to see how the fabric is constructed. A piece of cloth is made up of two types of thread, the warp and the weft. The warp is the stronger one. The weft runs from selvedge to selvedge (the selvedge is the finished edge of the cloth) and the weft thread is woven in and out of the warp thread. Warp threads are designed to take the strain on a piece of material.

Generally speaking, dress fabrics are not suitable for home furnishings. Firstly, they can be impractical as they are often only 90cm (36in) wide as opposed to furnishing fabrics at between 140/150cm (56/60in) wide. Secondly, they can be considerably more expensive. Cushions and covers designed for plenty of hard wear should be made from furnishing fabrics, but dress fabrics can be used for decorative items such as a bedroom throwover cover or cushions.

When shopping for fabric always buy the best quality you can afford and avoid being side-tracked by fancy names or designs.

Natural or man-made?

Natural fabrics are those made solely from natural fibres from animal or vegetable sources, whereas man-made ones are natural fibres that have been chemically treated (synthetic fibres are ones made entirely from chemicals). Both types of fabric have their advantages. Natural fabrics tend to respond well when cleaned but are more likely to shrink and crease. Man-made fabrics attract dirt more easily but they are unlikely to shrink and less likely to crease. The main groups of man-made fibres are acetate, acrylics, nylons and polyesters. The main groups of natural fibres are cotton, linen, wool and silk.

NATURAL FABRICS

Cotton

Cotton fabrics are very popular for home furnishing and have a traditional following. They are also extremely tough and can withstand plenty of rough treatment. However, cotton does have a tendency to shrink, so wash the fabric before you cut it. Also, if time is at a premium, cotton does require careful ironing. The following are the most popular cotton-based fabrics.

Brocade is a rich heavy-looking cloth that has a pattern woven into it. Cotton brocade is often woven with other yarns to give a silky pattern on a dullish background.

Bedford cord is often simply referred to as corduroy. This cloth is identified by the surface rib effect that can vary in width.

Calico is an inexpensive cloth that can be dyed or printed. It is used mainly for inner covers for cushions.

Chintz is a very popular choice for home furnishings. It has a glazed finish and is available in a printed or plain cloth.

Cretonne is a firmly-woven fabric not unlike chintz but without the glazed finish. The fabric is often reversible.

Damask is similar in weight to brocade. It usually features a matt pattern on a satin weave background.

Gingham is an inexpensive cloth, ideal for beginners. It can be cut on the cross for an effective finish. It is a very lightweight cloth only suitable for cushions or a bedroom throwover.

Lace is a delicate cloth where a pattern is applied to a mesh background, suitable only for decorative purposes.

Madras is a woven design fabric, often in a check or stripe, usually dyed in a variety of bright colours.

Sateen is a strong shiny fabric with a matt surface on the reverse side. It can be used for cushion inner covers and linings.

Ticking is a very strong fabric closely woven in twill, herringbone or satin weaves. It can often be found woven into stripes with coloured yarn. It is suitable for cushion inner covers provided the main fabric is not too sheer.

Velvet and velveteen are rich, soft-to-the-touch cloths that are ideal for formal chairs and sofas.

Linen

Linen, like cotton, is also a popular choice for loose covers. Although it can be expensive it is extremely hard-wearing. (Chintz, damask and brocade can be bought with a linen base.)

Wool

Woollen fabrics create a feeling of warmth, but wool fibres are not strong enough for most home-furnishing projects. However, light woollen cloths, frayed at the edges, may make attractive throwover covers for a sofa or chair. To make it more durable, wool is sometimes mixed with other fibres. Plush, a velour woollen fabric with a heavy pile is sometimes used in soft furnishings.

Silk

Silk-based fabrics have an air of luxury about them. Although silk is strong it is also very expensive so it is often mixed with other fibres.

Brocade can be bought as a silk-based fabric, often to be found with a silver or gold thread woven into it.

Crepe de Chine is a very soft silky fabric and can be used for a bedroom throwover cover or decorative cushions.

Taffeta and moiré are firmer types of silk fabric. Moiré can be identified by a ripple effect that seems to run across the surface of the cloth. Both are suitable for throwover covers or cushions.

Velvet can also be purchased with a silk base but it is expensive.

MAN-MADE FABRICS

Acetate is constructed by treating cotton linters. Like so many man-made fibres it is easy to care for and will not shrink. It can often be found in imitation silks such as brocades and moirés. Acetate is often combined with silk and cotton.

Acrylic is a bulky fabric with a soft quality. It has a resemblance to wool, and it is warm, strong and crease resistant. It is often mixed with other fabrics, such as wool or cotton.

Nylon is a by-product of coal. It is a strong but lightweight cloth, easy to use and hard to crease. Nylon can be drip-dried and requires little ironing. It is often mixed with other fibres and can be used for synthetic lace, net or satin – all are suitable for cushion covers or throwovers.

Polyester is a hard-wearing fabric often combined with other natural fabrics such as wool, silk, cotton or linen. It is both hard wearing and crease resistant.

3 EQUIPMENT

Working with the correct tools rather than having to make do will make sewing far more pleasurable; it will also give a much more professional look to your cushions and covers. It is a long-term investment, so always buy the best tools you can afford and keep them in tiptop condition.

SEWING TOOLS

Storage of your hand-sewing tools is very important – there is nothing more frustrating than not being able to find things when you need them. A wooden box with a lid or a deep-sided plastic tray with a handle is ideal. Avoid using a cloth bag as scissors are liable to tear it.

A sewing machine is essential for soft furnishings. Projects such as loose covers or 'throws' involve a great many seams and these are best completed on a machine. Working on a machine is far quicker than by hand and the stitches are much stronger. The most important thing to remember when you are buying a sewing machine is that you know exactly how it operates, so if you are buying an electric sewing machine and you are offered a course of lessons do take advantage of them. Many people feel more confident with a simple electric machine that offers a straight and zig-zag stitch and has a free-arm, which is very useful for tackling awkward corners. If you think you are unlikely to use the variety of embroidery stitches and gadgets provided with a very expensive machine, then opt for a more basic model. Before stitching your fabric always test that the tension on the machine is correct by working on a remnant.

Needles should be stored in a cloth book or tin. You will need a variety of needles, including a bodkin for threading cords and elastic through casings. An upholstery needle is also very useful. Its curved shape makes it ideal for sewing cushions or making repairs.

Pins A box of these is essential; steel ones are best as they are less likely to mark fabric. Glass-headed pins are easier to identify in thick fabrics but they are extremely sharp and need to be handled with care. A pin cushion attached to your wrist is useful if you need to make alterations to a loose cover and need pins quickly.

Threads are available in a wide choice and you need to match up the correct type to the fabric you are working with. All basting should be completed with tacking thread but, as this breaks easily, ordinary thread should be used for gathering. The range of synthetic threads should be used on synthetic fibres and cotton threads should be used on natural fibres. If you use cotton on a synthetic fabric it is liable to shrink and cause the seams to pucker slightly.

Scissors need to be razor sharp for sewing or they will damage the cloth when you are cutting it out, causing it to snag. An old pair of scissors should be kept for cutting out paper patterns and a large pair of dressmaking shears reserved for cutting out fabric only. Embroidery scissors are ideal for small areas of work, cutting threads and to remove tacking stitches. Alternatively, you can buy a stitch ripper, which is a plastic rod with a pointed metal end that efficiently removes tacking and machine stitches. Pinking shears are also useful for soft furnishing as a way of trimming seams. Never be tempted to cut out your fabric with pinking shears, reserve these for trimming.

Tape measure This is a necessary part of your equipment. Choose one made of linen or fibreglass rather than stiffened paper so that it will not tear easily. A wooden ruler is also very useful, especially for measuring out quantities of fabric.

Dressmaker's squared paper is much easier to work with than plain paper if you are making your own patterns. You will only need a small quantity of squared paper if you are making and designing a cushion or trimming. Always mark your patterns clearly and store them in a labelled envelope so that the patterns can then be re-used.

French chalk, also known as tailor's chalk, is necessary for marking lines and instructions on cloth. Never be tempted to use biro or felt tip as both are difficult to remove. French chalk can be removed with a stiff brush. It can also be bought in the form of a pencil with a brush at one end.

A thimble is necessary when working with soft furnishing fabrics because you are liable to sew with heavier weight fabrics than in dressmaking. For this reason it is easier to work with a thimble, preferably a metal rather than a plastic one, worn on the middle finger.

PRESSING EQUIPMENT

Pressing is just as important as sewing. A perfectly flat seam or pleated edging add the final touch to a soft furnishing design. Ideally, you should have an iron and ironing board permanently set up in a spare room to save time. If you haven't sufficient space then try to store your ironing equipment close to your machine. It is a good rule to always have an ironing board set up whenever you are sewing.

Steam irons are especially useful for bulky fabrics. Keep the base of the iron clean and always empty a steam iron after use. Always test the iron on a remnant to ensure that no rusty stains are likely to mark your fabric.

Sleeve board This is useful for pressing into smaller more awkward corners.

A pressing mitt is ideal for darts or perhaps a cushion corner. It can be used by attaching it onto the narrower end of your sleeve board. On fabrics other than cottons and linens it is advisable to work with a pressing cloth made from muslin, cheesecloth or fine cotton.

A fine mist spray bottle can be used in conjunction with a dry iron, or to dampen areas when using a steam iron.

4 SEWING TECHNIQUES

BASIC HAND-SEWING STITCHES

Although the major part of sewing home furnishings is performed on a sewing machine certain steps need to be completed by hand.

Tacking, sometimes referred to as basting, is considered only as a temporary stitch for holding two pieces of fabric in place. Once you are an accomplished sewer it is possible to dispense with the tacking stage. Tacking stitches can be worked either with long equal stitches of about 1.5 cm (½ in) each or two stitches of 1.5 cm (½ in) each and one 2.5 cm (1 in) long. Tacking is used as a guide to provide a straight seam for machining and should be worked from right to left.

Running stitch is a smaller neater version of tacking and is used essentially for gathering an area of cloth. To ensure neat even gathers the stitches should be of equal length.

Back stitch is a strong stitch and is performed by working from left to right. It causes a continuous line of stitches on the right side of the fabric and overlapped stitches on the wrong side. Working from right to left bring the needle through from the back of the material about 3 mm (⅛ in) forward along the seam, then re-insert the needle this time about 3 mm (⅛ in) behind the point where the thread came through and bring it out 3 mm (⅛ in) forward on the seam line. As back stitch is such a strong stitch it can be used on seams where it is difficult to manoeuvre the machine.

Slip stitch is used for joining edges of fabric together such as on a mitred corner. Bring the needle through under the folded edge of the fabric, slide the needle along for about 5 mm (¼ in) and then put the needle into the other fold and draw up the thread. This stitch needs to be worked rather loosely.

Blanket stitch is often used for decorative purposes such as on the perimeter of a woollen throwover cover or blanket. It is worked on the right side of the cloth, stitching from left to right. Insert the needle at a right angle to the fabric, take the thread and, once the needle is pushed halfway out of the cloth, wind the thread under the needle. Then pull the needle the remainder of the way out of the cloth.

Overcasting is a stitch used to prevent edges of a cloth from fraying. Working from left to right, bring the needle through at an angle to the cloth, drawing the thread over the edge of the cloth.

Hemming is worked on the wrong side of the fabric and from right to left. Insert the needle a little way under the folded edge picking up a thread of fabric, take the needle into the hem and push it out. Do not pull the thread too tightly or the seam will pucker.

MACHINE-STITCHED SEAMS

Before stitching with your machine it is important to test that the tension is correct. Work a few rows of stitching on a spare piece of cloth rather than on your cushion or loose cover.

When sewing a **plain or open seam,** work with the right sides of the fabric facing each other, then pin and tack the edges together. Tacking stitches need to be worked about 1.5mm (½in) inside the actual machine line, in case they are liable to mark it. Stitch the seam and make sure both ends of the stitching are quite secure. Remove the tacking stitches. Press the seam open, pressing on the wrong side of the cloth. To strengthen the seams you may wish to neaten the edges.

A french seam is a particularly strong seam, generally used on lighter-weight fabrics, and suitable for cushion covers, pillow cases or bed covers. Take the two pieces of fabric, with *wrong* sides together, and make a seam about 5mm (¼in) from the edge. Carefully trim the seam close to the stitching and turn it through so that the right sides are now facing. Work another row of stitching to enclose the raw edges of the material.

A flat fell seam is another strong seam but better suited to firmer heavier fabrics. When using this seam, bear in mind that the stitching is visible on the right side of the fabric. Position the *wrong* sides of the fabric together and machine 1.5cm (½in) from the edge. Press the seam open and then carefully trim one side of the seam only close to the machining. Take the other seam edge (the one that has not been trimmed) and fold it over the trimmed one then machine it close to the fold.

Seam finishes

To both strengthen and neaten seams, any of the following methods can be used. The quickest and easiest way to finish a seam is by using pinking shears. Once the seam has been pressed open simply trim the seam edges with the shears. Remember this method is not ideal for fabrics that fray easily. Another method is to work machine zig-zag stitches along the seam edges. Seams can also be finished by turning the seam edge under and stitching it in place.

MACHINE-STITCHED HEMS

Unlike dressmaking most soft furnishing designs need to be finished by machined hems. A hand-sewn hem is rarely strong enough to cope with the hard wear that cushions and covers have to withstand. To make a double hem, take your raw edge and make a narrow turning to the inside of 5mm (¼in), then press this turning in place. Turn the fabric over again to the depth of hem you require and press the hem again. Machine stitch the hem in place close to the folded edge. On thick woollen fabrics, felt and other cloths that are not liable to fray, simply pink the raw edge then turn the cloth up to the length you require, machining close to the pinked edge to finish.

For a less bulky finish use the zig-zag on your machine and make two rows of machining over the raw edge. Turn the fabric to the inside, to the length you require, and machine the hem in place stitching close to the neatened raw edge.

Mastering the various techniques involved in constructing a cushion or loose cover can give your design a really professional finish, but it is techniques such as frills, piping and pleats that can turn a very simple design into something far more decorative and interesting.

Cot bumpers, scatter cushions and dressing table cover all in matching fabric create a startling effect in this child's room

PIPING

Piping is essentially used to emphasize the outline of a piece of furniture or covering. It can either be made in co-ordinating fabric or in a contrasting colour for a more dramatic effect. Piping can add extra strength to covers on areas that might receive constant hard wear, such as around the arms and the cushions on a sofa.

Preparing piping

Piping is prepared by covering cord or twine with strips of fabric cut on the bias. The bias strip has some stretch and can be shaped round curves. To find the true bias of a piece of cloth, fold it diagonally so that a straight edge (or horizontal grain) is parallel to the vertical grain. Press the fabric on the diagonal fold, open it out and use the crease as a guide to mark parallel lines the desired width of the strip plus 1.5 cm (½ in) for seams (fig. 2). Most cord available today should be pre-shrunk. If you are unsure it is best to wash the cord and dry it thoroughly before using it for your cushions or covers.

Once you have cut strips of bias fabric you will then need to join them together. Take the ends of two strips and place them right sides together making sure that the two ends form an angle, like an arched shape, then stitch the ends together, making sure you leave a seam (fig. 3). Press the seam open, on both the right and wrong side of the cloth to ensure that it lays absolutely flat, and trim the ends.

With wrong sides of the fabric together fold the bias strip in half and lightly press. Open out the strip, place the length of cord onto the pressed line, then close the strip with the cord inside. The strip is now ready to be machined (fig. 4). To make sewing easier it is advisable to work with a zip foot to enable the stitching to sit closely to the covered cord. If you find handling the piping strip rather awkward, first

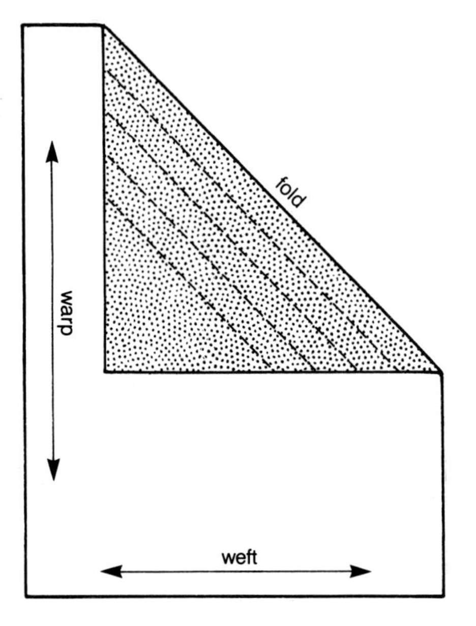

2 *Making the piping: cut strips along crossway fold making them wide enough to cover the cord plus 1.5 cm (½ in) for seams*

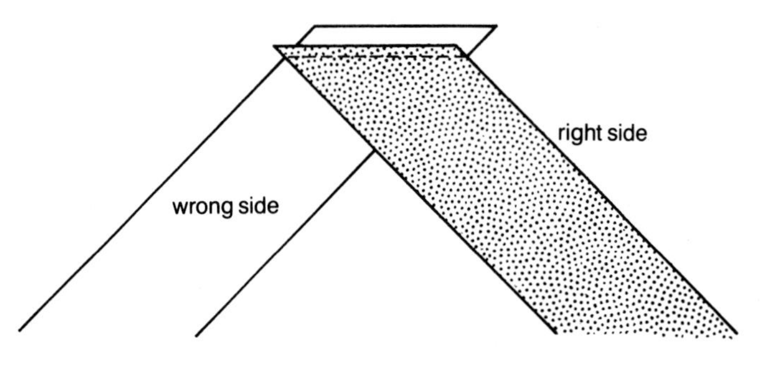

3 *Join the bias strips, stitching the ends together in an arched shape*

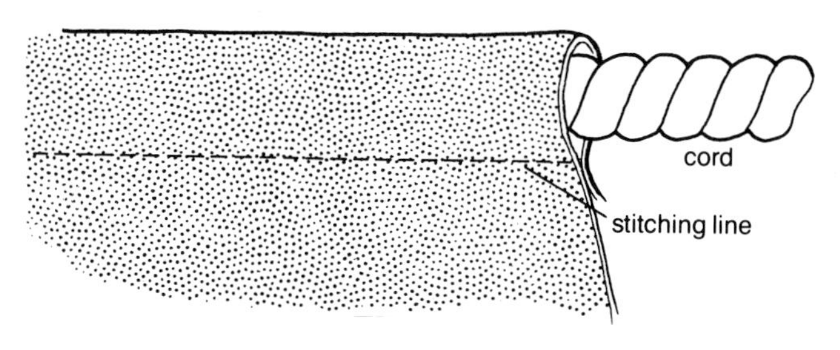

4 *Insert cord in piping, and then stitch close to the cord*

pin then tack the cord into place, remembering to remove the tacking once the machining has been completed.

Joining the piping to the fabric

Having made the piping it needs to be carefully joined to the main fabric to ensure that it lays quite smoothly in place. When attaching piping to your work always begin on a straight edge rather than a curved one. Once you are proficient at working with piping it will be possible for the cord and its casing to be pinned with the fabric and sewn in one operation. However, if you are inexperienced always make the piping carefully first, then attach it to the fabric with a second set of machining.

Take your length of piping and pin it to your fabric, pinning it to the right side of the cloth. Keep the raw edges even, then machine the pieces together. Take the second piece of fabric, and, with right sides together, place it over the piping so that the piping is now sandwiched between the two pieces of fabric. Make a second row of machining. Remove any pins or tacking stitches and turn the work through to the right side. When you come to a corner you will need to make a cut about 1 cm (3⁄8 in) in from the corner edge to allow for ease,

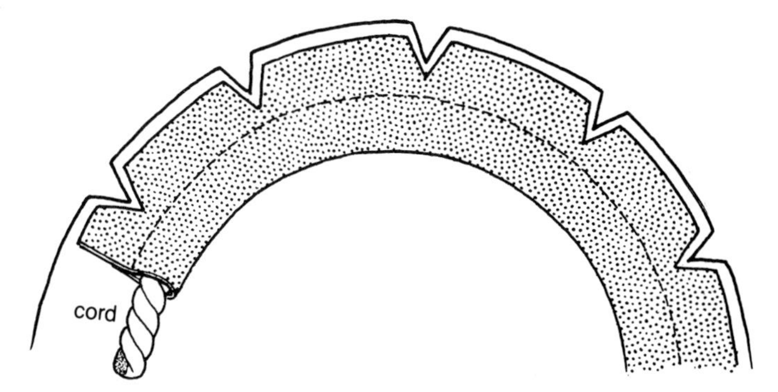

5 *Slash bias strip before adding cord for fitting on a curved edge*

and, as a precaution, make one or two back stitches inside the seam at the corner for added strength. If your work involves a continuous curved edge, such as a round cushion, you need to slash the bias strip at regular intervals of 3 cm (1 1⁄8 in), before wrapping it around the cord (fig. 5). Creating this extra ease in the strip will ensure that it moulds itself to the very shape you require.

Joining cord edges

Firstly trim off any excess strands of yarn and neaten the ends so that they are even. Position the two cord ends together, then bind them with matching sewing thread (fig. 6). Bind as neatly and smoothly as possible to avoid a lumpy finish

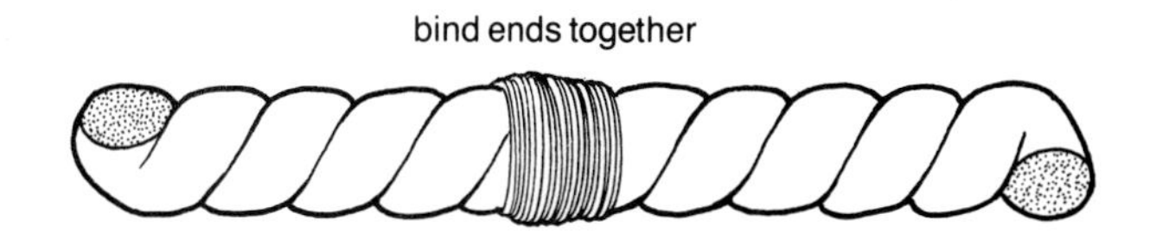

6 *Joining edges of cord together: butt the two ends of the cord and bind with matching thread*

showing through the piping. To join the fabric pieces, make narrow turnings to neaten on one edge, lay the other edge inside the neatened one and machine them together.

A continuous strip of bias fabric for use on a larger project such as piping around the edge of a throwover cover, or on a sofa, can be made in the following way. Take your strip of fabric and fold the right hand corner to the top edge, to obtain the true bias. Make a thumb crease to mark the fold line, then unfold the fabric. Cut along the crease line and then attach this triangle to the other end of the strip with the freshly-cut edge facing outwards (fig. 7). Stitch the triangle in place, press the seam and trim it. Mark off your bias strips on the fabric, using french chalk and working on the wrong side of the cloth. Take the top edge of the strip and with right sides together, fold it over, positioning the right hand top corner edge to meet the second bias line marked on your fabric, not the first. Pin along the seam, making sure that the lines match up exactly, then tack and seam the fabric. This will form a tube. (When cutting the fabric to make the continuous strip, this will create a spiral effect.) Starting at the right hand end of the tube and working with small scissors, cut along the chalk lines to make your continuous strip of binding.

7 *Making piping for a larger project: attach cut-off triangle to other end of fabric*

FRILLS

Frills bring a softening effect to any room. They are highly decorative and can instantly create an informal atmosphere.

In order for frills to hang correctly they should be cut from the width of the fabric, with the selvedge running down the depth of the strip. Decide on the width of the frill you need then add the seam allowances. If you are using a single frill, firstly neaten one edge of the strip by turning under the raw edge and machining it in place. On more delicate fabrics you may wish to hand-sew the hem as it will be visible. For a double frill calculate the finished width you require, double this and add the seam allowances. Fold the strip in half lengthways with wrong sides together. Work a row of gathering threads, either by hand or using the largest stitch on your machine inside the seam allowance, stitching through both thicknesses of cloth (fig. 8).

Having made the first row of gathering stitches about 3 mm (1/8 in) inside the seam allowance, make a second row 3 mm (1/8 in) below the first. Draw up the thread ends to the length you require, adjust the level of fullness equally and pin the frill to your

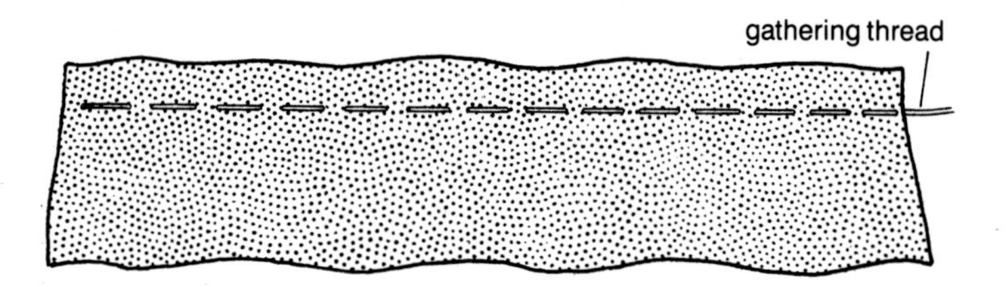

8 *A double frill: work gathering thread completed on the machine on inside of seam allowance*

This attractive but awkward-shaped seat has been made more comfortable with the addition of fabric-covered foam cushions

fabric making sure the thread ends have been securely tied. Allow a little extra fullness if your frill is on a corner.

PLEATS

To ensure that pleats have that really professional touch it is vitally important that they are spaced at equal distances apart. Pleats are most often found on the bottom edge of loose covers or throwovers for the bedroom.

Decide on the depth of pleat you need then add the seam allowance for the top edge and hem for the lower one. Hem the lower edge of the strip and then iron it quite firmly to eliminate any wrinkles. For box pleats cut a piece of stiff card to the width of pleat you require, for example 7 cm (2¾ in). With tailor's chalk mark the pleat every 8 cm (3 in), marking both the top and lower edge of the strip of fabric (fig. 9). Once the entire strip has been marked fold it into pleats, first pinning then tacking them into position, leaving a small space between pleats (fig. 10). This should be done along the top and lower edge of the pleat to hold it securely in place. Having removed the pins, press the pleats firmly in place. Then machine along the top edge only. Remove the tacking and, with right sides together, pin the pleats to your fabric.

The size of pleats can be varied to suit your taste and you can experiment with different widths by using strips of paper before marking your fabric.

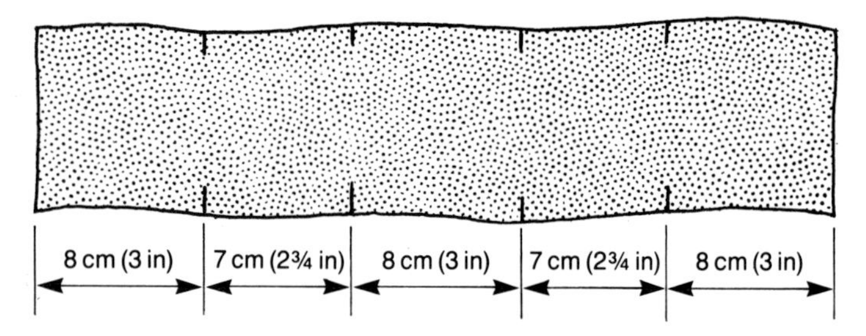

9 *With tailor's chalk mark the pleat every 8 cm (3 in), marking both the top and lower edge of the fabric*

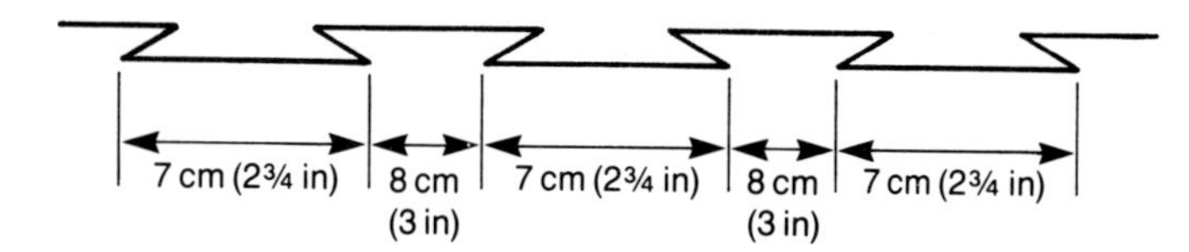

10 *Fold the pleats into position then press firmly*

MITRING

Being able to make a neat corner and to keep it flat is a great asset in sewing home furnishings. It is a technique commonly known as mitring. This skill can be employed when making openings for loose covers or bed covers. Mitring is especially suitable for thick fabrics to help to eliminate bulk.

Take the piece of fabric to be folded and then make two fold lines, first one then the other of equal widths. It is essential that the turnings are equal or the corner will not be perfectly finished. Press both the turnings lightly to set the fold lines. Open the

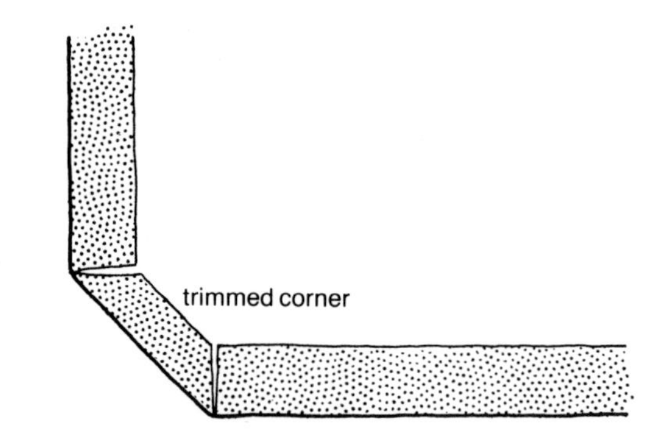

11 *Trim away the upper part of the corner to reduce bulk*

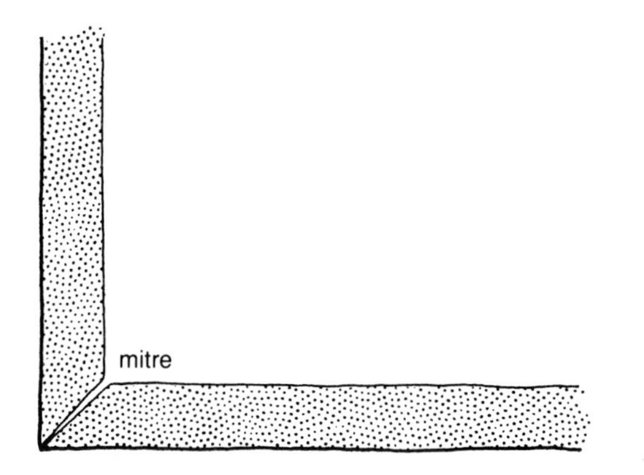

12 *Re-fold the original turnings to form the mitre*

piece of fabric out flat again and fold the corner in and trim away the upper part of the corner to reduce bulk (fig. 11). Now re-fold the original turnings along the crease lines to form the mitre (fig. 12). Hand-sew the folded edges together using a slip stitch and press lightly to re-define the edge.

SCALLOPED EDGES

This very attractive type of edging can be used to trim the corners of a throwover cover.

Like pleats, the success of a scalloped edge is determined by scallops being the same depth and an equal distance apart. Ideally it is best to make a paper pattern of your scalloped edge before transferring it on to fabric. Decide on the depth of your scallop which can be made by tracing around a small plate, saucer or cup and allow for your seam. Cut out the paper pattern and then pin it to your fabric and cut out the scalloped edge. The raw edge can be simply finished by machining around the raw curved edge with a small zig-zag stitch. You will need to do this twice in order to secure the raw edge effectively.

For a firmer finish, cut out two strips of fabric with a scalloped edge, one can be from lining fabric if you haven't sufficient furnishing fabric. With right sides together stitch the scalloped edges together, clipping into the corners (fig. 13) and trimming close to the stitching before turning the scallops through to the right side. Gently pull the scallops into shape and then press firmly before attaching the shaped edge to your main piece of work.

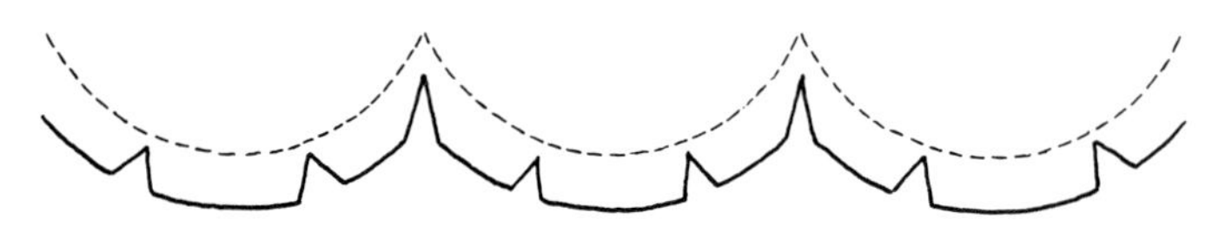

13 *Clipping into the edges of the scallops*

BOUND EDGES

Contrasting strips of bias binding can make an inexpensive yet colourful trim for cushions or 'throws'. You can either buy the binding ready-made or make your own from oddments of fabric. You might like to trim a throwover cover with a variety of different prints joined together. This would provide an eye-catching contrast to a plain cover.

If the binding is being sandwiched between two layers of fabric it can be applied in the same way as piping but omitting the cord. If binding is used to finish a single layer of fabric, first, stitch it to your fabric with right sides together. Bring the remaining longer edge to the wrong side of the fabric and, making a narrow turning, either machine or hand-sew in place. Join strips of bias binding following the method given in the piping section.

PART II

5 *MAKING A BASIC CUSHION*

You can either make a new cushion right from scratch, or you can simply cover an existing one in a new fabric. In either case the first cushion you choose to make should be a simple square. More complicated shapes are better left until you have gained confidence with a basic design.

THE INNER COVER

Having decided on the size of cushion you need, you will then need to measure for the inner cover. Sateen and calico are the most suitable coverings for all types of filling apart from down and feathers. Both of these should be covered with either downproof cambric or ticking.

To create an attractive plump appearance, cushions with loose fillings such as feathers, down, kapok, wadding and foam chips need to have an inner cover 1 cm (3⁄8 in) larger on all the seams than the outer cover. Solid fillings such as foam, and their inner covers, need to be made to exactly the same size as the cushion cover. Inner covers need to be kept as smooth and neat as possible, particularly if the cushion cover is in a lightweight cloth. Any unsightly bumps or ridges from the filling will be visible from the outside of the cushion and will make the resulting cushion look home-made.

Having marked out the size of your inner cover plus 1.5 cm (1⁄2 in) seam allowances, cut two pieces of cloth. With right sides together, pin, tack and then machine the seams leaving one edge free. Stitch along both remaining ends of the free edge for just 3 cm (1 1⁄8 in). Make a second row of stitching just inside the seam allowance for added strength. Secure the stitches either end of the opening. Trim the corners and pink the seams and turn the cover to the right side (fig. 14). Push out all the corners with the end of a knitting needle and press the cushion to remove creases.

Insert the filling and ensure that the pad feels quite firm. Keeping edges in line with the seam, close the opening with a neat even slip stitch in a toning thread.

THE CUSHION COVER

Taking a sheet of dressmaker's squared paper, draw out your cushion pattern, allowing 1.5 cm (1⁄2 in) for seams. Cut out the pattern and place it on your fabric, reserving the selvedge for the opening if possible. In this way you will avoid having to neaten the raw edge for the opening. For patterned cloth you will need more material than for plain cloth, so that you can cut each cover piece separately so that any attractive motif can be positioned in the centre of the cushion.

With right sides together, pin and then tack the edges together. If you feel proficient enough to

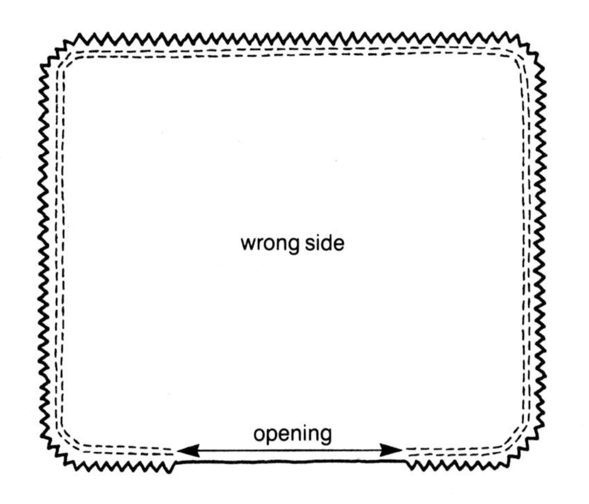

14 *Making the inner cover: pink the seams and trim the corners, and turn the cover to the right side*

avoid the tacking stage, insert your pins at right angles to the fabric edge and your sewing machine should stitch over the pins without you having to remove them first. This will ensure that you have an even line of stitching, which is harder to achieve when removing pins. Stitch around three edges of the cushion, leaving the opening edge free. Stitch for 3 cm (1⅛ in) along both remaining ends (in the same way as the inner cover).

Trim the corners and trim the seam allowances to 1 cm (⅜ in), then zig-zag the seam edges to neaten and strengthen them.

OPENINGS AND FASTENINGS

A sufficiently wide opening is one of the most important points to consider when sewing a cushion. As you will want to be able to remove the inner cover easily it is necessary for almost one complete side of the cover to be reserved for the opening.

Slip stitch fastening

One of the simplest methods of fastening a cushion cover is to use a hand-sewn slip stitch. First, neaten the raw edges of the opening either with the zig-zag stitch on your machine or making a narrow hem and machining it in place. If you have used the selvedges for the opening the fabric edges will not need to be neatened.

Insert the filling into the cushion cover and then slip stitch the opening to close it. Work with thread that matches the colour of the cushion and keep the stitches small and even, keeping the edges in line with the seam. This type of fastening is suitable for decorative cushions in lightweight fabrics only. It is not particularly strong and if the cushion receives plenty of hard wear and needs frequent washing, constantly unpicking the stitching will prove very tiresome.

Press fasteners

These are mainly suitable for decorative cushions that will not receive too much hard wear or the fasteners are likely to pop open. They are suitable for lightweight fabrics but are more convenient than using a slip stitch. To provide a firm backing for the fasteners make a double hem on the opening seams by turning the fabric under once, then again, and then machining it in place.

Fastening tape

Press studs can be purchased on a canvas strip and sewn into place by stitching down either side of the strip. As the strips are about 2.5 cm (1 in) wide you will need to make a flap for the opening edge. To do this take your paper pattern and add 3 cm (1⅛ in) to the opening area only. Make up the cushion in the usual way. Make a narrow hem on the flap edge and then machine the fastening tape in place turning the ends under to prevent them fraying.

Velcro touch-and-close spots and strips
Velcro can be purchased in strips and machined in place in the same way as the fastening tape or it can be hand-sewn in place by using small Velcro spots. Velcro is made from two tapes with different surfaces, one has small nylon hooks, the other has a coarse brush-like surface. The two surfaces 'lock' together when pressed firmly. Velcro is suitable for most types of fastening but is not ideal for sheer fabrics. It is worth noting that Velcro spots and strips should be fastened before being put in the washing machine or the hooks are liable to snag other fabrics. As Velcro is 2 cm (¾ in) wide it will be necessary to add a flap to your cushion opening as described for the fastening tape. Strips should be machined in place and spots can be secured with tiny back stitches worked in the shape of a square.

Zip fasteners
Zips are perhaps the most widely used type of fastening. They are neat and strong and you can generally colour-match them to your fabric. As zips can be slightly awkward to sew into a seam you may prefer to finish your opening edge before stitching the remaining seams. The zip will need to be 6 cm (2⅜ in) shorter than the entire length of the opening edge. Where possible try to position the zip on a straight edge of your cushion. For greater ease you may prefer to stitch the zip in place using a small back stitch.

With right sides together pin, tack and then machine along the opening ends for 3 cm (1⅛ in). Then tack the remaining opening edges together along the seam line. With the wrong side of the fabric uppermost, position the zip in place. Tack, then machine the zip in place, making a double row of stitching at the top edges and base of the zip to strengthen it. Remove the tacking and then proceed to stitch the remaining edges of the cushion.

If you have a cushion with an embroidered or appliquéd front and a plain back you may prefer to attach your zip to the back to avoid any strain being placed on the edge of the work. Take your pattern piece and cut it in half then add an extra 1.5 cm (½ in) to the centre back edge. Insert the zip as you would for a side opening but working on the centre back seam of the cushion.

Back vent opening
This type of opening is mainly suitable for decorative cushions in lightweight fabrics only. It provides a quick and easy finish and enables the

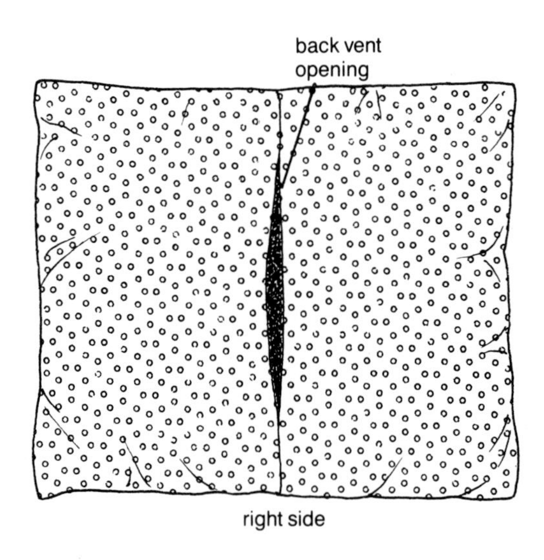

15 *Back vent opening: leave open to insert filling*

inner cover to be removed easily. Cut out the front cover piece, then cut out the back piece twice. Neaten the centre back edge of each back piece by making a double hem and machining or hand-sewing it in place. With right sides together stitch a back piece to either side of the front piece. Overlap the back pieces so that they line up with the front then stitch down the vent for just 5 cm (2 in), and complete stitching the remaining side seams. Turn to the right side and insert the filling (fig. 15). The two halves of the back will lie together as if closed without further fastening, and the inner filling is easy to remove when necessary.

Fastenings as a feature

For most projects it is likely that you will want to disguise the opening area as much as possible. However, you may wish to design your cushion so that the fastening becomes a feature of the cushion.

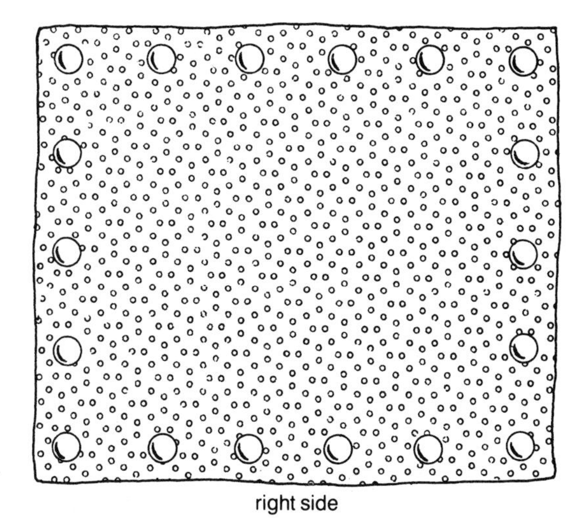

16 *Using snap-on fasteners to secure the edges of your cushion pieces together*

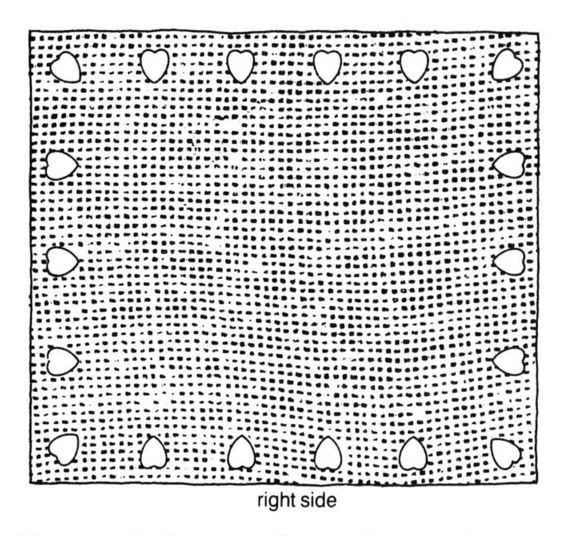

17 *Using novelty buttons to fasten edges together*

Snap-on fasteners are colourful easy-to-apply studs which would make a colourful finish to a cushion for a teenager's room. Take your two cushion cover pieces and, instead of stitching them together, make a double hem and mitre the corners. Press the cushion edges firmly. With wrong sides together position the front and back pieces together and secure around all the edges with snap-on fasteners (fig. 16).

Button fastenings are easy to make and look very attractive. Neaten your two cushion covers as described for the snap-on fasteners. Then sew pretty-coloured buttons to the wrong side of the back cushion edges and corresponding buttonholes on the front edges. Insert the inner cushion and button the edges to finish (fig. 17).

Ribbon is an alternative to buttons and gives a more delicate finish on lace and silk fabrics. Sew lengths of ribbon at 4 cm (1½ in) intervals on the front and back pieces to hold them together and tie

The floral design on this cushion is echoed in a stencil motif which carries right round the walls, door and onto the furniture

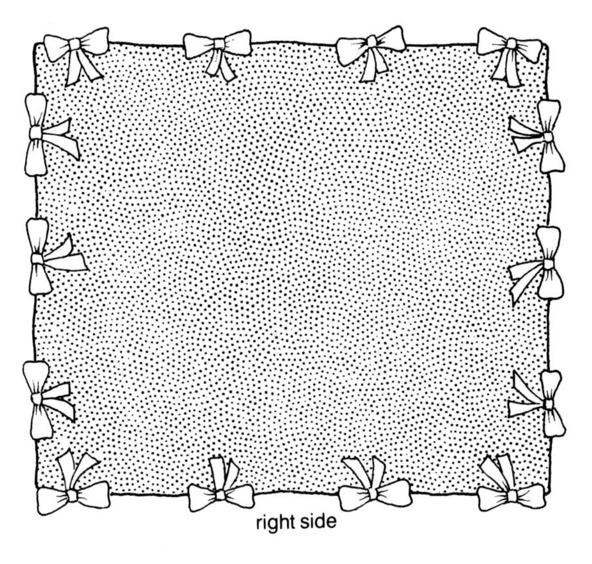

18 *Alternatively, the edges can be tied together with lengths of ribbon*

with decorative bows (fig. 18). If you are working with a brightly-coloured print you may like to use a variety of different coloured ribbons and on firmer heavier fabrics use coloured braid instead of ribbon.

Alternatively, punch eyelet holes through the fabric at regular intervals making sure they correspond on the front and back cushion edges, then thread ribbon through the holes and tie it at one corner.

6 *ALTERNATIVE SHAPES FOR CUSHIONS*

No matter how proficient you may be about making soft furnishings, it is wise to make a paper pattern for everything. Proportions can easily be rectified on paper, but it is impossible to re-shape fabric once it has been cut.

ROUND CUSHIONS

Round cushions need to be made from a perfect circle. If you are making a small cushion you may have some household utensil available that you can draw round, perhaps the rim of a large mixing bowl or saucepan. However, if you are drawing a circle free-hand always work with dressmaker's squared paper. First, measure out a square of paper roughly to the size of cushion you require. Fold the paper in half and then half again. Using a rounded object such as a saucer or plate, trace a curve from one corner of the folded paper to the other, then cut along the curved line (fig. 19). Open out the paper and you have a circle. You will need to add 1.5 cm (½ in) round the edge for your seam allowance.

You can choose to position your opening on a round cushion in the seam, but it is easier to have an opening in the back piece, especially if you are inserting a zip. Take the pattern and slash it in half widthways. Make an allowance for 1.5 cm (½ in) on all edges for seams and insert the zip before joining the front and back pieces together.

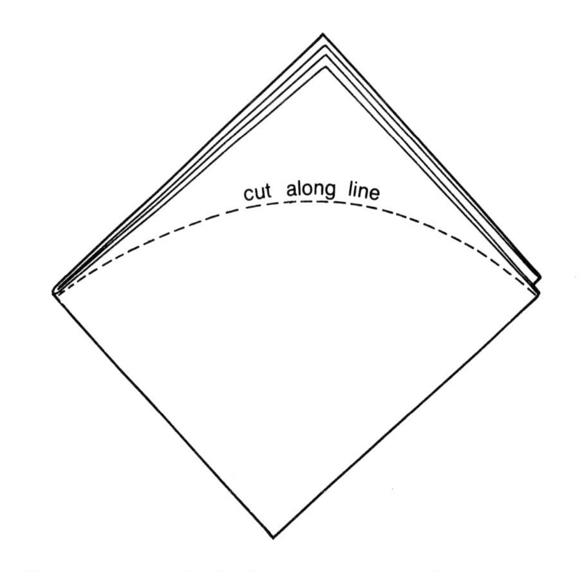

19 *To create a circle, fold a square piece of paper in half, and then in half again, and trace a curve from one corner to the other*

TRIANGULAR AND HEART-SHAPED CUSHIONS

Measure out a square of paper roughly to the size you require. Fold the paper in half and measure out half of your triangle or heart, then cut the pattern out omitting to cut along the folded edge. An opening for a triangular-shaped cushion is sewn into the base. For a heart-shaped cushion the zip is sewn into the back piece one quarter of the way down from the top of the heart.

BORDER CUSHIONS

Moving one step on from a basic square cushion are border cushions. This type of cushion requires no piped or frilled edge because the decorative edging is cut in one with the cushion piece. The variations on this type of design mean that you can choose to have a single or double border.

Single border cushions

To make your pattern, measure out the size of cushion you need, add to this amount an extra 6 cm (2⅜ in) for your border (you can make the border wider if you wish) plus your seam allowance. Cut out your paper pattern to these dimensions, then place the pattern on your fabric and cut out the front piece. Slash the pattern in half and add an extra 1.5 cm (½ in) for the centre back seam then cut out two pieces for the back. With right sides together stitch the centre back seam leaving an opening for a zip, then insert the zip (fig. 20). With right sides together stitch the cushion pieces together. Turn the cover through to the right side and press. Measure and mark, using tailor's chalk, your stitching lines on the right side of the cover 6 cm (2⅜ in) from the outside edge. Stitch over the chalk lines again.

Double border cushions

To make your pattern, measure out the size of cushion you need, add to this an extra 12 cm (4¾ in) for your border (this will give a finished

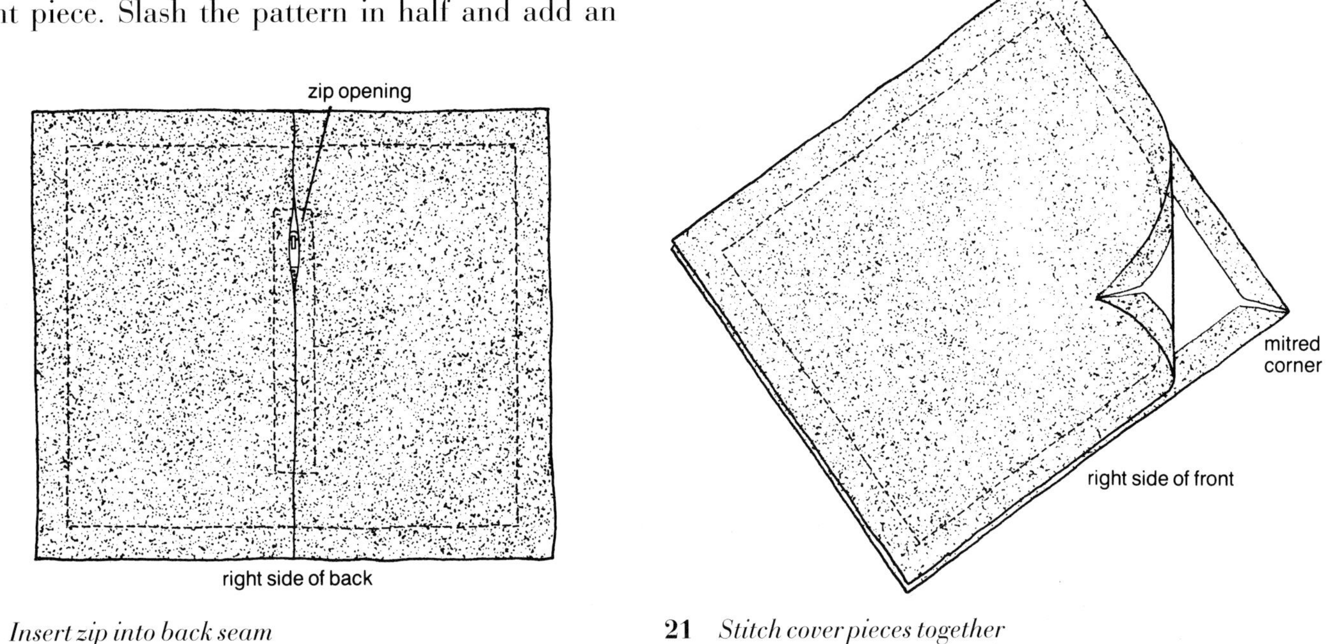

20 *Insert zip into back seam*

21 *Stitch cover pieces together*

border width of 6 cm (2⅜ in)), plus your seam allowance. Cut out your paper pattern to these dimensions, then place the pattern on your fabric and cut out the front piece. Make up the back piece and put in a zip for the opening, as described for a single border cushion. Make a 6 cm (2⅜ in) turning, plus seam allowance, to the wrong side of the fabric on all the raw edges of the cushion. Press under the turnings and mitre the corners (fig. 21). Measure and mark, using tailor's chalk, your stitching line on the right side of the front piece. Pin the two cushion pieces together, wrong sides facing, and stitch over the chalk lines.

PIPED CUSHIONS

Piped cushions are one of the most popular types of cushion. Once you have made a simple square-shaped cushion you need only add a length of piping for a really professional finish. You can choose to work your piping in co-ordinating or contrasting fabric. For a first attempt it would be advisable to work with co-ordinating fabric to disguise less-than-perfect seams.

Begin by taking your cushion pattern and, allowing for your seams, measure round the outside edge. To this figure add another 10 cm (4 in) for ease and joining the ends of the piping. Your strip of bias-cut fabric and cord should be cut to this length. You can choose to pipe your cushion with a thick wide cord or a narrow one. Narrow cord is suitable for lightweight fabrics, a medium cord is ideal for firmer fabrics such as linens and cottons and a wide cord is usually reserved for loose covers.

Take the front piece of your cushion cover and start to pin the cord around the edges on the right side of the fabric. It is best to join cord away from a corner and not near an opening. Ease the cord carefully at the corners snipping into the bias strip so that it sits neatly at the edges. Having pinned the cord in place then tack it. Butt the ends of the cord together and secure following the method given on page **183.**

Replace the foot on your machine with a zip foot, then stitch the piping in place (fig. 22). With right sides together pin then tack the back piece of your cushion cover in place, then machine it leaving the opening edge free. Complete the fastening using one of the methods given. A zip fastener or a hand-sewn slip stitched finish are the most common types of fastening for a piped cushion as they avoid extra bulk. A piped round cushion is prepared in the same way as the square one but the strip of bias fabric that encloses the cord should be snipped at 3 cm (1⅛ in) intervals so that the piping moulds itself to the shape of the cushion.

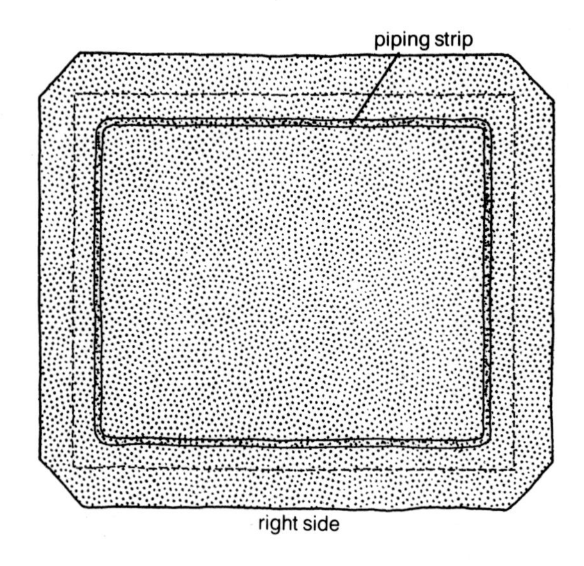

22 *Stitch piping to the right side of the front cushion piece, keeping all raw edges even*

Two contrasting fabrics are used with dazzling effect in this room. Behind them is draped a Paisley patterned throwover

If you feel rather nervous about using a piped edging you can create a similar effect by adding colourful cord and hand-sewing it in place. Make up your square or round cushion in the usual way. Measure round the finished edge of the cushion and allow 10 cm (4 in) for ease and securing the ends and buy some attractive cord or braiding to this length. Position the cord on the cushion seams, tack it in place, then hand-sew it in place stitching both sides of the cord into position to the front and back of the cushion cover. For a more decorative finish begin and end sewing your cord at one corner and make a tassel by unwinding the cord end and then re-tying a knot.

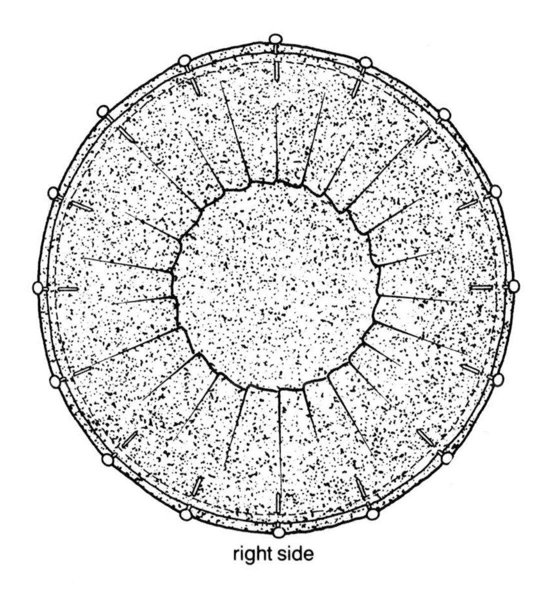

23 *Fixing a frill to a round cushion: ease gathers to fit front cushion piece, then pin in place*

FRILLED CUSHIONS

Plain frill

A frilled edge makes a very attractive finish to a simple round or square cushion. However, you will need to allow for extra cloth depending on the width of your frill.

For a single frill take your paper pattern and, allowing for seams, measure the outside edge. Double this measurement and cut a strip of fabric to this length plus 3 cm (1⅛ in) seam allowance for joining the strip. Neaten one raw edge by making a double hem and machining it in place. Then join the strip of fabric to make a circle, trim the seam and press it flat. Run a gathering thread around the remaining raw edge. Take your front cushion cover piece and, with right sides together, draw up the gathering thread so that the frill fits the circumference of the cushion (fig. 23), allowing slightly more gathers at the corners on a square cushion. Pin, tack and then machine the gathers in position. On a large cushion it is easier to divide the frill into four sections before pulling up the gathers, then pin each section to a side of the cushion. For a round cushion mark the cushion into quarters before pinning the frill in place. On firmer fabrics where the thread may break it is advisable to work two rows of gathering thread.

Take the back cushion cover piece and place it over the front one, with all edges even, stitch the frill in place leaving the opening area free.

For a double frill, take the measurement for the single frill for the length. Calculate the width of frill you need then double it. With right sides together join the ends of your frill, trim and press the seam. Then fold the strip in half with wrong sides together and lightly press the fold line. Work a gathering thread along the raw edges and attach to the cushion as described for a single frill.

Pleated frill

A pleated frill creates a slightly more formal image than a plain one. A pleated frill is time consuming so allow for this as all the pleats need to be made an equal size. To calculate the amount of fabric you need, first measure the outside edge of your cushion. Decide on the width of your pleat and multiply this by the total measurement of the outside edge, allow an extra two pleats for each corner and a seam allowance where the ends will be joined. Cut out your strip of fabric, neaten one raw edge, pin your pleats into position, then tack them and press firmly in place. Join the strip to form a circle and, with right sides together, pin it to the front cushion cover piece. Overlap the pleats at the corners, then machine the pleats in place.

Frilled and piped cushions

Taking your front cushion cover piece, attach the piping in place and then stitch the frill in position over the piping, before adding the back cushion cover piece.

BOLSTER CUSHIONS

These round sausage-shaped cushions have been traditionally used to support pillows on a bed. Bolsters can also be used as a means of support on an open-ended sofa. A bolster pad can be bought ready-made.

If you want to make your own bolster, use calico or sateen fabric and fill with polystyrene granules. To make your pattern, decide on the length of your bolster and the depth. Draw out the main piece of the cushion and then draw the circle for the ends. Cut the main piece once and the circle twice. With right sides together stitch the main piece to form a tube leaving a small opening to insert the granules.

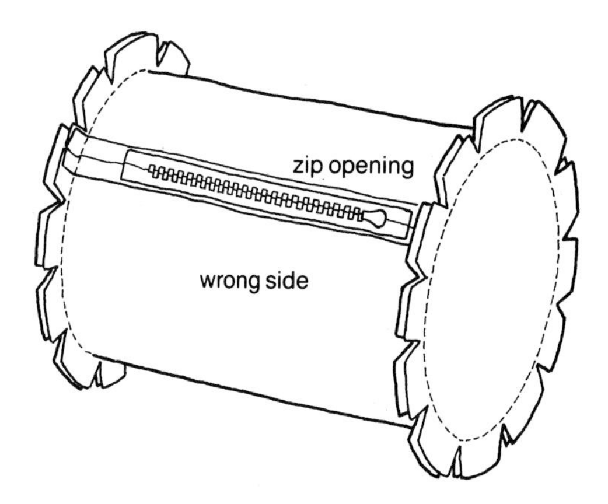

24 *Making a bolster cushion. Add the end pieces to the bolster snipping in at the seam allowance for ease*

Attach the circles to each end, snipping in at the seam allowance to allow for ease. Turn the cover through to the right side, insert the filling and slip stitch the opening to close it.

Place your pattern on your fabric and cut out as for the inner cover, and adding 1.5 cm (½ in) seam allowance. Using a zip 6 cm (2⅜ in) shorter than the length of the bolster, insert it in position. Stitch the seam either end of the zip to complete the tube. Stitch the end pieces to the bolster, snipping in at the seam allowance to allow for ease (fig. 24). Turn the bolster through to the right side, insert the filling pad and close the zip.

Gathered bolster cushions

This type of cushion is used for decorative purposes and, as the gathered end is likely to be hidden underneath pillows, it is used mainly on sofas.

Take your paper pattern for the main part of your bolster cushion and add 3 cm (1⅛ in) to each end. Cut out one piece of fabric to this size. Insert the zip as described previously and finish the seam. Neaten the ends of the tube with a double hem. Then stitch a gathering thread close to the folded edge. Gently draw up the gathering threads at each end so that the edges of the fabric meet. Position a covered button or tassel at each end of the bolster enclosing the gathered ends and stitch them firmly in position. Insert the filling and close the zip to finish.

Instead of gathering the ends of your bolster you may like to extend the main part for a further 7 cm (2¾ in) each end, neaten the ends and tie them with a pretty ribbon or cord into a cracker shape. This type of finish is ideal for decorative cushions and not for those liable to receive hard wear.

BOX CUSHIONS

Cushions of this kind have a welt running around the circumference creating a box effect. The cushion can either be square or round. Box cushions are most often filled with a foam pad that has been cut to the exact size of the cushion. To enable the foam filling to be removed easily a zip is positioned in the welt and, unlike the simple square cushion, the zip continues around the adjoining two corners for 6 cm (2⅜ in).

Square box cushions

Using squared paper calculate the length and width of your cushion and draw out your pattern. Decide on the depth of your welt and make it long enough to equal the circumference of your cushion. To create a more structured finish cut your welt strip into four pieces following the diagram. Then slash the piece where the opening is to go in half (fig. 25). Position your pattern pieces on your fabric and cut out allowing for all seams. Stitch the zip in place following the method given for a square cushion.

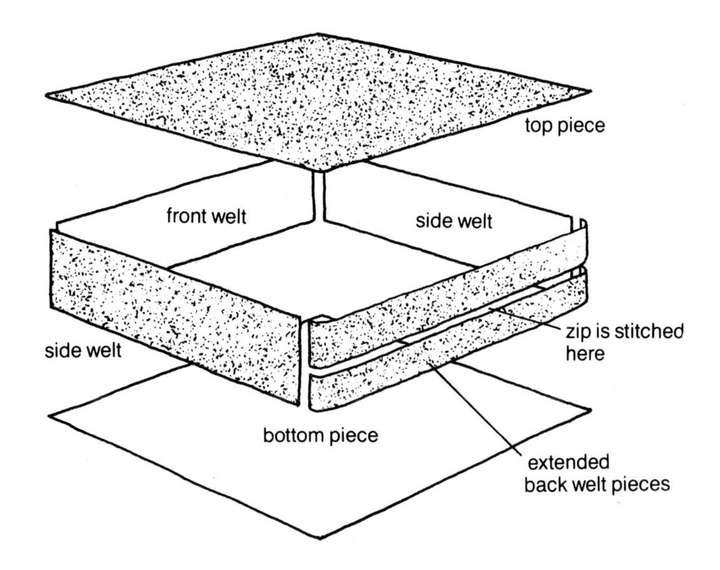

25 *The pieces which make up a square box cushion*

With right sides together join the remaining welt pieces together to form a strip. With right sides together attach the bottom cushion piece in place, clipping the seam allowance of the welt and trimming the corners to allow for ease. Then with right sides together stitch the top cushion piece in place, again trimming corners and clipping the seam allowance. Turn the cushion right side out, gently pushing the corners out, insert the filling and close the zip to finish.

Round box cushions

These are made in the same way as the square cushions, however the welt is made from two not four strips joined together. One strip houses the zip, which is half the circumference of the cushion.

Cut out your paper pattern for the top and bottom pieces plus the welt pieces. Slash the welt piece that houses the zip in half lengthways and

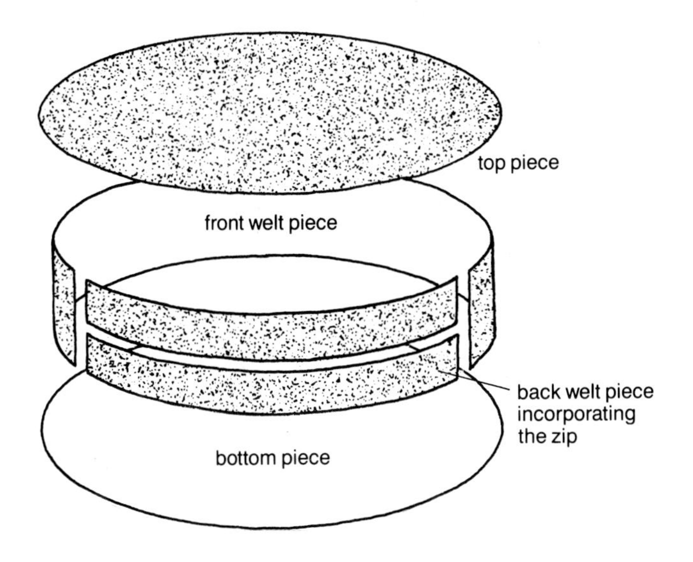

26 *The pieces which make up a round box cushion*

insert the zip (fig. 26). With right sides together join the two welt pieces together to form a circle. With right sides together join the welt to the bottom piece of the round cushion. Snip at 3 cm (1⅛ in) intervals into the seam allowance to allow for ease, repeat this with the top piece. Insert the filling and close the zip to finish.

SQUAB CUSHIONS

This type of cushion is designed to be cut to the exact shape of the chair seat, ties are then attached to the cushion to secure it in position. The opening is most often put across the back piece.

Taking your squared paper lay it over the seat of your chair and trace around the exact shape of the top. Mark the position of the arms and legs so that you know where to attach the ties.

Place your pattern on your fabric and, allowing for seams, cut out a front piece. Slash the pattern in half widthways, position the two pieces on your fabric and cut them out allowing for seams on all the edges.

Insert the zip into the centre back seam. Cut strips of bias binding, ribbon or narrow tubes of matching fabric and pin them to the back piece over the markings. The ties should be long enough to tie in a bow. They should be folded in half and the folded edge pinned to the seam allowance of the cushion.

With right sides together position the front and back cushion pieces together and stitch incorporating the ties. Turn through to the right side, insert the filling and close the zip to finish (fig. 27).

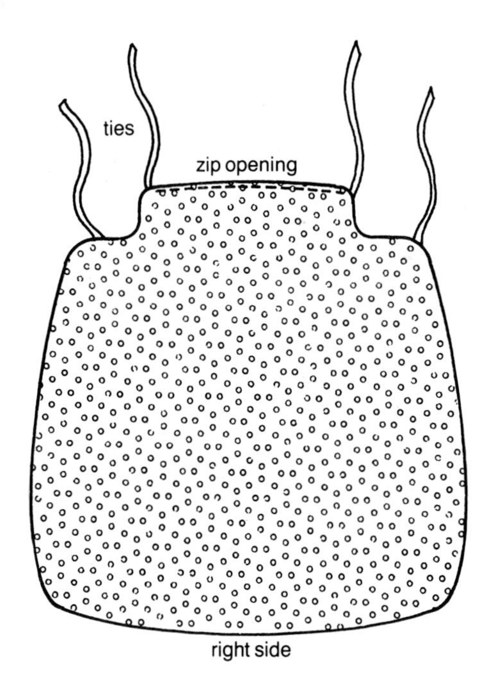

27 *A squab cushion: the cushion is made to the exact shape of the chair*

Piping on squab, box and bolster cushions
Piping can be used on squab, bolster and box cushions. You will need to measure the circumference of the cushion once for a squab cushion. For a box cushion measure the circumference and double the amount as the piping will need to be sewn with the top and lower edge of the welt. Both ends of the bolster cushion can be piped before stitching the round ends in position.

Fillings for squab and box cushions
Both squab and box cushions are best filled with a piece of foam cut to exactly the same shape and size as the cushion cover. As both types of cushion demand a smooth finish an inner cover is not necessary.

PILLOW CASES
Making a pillow case is an ideal project for a beginner as it requires no fastenings. Pillow cases can be made from soft silky fabrics or easy-care cottons.

Using squared paper draw out the size of your pillow case measuring around your pillow as a guide. Cut out your front pillow piece, allowing for seams. Add an extra 18 cm (7 in) to the length of your back pillow piece for the tuck-in flap. Cut the pillow out allowing for seams. Neaten the shorter end of the flap and one shorter end of the front piece with a double hem. With right sides together pin the front to the back bringing the flap over to sit on the front piece. Stitch the side seams and zig-zag stitch to neaten. Turn the pillow case to the right side pushing out the corners and press to finish.

Pillow cases with frilled edging
Cut out a frilled edge to fit your pillow case. With right sides together pin it to the front section only. Tack, then machine the frill in place easing the gathers evenly around the sides. Cut the back and flap pieces separately this time, adding a 1.5 cm (½ in) seam allowance to the cut edges. Neaten one long edge of the flap piece. Position the flap piece on the front piece with right sides together and the frill between them, stitch along the remaining longer edge. Turn through to the right side. Take the back piece and neaten one short edge. With right sides together pin the front and back pieces together then stitch around the edges, leaving the opening area with the flap free (fig. 28).

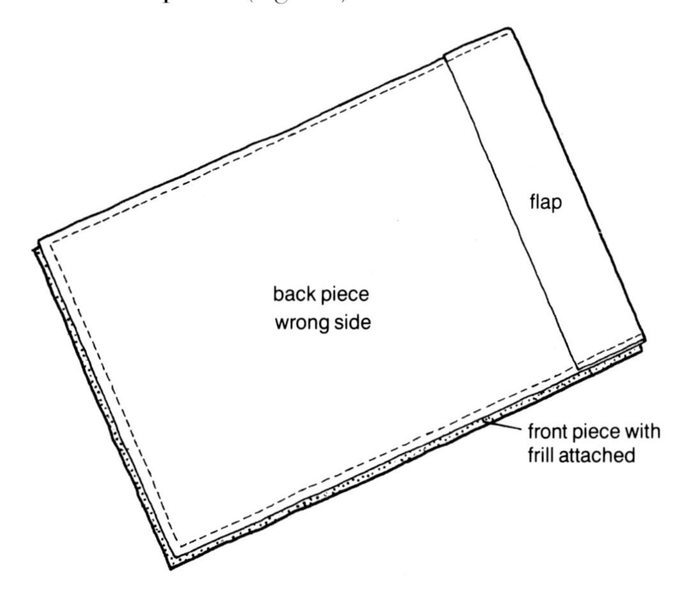

28 *Pillow case with frill: stitch front and back together, incorporating the flap*

7 *DECORATING CUSHIONS*

Using piping and adding frills are attractive ways of trimming cushions, but there are also many other techniques that you could experiment with.

RIBBONS AND BRAIDS

Ribbons and braids make an easy-to-apply decoration to a cushion cover. Take your front cushion piece and pin ribbon or braid around the edges. Cut the ribbon into four pieces and mitre it at the corners for a professional finish (fig. 29). When you pin the ribbon in place, do so making an allowance for the seams. Tack the ribbon and then machine it in place, working two rows of stitching either side of the ribbon. On a plain-coloured cushion cover cut strips from a remnant of fabric as an alternative to ribbon. Cut the fabric into strips to the width you require, allowing for turnings. Press under a turning on the raw edges, mitring the corners. Tack, then machine the strips in place on a plain-coloured cushion cover.

If you have velvet curtains or suite, you can use strips of velvet ribbon to co-ordinate with your furnishings. Stitch the velvet ribbon around the edges of your front cushion piece over a plain-coloured fabric.

Children's ribbons can be stitched onto brightly-coloured cushions to brighten up a bedroom.

Ribbons tied in bows make an attractive finish for a cushion. Narrow satin ribbon can be cut into several small lengths, tied in short bows and stitched at random over the front of a cushion piece. Alternatively a wide floppy bow can be stitched to the centre or corner of a cushion and used for decorative purposes in a bedroom. Oddments of ribbon can also be used by stitching them in separate lengths to the front cushion piece covering the piece entirely. Machine stitch the lines of ribbon together overlapping them slightly (fig. 30).

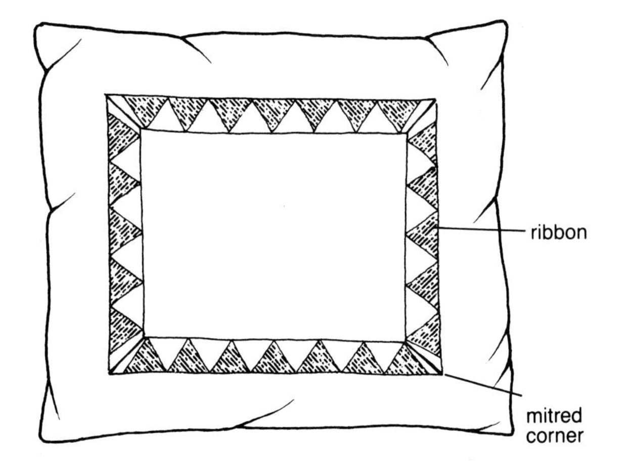

29 *Stitch ribbon to the front cushion pieces mitring the corners*

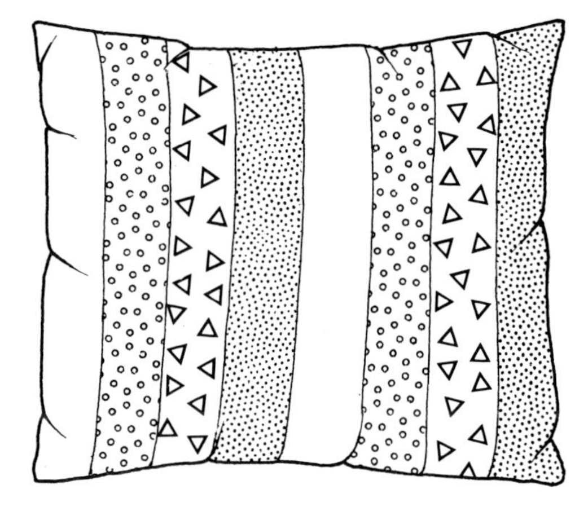

30 *Oddments of ribbon can be stitched together to cover the front cushion piece entirely*

BEADING

Beading is a very attactive way of making a cushion eye-catching. However, if your cushion is not purely for decoration then choose small beads and work them in the corners, or perhaps just one corner of your front piece so that it will not be uncomfortable to sit against. If your cushion is used solely for decoration then you can work a motif over the entire front area. Always design your motif on paper first. Alternatively you might like to use a rich dark-coloured velvet cloth and sew small glass beads at random onto the velvet background.

TASSELS AND FRINGING

Fringing can be sewn to the perimeter of the cushion to accentuate the shape of the cushion and to co-ordinate a room. The fringing is hand-sewn into position once the cover has been completed. Most types of fringing have a heading and it is this part which is sewn to the cushion.

Tassels can also be used to decorate cushions – they are most often used for trimming the ends of gathered bolsters. Tassels can also be stitched to the corners of a cushion, or stitched around the circular ends of a bolster.

BUTTONING

Buttoning is a traditional and popular way of finishing a cushion particularly in fabrics such as dralon and velvet. Make up your cushion and decide how many buttons you want to use for decoration. You may only require one in the centre or several positioned at random. Choose a button with a shank, you will need at least two, one either side of the cushion. Insert the needle through the cushion and through the shank of one button, then take the needle back through the cushion to secure the other shank in place. Use button thread for this type of work to prevent the thread snapping under stress.

If you prefer you can use a covered button to finish your cushion. To cover a button, first place it on your fabric, draw around the outside edge allowing an extra 1.5 cm (½ in). Cut the circle out and work a gathering stitch around the outside edge. Position the button on the wrong side of the cloth and draw up the thread so that the fabric over the button is quite tight. Keep the raw edges to the inside of the button and tie the ends securely to finish.

APPLIQUÉ

Appliquéd motifs can be used to echo the theme of a room. In a child's room, why not cut out motifs from curtain remnants, of their favourite television or cartoon characters for instance. When cutting out the motif allow a 1.5 cm (½ in) border around the edge. Press medium-weight iron-on Vilene to the

This bedroom throw is decorated with ribbon and a broderie anglaise frill. Pillow slips and quilted cushions match

wrong side of the motif to prevent it from fraying. When the Vilene is quite cold cut around the motif eliminating the 1.5 cm (½ in) border. Pin the motif to the right side of the cushion piece, using a plain-coloured fabric for the background, and then tack them in place. Either hand-sew or zig-zag the motifs in place.

Appliqué can also be used in other rooms. Cut out the central motif from curtain or loose cover remnants, using Vilene as a backing to prevent the edges fraying. Pin the motif to a corner or centre of your cushion, using a plain background to emphasize your motif and hand-sew or machine it in place. For very simple shapes add a hem allowance of 8 mm (⅜ in) and, instead of using Vilene, baste all the raw edges into position on the wrong side of the cloth, before sewing them to the cushion cover. Appliqué can also be used for cutting out lace and stitching the motifs to a cushion cover for an effective trimming.

PATCHWORK

Small hand- or machine-sewn patchwork can be put to effective use on cushion covers. You can choose to make the entire cover in patchwork, just the front piece or use a central motif on a plain background. If your cushion is not purely for decoration machine-sewn patchwork is recommended. The simplest patchwork is different coloured squares sewn together. By incorporating scraps of curtain or loose cover fabrics into your patchwork the cover will co-ordinate with the room. If you want to create a less rigid effect cut out a number of paper shapes then re-arrange them until they fit the size of your cushion. This is known as a random patchwork design and should always be arranged on paper before cutting the different shapes out of fabric. One of the simplest types of patchwork is to use a central design on a plain background. Cut out seven hexagonal shapes and stitch them to the front cushion piece working on a plain-coloured background to emphasize the patchwork. This type of design could also be used for a set of squab cushions designed for dining-room chairs.

EMBROIDERY AND TAPESTRY

Small cushions make perfect samplers for embroidery. They can be used to decorate a baby's room, with the name and date of birth stitched onto the fabric. A small tapestry can be worked in the same way. Alternatively, a small tapestry can be set on a larger cushion by stitching it onto plain-coloured fabric and a narrow strip of ribbon hand-sewn around the edges of the tapestry to disguise the edges. Embroidery can be worked on pillow cases to identify his and her pillows. Or embroidered cushions can be arranged in a conservatory depicting flowers that can be found there. An attractive embroidered hanky could also be made up into a cushion cover provided it is stitched to a similar weight backing cloth. Old tablecloths that are no longer used but which have been worked with attractive designs can be cut up and used as cushion covers.

IRON-ON MOTIFS

For a very quick and simple method of decorating cushions, use a selection of iron-on motifs. There are soft furry animal shapes ideal for a nursery, or colourful cartoon characters and popular slogans for a teenager. For the bedroom use ready-made embroidered flowers that can be simply ironed into one corner of your cushion, then edged with co-ordinating ribbon to finish.

QUILTED CUSHIONS

Simple square cushions can be made more interesting if the surface has been quilted. If you haven't the time to quilt cloth but like the effect, then you can buy a small amount of ready-quilted fabric and perhaps use a piped border in bias binding of a contrasting colour.

To make quilted cushions you will need to make your paper pattern. Using the pattern cut out your main fabric twice, two pieces of wadding and two pieces of backing cloth. Using tailor's chalk and a rule draw out your pattern on the fabric pieces; lines running vertically and horizontally is the easiest type of quilting to begin with.

Take one fabric piece and, with the right side uppermost, place the wadding to the wrong side and the backing under the wadding. Pin all three layers of cloth together and tack the outer edges together to keep them in position. Machine along the chalk lines, using a quilting bar if you have one, then remove the tacking. Don't press quilting or it will loose its attractive plump appearance. Repeat this process with the remaining cushion pieces and then continue to make up the cushion using the method of your choice.

Once you have mastered the quilting technique you can then go on to stitch more elaborate patterns on your fabric. Alternatively, use patterned fabric and quilt around the motifs. Most types of fabric can be quilted but cottons are easier to handle; slippery cloths such as satins are more difficult and not to be recommended until you are proficient.

8 IDEAS WITH CUSHIONS

Cushions are such versatile furnishings that they can be used in virtually every room in the house.

IN THE BEDROOM

Cushions in a bedroom can range from under-pillow bolsters, pillow cases and window seats to decorative scatter cushions for the bed.

Pillow cases in plain-coloured cotton can be trimmed with lace that should be at least 5 cm (2 in) wide, and edged with narrow strips of satin ribbon. Strips of lace can either be incorporated into the side seams and applied in the same way as a frill, or they can be hand-sewn to the right side of the case once it has been completed. Lace and ribbon can also be worked in criss-cross or diagonal patterns over the front pillow piece. Select lace with a smooth surface or it will be too uncomfortable to sleep on. Take the right side of your front piece and pin strips of lace or ribbon in position, tack and then machine the strips in place working rows of stitching either side of the strips to ensure they lay flat.

Several different-sized cushions covered entirely with lace can be scattered around the head of the bed for decoration. Choose square, round or heart-shaped ones, make the inner cover in the usual way but use a backing fabric with lace or the inner cover will show through. If you want to emphasize the lace pattern choose a backing fabric in a contrasting colour. Cut out the backing fabric and your lace covering from your pattern, and then stitch the wrong side of the lace to the right side of the backing cloth before making up the cushion. To avoid the lace getting caught in a zip close the opening with a slip stitch. For a more co-ordinated look you may wish to use lace and backing cloth in the same colour.

A simple design worked in embroidery is another way to make an ordinary pillow case look special. Keep the design to the corners and edges of the pillow to avoid leaving an impression on your face while you sleep.

Pastel-coloured ribbons are a simple way of finishing the edges of a pillow or cushion. Once your cushion or pillow has been made up, measure enough ribbon to cover the perimeter. With wrong sides together press the ribbon in half lengthways. Slide the edges of the cushion or pillow into the ribbon so that it touches the crease line. Pin, tack and then machine the ribbon border in place.

For a more comfortable weekend lie-in, fix bedrest cushions above the bed. These are made from the box cushion pattern (see page 200) but two loops are stitched into the top welt seam. Cut two loops for each cushion 8×20 cm (3×8 in). With right sides together fold them in half lengthways and stitch along the length of the strip. Turn the

This bed has been transformed into a sofa with the addition of a two-tiered fitted cover and matching cushions in various shapes

loop to the right and press firmly. Pin the loops either side of the welt approximately 8 cm (3 in) in from the corner edge. Stitch the loops in place when you stitch the welt seams. The loops are then threaded onto a pole which is suspended above the bed.

Window seats are a good way of utilizing extra space. They are made from the box cushion pattern and filled with shallow pieces of foam between 4-6 cm (1½-2½ in) deep. Depending on the length of your sill it may be necessary to make more than one cushion. Window seats look particularly attractive when designed to co-ordinate with curtains and bedcovers.

Sweet-smelling herb cushions are a delightful way of making drawers fragrant. Small cushions can be made from cotton, lace or voile cut into hearts, circles or rectangles, edged with narrow strips of lace and filled with dried flowers or herbs. You might also like to slip a small bag of pot-pourri into a large cushion with the filling but remember to remove it before washing.

IN THE NURSERY

A child's room is definitely one area of the house where you can experiment with colour. The addition of one or two brightly-coloured floor cushions can be a focal point of the room and ideal for relaxing on or for props in imaginative play. These cushions should measure 90 cm (36 in) square and filled with foam chips. A tough washable cotton is most serviceable and all seams should be stitched twice for added strength. You could also make a sofa on the floor using square-shaped cushions to sit on and oblong shapes for the back part. Small children would also have plenty of fun with a long strip of foam covered using the box cushion method. This strip could be used for rolling around on, or, combined with a bolster, for a resting place for an afternoon nap.

Cushions in a child's room need to be fun. Furnishing fabrics depicting favourite cartoon or television characters will prove tremendously popular. Cushions for a playroom can also be made from fabric oddments, sewn together in blocks of different colours. Do remember that all fabrics for the nursery should be washable.

Cot bumpers

Cot bumpers are a practical way of protecting a baby from draughts. Bumpers are made in the same way as squab cushions and designed to a simple oblong shape. You can choose to line the entire cot or just the end where your baby sleeps. Bumpers are filled with wadding and held in place with ties fastened to the cot bars. To prevent toddlers undoing ties, replace them with shorter ones that are secured with poppers or Velcro

Changing mat

An oblong of foam covered with PVC makes a handy changing mat for a baby. Make sure that it is wide and long enough for your baby to roll on and insert fabric ties at either end so that the mat can be rolled up and secured for travelling.

Pyjama cases

To entice young children to put their night clothes away a pyjama bag can be very useful. Make it from just a back and front piece with the opening in the back so that it is easier for the child to find. Decorate the case with an animal or doll's face using remnants of wool and cloth for trimmings. Do not use small buttons or beads.

IN THE BATHROOM

If you enjoy a long relaxing bath then a cushion for your head makes the experience more comfortable. Ready-made bath cushion pads are available from most department stores, or you can cut your own from foam. Cover the pad with a light quick-to-dry material such as polyester cotton and make it more attractive by adding a short frill to the outer edge.

A bath mat can be made from a cushion pattern. Draw it to an oblong or circle shape to the size you require, cover it with brightly-coloured towelling using a piece of foam for the filling. Appliqué a motif on the front section if desired.

IN THE DINING-ROOM

Make the seats of wooden chairs more comfortable by tying squab cushions to them. A washable fabric should be used so that the covers can be laundered frequently. If you want the ties on your dining chairs to be a focal point, use wide strips of ribbon and tie elaborate bows. Alternatively, add long narrow strips of ribbon and wind them in a criss-cross pattern three-quarters of the way down the chair leg tying them in a bow at the end.

Chests, workboxes and wooden stools can be used as impromptu seats by adding a box cushion. Choose a hard-wearing cloth that will withstand constant friction against a wooden surface. Instead of the box cushion design, make a cushion to fit without a welt and insert a frill into the seams, one long enough to reach the floor.

IN THE LIVING-ROOM

Unlike the dining-room where it is necessary to work with practical fabrics, the living-room can be the focus of more expensive materials that perhaps require the occasional dry-cleaning.

If you are furnishing on a budget you can make an inexpensive sofa by adding cushions to a simple wooden frame comprising slats of wood secured to a raised plinth.

Bolster cushions, with tasselled trimmings, are an attractive way of making a large sofa more comfortable. They can also be used for dividing the sofa into separate seats. Make decorative cushions with large lengths of soft cotton or polyester crêpe de Chine material, tuck two sides in and then fold them onto the inner cushion. Take the remaining two ends and bring them to the centre and secure with a large bow or knot. Alternatively, cover a square cushion and tie lengths of ribbon around it to create a parcel effect securing the ribbon in the centre with a bow.

A rocking chair is more comfortable with squab cushions tied to the seat and back. If you wish you can make one long squab cushion but provide plenty of ties to prevent it from slipping.

IN THE GARDEN

You can make your own sun bed by simply covering a thick piece of foam using the box cushion method. Select a bright summery cotton cloth and one that will withstand plenty of hard wear. From a remnant of fabric you could also sew a simple square or round cushion to rest your head on.

A deck-chair with a cushioned lining looks more inviting than just canvas. Using the squab style of cushion, first measure the length of the canvas allowing for seams. Select a bright colourful cloth, perhaps a stripe or check pattern, and cut out a front and back piece. For decoration add a single or double frill, too. To keep the lining in place you might also like to add a flap for the top end of the chair, as for the pillow case.

Outdoor furniture tends to be rather basic and is made more comfortable by the addition of box cushions especially in bright primary colours. Squab cushions can be tied to cane furniture to make it more comfortable.

A HOME FOR ROVER

Dog and cat baskets can be expensive and your pet could be just as happy sleeping on a large sag bag floor cushion. This type of cushion moulds itself to the shape of the animal's body. Using the box cushion principle cut out your pattern to a round shape and the size you need. Then allow for a welt to a depth of at least 35cm (14in). Using a strong fabric, such as corduroy, denim or calico, sew the pieces together. Having made an inner cover fill it with polystyrene granules and slip stitch the opening to close it. It is advisable to make a second row of stitching around the inner cover to prevent the granules escaping. Fill the inner cover to three-quarters full to create a nice soft, squashy effect.

PART III

9 *LOOSE COVERS*

Loose covers are an inexpensive way of giving furniture a new lease of life, especially if you have acquired a second-hand bargain or a junk shop find. Although the prospect of making covers may seem quite daunting, the key to success lies in knowing how to measure-up for the pattern.

You can make loose covers for most styles of chair or sofa and, as their name implies, they have the advantage of being easy to remove for washing or dry cleaning.

Always work with furnishing and not dress fabrics which are not strong enough to withstand the constant wear-and-tear. Furnishing fabrics are also wider than dress fabrics and more economical. For your first project it is advisable to work with a plain fabric or one with an overall pattern. Fabrics with a large pattern have to be matched carefully and motifs need to be placed centrally on the furniture.

MEASURING UP

Taking the measurements for your loose cover pattern is the most crucial stage. You will need to be prepared to spend plenty of time ensuring that the measurements are exact – avoid working in a hurry. Loose covers require large quantities of fabric so always double check on the amount you need before you make a purchase.

Until you are experienced in making covers it is a wise precaution to make a calico pattern before you buy your fabric and certainly before you start cutting into it. If you make a calico pattern first, it gives you the opportunity to try it out on your seat and make any adjustments. Then you can lay the pattern out on an old sheet to the width of the fabric you intend to buy. Position the pattern pieces on the sheet, working with the grain line running in the same direction, so that you can calculate the amount of material you need. If you have a couple of discarded double sheets these can be used instead of calico. Any mistakes you make can then be rectified on the calico pattern instead of your fabric. When you take measurements do so from the widest point of each section. Make a brief sketch of your chair so that you can write in all the measurements as you take them. If your chair has a removable cushion seat take this out of position so that you can measure for the cover that sits underneath it, remembering to measure for the cushion, too.

If you are calculating the cost of covering a chair you can make a very rough total by estimating that you will need something in the region of five times the height of the back of the chair to the bottom edge.

At certain areas on your cover you will have to allow for a tuck-in. This is the extra piece of fabric, used at the back and sides of the chair, that helps to keep the cover in place. Also keep in mind that you will need extra cloth for covering the piping cord and perhaps an extra 50 cm (20 in) of cloth for any possible repairs later on. If you want matching cushions, arm caps and chair backs include them in your fabric measurements too. Arm caps and chair backs enable you to protect the areas of your cover that are likely to become heavily soiled and they can be washed and replaced without the entire cover having to be removed.

The seven main areas that you will need to measure are (fig. 31):

1 The outside back from the top of the chair to the bottom edge.

2 The inside back from the top of the chair to the base of the back piece, plus a 15 cm (6 in) tuck-in.

3 The seat area with a 15 cm (6 in) tuck-in either side and at the back edge.

4 The front of the seat.

5 The outside arm.*

6 The inside arm with a 15 cm (6 in) tuck-in.*

7 The front of the arm.*

*Double these measurements to allow for the two arms.

In addition to these measurements you should allow 2 cm (¾ in) for all the seams.

Finishing the bottom edge

You will also need to allow material for the type of finish you want on your chair. For a fitted look you can use a set of four flaps, one on each side of the chair, with ties attached that are tied in bows underneath the chair (fig. 32).

To measure for the flaps turn your chair upside down. Measure from the edge of the chair to 10 cm

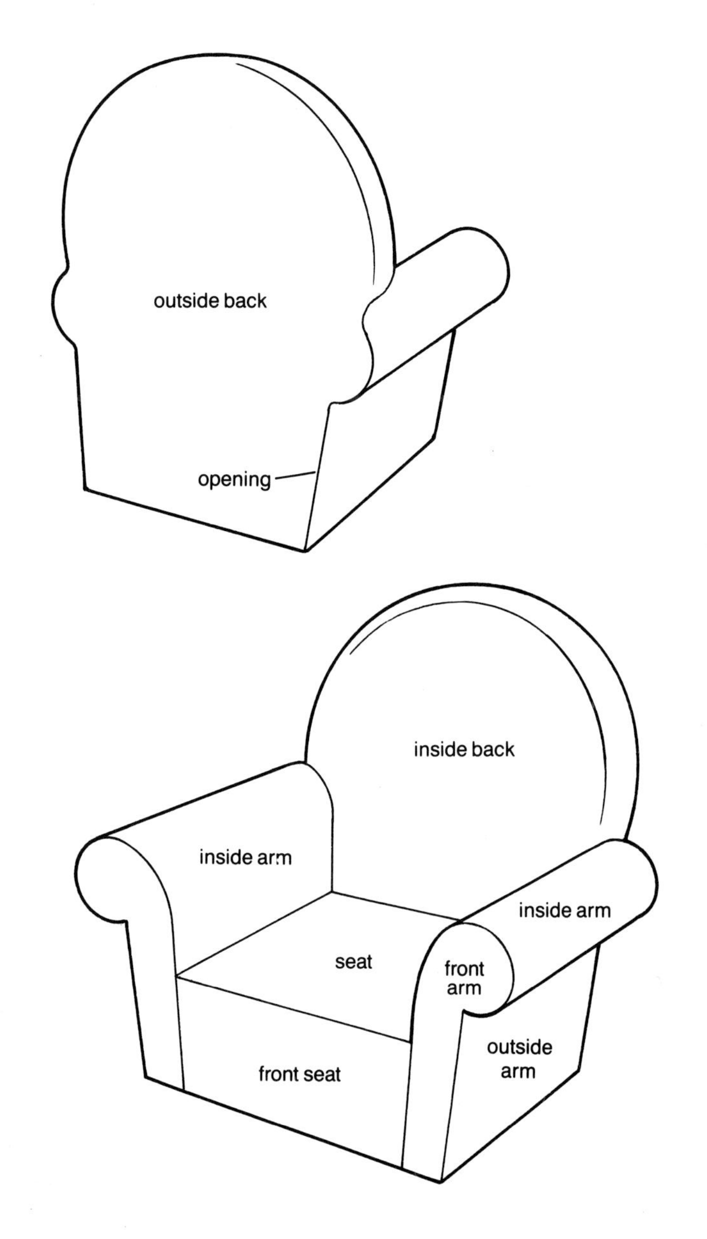

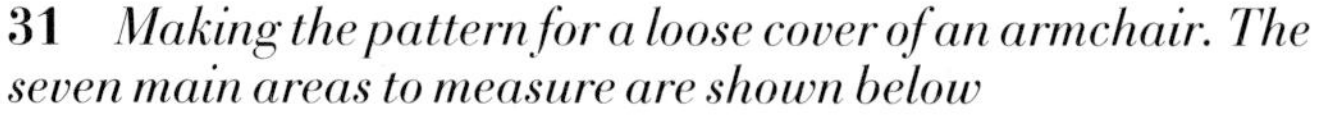
31 *Making the pattern for a loose cover of an armchair. The seven main areas to measure are shown below*

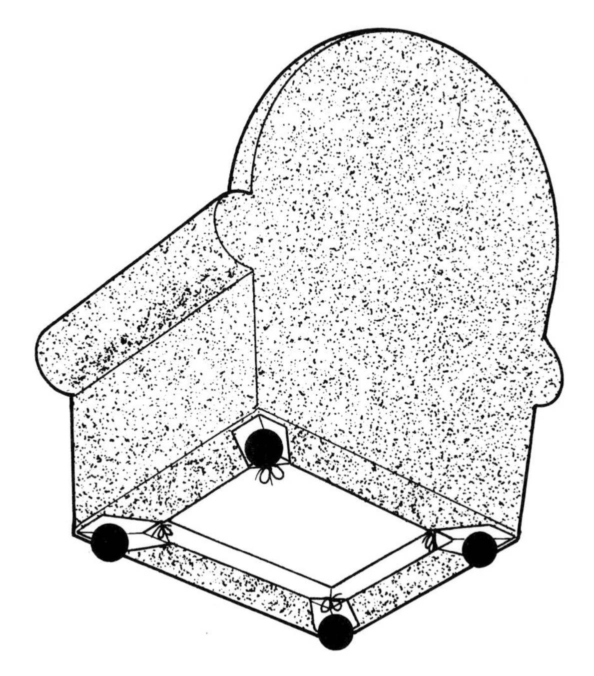

32 *Four flaps tied with bows on the underside of the chair provide a neat finish*

33 *A frill makes a decorative trimming on the loose cover for an armchair*

(4 in) beyond the leg, then measure the length of the side of the chair. Cut out the flaps, shaping them by tapering them slightly on each side. Make a double hem on each side edge and make a narrow 2 cm (¾ in) hem on the top edge incorporating the ties at either end. Flaps provide a simple uncluttered finish to the edge of a chair cover, but there are more decorative styles you can choose.

Provided you are working with a soft cloth then a frill makes a very decorative trimming (fig. 33). To determine the length of your frill take a piece of string and measure around the lower edge of the chair. For a soft fabric you will need twice this amount of fabric and for slightly firmer cloths use one and a half times the amount. Measure the depth from the bottom edge of the front seat piece to the floor allowing for seams. Make up the frill and attach it to the cover using piping sandwiched between the frill and lower edges of the cover. For a contrasting effect you can encase the hem of the cover in binding or ribbon.

Box pleats are a popular way of trimming the lower edge of loose covers. Measure the bottom edge of the chair as described for a frill then multiply this amount by the size of pleat you intend to use. Pleats for chair covers tend to be about 12 cm (4¾ in) wide. To measure their height, measure from the bottom edge of the front seat piece to 5 mm (¼ in)

This sofa has a loose cover with a frilled edging and separately covered cushions. The cushion piping matches

from the floor (box pleats are usually made to sit slightly off the floor). You will need to see that the outside edge of the pleat sits neatly on the corner of the chair. You may have to juggle with the pleats in order to get them to sit in the right position, making the corner pleat slightly above or below 12 cm (4¾ in). By working on a strip of calico first you can avoid making your fabric grubby and simply transfer your markings when you have fitted the strip exactly in position.

Scallops make a very fancy trimming ideal for a bedroom chair. Measure the length of strip you need as described before, then measure the length of your scallop from bottom edge of the front seat piece to 5 mm (¼ in) from the floor. Again, you will need to juggle with scallops so that they sit neatly on the corner of the chair.

THE CALICO PATTERN

Always make a separate calico pattern for each item of furniture you cover. Store the calico so that you can use it for reference when your cover needs replacing. Don't unpick an old loose cover as it is likely to have shrunk in the wash. If you have bought a washable fabric it is worth taking the time to put it through your machine in case it shrinks. Having taken the measurements for the various sections of the chair, cut large rectangles of calico or sheeting that will encompass these measurements, remembering to allow for seams and tuck-ins.

Working on one area at a time place the pieces of calico over the chair securing them in place with upholstery pins or sticky tape. Carefully draw around the outline of the section you are working on, using a pencil. Remove the calico and cut around the pencilled outline, allowing 2 cm (¾ in) for seams. Place the calico pieces back on the chair to ensure that the pieces have been traced exactly. Continue making a calico pattern for each section of the chair including the type of finish you want along the bottom edge.

Assembling the pieces

Pin all the pieces together and then join them with tacking stitches, as the pins are liable to drop out when you fit the calico on the chair.

With so many pattern pieces to work with it is helpful to sew them together in a set order to ensure that each piece is stitched in the right place. Label each piece either by name or by number with french chalk to avoid confusion. Begin by stitching the back piece to the inside back, then the inside back to the seat area. Then stitch the seat to the panel at the front of the seat. Next, stitch the seat area to the arms along the inside edge, then the inside arm to the outside arm, then stitch the front of the arms in place. Stitch the end of the arm pieces to the back and inside back leaving an opening on one back seam of approximately 35 cm (13¾ in). Your opening should run from the bottom edge of the chair to the beginning of the scroll (curve) on the arm of the chair. Finish stitching by adding your trimming to the bottom edge, whether it is pleats, a frill or flaps.

Slip the calico onto the chair. On the curved areas, such as the front of the arms, it may be necessary to ease out a small amount of fullness. To do this unpick the tacking stitches and make tiny pleats or gathering stitches on the wrong side of the cloth. Once you have made your pleats or gathers tack the edges together again to ensure the pieces fit comfortably.

Once you are satisfied that your cover fits well take it off the chair and unpick all the tacking so that the calico is in pieces.

MAKING THE COVER

Having bought your fabric lay it out on the floor with the right side facing you. Put the calico pieces on it, checking that the grain is correct (fig. 34). You may find it helpful to number all your pattern pieces with chalk on the wrong side of the cloth to ensure that you stitch them together in the correct order. Also add a chalk arrow to indicate the top and bottom edge of each piece. You could even write the name of each section on the back. Sections that need to be piped could be identified by a small cross on the back. Once all the pattern pieces have been marked cut them out.

Inserting piping

Areas of the loose cover that require piping are the top edge of the front of the seat, the front arm pieces, between the inside and outside arm pieces, between the inside and outside back pieces along the top edge and between the bottom edge of the cover and the finishing trim. It isn't essential to use piping, but it does strengthen the covers at the seam areas and helps to exaggerate the outline of the chair.

Attach the piping to the areas of the chair that you have indicated, then stitch all the sections together. Trim any bulky seams and clip around the curved edges of the front arm pieces.

Fastenings for loose covers

The most durable type of fastening for covers are hooks and eyes or Velcro. Although zips can provide a neat inconspicuous finish they are not sufficiently strong for loose covers, especially as the covers, after they have been washed, need to be stretched slightly to ease them back into place.

Neaten the chair opening with a double hem on

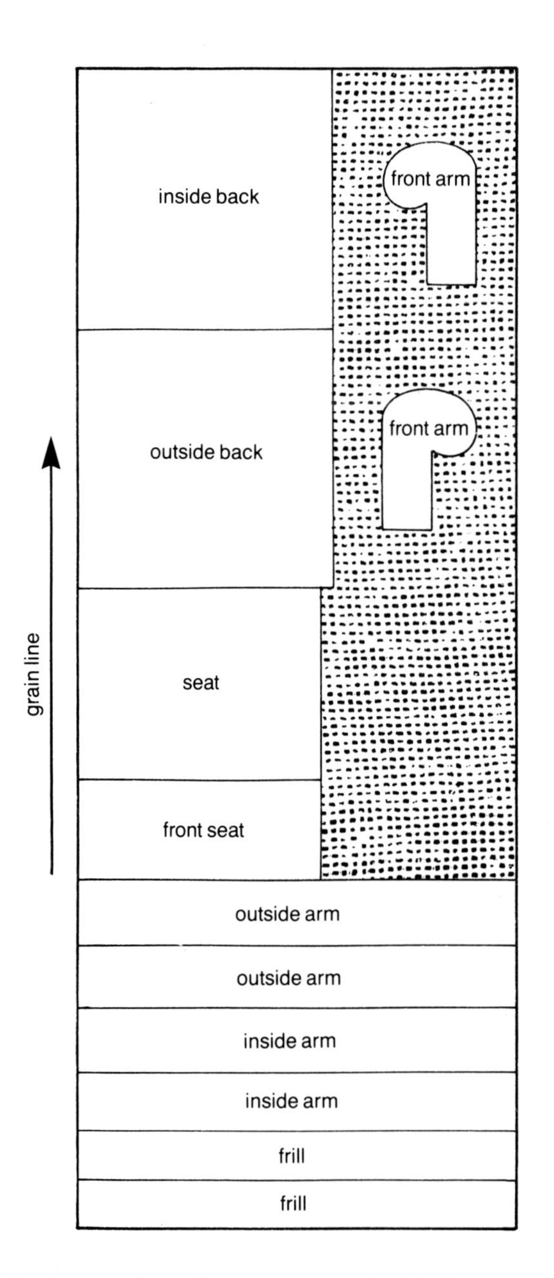

34 *Laying out the calico pieces onto the fabric*

the raw edges, sew hooks and eyes the length of the opening using a heavy duty cotton, sewing them approximately 12 cm (4¾ in) apart. Alternatively you can use strips of Velcro that should be machined rather than hand-sewn in place.

Finishing the flaps

If you have chosen to finish your chair with flaps you will need to neaten the remaining raw edges with a machined double hem. Incorporate ties made from strips of bias binding. You will need eight ties each 25 cm (10 in) long. The ties are secured in bows at each corner and should not be visible once the chair is in position.

Making arm caps and chair backs

If you have allowed sufficient material for arm caps they should be made for chairs and sofas. The pattern can be taken from the outline of the inside arm, outside arm and front arm pieces. The length of the cap should be two-thirds of the total length of the arm of the chair.

Using the calico pattern for the front arm piece cut off the head of the scroll allowing 1.5 cm (½ in) for a hem. Take the outside arm piece and measure down for 11 cm (4¼ in) plus seams and cut off at this point. With right sides together stitch the outside and inside arm pieces, using piping if you wish to, then add the front arm piece, again piping around the curved edge. Make a double hem on all the edges, and clip the curved area on the front arm piece (fig. 35).

To make a chair back cut a piece of fabric 30×38 cm (12×15 in). Hem all the raw edges mitring the corners. Lay the cloth on the chair with the extra 8 cm (3 in) on the longer edge taken over to the back of the chair to hold it in position.

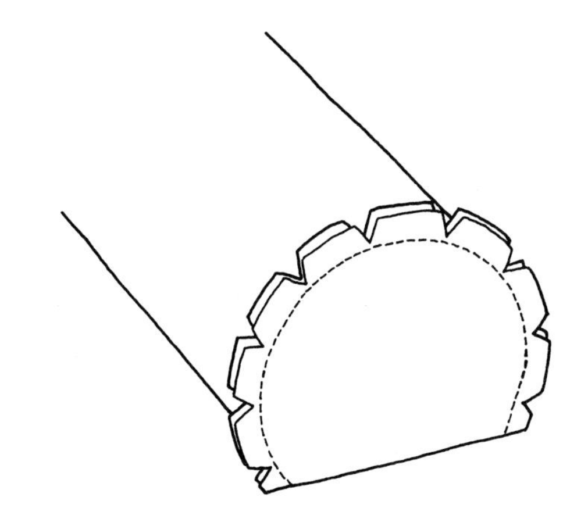

35 *Making an arm cap from the calico pieces, using the inside arm and the adapted front arm and outside arm pieces. The curved area on the front arm piece is clipped*

COVERING A SOFA

The same basic principles used when making a cover for a chair are used for a sofa. You will be working with twice as much fabric, so you need to allow plenty of room for cutting out and sewing the pieces together.

On a three-seater sofa it may be necessary to make seams in the back and seat pieces as these areas are very wide. If you have to allow for seams in the cover, position them so that the area is divided into thirds or perhaps a central seam. If your sofa has separate cushions you will need to ensure that the seams on the inside back sofa piece correspond with the seam edges on the cushions.

As longer flaps are required on the bottom of a sofa they can be neatly secured with one piece of cord rather than several ties. On the flap pieces make a narrow casing on the top edge about 2 cm (¾ in) deep. Take several metres of binding and attach a safety pin to one end, push the pin through

This living room is a blaze of matching blues. The cushions are highlighted with appliqué, frills, ribbon and single borders

the casing on all the flaps. Pull the cover over the sofa and turn the sofa upside down or on its side. Pull the bias binding until the flaps are neatly in place, then tie the two ends of the binding together.

Cushions for a sofa are made using the box cushion method and are fastened with a zip incorporated in the back welt piece.

COVERING A SUITE

If you are planning to cover a suite of furniture make a calico pattern for each piece first so that you can order sufficient fabric to cover them all. If you buy fabric for each item separately there is a chance that you will be buying from a different roll of fabric and the dye may be slightly different.

Even though two chairs may look identical it is worthwhile to make individual patterns for each one. Don't assume that one cover will fit the other, especially if you are covering old furniture. Always make your first project a chair rather than a sofa so that you can gain experience with a smaller area. If you have selected a patterned fabric with a central motif ensure that it sits in the same position on every piece of furniture.

10 MORE IDEAS FOR COVERS

Loose covers tend to be thought of in terms of a covering for a suite. However, there are a variety of other types of furniture that can be given a new image with a loose cover. Furniture not constantly in use can be covered with less practical dress fabrics and trimmed with elaborate bows, swags and ribbons.

A CHAIR WITHOUT ARMS

A smaller item of furniture such as a chair without arms is an ideal project for a beginner. It requires far less fabric than a sofa or armchair and fewer pattern pieces.

You will need to measure for a back, inside back, seat, front seat, side seat and any finishing trim you may want. If you want to disguise the legs you can use a frill or pleats (fig. 36). However, if the legs of the chair are to remain visible use flaps and tie them together underneath.

Although this type of cover is simpler than an armchair it is worthwhile making a calico pattern. Alternatively, you could use a paper pattern as the fitting stage is not so complicated. Allow for piping around the top and lower edge of the front seat and side pieces. You can also choose to pipe the back and inside back pieces along the side edges.

Begin by stitching the front seat part to the two sides. Stitch on the seat part incorporating the

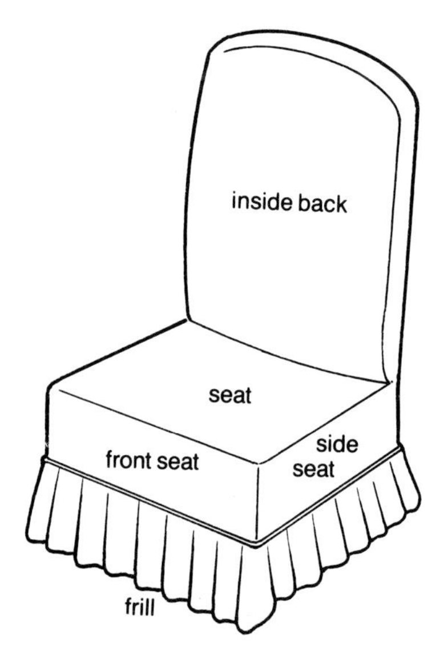

36 *Measuring for a chair without arms*

piping, stitch the inside back to the seat, then the back piece to the inside back and side ends. Take the cover and slip it on the chair and pin the finishing edge in place, marking the exact length you require. Make up the finishing edge and stitch it to the cover.

If your chair is rather worn then add a piece of foam cut to the exact size and shape of the chair. Simply place it on the chair and make up the cover.

Once the cover is in place it will keep the foam in position.

As a more decorative finish you can choose to neaten the side seams of the back and inside back pieces with a double hem. Then, stitch lengths of ribbon at intervals down the side of the chair tying them in bows once the cover is complete. This is suitable for bedroom furniture and the final touch is a deep frill round the lower edge. For a very stylish look, stitch one large bow to the back section of the chair, or tie one with wide strips of fabric stitched between the inside and outside back pieces.

A STOOL

Covering a stool whether it is for the bedroom or kitchen is a simple project to attempt. In the kitchen it may be advisable and more practical to add a round box cushion or a squab cushion with ties to the stool. However in the bedroom you can afford to be more impractical and use a long decorative frill.

To make a cover for a stool, first turn it upside down and trace around the top piece onto a sheet of paper. Cut around the shape allowing 1.5 cm (½ in) for seams. Cut a welt to the circumference of the top allowing for seams, then make up piping to twice the length of the welt. Stitch the welt to the circle of fabric inserting the piping. Place these pieces on the stool and measure for the length of the frill noting the exact length you require. Make up the finishing trim and stitch it to the lower edge of the welt piece incorporating the piping.

A DRESSING-TABLE

A prettily covered stool and dressing-table can be made the focal point in a bedroom. You could cover an old desk, small table or simply use a wooden shelf secured to the wall and adapt them as dressing-tables if you are working to a budget.

To get the exact dimensions of the top of your dressing-table a paper pattern is necessary, particularly for one that is kidney-shaped, in order to cut the curved shape correctly. Lightly tape the paper to your table and trace around the shape. If your dressing-table has a removable plate glass top then you can use this. Cut out your pattern, placing it on your fabric and allowing 1.5 cm (½ in) for seams. It is not necessary to think only in terms of furnishing fabrics for this type of cover as it will receive little wear and tear and lighter-weight dress fabrics are ideal.

Cut out the top cover for the table and line it with iron-on medium-weight Vilene for extra body. Alternatively, you could quilt this section of the cover. Neaten the back edge of the top cover piece with a double hem. Measure round the dressing-table for the frill omitting the back edge. Cut a strip of fabric to twice this measurement, noting the length you require. Neaten the side edges of the frill with a double hem and gather one longer edge. Pin the frill to the top easing out the gathers evenly and stitch in place. Fit the cover onto the table, check the length, then hem to the length you require.

If you have a dressing-table with a curtain track then you will need to attach a frill of just 15 cm (6 in) and make two separate curtains to hang onto the track.

Dressing-table covers can be decorated with bows stitched to the lower edge of the frill or the hem can be encased with ribbon binding and small bows stitched at random onto the frill. You might like to make the entire cover in lace or a soft satin fabric. The fabric you choose could also be used for making scatter cushions for the bed.

A BED

Although you are required to work with large pieces of fabric, making a cover for a bed or divan is very easy and is an ideal project for a beginner to learn the basic techniques of measuring and sewing covers. It is simply a rectangular piece of fabric edged with a frill or pleated trimming. You can choose to make your cover in a pretty fabric suitable for the bedroom or, if the bed doubles as a couch during the day, use a more practical cloth and decorate it with a variety of cushions.

Measure out the size of your bed and allow for seams. If your fabric is not wide enough to cover the width of your bed then choose either to have a centre seam or two seams with the area divided into thirds. Measure around the circumference of the top, but do not include the top edge of the bed. Make up a strip of fabric for the frill twice the circumference measurement and allowing for the depth which is measured from the top of the mattress to the floor. Make a double hem on the top edge of the cover piece to neaten. Then neaten the side and one longer edge of the frill piece with a double hem. Gather the remaining raw edge of the frill and pin it to the cover, allowing slightly more gathers at the corners. Stitch the frill to the cover. For a more fitted effect use ready-quilted fabric for the top cover piece, unquilted fabric for the frill, and contrasting piping sandwiched into the top edge of the frill.

Informal throwover covers are ideal and distinctive as bed covers. Experiment with favourite shades and designs which pick up decorative themes from the rest of the room, or select a colour which contrasts with its surrounds to dramatic effect. Scalloped, tassled or even pleated frills make ideal edgings for this type of bed covering.

A DIVAN

A divan is covered using the same principle as the box cushion, although there is no zip or fastening required. If you prefer the divan can be piped to emphasize the shape. This treatment, particularly

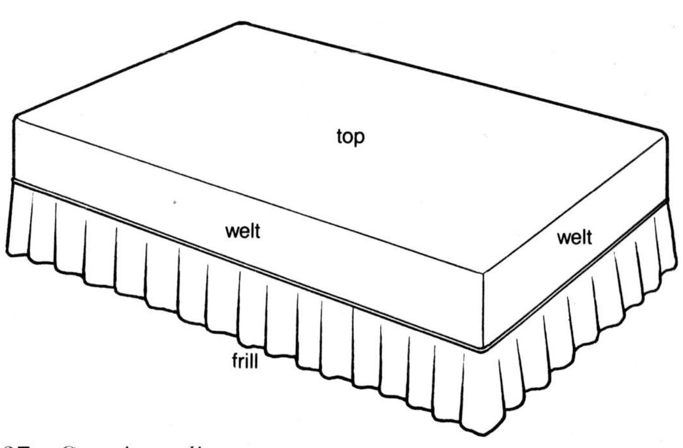

37 *Covering a divan*

with the addition of matching box cushions, will turn your divan into a comfortable day time sofa.

Begin by taking the measurements for the top of the divan allowing for seams on each side. Then measure the depth of the mattress allowing for two seams, then measure the length of the mattress plus a seam allowance. Measure for the frill from the lower edge of the mattress to the floor allowing for seams (fig. 37).

Join the edges of the welt together and press the seam open. Then stitch one edge of the welt to the top of the divan inserting piping if you wish. Stitch the ends of the frill together and neaten one longer edge with a double hem. Work a row of gathering stitches inside the seam allowance on the remaining raw edge of the frill. Pin the frill to the remaining

A simple, lightly pleated valance sets off the more elaborate but similarly coloured duvet cover

raw edge of the welt, easing gathers around evenly and inserting piping.

For a more formal room the lower edge of the cover, known as the valance, can be made from strips of fabric with a pleat at each corner. To calculate the amount of fabric you will need use the length measurement taken for the welt plus four times the depth of each pleat.

As a divan cover requires a considerable amount of fabric either design your cover so that seams are made at each corner, or so that they are concealed in the side edges.

11 THROWOVER COVERS

If you want to transform the appearance of your furniture instantly and you are short of time, then a throwover cover is the answer. Throwover covers, often referred to as throws, are also an attractive alternative to loose covers if your sewing skills are rather limited.

Throws can be used to cover beds, tables, chairs and sofas. Because we have been conditioned to accept that covers on chairs should be fitted it may take a little while to get used to this type of covering. You need to be bold about using fabric, arranging the cloth and then leaving it alone, resisting the temptation to constantly pull it about!

FABRICS

If your throw is for purely decorative purposes, such as a covering for a table or bed, then you can select a lightweight cloth. Bulky fabrics would be too difficult to arrange neatly over a table or dressing-table surface. Furnishing fabrics are a good choice because they are wide and they avoid the need for too many seams, but dress fabrics will provide you with a much greater variety of patterns and textures.

Lightweight fabrics are suitable for chairs and sofas provided they are not going to receive too much wear. A suite used for every-day purposes should be draped with a firmer linen or cotton. Cane and wood furniture needs to have some sort of padded covering or it will be too uncomfortable.

Soft woollen blankets can also be used as throws. You could stitch contrasting braiding to the outside edge for an attractive finish. Shawls with heavily fringed edges can also look very attractive casually draped, or perhaps partially covering a chair or sofa. A brightly-coloured sleeping bag, unzipped and placed over a chair or sofa, could also make a versatile covering. Appliquéd cot quilts are ideal for children's rooms draped over chairs or the centre of the bed. Old tablecloths with embroidery would make a lovely throw for a small chair or stool, and an antique bedcover with lace edging could be used on a sofa. If you want to create a nostalgic look by using antique or old-fashioned materials do have them cleaned first, repair any small tears and deal with any obvious stains or they will detract from the appeal of this type of cover. A quilt would make a lovely squashy cover for a dilapidated sofa and you could decorate it with an assortment of scatter cushions.

You need not only think in terms of using just one fabric, for example two or three shawls thrown together over a sofa could create a very dramatic effect. Or several floral prints draped together might be far more interesting than just one. The main point to remember when you are using more than one cloth is that they blend together. Fabrics should not fight with each other, rather they should blend together giving a casual but deliberately co-ordinated effect. It is not necessary to stitch lengths of fabric together – they can be draped on top of each other.

MAKING THE THROW

To cover your furniture with a throw you will need to decide whether you want to partially or entirely cover it. If you choose to cover the furniture entirely then you will need to use several metres of fabric. Partially covering a chair is fine provided the chair itself is still in a reasonable condition. A thread-bare cover, with stuffing showing through, and left showing when the chair is only half covered, will look most unattractive. If only one area of your chair is worn then you can use your throw to conceal it. If the chair is worn all over then you will need to use a sufficiently large throw to cover it completely.

With a young active family it might be more practical to use a throw to cover your furniture completely. You might otherwise find yourself constantly re-arranging your throw while young ones wriggle and put it out of position.

To decide just how much cloth you will need take an old sheet and drape it over your chair or sofa. Allow for enough material so that it can be tucked in at the back of the seat and the inside arm areas. This will help to keep the throw in place. You will then need to have enough cloth to take over the back of the chair and touch the ground and enough to drape over the arms and onto the floor if you wish. Use another sheet if you are running out of cloth pinning them together before laying them over the chair again. With young children about it might be advisable to seam separate lengths of cloth together. Once you have covered your chair or sofa remove the sheet and measure out the amount of fabric you will need.

Before placing your cover in position you may like to neaten the edges. You can simply pink the edges of the fabric if you wish. This type of finish is suitable for thick wool fabrics that are unlikely to fray or for felt. However, most household materials are liable to fray especially during washing so it is advisable to neaten the edges of the cloth. If you really are short on time then you can stick the hems of the throw in place with an adhesive hemming tape from Vilene. A stitched hem is stronger than a glued one and you simply need to make a double hem on each edge mitring the corners for a neat finish.

Ties and fastenings

If you want to emphasize the design of an attractively curved chair or one with scroll arms then the addition of a few ties and careful draping of the fabric will make this possible even on a throw. You can reveal the shape of the arms by pleating layers of fabric around it and making a few running stitches to hold those pleats in position. Pleating can also be used along the back area of the chair at either side. Take a small quantity of fabric in each hand, make a pleat by folding the cloth in your hand then pinning it. Attach ties made from strips of bias binding or narrow satin ribbon at intervals down the side of the chair to hold the pleats together. On geometric or broad striped patterns you might like to use press-on fasteners for a more modern finish.

COVERING A BED

Because a fitted bedcover involves using large quantities of fabric and attaching a frill or pleated edging, using a throw on a bed can minimize that

This table is disguised with two throws in contrasting colours. The theme is emphasized by matching blue and cream chair cushions

amount of work. If the frame of your bed is in good condition you may simply like to use a pretty piece of fabric and lay it diagonally over and not worry whether it touches the floor. This type of throw is suitable for a low bed. Ready-quilted fabric is ideal for bedding as it provides an attractive and warm cover and the edges of the quilting can be finished with strips of wide bias binding or ribbon to prevent them fraying.

If your room is decorated with several items of wooden furniture then a tartan rug with a fringed edging would help to convey a rustic look. Samples of patchwork also make suitable throws for a bed, while smaller samples can be used as cot throws in a child's room. An old fur coat or piece of fake fur fabric could also be used for throwing over a bed to create a cosy atmosphere.

Before measuring for the amount of fabric you will need for your throw, you will have to decide whether you want the cover to touch the floor or end just below the mattress. Although a throw designed to touch the ground looks very neat you may want to make a feature of some attractively carved legs on your bed.

Take your tape and measure from the centre of the bed to the floor or end of the mattress, then double this amount to give you the width of the throw. Then, measure from the floor at the end of the bed to the head of the bed for the length, allowing for hems on all the edges. If you want to be able to secure the throw in place by tucking it under the top edge of the pillow add an extra 20 cm (8 in) to the length measurement. If your fabric is not sufficiently wide to cover your bed then you can choose to make a centre seam or divide the area into thirds making two seams. Neaten the edges of the throw with a double hem and place it in position.

VERSATILE THROWS

Throws can be used throughout the house. Small circles or rectangles of fabric can be used to cover fancy tables, pianos, stools, in fact most items of furniture that have seen better days. Quilted throws once discarded from the bedroom or sofa can be folded into a square and used as an extra cushion, quilted fabric can also be used as an impromptu playmat for a young child on a vinyl or wooden floor.

If you order twice the amount of fabric you need for your throw you can use the second length for decorating walls. Use cloth with an interesting texture or intricate pattern. Secure the cloth to the wall by stapling it to wooden battens which are then screwed to the wall. This type of furnishing is suitable for a lounge or bedroom. In a child's bedroom a bright jazzy print could be used over the bed and repeated with the separate throw secured above the head of the bed.

By taking a couple of lengths of cloth and walking around the house you can begin to discover areas that can be covered. Try the fabric in all sorts of places, making a few pleats or folds where necessary, and you will begin to realize that the possibilities for using this type of cover are endless. Surfaces in a child's room or kitchen could be draped with PVC that requires no hemming. An over-stuffed chair can look quite luxurious draped with a velvet curtain or a shawl with a Paisley pattern.

Using throws means looking at your furniture in a new light and accepting that covers do not have to be formal and very fitted. It means you can act on impulse if you fall in love with a remnant – it is easy enough to find something to cover in the house!

GLOSSARY

Accommodate......make room for
Back tack......tack invisibly
Back tack strip......length of plastic or metal used to make a smooth edge
Back up......to fill in a section and reinforce the fabric
Basting......a long running stitch for temporarily holding two surfaces together
Beading......a semi-circular moulding used to finish edges
Blanket Stitch......used to neaten raw edges and provide a decorative finish
Blind Stitching......used to hold the filling in place in a seat
Bridle Stitch......stitch sewn into hessian to hold stuffing in place
Buckram......hessian impregnated with glue to form a stiff cloth
Buttoning......application of buttons through fabric to hold pleats or to decorate
Clean out......to make smooth by pulling the fabric to remove puckering
Close nail......decorative nails placed together to form a continuous line
Collar......extra piece of fabric joined to a curve to make a smooth tuck in
Cord Edging......used to emphasise and strengthen edges of chairs and sofas
Cut sheet......cutting and estimating plan
Ease in......work fabric into a smaller area
Edge Stitching......machining as close to the edge of a hem or seam as possible
Facing......covered shape, used to tidy or decorate front or back scrolls
First stuffing......first stage of stuffing
Flat Fell Seam......self-neatening seam with two rows of stitching visible on the right side of the cloth
Float Buttoning......button left slightly loose on a headboard or chair to keep stuffing in place
Flush......level with

Fluting...a stuffing and stitching method used to provide extra padding
Flys...piece of fabric sewn on to make extra length in tuck-in-area
Gimp...a narrow braid
Gimping..applying gimp trimming
Girt...a tight line across the fabric caused by packing stuffing down too hard
Interlining.......................................to give extra body to curtains
Lashing...a stitching pattern used to keep springs in place
Lip...front edge of seat joined to platform
Marking up.....................................marking fabric with chalk or marker
Mitre...folding a corner to make fabric lie flat
Notch..V-shaped cut in seam allowance
Overcasting....................................used for neatening raw edges by taking thread over the edge of the fabric
Piping...made by covering cord with fabric
Piping used as trimming.....................crossways strips with cord inserted
Platform cloth.................................cloth used instead of main fabric usually on the seat
Proud..in front of
Purchase...obtain maximum power
Running Stitch................................used for hand gathering
Scroll..a curved shape usually on chair front (see facing)
Second stuffing...............................after the stitched edge comes the second stuffing
Shy..just short of (opposite of proud)
Skewer..a long type of pin which holds fabric in place
Slipping thread...............................fine lining thread used for slip stitching
Slip Stitch......................................used to hold a folded edge to a flat one or two folded edges together
Sound..in good order
Stuffing ties....................................ties of twine sewn right through stuffing to hold it in place
Swell...protruding layer of stuffing
Tacking...another word for basting
Tack home......................................tack right into the frame
Tack line...line of tacks in the frame
Take-up...extra fabric used when quilting or fluting
Temporary tack...............................tack only halfway just to hold the fabric
Tie off..knot ends to secure
Top cover..finishing fabric
To the thread...................................to the line of the thread across the weft of the fabric

To trim..apply trimming
Trim...cut fabric back to seam line
Tuck-in..areas between seat back and inside arm, where fabric tucks out of sight
Up to calico......................................ready for top cover
'W' formation...................................tacks placed to form a 'W' shape
Welt..used as a trimming on leather or fabric (see piping)

USEFUL ADDRESSES

Habitat
Hithercroft Road
Wallingford
Oxfordshire OX10 9DQ
0491 35511

Laura Ashley
Braywick House
Braywick Road
Maidenhead
Berkshire SL6 1DW
0628 39151

Next
Desford Road
Enderby
Leicester LE9 5AT
0533 866411

The Association of Master Upholsterers
564 North Circular Road
Neasden
London NW2 7QB
01-205 0465

Surrey Trimmings Ltd (upholstery sundries)
16 St Dunstans Hill
Sutton
Surrey
01-644 9201

Pilgrim Payne and Co Ltd (specialist cleaners)
Park Street Works
Latimer Place
Latimer Road
London W10 6QA
01-960 5656

Distinctive Trimmings (trimmings, fringes)
17D Kensington Church Street
London W8 6QA
01-937 6174

D L Forester Ltd
(DIY upholstery sundries, mail order service)
12 The Ongar Trading Estate
20 Ongar Road
Great Dunmow
Essex CM6 1EU
0371 5201

PICTURE ACKNOWLEDGEMENTS

The authors and publishers would like to thank the following for the use of photographs in this book:
Bill Batten page 229;
Michael Boys Syndication pages 43, 51, 74;
Colefax & Fowler page 168;
Crown Paints page 205;
Harrison Drape pages 119, 225;
ICI Fabrics pages 185, 192;
Interior Selection pages 209, 220;
London Interior Design Centre page 229;
Tom Mannion pages 23, 28, 30, 32, 34, 40, 41, 44, 52, 55, 59, 62, 77, 82, 91;
Osborne & Little pages 99, 137, 141;
Poppy Limited, Yarm page 181;
Sanderson page 159;
Smallbone Kitchens page 165;
Sunway Blinds pages 123, 151, 157, 165;
Swish pages 102, 113;
Syndication International pages 109, 143;
Syndication International/Homes & Gardens page 172;
Warner Fabrics, from their Claremont Collection page 216;
World of Interiors page 229;
Brian Yates Interiors, from the Silverdale Collection page 197;

Thanks also to Gatestone Upholstery for supplying the furniture photographed in the upholstery section, and to Parker Knoll Textiles Ltd for supplying the fabric in the photograph on page 59.

INDEX

Page numbers in *italics* refer to diagrams and illustrations